# The Portuguese Economy Towards 1992

# The Portuguese Economy Towards 1992

Proceedings of a conference sponsored by Junta Nacional de Investigação Científica e Tecnológica and Banco de Portugal.

Edited by João Ferreira do Amaral
Diogo Lucena
António S. Mello

SPRINGER SCIENCE+BUSINESS MEDIA, LLC

**Library of Congress Cataloging-in-Publication Data**

The Portuguese economy towards 1992 : proceedings of a conference sponsored by Junta Nacional de Investigação Científica e Tecnológica and Banco de Portugal / edited by João Ferreira do Amaral, Diogo Lucena, António S. Mello.
p. cm.
ISBN 978-1-4613-6618-8 ISBN 978-1-4615-3638-3 (eBook)
DOI 10.1007/978-1-4615-3638-3
1. Portugal—Economic conditions—1974- —Congresses. 2. European Economic Community—Portugal—Congresses. 3. Labor market--Portugal—Congresses. I. Amaral, João Ferreira do. II. Lucena, Diogo de. III. Mello, António Sampaio. IV. Junta Nacional de Investigação Científica e Technológica (Portugal) V. Banco de Portugal.
HC392.P699 1992
330.9469'12—dc20 91-39506

---


Originally published by Kluwer Academic Publishers in 1992
Softcover reprint of the hardcover 1st edition 1992



*Printed on acid-free paper.*

# Contents

# Preface

This book contains papers presented at a conference held in Vimeiro, Portugal, on March 23 and 24, 1991. The purpose of this conference was to discuss several aspects of the portuguese economy, namely issues and problems related with the european integration of 1992. The sponsorship has been provided by the Junta Nacional de Investigação Científica e Tecnológica, the portuguese science and technology foundation, as well as by the Banco de Portugal, the central bank.

The first paper, by Horta Correia, César das Neves and Rebelo represents an attempt to characterize and to analyze the main features of the portuguese business cycles. Making use of the real business cycle methodology, the authors contrast the properties of the portuguese empirical regularities with those of other OECD countries and conclude that the economic fluctuations in Portugal seem much more severe. On the other hand, the relative volatility of the various series analyzed, as well as their co-movement and serial correlation properties, are of the same order of those in other OECD countries. Horta Correia, César das Neves and Rebelo evaluate the properties of the portuguese time series in light of the predictions of two dynamic general equilibrium models: a closed economy model and a model of a small open economy. Surprisingly, their closed economy model provides a good fit for the portuguese fluctuations, while the small open economy model predicts unplausibly low volatilities for both aggregate consumption and the trade balance.

The next paper, by Antão and Brito, analyses the effects on the portuguese economy of both the liberalization of capital movements within the EEC and the adhesion to the European Monetary System. Two scenarios are compared in this work: full liberalization with immediate EMS adhesion, and liberalization with precommitment to EMS adhesion at a future date. The authors find that the latter strategy will likely imply a smoother transition from lower losses in the country's competitive position, provided that the announcement of the EMS timely adhesion is credible. From the model, a dynamic relationship between the real exchange rate and the real interest rate parity is derived. Antão and Brito successively test the hypothesis that the former causes the latter with recourse to co-integration techniques: real exchange rate disturbances significantly determine the variations in the Fisher open gap, as it is suggested by the study of impulse response functions. Interestingly, a strategy of preannouncement of EMS adhesion coupled with increasing liberalization of exchange controls characterizes the strategy followed by Portugal in recent years.

The third paper, by Barros and Cabral, focuses on the welfare aspects of foreign direct investment. The authors develop a theoretical model which is then applied to measure the effects of recent foreign penetration in the portuguese insurance market. Barros and Cabral show that the marginal effect of entry is welfare improving if and only if foreign firms' market share is above some threshold level. Also, they show that the global effect of foreign entry is only positive when the consumer's surplus effect from greater competition compensates the transfer of profits from domestic to foreign firms. In their model de-novo entry is contrasted with entry by acquisition. By applying their model to the case of the portuguese life-insurance sector, which has been the target of intense penetration by foreign firms and subject to a significant restructuring in light of the recent european financial reforms, the authors conclude that, in general, the global effect is negative but the marginal effect is positive. Consequently, although recent foreign entry has decreased domestic welfare, additional foreign entry can contribute to improve it.

José Mata provides an empirical analysis of entry and exit flows of firms in the portuguese manufacturing industry, in recent years. Using different measures of firms' mobility the author concludes that resources in Portugal seem to display much less rigidity than it is suggested in a country where layoffs, bankruptcies and reorganizations are often subject to difficulties of various types. An appreciable capacity for adjustments and some degree of flexibility in the alternative use of resources are crucial features to accommodate rapidly and decisively the reforms required in the process of economic integration created by 1992.

The next four papers are devoted to the analysis of the portuguese labor market. First, Branco and Mello attempt to explain why wages are much lower in Portugal than in other EEC countries. The authors decompose the wage gap in three main components: the exchange rate, productivity and industrial relations. Productivity seems to matter more than any other factor, while industrial relations shows a negative contribution to the wage gap, perhaps because unions have greater power and labor laws are relatively more stringent in Portugal. Branco and Mello observe a narrowing of the wage gap since Portugal's joined the EEC, a fact that gives credit to the convergence argument in favor of european integration. Next,

Modesto, Monteiro and César das Neves discuss the neutrality hypothesis and conclude that in the long run, productivity changes are almost completely reflected in increases in wages, although that is far from true in the short run. Labor markets in Portugal also reveal imperfections which seem to be characteristic of situations where unions give priority to active membership, in detriment of outsiders.

In both the papers by Alfredo Pereira and Barosa and Pedro T. Pereira the issue of labor mobility across borders is raised. The first studies the effects of emigration in the 1960's on the portuguese economic growth and welfare. By analyzing the experience of a large migration of workers to Central Europe, the author is able to draw conclusions, of course temptative, from the liberalization of labor force movements brought about by the european integration. The study emphasizes two opposite effects of emigration: one negative from slower economic growth resulting from lower labor force and one positive due to the remittances sent home by the emigrated workers. In the work by Barosa and Pedro T. Pereira the choice between working at home or abroad is modelled and tested. They show that wage differentials and its expectations, as well as capital market imperfections are important variables that help to explain domestic labor supply and emigration in the case of the portuguese worker.

Gaspar and Pinheiro estimate a consumption function for Portugal using co-integration relations between consumption, interest rates and aggregate income. They measure the short run dynamics of real private consumption and identify how it relates with the long run behavior of this variable. The next paper is by Lucena, Leite and Gaspar and focuses on the allocation of common costs among Portugal's long distance telephone operators. Their paper is topical in a time of greater deregulation of markets and increased competition.

Finally, Courakis and Roque study the pattern and evolution of trade of the portuguese economy and conclude that Portugal has a comparative advantage in products of industries that are intensive in unskilled labor coupled with a comparative disadvantage in products of industries that are intensive in skilled labor or display economies of scale; the disadvantage in skilled labor intensive products seems more pronounced in products requiring intensive lower quality, as opposed to higher quality. Moreover, in recent years, the country has evolved from a pattern of trade characterized by a comparative disadvantage in physical capital intensive products to a stage of comparative neutrality.

As always in a project of this type there are many people to thank: the authors of the papers, who promptly responded to the call, and the discussants, António Pinto Barbosa, José Ferreira Machado, Ana Paula Martins, Vasco D'Orey, João Pontes, Vasco Santos, Victor Santos. Fátima Branco for the excellent preparation of the manuscript. David McConnell, the editor, always enthusiastic about Europe. António Borges, Vice-Chairman of the Banco de Portugal and Ramôa Ribeiro, Vice-President of JNICT, for their support. All these people have contributed to make better known the experiences of the small, highly open and semi-developed portuguese economy in its path towards Europe 1992.

João Ferreira Amaral
Diogo Lucena
António S. Mello

# The Portuguese Economy Towards 1992

# Business Cycles in Portugal: Theory and Evidence

Isabel Horta Correia
João César das Neves
Sérgio Rebelo

## 1 Introduction

The main objective of this article is to describe the most important features of business cycles in Portugal during the period 1958-1989. We compare these features with the empirical regularities of economic fluctuations in other OECD countries and with the predictions of two benchmark dynamic general equilibrium models.

Our analysis builds on two strands of research. The first is the analysis of the business cycle phenomenon pursued by pioneers such as Juglar (1862), Schumpeter (1939), Slutsky (1937) and Frisch (1933), and recently revived by the work of Lucas (1977, 1980) and Kydland and Prescott (1982). The second line of research is the accumulated wealth of studies on the Portuguese economy.[1]

Investigating the key features of business cycles in Portugal is a difficult task given the scarcity of long macroeconomic series. Most series are available only since 1958 and at an annual frequency, rather than at the quarterly frequency which is standard in business cycle analysis. Information on some variables of interest is unavailable (e.g., hours worked, capital

We wish to thank, without implicating, Marianne Baxter, Robert King and José Machado for their comments and suggestions.

[1]Some of these studies use different methodologies to provide a general characterization of the Portuguese economy (e.g., Moura and Pinto (1958), Pintado (1964), Moura (1969), A. M. P. Barbosa (1971, 1972), Marques and Romão (1983), Gomes (1984), A. S. P. Barbosa (1985), Macedo et al. (1986), Neves and Confraria (1988)), and Pereira and Gaspar (1990)). Other studies focus on particular historical episodes (e.g., Lopes (1981) and Rocha (1981, 1984)), while some recent research has attempted to provide a long run perspective (e.g., Justino (1988), Nunes et al. (1989) and Neves (1990)).

utilization), while measurement of other variables is plagued by serious statistical problems (e.g., employment rate). Yet, it is hard to believe that these difficulties are greater than those encountered by Wesley Mitchell and Arthur Burns in their pioneer work on business cycles. During the 20's and 30's Burns, Mitchell and their team of researchers at the National Bureau of Economic Research were the first to characterize the length, variability and co-movement properties of American business cycles.[2] Their findings, which continue to be influential today, were obtained at a time when there were no aggregate production measures, such as GNP.

To characterize the key features of the Portuguese business cycle we use a modern counterpart to the methods of Burns and Mitchell: the Hodrick-Prescott (1980) filter. This filter extracts a smooth trend from the data and has the advantage of rendering stationary series that are integrated up to fourth order. This happens to be an advantage in examining the Portuguese data given that most of the variables are not trend-stationary in the sense of Nelson and Plosser (1982).

We compare our findings to those of other researchers who have used the Hodrick-Prescott filter in their business cycle investigations: Kydland and Prescott (1982, 1989) for the U.S., Blackburn and Ravn (1990) for the U.K., Danthine and Girardin (1989) for Switzerland, Brandner and Neusser (1990) for Austria and Germany, and Baxter and Crucini (1990) and Backus, Kehoe and Kydland (1989) for other OECD countries.

Empirical facts are always interesting in their own right but are hard to evaluate without a well articulated theory. One cannot say that the volatility of consumption seems too high or that the capital-output ratio seems too low in the absence of a theory that has predictions for what these statistics should be. For this reason we compare the main statistical properties of Portuguese time series with those predicted by two dynamic general equilibrium models.

The first model that we consider is a standard closed economy model, driven by shocks to productivity and to government expenditures. This model, studied in King, Plosser and Rebelo (1988a), is a descendent of the economies of Kydland and Prescott (1982) and Long and Plosser (1983). Until recently, models of this type emphasized the role of productivity shocks in shaping the business cycle, abstracting from what was previously regarded by many macroeconomists as the main cause of economic fluctua-

[2] The methodology and empirical findings of the Burns and Mitchell research program are described in a large number of books and articles. A key reference is Burns and Mitchell (1946). King and Plosser (1989) have recently provided an excellent description and evaluation of the Burns and Mitchell methodology. Kydland and Prescott (1989) situate the contributions of Burns and Mitchell in the context of the modern business cycle research program.

tions: monetary shocks. For this reason these models are often referred to as "real business cycle models".[3]

The second model that we examine is that of a small open economy that can borrow or lend to the rest of the world at an exogenous real rate of interest. This model, which is part of our ongoing research on dynamic models for small open economies (Correia, Neves and Rebelo (1991)), provides the simplest framework that allows us to think about the cyclical properties of the current account.

The paper is organized as follows. Section 2 describes the main features of the Portuguese data and compares those features with the empirical regularities of the business cycle in the U.S. and in other OECD countries. In section 3 we discuss why dynamic stochastic general equilibrium models are a natural first candidate to organize the facts uncovered in the previous section. We also describe the closed economy model and calibrate it to reproduce the most important long-term features of the Portuguese economy. This model is then used to generate predictions for the second moments of the various macroeconomic variables which we compare with the second moments of the detrended Portuguese data. Section 4 repeats this analysis for the small open economy model. Section 5 summarizes our main findings and outlines directions for future research.

# 2 Stylized Facts of Portuguese Business Cycle

Our data sources have two main components: the time series for the period 1833-1985 produced by Nunes, Mata and Valério (1989) and the National Accounts series for the period 1958–1989. Detailed information on all the data sources that we used can be found in the data appendix. Unless otherwise is stated, all variables described in the text, tables and figures are expressed in logarithms.

## 2.1 The Secular Series

The long series produced by Nunes, Mata and Valério (1989) allow us to characterize the broad lines of the evolution of the Portuguese economy since the early 19th century. We used them to produce our first three graphs.

Figures 1.1 and 1.2 show the logarithm of per capita output, its linear trend and the deviations from this trend. The detrended series reflects,

[3] Recent discussions of this line of research are provided by Lucas (1987) and McCallum (1989).

as is natural, the character of the different historical periods: the "good" decades of the 19th century, which were the 1840's, 60's, 80's and 90's; the economic and social turmoil of the early decades of the 20th century; and the fast growth that took place between the 50's and the early 70's.

The linearly detrended series are not stationary. This property, which also holds for the period 1958-1989, prevents us from computing meaningful statistics to describe the characteristics of business cycles. To surpass this problem we use the Hodrick-Prescott (1980) filter to detrend the data. This filter removes a smooth trend from the data, rendering stationary stochastic processes that are integrated up to fourth order.[4] The Hodrick-Prescott (HP) trend is obtained by solving the following minimization problem:

$$\min_{\{y_t^g\}} \sum_{t=1}^{T}(y_t - y_t^g)^2 + \lambda \sum_{t=2}^{T-1}[(y_{t+1}^g - y_t^g) - (y_t^g - y_{t-1}^g)]$$

where $y_t$ represents the original series (e.g., the logarithm of GNP) and $y_t^g$ its trend. The smoothing parameter $\lambda$ penalizes changes in the first difference of the trend component. For this reason high values of $\lambda$ generate smooth trends while low values produce erratic trends. In the limit case of $\lambda = \infty$ the HP filter extracts a linear trend from the data, while if $\lambda = 0$ the trend coincides with the original variable. The standard value of $\lambda$ used for detrending quarterly series is 1600. We used a value of 400 to detrend our annual data since it produces trends that are similar to those that are obtained from quarterly series with $\lambda = 1600$.[5]

Figure 1.1 also depicts output per capita against its HP trend. This trend is a smooth line that captures the main low frequency movements in the data. It reveals four long cycles of the Portuguese economy: 1830–1860, 1860–1920, 1920–1950 and 1950 until present. It also suggests an acceleration of the growth process since 1920. These long term swings in Portuguese economic activity uncovered by the HP filter clearly deserve further examination.

Table 1 compares our growth performance during the period 1870–1979 with that of a group of other OECD countries. In this comparison the country most similar to Portugal is Italy. Both economies had slightly below average growth performance and relatively high output volatility.

Figures 2.1 to 2.4 describe the evolution of the shares in GNP of the trade balance ($TB$), tax receipts ($T$), government expenditures ($G$), exports

[4] See Hodrick and Prescott (1980) and King and Rebelo (1989) for a detailed description of the properties of the Hodrick-Prescott filter.

[5] The value of $\lambda$ that makes the frequency response function of the filter for annual data correspond to the frequency response of the filter with $\lambda = 1600$ and quarterly data is approximately 6. This value of $\lambda$ produces, however, extremely erratic trends.

Table 1: Per-capita GNP 1870–1979: summary statistics.

| Countries | Time Trend | Standard Deviation of log $Y$ HP detrended |
|---|---|---|
| Portugal | 1.53 | 7.49 |
| Australia | 0.90 | 5.02 |
| Canada | 1.77 | 8.46 |
| Denmark | 1.74 | 4.21 |
| France | 1.53 | 8.94 |
| Germany | 2.45 | 10.39 |
| Italy | 1.52 | 7.26 |
| Norway | 2.10 | 4.20 |
| Sweden | 4.60 | 2.30 |
| United Kingdom | 1.24 | 3.96 |
| USA | 1.78 | 7.12 |

*Source:* Nunes, Mata and Valério (1989) for Portugal; Maddison (1982) for all other countries.

($E$) and imports ($Im$). The first salient feature that these figures illustrates is the opening of the economy to international trade that has occurred since 1920. The second feature is the increase in the share of government expenditures in GNP. This increase, sometimes referred to as Wagner's law, is commonly found in other countries, being usually associated with an expansion of systems of transfer payments, such as the Social Security system (see, for instance, Barro (1988), fig. 12.1). Since 1958 an increase in transfer payments seems, in fact, to explain most of the increase in government share that has occurred in Portugal. This can be seen by comparing for the period 1958-1989 the evolution of the government share in Figure 2.1 (which includes transfer payments in the definition of government expenditures) and in Figure 7.2 (in which only purchases of goods and services by the government are considered).

Figures 3 to 6 show the dramatic volatility that characterized nominal variables in the first two decades of this century. The success of the Salazar regime (1926–1974) in achieving monetary stability is also clear in this graph. This stability which was maintained even during the growth decades, the 50's and 60's, was greatly reduced in the 70's as a result of the 1974 revolution and the oil shock.

## 2.2 The Period 1958–1989

The data available for the period 1958–1989 are described in detail in Figures 7.1 through 15.4. Figure 7.1 represents GDP and its components. These figures show an increase in the GDP share of government expenditures, imports and exports, and a somewhat puzzling decrease in the consumption share.[6] The investment share shows no clear trend.

[6] Our measure of consumption includes both durables and non-durables. For the period 1958 to 1981 it is possible to use the estimates in Santos (1984b) to disaggregate

During this period output per capita grew at an average rate of 4% per annum. Our growth performance since 1958 is remarkably similar to that of other European countries such as Austria, Denmark, France, West Germany, Italy and Spain (see Barro (1987)).

Figure 8 depicts the evolution of investment and "basic savings" which, following Baxter and Crucini (1990), we define as:[7]

$$S_t = Y_t - C_t - G_t = I_t + X_t - Im_t \ .$$

This figure might suggest that there is a significant co-movement between savings and investment but the correlation between these two series is only 0.31 if we linearly detrend them and 0.10 if we detrend with the HP filter. These values are smaller than most of those reported in Baxter and Crucini (1990) for other OECD countries.[8] These low correlations are essentially due to the behavior of savings and investment in response to the most important shocks that occurred in the last three decades. During the Colonial War a reduction in savings was accompanied by an increase in investment, while the opposite took place during the 1974 revolution and the two IMF stabilization programs (1977–79 and 1983–85).

The behavior of the real wage rate and of the real rate of return to capital (gross of depreciation) is depicted in Figure 9 . The wage rate grew steadily during the period 1958 to 1973, and then stagnated during the past two decades. The real return to capital declined in 1973 as a result of the first oil shock and then dropped dramatically in 1974–76.[9]

Figures 10.1 through 10.9 describe the behavior of the most important real macroeconomic series. All series are expressed in logs and were detrended with the HP filter. Not surprisingly, the detrended series reflect the most important shocks that have occurred during the last three decades:

---

the two components of consumption. Since these estimates indicate that the acquisition of durable goods represents only about 8% of total consumption it is unlikely that this refinement would significantly alter the behavior of consumption described in the text.

[7] A description of different savings concepts can be found in Baxter (1991) and in Stockman and Svensson (1987).

[8] In a famous article Feldstein and Horioka (1980) claimed that the high correlation between savings and investment found for most countries implied that international capital markets were unimportant and hence that closed economy models were the appropriate paradigm for policy analysis. A criticism of this view can be found in Baxter and Crucini (1990).

[9] One interesting feature of this rate of return measure (computed by dividing income accrued to capital by the capital stock measure in Santos (1984a)) is that, if we assume the standard value for the rate of depreciation used in the literature (10%), it implies that the mean net rate of return to capital was 6%. This value is remarkably close to the real return to common stock in the US for the same period, which was 6.5% (see Ibbotson and Sinquefield (1988)).

Table 2: Portuguese data.

| | St. Dev. | St.D. rel.$Y$ | Autocorrel. 1 | 2 | Cross-correlations with $y(t+i)$ -2 | -1 | 0 | 1 | 2 |
|---|---|---|---|---|---|---|---|---|---|
| $y$ | 4.66 | 1.00 | 0.69 | 0.26 | 0.26 | 0.69 | 1.00 | 0.69 | 0.26 |
| $c$ | 4.38 | 0.94 | 0.72 | 0.41 | 0.67 | 0.75 | 0.69 | 0.31 | -0.01 |
| $g$ | 3.82 | 0.82 | 0.49 | 0.12 | 0.34 | 0.42 | 0.32 | 0.04 | -0.10 |
| $s$ | 17.20 | 3.70 | 0.42 | 0.12 | -0.18 | 0.03 | 0.32 | 0.47 | 0.28 |
| $i$ | 15.13 | 3.25 | 0.57 | 0.02 | 0.03 | 0.51 | 0.83 | 0.56 | 0.18 |
| $x$ | 12.84 | 2.76 | 0.74 | 0.31 | -0.10 | 0.31 | 0.65 | 0.61 | 0.38 |
| $im$ | 12.50 | 2.69 | 0.63 | 0.20 | 0.12 | 0.56 | 0.81 | 0.63 | 0.33 |
| $TB$ | 48.40 | 10.40 | 0.63 | 0.04 | -0.21 | -0.41 | -0.42 | -0.19 | 0.03 |
| $N$ | 2.58 | 0.55 | 0.75 | 0.43 | -0.13 | 0.25 | 0.54 | 0.48 | 0.33 |
| $k$ | 1.94 | 0.42 | 0.89 | 0.63 | 0.71 | 0.69 | 0.44 | 0.06 | -0.28 |
| $w$ | 7.87 | 1.69 | 0.79 | 0.53 | 0.65 | 0.43 | 0.17 | -0.02 | -0.17 |
| $r$ | 11.98 | 2.57 | 0.59 | 0.03 | -0.53 | -0.02 | 0.47 | 0.48 | 0.37 |
| $M1$ | 7.34 | 1.53 | 0.57 | 0.15 | -0.04 | -0.12 | -0.23 | -0.38 | -0.55 |
| $M2$ | 9.60 | 2.00 | 0.83 | 0.47 | -0.14 | -0.08 | -0.15 | -0.30 | -0.49 |
| $MB$ | 12.68 | 2.64 | 0.53 | 0.18 | 0.30 | 0.08 | -0.23 | -0.59 | -0.67 |
| $TD$ | 13.99 | 2.91 | 0.77 | 0.39 | -0.13 | 0.08 | 0.19 | 0.16 | 0.04 |
| $V1$ | 7.62 | 1.59 | 0.60 | 0.27 | -0.50 | -0.40 | -0.25 | -0.15 | 0.05 |
| $V2$ | 6.45 | 1.34 | 0.73 | 0.28 | -0.45 | -0.48 | -0.33 | -0.20 | 0.11 |
| $Vb$ | 12.78 | 2.66 | 0.41 | -0.10 | -0.61 | -0.38 | -0.05 | 0.25 | 0.35 |
| $Py$ | 8.34 | 1.79 | 0.91 | 0.73 | -0.56 | -0.64 | -0.68 | -0.61 | -0.42 |
| $Pc$ | 10.29 | 2.21 | 0.90 | 0.70 | -0.33 | -0.50 | -0.67 | -0.69 | -0.53 |

*Note:* $y-$ output; $c-$ private consumption; $g-$ government consumption; $s-$ savings; $i-$ investment; $x-$ exports; $im-$ imports; $N-$ employment; $k-$ capital stock; $w-$ wage rate; $r-$ capital returns; $M1-$ money stock; $TD-$ time deposits ($= M2 - M1$); $Vi = (PyY)/Mi$; $Py-$ GDP deflator; $Pc-$ Consumers Price Index.

the Colonial War (early 60's), the 1974 revolution and the two IMF stabilization programs (1977–79, 1983–85). The effects of our entry to the EEC and of the favorable internal and external economic environment are also visible in the latter part of the sample.

Figures 11 to 15.4 depict the evolution of the most important nominal variables, $M1$, $M2$ and the monetary base ($MB$). Figure 12 shows the increasing importance of time deposits ($M2 - M1$) and the increase in the credit multiplier ($M2/MB$). The velocity of circulation, measured with the various definitions of money, has a stable pattern, only disturbed by the four major shocks to the portuguese economy, and by the evolution of the financial system, which caused the rise in $V1$ and a slight reduction in $V2$.

Table 2 confirms the patterns suggested by Figures 15.1 to 15.4. All nominal variables are strongly counter-cyclical and more volatile than output. Time deposits ($TD$), which equal $M2 - M1$, are the only nominal variable that is pro-cyclical. Some additional features are made clear in this Table. $M2$ displays much higher persistence than $M1$ and $MB$. The monetary variables $M1$, $M2$ and $MB$ lead the cycle, while the velocity of circulation is a lagging variable.

The two price measures (the GDP deflator and the Consumer Price

Index) show the highest degree of persistence in the reported variables and the absence of a time-shift. But the most striking feature of the behavior of nominal prices is their volatility: these prices are twice as volatile as output in Portugal, while they are less volatile than output in the U.S. (Kydland and Prescott (1989)). Sorting out the role played by monetary policy and by changes in relative prices in the variability of Portuguese nominal prices is a challenge to future research.

The main stylized facts of the business cycle — the ones most macroeconomists would manage to recall during a surprise quiz — are that:

(i) investment is 2 to 3 times more volatile than output, while consumption is less volatile than output;

(ii) there is a positive correlation between consumption, investment, output and labor effort;

(iii) all of these variables show significant serial correlation.

Figures 15.1 to 17.4 and the statistics reported in Table 2 demonstrate that the Portuguese business cycle conforms with these general patterns. Other salient features of the moments reported in this Table are the high volatility of exports and imports and the presence of leading and lagging variables. Employment and returns to capital seem to leading variables, while the capital stock and real wages seem to lag the cycle.

To investigate whether there is something unique about Portuguese fluctuations we compare the statistics computed for Portugal with those for a variety of other OECD countries. We must warn the reader that, while the Portuguese data have annual frequency, the data for all other countries have quarterly frequency. Since all variables are expressed in logs the magnitudes of the standard deviations are directly comparable, although they could be affected by the time aggregation phenomenon. The first lagged (and leaded) correlations are, however, not directly comparable, since they refer to the previous (following) year in the case of Portugal and to the previous (following) quarter in the case of all the other countries.

Another important difference between the statistics for Portugal and those for all the other countries is with respect to the smoothing parameter $\lambda$ associated with the HP filter. As we mentioned before, we used $\lambda = 400$ to detrend the Portuguese annual data, while the data of all the other countries (which has quarterly frequency) was detrended with $\lambda = 1600$. Luckily, the features that we emphasize below (in particular the high volatility of Portuguese macroeconomic variables) hold for a very large range of values for $\lambda$.

Table 3 collects the most important second moments of macro series of OECD countries detrended with the HP filter. We use these countries

Table 3: International comparisons.

3.1: Standard deviations.

| | *y* | *c* | *g* | *s* | *i* | *x* | *im* |
|---|---|---|---|---|---|---|---|
| Portugal | 4.66 | 4.38 | 3.82 | 17.20 | 15.13 | 12.84 | 12.50 |
| USA | 1.84 | 1.24 | 2.04 | 7.41 | 5.52 | 6.94 | 5.55 |
| Japan | 1.71 | 1.92 | 2.20 | 4.50 | 3.95 | 6.88 | 9.88 |
| Germany | 1.70 | 1.19 | 2.09 | 5.47 | 5.78 | 3.87 | 1.64 |
| U.Kingdom | 1.49 | 1.60 | 1.47 | | 6.69 | 3.12 | 3.83 |
| France | 0.99 | 0.88 | 1.23 | 3.62 | 1.90 | 4.06 | 6.14 |
| Canada | 1.66 | 1.47 | 2.17 | 6.22 | 4.71 | 5.01 | 3.32 |
| Italy | 2.21 | 1.81 | 3.12 | 8.15 | 5.51 | 4.97 | 9.09 |
| Austria | 1.18 | 1.47 | 0.59 | 4.17 | 3.64 | 3.52* | |
| Australia | 1.70 | 1.17 | 2.80 | 5.79 | 3.69 | 6.09 | 7.62 |
| Switzerland | 2.15 | 1.64 | 1.81 | 5.72 | 6.20 | 4.42 | 7.29 |

3.2: Standard deviations relative to output.

| | *c* | *g* | *s* | *i* | *x* | *im* |
|---|---|---|---|---|---|---|
| Portugal | 0.94 | 0.82 | 3.70 | 3.25 | 2.76 | 2.69 |
| USA | 0.67 | 1.11 | 4.03 | 3.00 | 3.77 | 3.02 |
| Japan | 1.12 | 1.29 | 2.63 | 2.31 | 4.02 | 5.78 |
| Germany | 0.70 | 1.23 | 3.22 | 3.40 | 2.28 | 0.96 |
| U.Kingdom | 1.07 | 0.99 | | 4.49 | 2.09 | 2.57 |
| France | 0.89 | 1.24 | 3.66 | 1.92 | 4.10 | 6.20 |
| Canada | 0.89 | 1.31 | 3.75 | 2.84 | 3.02 | 2.00 |
| Italy | 0.82 | 1.41 | 3.69 | 2.49 | 2.25 | 4.11 |
| Austria | 1.24 | 0.50 | 3.52 | 3.08 | 2.97* | |
| Australia | 0.69 | 1.65 | 3.41 | 2.17 | 3.58 | 4.48 |
| Switzerland | 0.76 | 0.84 | 2.66 | 2.88 | 2.06 | 3.39 |

3.3: Cross correlations with output.

| | *c* | *g* | *s* | *i* | *x* | *im* |
|---|---|---|---|---|---|---|
| Portugal | 0.69 | 0.32 | 0.32 | 0.83 | 0.65 | 0.81 |
| USA | 0.88 | 0.06 | 0.90 | 0.90 | 0.17 | 0.55 |
| Japan | 0.47 | -0.29 | 0.77 | 0.60 | -0.10 | -0.02 |
| Germany | 0.64 | -0.03 | 0.90 | 0.80 | 0.19 | 0.45 |
| U.Kingdom | 0.68 | 0.14 | | 0.74 | 0.49 | 0.56 |
| France | 0.58 | 0.10 | 0.78 | 0.45 | 0.34 | 0.29 |
| Canada | 0.72 | -0.21 | 0.82 | 0.62 | 0.67 | 0.77 |
| Italy | 0.70 | 0.17 | 0.80 | 0.80 | 0.42 | 0.81 |
| Austria | 0.54 | -0.18 | 0.70 | 0.74 | -0.34* | |
| Australia | 0.62 | -0.17 | 0.88 | 0.55 | 0.34 | 0.43 |
| Switzerland | 0.74 | 0.29 | 0.87 | 0.73 | 0.68 | 0.83 |

3.4: First order autocorrelations.

| | *y* | *c* | *g* | *s* | *i* | *x* | *im* |
|---|---|---|---|---|---|---|---|
| Portugal | 0.69 | 0.72 | 0.49 | 0.42 | 0.57 | 0.74 | 0.63 |
| USA | 0.84 | 0.83 | 0.85 | 0.75 | 0.89 | 0.76 | 0.68 |
| Japan | 0.74 | 0.79 | 0.31 | 0.75 | 0.83 | 0.82 | 0.88 |
| Germany | 0.71 | 0.50 | 0.45 | 0.65 | 0.68 | 0.63 | 0.73 |
| U.Kingdom | 0.58 | 0.73 | 0.61 | | 0.68 | 0.33 | 0.63 |
| France | 0.79 | 0.49 | 0.10 | 0.67 | 0.70 | 0.72 | 0.75 |
| Canada | 0.79 | 0.75 | 0.61 | 0.74 | 0.87 | 0.74 | 0.81 |
| Italy | 0.78 | 0.66 | 0.82 | 0.44 | 0.86 | 0.61 | 0.76 |
| Austria | 0.61 | 0.26 | 0.68 | 0.57 | 0.55 | 0.30* | |
| Australia | 0.67 | 0.47 | 0.49 | 0.63 | 0.74 | 0.67 | 0.77 |
| Switzerland | 0.70 | 0.52 | 0.11 | 0.41 | 0.81 | 0.76 | 0.83 |

* The data for Austria in the column of the Exports, refers to the Trade Balance.

*Source:* Portugal: Table 1; U.Kingdom: Blackburn and Ravn (1990); Austria: Brandner and Neusser (1990); Other countries: Baxter and Crucini (1990).

as a control group against which we compare the Portuguese economy. A few ideas emerge clearly from this comparison. The variability of all the variables, as measured by their standard deviation, is more than double the average volatility in the control group. This observation accords with evidence that less developed countries tend to have higher output volatility. In the Summers and Heston (1984) cross–country data set the standard deviation of real GDP growth for the 1/3 poorest countries is 50% higher than the same standard deviation for the 1/3 richest countries (5.7% versus 4%).

There is, however, reason to believe that the high volatility of Portuguese macroeconomic indicators might partly be associated with the sample period that we have available. The period 1958–1990 was one of stability for most OECD countries included in the control group, since events such as the two World Wars and the Great Depression were excluded from the sample. In contrast, this period includes events, such as the Colonial War and the 1974 revolution, that had a significant impact in the Portuguese economy. The idea that sample selection is one of the factors that can account for the pattern of volatility that we uncovered receives some support from Table 1. The standard deviation of GDP (detrended with the HP filter) reported in this Table for the period 1870–1979 is not out of line with the volatility of output in other countries during this period.[10]

The relative variability of all the Portuguese macroeconomic variables (standard deviation of variable relative to the standard deviation of output) is similar to those of the other countries. The relative volatility of exports and imports is lower than average while the relative variability of private consumption, savings and investment is higher than average. The relative volatility of government consumption is the lowest in the sample. Portuguese relative variabilities are most similar to those found in Switzerland (for government consumption and imports), Canada (for savings), US (for savings and imports), UK (for government consumption and imports) and Germany (for investment).

The cross correlations with output have values that are higher than average for all the variables expect for consumption and savings. The correlation of consumption with output is about average, while the correlation between savings and output is by far the lowest in the sample. The countries with similar patterns of co-movement with output are: Switzerland (for private and government consumption, imports and exports), Canada (private consumption, exports and imports), Italy (investment and imports) and Germany (private consumption and investment).

[10] Further uncertainty on this issue is associated with C. Romer's (1989) demonstration that the difference in U.S. output variability before and after World War II is in part an artifact of the methods used to estimate pre-war output.

In summary, the volatility of the Portuguese economy seems to be substantially higher that the volatility of other OECD countries. All other statistics seem to be in line with the cross-country evidence. Not surprisingly, Portuguese fluctuations seem to be closest in pattern to those of other small open economies, such as Switzerland and Canada, and to those of other European economies such as the UK, Germany and Italy.

These international comparisons give us a sense of the dimensions along which the Portuguese business cycle is peculiar and the ones that abide by the general pattern. To evaluate whether these peculiar aspects are a natural consequence of the characteristics of the Portuguese economy, its openness to international trade, its labor share in national income, its share of government expenditures in GNP, etc. we need a model that links the properties of macro time series to the main structural parameters of the economy. In sections 3 and 4 we provide two such models . Both of these models are extremely simple and could easily be complicated along a large number of directions. But one has to start with the simplest possible model to evaluate which of these directions are likely to be fruitful. As in physics, it makes sense first to study a world with no frictions to evaluate which sources of attrition are likely to be most relevant to understand the phenomena under examination.

# 3 A Closed Economy Model

This section describes a closed economy model which we use to organize the main empirical regularities uncovered in section 2. This model is similar to the one studied in detail in King, Plosser and Rebelo (1987,1988a) so our presentation will be brief.

The economy is populated by a large number of identical agents who perceive their influence on prices to be negligible. Population ($M_t$) increases at an exogenous gross rate $\gamma_m$.

Each individual seeks to maximize his expected lifetime utility

$$U = E_0 \left[ \sum_{t=0}^{\infty} \beta^t [u(C_t, L_t) + \phi(G_t)] \right] \quad , \quad \beta = \tilde{\beta} \gamma_m^{\eta} \tag{1}$$

defined over sequences of per capita private consumption ($C_t$), leisure ($L_t$), and government expenditures ($G_t$),[11] where $\phi$ maps $\mathbf{R}^+$ into a bounded

[11] This formulation, in which utility is a function of per capita government expenditures, assumes that the consumption of goods provided by the government is rival. Since we will take the stochastic process for $G$ as exogenous, considering pure public goods in the Samuelson sense would not change the conclusions of our analysis.

subset of $\mathbf{R}$. The operator $E_0$ denotes the expectation conditional on the time zero information set which comprises present and past values of all the variables.

The discount factor $\beta$ embodies two components. The first, $\tilde{\beta}$, corresponds to the Fisherian pure rate of time preference, while the second component ($\gamma_m^\eta$) reflects the nature of the links between the utility of the present generation and that of future generations.[12]

In the analysis that follows we only need to take a stand on the value of $\beta$, instead of parameterizing $\tilde{\beta}$ and $\eta$ separately.

We assume that the function $u(\cdot)$ takes the following isoelastic form

$$u(C,L) = \frac{(C_t L_t^\theta)^{1-\sigma} - 1}{1-\sigma} .$$

The values of $\theta$ and $\sigma$ are positive and we assume that $\theta(1-\sigma) < 1$ and $\theta(1-\sigma) < \sigma$ to ensure that $u(\cdot)$ is strictly concave.

Each individual has an annual time endowment which is normalized to one, so:

$$N_t + L_t = 1 . \tag{2}$$

where $N_t$ is the number of hours devoted to work. There is a single good in the economy that can be produced by combining labor and per capita capital ($K_t$) according to a Cobb-Douglas production function. Per capita output is given by:

$$Y_t = AK_t^{1-\alpha}(N_t X_t)^\alpha . \tag{3}$$

The variable $X_t$ represents the level of technical progress. This level expands at an exogenous gross rate $\gamma_x$ and represents the secular increases in productivity associated with the process of technical innovation.[13] The variable $A_t$ , which represents exogenous shocks to productivity, is such that $\log(A_t)$ follows an $AR(1)$ process.

Output can be devoted to private consumption, to public expenditures, or to investment ($I_t$):

$$Y_t = C_t + I_t + G_t . \tag{4}$$

[12] In his work on money and growth Sidrauski (1967) chose $\eta = 0$, which corresponds to the assumption that current generations attribute utility only to the per capita utility of future generations. Other authors, such as Lucas (1988), chose $\eta = 1$ (current generation care for the total utility of future generations). Finally, in their work on fertility, Barro and Becker (1989) considered the intermediate case in which $0 < \eta < 1$.

[13] We assume that $\beta\gamma_x^{1-\sigma} < 1$ to ensure that expected life time utility is finite. If this restriction did not hold there would be a continuum of paths that would generate an infinite value for $U$. Notice that the restriction $\beta\gamma_x^{1-\sigma} < 1$ does not generally imply that $\tilde{\beta}$ must be less than one (see Kocherlakota (1988)).

The law of motion for the per capita capital stock is:

$$\gamma_m K_{t+1} = I_t + (1 - \delta)K_t \ , \tag{5}$$

where $\delta$ denotes the rate of depreciation.

Government expenditures follow an exogenous stochastic process:

$$\log G_t = \log G_{t-1} + \log \gamma_{gt} \tag{6}$$

$$\log \gamma_{gt} = \log \gamma_x + \varphi_t \ , \tag{7}$$

where $\varphi_t$ is an $AR(1)$ process. Equations (6) and (7) imply that the mean growth rate of government expenditures is $\gamma_x$, which coincides with the mean growth rate of output. We impose this restriction to ensure that the share of government expenditures in GNP is stationary.[14]

To understand the economic mechanisms that generate the laws of motion for the different variables in this model it is useful to start by describing what a fictitious planner, who seeks to maximize welfare, would do. The planner's problem is to maximize the welfare of the representative agent defined in (1), subject to the constraints (2)–(7). In this problem the stochastic process for government expenditures will be taken as exogenous, i.e., $G_t$ will not be chosen to maximize welfare as in Ambler and Paquet (1990). The reason for this is that we want to use as a description of the behavior of $G_t$ the actual stochastic process that represents the evolution of $G_t$ in Portugal.

The planner's problem is one in which decisions are made sequentially on the basis of information about the nature of the shocks that is revealed as time goes by. The optimal level of consumption at time $t$ is decided on the basis of the time $t$ capital stock and of the realizations of the shocks to government expenditures and productivity. A solution to the planning problem is then a set of decision rules that express what the optimal levels for the different variables should be as a function of $K_t$, $A_t$ and $G_t$. These rules generate stochastic processes for $C_t$, $Y_t$, $I_t$, etc. whose first and second moments (after appropriate detrending to ensure stationarity) can be confronted with those of the data.

The planning problem just described is only useful as an expositional and computational device. We are not interested in using this model to interpret the evolution of a planned economy in which all allocations are dictated by the government. Instead, we want to compute a competitive equilibrium under rational expectations. In this competitive equilibrium all

[14] As Figure 7.2 illustrates, there is no pronounced trend in the share of GNP (narrowly defined to include only purchases of goods and services by the government) during the 1958–1989 period.

markets clear, and all agents make optimal decisions taking prices as given and making the best possible use of the information that is available to them to forecast the future. The rational expectations assumption means, in our specific context, that agents know the stochastic processes that rule the behavior of prices (interest rates and wage rates) and so are able to make optimal (though not perfect!) predictions about the future values of these variables on the basis of their past observations. This may seem a stringent requirement but prices in this economy follow low order ARMA processes that would certainly belong to the tool kit of any forecasting service, government agency or financial institution.

By virtue of the second welfare theorem the evolution of all quantity variables in the competitive equilibrium is the same as the evolution of these variables that would be chosen by our benevolent planner. This means that we can study the evolution of the quantity variables in our economy without being specific about what set of markets is being used to decentralize the competitive equilibrium. This is fortunate since the vast majority of the variables that we studied in section 2 are quantities, not prices.

Producing predictions about the evolution of prices requires that we grapple with all the details of the market structure that prevails in the economy. Perhaps the simplest market structure that would support the competitive equilibrium that we describe is one with spot labor markets (cleared by the wage rate $w_t$), a stock market in which claims to firms are traded (cleared by the rate of return, $r_t$) and a system of lump sum taxes that finances public expenditures. It is important to stress that many other, more realistic, market structures are compatible with the properties of the quantity variables that we describe. It is possible for instance to expand the number of assets that are traded in the stock market, to include bonds, options, futures, etc. The spot labor market can also be replaced by a system in which firms smooth out the wage payments to their workers establishing long-term relations with these. We can also allow the government to issue public debt so that tax revenues and expenditures do not have to coincide in every period.

The optimal decision rules of the planning problem described above cannot be computed analytically unless one imposes stringent restriction on the functional forms that describe preferences and technology (as in Radner (1966) and in Long and Plosser (1983)). For this reason we resort to the numerical method developed by King, Plosser and Rebelo (1987, 1988a) to solve the problem. This method, which has proved to be surprisingly accurate for the type of model that we consider, involves linearizing the equations that describe the competitive equilibrium around the steady state.[15]

[15] This procedure is equivalent to the linear-quadratic approximations originally used

Although we will skip over the details of the application of this numerical method it is useful to describe the steady state of the economy, since this will be used as a guide to choose many of the parameters of the model.

## 3.1 The Steady State

To characterize the steady state of this economy we set all stochastic variables ($A_t$ and $G_t$) to their unconditional mean ($A$ and $G$) and look for a solution to the planning problem in which all variables grow at a constant rate. It is easy to see that $N$ and $L$ have to be constant, i.e., to expand at rate zero. It is also easy to show that the only sustainable growth rate for per capita consumption, output and investment is the rate of technical progress $\gamma_x$.

We have previously assumed that (abstracting from stochastic shocks) $G_t$ grows also at rate $\gamma_x$. If this were not the case a steady state would not exist for this economy. This would mean that model's variables would not possess a stationary distribution even after appropriate detrending, making it virtually impossible to compute any meaningful statistics that could be compared to the data

The conditions that characterize the steady state are:

$$C_{t+1}/C_t = [\beta(1+r)/\gamma_N]^{1/\sigma} \tag{8}$$
$$r = (1-\alpha)A[K_t/(X_tN)]^{-\alpha} - \delta \tag{9}$$
$$\gamma_m(K_{t+1}/K_t) = (1-\delta) + I_t/K_t \tag{10}$$
$$K_t/Y_t = [K_t/(X_tN)]^{\alpha}/A \tag{11}$$
$$\theta C_t/(1-N_t) = \alpha A(K_t/N_t)^{1-\alpha}X_t^{\alpha} \tag{12}$$
$$C_t/Y_t + I_t/Y_t + G_t/Y_T = 1 \tag{13}$$

Equation (8) is the standard Fisherian condition for the growth rate of consumption. This equation determines the steady state value of the real interest rate, $r$: this rate has to be such that individuals will be led to expand their consumption at rate $\gamma_x$. Hence, the steady state real interest rate is given by:

$$r = \gamma_m\gamma_x^{\sigma}/\beta - 1 \; .$$

Given this rate of interest equation (9), familiar from the firms maximization problem (it requires that the net marginal product of capital be

by Kydland and Prescott (1982). On the accuracy of these approximations see Christiano (1988), Dotsey and Mao (1990), and Danthine, Donaldson and Mehra (1989). The January 1990 issue of the *Journal of Business and Economic Statistics* is an excellent source of information on numerical methods that are suitable to solve the planning problem described in the text.

equal to the real interest rate) determines the steady state capital-labor ratio, $(K_t/NX_t)$, where $NX_t$ represents labor in efficiency units. Equation (10) and the fact that capital expands at rate $\gamma_x$ determines the steady state investment-capital ratio. Equation (11) determines the capital-output ratio, which, together with $I/K$ determines the share of investment in income. Equation (13) determines the share of consumption in output that corresponds to a given exogenous government share, $G_t/Y_t$. Finally, equation (12) (which corresponds to the requirement that the marginal rate of substitution between consumption and leisure be equal to the wage rate) determines the steady state value of $N$.

## 3.2 Parameterizing the Model

Before we compare the statistical properties of our artificial economy with those of the Portuguese data, we parameterize the model so that it reproduces the most important long-run features of the Portuguese economy. The list of parameter values adopted is provided in Table 4.

We want the model to reproduce the mean growth rate of per capita output (4%) and population growth (0.6%) that we found in the data. To this end we set $\gamma_x = 1.04$ and $\gamma_m = 1.006$. We also choose $\beta$ so that $r + \delta$, the mean real rate of return to capital (gross of depreciation) coincides in the model and in the data ($r + \delta = 16\%$). We choose $\alpha$ to be 53%, which is the mean share of labor in the data and set the share of government in output to its mean value, 12%. We choose $\delta$ to be such that the investment

Table 4: Parameterizations.

| Parameters | Closed Economy Case A (lump sum taxes) | Closed Economy Case B (income taxes) | Open Economy |
|---|---|---|---|
| $\alpha$ | 0.5300 | 0.5300 | 0.5300 |
| $\gamma_m$ | 1.0060 | 1.0060 | 1.0060 |
| $\gamma_x$ | 1.0400 | 1.0400 | 1.0400 |
| $\sigma$ | 1.0000 | 1.0000 | 1.0000 |
| $\delta$ | 0.0500 | 0.0500 | 0.0500 |
| $\beta$ | 0.9426 | 0.9539 | 0.9824 |
| $G/Y$ | 0.1200 | 0.1200 | 0.1200 |
| $\tau$ | 0.0000 | 0.1200 | 0.1200 |
| Benchmark Indicators | | | |
| $I/Y$ | 0.2827 | 0.2712 | 0.3461 |
| Basic Savings Rate | 0.2827 | 0.2712 | 0.1718 |
| $C/Y$ | 0.5973 | 0.6088 | 0.6900 |
| $TB/Y$ | | | -0.1561 |
| $B/Y$ | 0.0000 | 0.0000 | 8.3225 |
| $r$ | 0.1100 | 0.0968 | 0.0650 |
| $r^*$ | | | 0.0650 |
| $N$ | 0.2000 | 0.2000 | 0.2000 |

share coincides with its average value in the data, 27%. This requires that we set the rate of depreciation, $\delta$ to 5%. This value is lower than the standard 10% commonly employed in the literature but it is well within the range of values reported by Santos (1984a) for Portugal and accords with the values that Romer (1989) found to be consistent with observed capital-output ratios. We normalize the constant $A$, which has no bearing on the statistics that we report, to one. We know of no information concerning the value of $N$ (the mean fraction of hours worked) so we chose a value of $\theta$ such that the steady state number of hours worked in our model is the same as that reported in King, Plosser and Rebelo (1988a): $N = 0.20$.

We estimated the value of $\sigma$ using Hansen's (1982) Generalized Method of Moments applied to the orthogonality condition that describes the optimal growth of consumption:

$$E_t \left\{ \beta [C_{t+1}/C_t]^{-\sigma} (1 + r_{t+1}) - \gamma_m \right\} = 0 \, .$$

Depending on the instrument used (a constant, lagged consumption or lagged returns) we obtained point estimates of $\sigma$ that ranged between 0.6 and 3. This led us to choose a value of $\sigma$ equal to one, which is the standard value used in the literature.[16]

Our estimates for $\sigma$ contrast with those obtained by Giovannini (1985) for Portugal, which range between $\sigma = 7$ and $\sigma = 20$ and are not significantly different from $\sigma = \infty$ (i.e., no intertemporal substitution). The difference between our estimates and those of Giovannini is mainly due to the different rate of return series employed. We used our measure of the real rate of return to capital (which was constructed dividing income accrued to capital by the capital stock), while Giovannini (1985) used the real return to one year time deposits. We believe that the real return to one year time deposits severely underestimates the returns to savings in Portugal. For most of Giovannini's sample period, investment in time deposits represented a relatively small fraction of private savings.[17] During this period firms resorted heavily to internal financing to implement investment projects whose mean rate of return was clearly much higher than the real interest rate associated with time deposits.

To complete the parameterization of the model we need to choose the stochastic processes for $A_t$ and $G_t$. In the case of $G_t$ our task was simple: we linearly detrended our series for $\log(G_t)$ and estimated an $AR(1)$ with the detrended data. We used our estimates for the first order correlation (0.6)

[16] Given that data on hours worked is not available we abstracted from leisure choice, assuming $N$ to be constant, in these computations.

[17] The change in the stock of time deposits as a fraction of total savings by Portuguese residents was smaller in the 60's and 70's (26% in 1965, 35% in 1970, 18% in 1973) than in the 80's (75% in 1981 and 42% in 1985).

and for the variance of the innovation (0.12) to parameterize the stochastic process for $\varphi_t$ in equation (7).

If a time series for $N$ were available we could have parameterized the stochastic process for $A$ in a similar manner. Using the series for $K$, $N$ and $Y$ we could have computed the Solow residual, as in Prescott (1986), and used this to estimate the process for $A_t$.[18] Without an available series for $N$ we resorted to the Kydland-Prescott (1982) method of choosing the stochastic process for $A_t$ so that the variance and serial correlation of output (HP detrended) coincides in the model and the data.

## 3.3 Introducing Income Taxation

We have explored a second parameterization that involves replacing the lump sum taxes used to finance public expenditures by income taxes (see Table 4). We chose the income tax rate to coincide with the government share so that, on average, the budget is balanced. Outside the steady state the difference between government revenue and government expenditure is eliminated through lump sum transfers. The equilibrium that we describe is also consistent with the alternative assumption that the government uses public debt as a buffer that compensates deficits and surpluses.

We left all the parameters of the model unchanged but adjusted $\beta$ so that the average before tax rate of return on capital (gross of depreciation) continues to be 16%.[19] The model with lump sum taxes has statistical properties that are virtually identical to the model with income taxes so we discuss only the results for the latter.

## 3.4 Second Moment Properties

The standard method used in the literature for evaluating the model is to compare the second moment properties of the variables generated by the model with those of the data. As has been the case in studies for many other countries, this very simple model demonstrates a surprising ability to mimic reality. A few important differences between the two sets of moments will be noted, but it must be stressed that these "failures" of the model are embedded in a general picture of adherence.

We must emphasize that all the second moments that we discuss were obtained after detrending the variables with the HP filter. Our theoretical

[18] Recent results obtained by Gordon (1990) indicate that is important to control for capacity utilization in computing the Solow residual.

[19] The second welfare theorem does not hold for this economy due to the presence of distorting taxes. This implies that the competitive equilibrium cannot be computed simply by solving a planning problem. Romer (1989) and King, Plosser and Rebelo (1988b) describe a computational strategy that works for this case.

Table 5: Closed economy with income taxes.

| | St. Dev. | St.D. rel.$Y$ | Autocorrel. 1 | 2 | Cross-correlations with $y(t+i)$ -2 | -1 | 0 | 1 | 2 |
|---|---|---|---|---|---|---|---|---|---|
| $y$ | 4.60 | 1.00 | 0.69 | 0.45 | 0.45 | 0.69 | 1.00 | 0.69 | 0.45 |
| $c$ | 4.01 | 0.89 | 0.79 | 0.61 | 0.61 | 0.78 | 0.96 | 0.64 | 0.40 |
| $g$ | 3.80 | 0.82 | 0.49 | 0.16 | 0.01 | 0.02 | 0.03 | 0.01 | 0.00 |
| $i$ | 8.63 | 1.85 | 0.61 | 0.32 | 0.25 | 0.55 | 0.96 | 0.69 | 0.46 |
| $N$ | 1.10 | 0.24 | 0.63 | 0.35 | -0.27 | 0.07 | 0.59 | 0.47 | 0.34 |
| $k$ | 2.47 | 0.53 | 0.96 | 0.90 | 0.80 | 0.66 | 0.38 | 0.18 | 0.07 |
| $w$ | 4.11 | 0.88 | 0.77 | 0.57 | 0.58 | 0.76 | 0.98 | 0.66 | 0.41 |
| $r$ | 0.55 | 0.12 | 0.58 | 0.27 | 0.02 | 0.36 | 0.85 | 0.63 | 0.44 |

*Note:* $y$– output; $c$– private consumption; $g$– government consumption; $i$– investment; $N$– employment; $k$– capital stock; $w$– wage rate; $r$– capital returns.

model implies that if we extracted a common linear trend to all series (with the exception of $r$ and $N$) we should obtain stationary variables. This implication of the model is not satisfied by the Portuguese data. The model economy considered in the section 4 is, in part, an attempt to eliminate this counterfactual implication.[20]

The most important differences between the model and the data concern the behavior of the real return to capital ($r_t$) and the real wage ($w_t$). The standard deviations of $r_t$ and $w_t$ are 12% and 8%, respectively, while the model predicts values around 0.5% and 4%. In the data the path for both of these variables is smooth except for the severe shock occurred in 1974.

As in the analyzes of Kydland and Prescott (1982) and Hansen (1985) for the US economy, our model underestimates the volatility of consumption and produces a standard deviation of investment that is smaller than that in the data.

The serial correlation properties are very similar in the model and in the data. In terms of the comovement properties of the different variables the model generally overestimated the cross-correlations with output. One notable exception is government expenditures which are more correlated with output in the data than in the model.

As a general conclusion this model performed extremely well, specially if we take into consideration its intrinsic simplicity and elementary character.

## 3.5 Impulse Response Functions

Figures 16.1 to 17.4 depict the impulse response functions associated with a 1% innovation to $A$ and $G$, respectively. All variables are represented as

[20] Another possible avenue for dealing with this problem is to assume that the shocks to productivity follow a random walk as in King, Plosser and Rebelo (1988b). This would imply that all components of the National Income accounts would be cointegrated in the sense of Engle and Granger (1987).

percent deviations from the steady state. These impulse response functions illustrate well the mechanisms at work in this economy. Figures 16.1 to 16.4 describe the effects of a shock to productivity. This shock has almost a permanent character, since its serial correlation is close to one. These figuree contain all the ingredients of an economic boom: the economy responds to the shock by increasing its investment, consumption, work effort and output. The wage rate and the real interest rate also rise. During this period the response of investment is higher than that of output which in turn is higher than that of consumption. These patterns are the result of income effects (which dominate the behavior of consumption), intertemporal substitution effects (associated with the interest rate path and with the evolution of wages which induce an upward sloping path both consumption and leisure), and intratemporal substitution effects (that lead agents to increase consumption and reduce leisure in response to the increase in labor productivity).[21]

The effects of a shock to government expenditures are perhaps easier to describe. Since the taxes levied to finance this surge in government expenditure are lump sum the main effect that is operating is an income effect. This makes private agents decrease their leisure and their consumption both now and in the future. The decline in future consumption is accomplished through a reduction in the level of investment. It is worthwhile noticing that the short term "multiplier" effect of a 1% increase in $G$ is only a 0.04% increase in output. The response of all the other variables to this shock is also dramatically lower than in the case of a productivity shock. The long run effect of this temporary increase in government expenditures is zero. The response of the economy to this increase in $G$ does not have the typical pattern of an expansion: output and labor increase but investment, consumption and wages decrease.

## 3.6 The Productivity Shock

Our model generates a contingent decision rule for output that has the form $Y_t = \Phi(K_t, A_t, G_t, X_t)$. Using the observed time series for $Y_t$, $K_t$, $G_t$, and the fact that $X_t = X_0\gamma_x^t$, (where $X_0$ is an irrelevant scale factor) we can uncover the path of the exogenous productivity shifter $A$ that is implied by the model. This path is depicted in Figure 18.1, together with the evolution of linearly detrended $G_t$ ($A_t$ is expressed in terms of percentage deviations from its mean value).[22]

[21] A method for decomposing the impact of these various effects is described in King (1990a).

[22] The path for $A$ in Figure 18.1 was computed using the decision rule for $Y_t$ and $C_t$ to avoid using the capital stock data, which is always the most problematic series in terms of measurement error.

Critics of the real business cycle literature often remark that to generate plausible cycles these models need to rely on frequent total decreases in productivity (see Mankiw (1989)). It turns out that the behavior of this unobservable shock is extremely plausible in our model.

There are six instances in which the model predicts a decrease in productivity, but only four of these are larger in absolute value than 0.5%: the oil shock in 1973 (-7.4%), the revolution in 1974 (-15.2%), the 1980 currency appreciation with its negative effects on the terms of trade (-2.9%) and the second IMF stabilization program in 1983 (-2.3%).[23]

# 4 A Small Open Economy Model

In this section we investigate the effects of allowing the economy described in section 3 to trade in the international capital markets. Our motivations to pursue this modification of the standard real business cycle model are as follows. First, international trade and the behavior of the current account are important phenomena in the Portuguese economy. Second, our empirical analysis seems to indicate that small open economies share some peculiar business cycle patterns. Finally, the model that we consider in this section implies that all variables in the economy are first order integrated processes, even though the shocks that drive the model are trend-stationary.

This generalization of the basic neoclassical model of section 3 involves replacing equation (4) by:

$$\begin{aligned} Y_t &= C_t + G_t + I_t + TB_t \\ \gamma_m B_{t+1} &= TB_t + (1 + r_t^*) B_t \ , \end{aligned}$$

where $TB_t$ denotes the trade balance and $B_t$ the domestic per capita foreign asset holdings. The rate of return to these foreign assets is $r_t^*$.

We also replace equation (5) by:

$$\gamma_m K_{t+1} = \phi(I_t/K_t)K_t + (1-\delta)K_t \ , \quad \phi\prime(\cdot) > 0, \phi''(\cdot) < 0$$

where the function $\phi(\cdot)$ reflects adjustment costs associated with the investment process as in Abel and Blanchard (1985), and Baxter and Crucini (1990). These adjustment costs are indispensable to generate empirically plausible investment volatilities.

Our economy cannot trade in the complete set of international markets present in the economies of Baxter and Crucini (1990). For this reason,

[23] In terms of our notation an absolute fall in productivity occurs when $(X_0\gamma_x^t)^\alpha A_t > (X_0\gamma_x^{t+1})^\alpha A_{t+1}$.

agents in our model will bear risk that would be diversifiable in the Baxter-Crucini world. This has important consequences that we explore in detail in our work in progress, Correia, Neves and Rebelo (1990).

The main difficulty involved in solving this model is due to the fact that consumption, and consequently all other GDP components, are random walks. The reason for this non-stationarity is the same that underlies the random walk behavior of consumption of a household that can trade in the credit market at an exogenous real interest rate (see Hall (1989)).

In an appendix (available on request) we describe in detail how our method for computing the competitive equilibrium for this economy maps into the approximation strategy of King, Plosser and Rebelo (1987,1988). Here we limit ourselves to a description of the steady state and of our parameterization procedure.

## 4.1 The Steady State

For convenience, we assume that in the steady state there are no adjustment costs associated with the investment process. This assumption results in steady state equations that are very similar to those of the closed economy model; equations (9), (10) and (12) continue to be part of the steady state characterization, while equations (8), (9) and (13) suffer some minor adjustments. In equations (8) and (9) the steady state domestic interest rate $r$ replaced by the steady state international interest rate $r^*$. This reflects the Fisherian separation at work in this economy: the growth rate of consumption and the domestic investment decisions are solely determined by the foreign real rate of interest. The analogous to equation (13) is now:

$$C_t/Y_t + I_t/Y_t + G_t/Y_t + TB_t/Y_t = 1 \, .$$

As before, this equation determines the consumption share given the investment share implied by (10) and (11), the exogenous government share and the share of the balance of trade in GDP. The steady state value of the balance of trade share in output is determined by:

$$TB_t/Y_t = (B_t/Y_t)[\gamma_m - (1 + r^*)] \, .$$

As one would expect, the steady state consumption share depends on $B_t/Y_t$, the share of foreign assets in the country's portfolio. Any value of $B/Y$ is consistent with the steady state; countries with a higher stock of foreign assets will have higher levels of consumption but the same investment share and capital-labor ratios.

## 4.2 Parameterizing the Model

The parameter values chosen for this model are reported in Table 4. These values are identical to those of the closed economy with income taxes with two exceptions: the discount factor $\beta$ and the parameter $\xi$ which has to do with the presence of adjustment costs. We also have to choose a value for the share of the balance of trade in GDP, which in section 3 is equal to zero. We have chosen $TB/Y$ so that the consumption share coincides in the model and in the data ($C/Y = 0.69$).

To choose the parameter $\beta$ we need data on the international real interest rate $r_t^*$. As a first approximation, we identified $r_t^*$ with the real return to a portfolio of common stock in the 500 largest American companies (the Standard and Poors 500 index).[24] This portfolio is one that is available to international investors and hence must reflect the behavior of the world real interest rate.[25] Its mean real rate of return was approximately 6.5% for the period 1929–1989 (see Ibbotson and Sinquefield (1988)). We chose $\beta$ so that, faced with a 6.5% real return, our economy chooses to expand its per capita consumption at the rate of technical progress: $\beta = \gamma_m \gamma_x^\sigma/(1 + r^*)$. A higher value of $\beta$ would imply that our economy would lend to the rest of the world until, asymptotically, it owned all of world's wealth. A lower value of $\beta$ would imply that our country would borrow from the rest of the world until it exhausted all of its wealth (including the present value of all future labor income). Our choice of $\beta$ avoids these implausible asymptotic implications, first demonstrated by Becker (1980), and guarantees that, as in our closed economy, all components of GDP have a steady state growth rate of $\gamma_x$.[26]

The mean value of our $r_t^*$ series (6.5%) is different from the steady state real interest rate in the economy of section 3 (11%). Since we maintained the rate of depreciation at 5%, this economy has a steady state value of $I/Y$ that is higher than that of the data (34% versus 27%). To obtain a value of the investment share similar to that suggested by the data we would have to have chosen an extremely low rate of depreciation (about 2%).

To solve the model all we need to specify about the adjustment cost technology is the elasticity of $1/\phi'(\cdot)$ with respect to its argument. We

[24] Baxter and Crucini (1990) show that the correlation between the international real interest rate and the productivity shocks play an important role in determining some properties of open economy models. For this reason, we plan to explore alternative measures of the world real interest rate in future work.

[25] Implicitly we assume that relative purchasing power parity holds so that we can use the real rate of return for dollar — denominated assets as a measure of $r_t^*$.

[26] An alternative to this strategy would be to abandon our time-separable preferences and employ recursive preferences of the Epstein (1983) variety, as in the work of Mendoza (1990).

denote this elasticity by $\xi$ and set it equal to 0.075. This is the lower value used by Baxter and Crucini (1990) and has the advantage of generating a realistic behavior for investment.

The value of $1/\phi'(\cdot)$ is equal to Tobin's $q$, the ratio of the value of capital to its replacement cost. We report the model's implications for this statistic although, at present, there are no measures of Tobin's $q$ available for Portugal. It is important to note that the presence of adjustment costs makes our measure of the rate of return to capital not comparable to the rate of return predicted by the model.

As in section 3 we have chosen parameters for the $AR(1)$ stochastic process that describes $A_t$ so that the standard deviation and serial correlation of output coincide in the model and in the data.[27] We have also chosen this shock to be orthogonal to $r_t^*$.

## 4.3 Second Moments

The performance of this model, in terms of replicating the second moments of the most important macroeconomic variables, is significantly weaker than that of the closed economy model. In particular, our open economy generates a volatility for consumption that is much lower than that of the data (4.38 versus 0.4). The reason for this is that private agents have more opportunities to smooth their consumption than in a closed economy. By borrowing and lending in the international capital market they can eliminate almost completely fluctuations in consumption.

As a consequence of the introduction of adjustment costs, the model is able to replicate the volatility and serial correlation of investment and savings. Despite this, the model underestimates significantly the balance of trade volatility. This is related to the fact that the savings-investment correlation is much higher in the model (85%) than in the data (10%).

The model performs extremely well in terms of the serial correlation properties. As for the co-movement properties,the model exaggerates the correlation between output and savings and between output and employment. A significant failure of the model is with respect to the correlation of the trade balance with output, which is negative in the data (−40%) and positive in the model (15%). The main driving force of the balance of trade in the model are capital flows which arbitrage out real interest rate differentials between the home country and the rest of the world. As is clear in

[27] While in section 3 the model statistics are population moments which were computed without simulating the model, here the statistics correspond to the outcome of model simulations. For this reason there is a very small difference between the variance of output in the data and in the model which we did not attempt to fine tune by producing more simulations for new values of the parameters of the stochastic process for $A_t$.

Table 6: Open economy.

| | St. Dev. | St.D. rel.Y | Autocorrel. 1 | 2 | Cross-correlations with $y(t+i)$ -2 | -1 | 0 | 1 | 2 |
|---|---|---|---|---|---|---|---|---|---|
| $y$ | 4.60 | 1.00 | 0.71 | 0.44 | 0.44 | 0.71 | 1.00 | 0.71 | 0.44 |
| $c$ | 0.40 | 0.09 | 0.59 | 0.29 | 0.24 | 0.56 | 0.97 | 0.71 | 0.46 |
| $Ns$ | 21.07 | 4.58 | 0.69 | 0.40 | 0.43 | 0.70 | 1.00 | 0.69 | 0.41 |
| $Bs$ | 22.76 | 4.95 | 0.72 | 0.45 | 0.45 | 0.72 | 1.00 | 0.71 | 0.44 |
| $i$ | 13.31 | 2.90 | 0.57 | 0.25 | -0.03 | 0.33 | 0.86 | 0.71 | 0.55 |
| $Tb$ | 15.79 | 3.44 | 0.80 | 0.55 | 0.84 | 0.65 | 0.15 | -0.08 | -0.25 |
| $Ca$ | 6.26 | 1.36 | 0.80 | 0.55 | 0.77 | 0.54 | 0.02 | -0.21 | -0.41 |
| $N$ | 3.36 | 0.73 | 0.73 | 0.46 | 0.46 | 0.73 | 1.00 | 0.71 | 0.44 |
| $Mk$ | 4.03 | 0.88 | 0.55 | 0.24 | -0.10 | 0.26 | 0.81 | 0.68 | 0.55 |
| $w$ | 1.23 | 0.27 | 0.68 | 0.40 | 0.39 | 0.68 | 1.00 | 0.72 | 0.45 |
| $q$ | 1.02 | 0.22 | 0.55 | 0.23 | -0.20 | 0.16 | 0.74 | 0.66 | 0.54 |
| $r$ | 1.12 | 0.24 | -0.13 | -0.08 | -0.34 | -0.45 | 0.29 | 0.28 | 0.27 |

*Note:* $y-$ output; $c-$ private consumption; $Ns-$ NIA savings; $BS-$ basic savings; $i-$ investment; $Tb-$ trade balance; $Ca-$ current account; $N-$ employment; $Mk-$ marginal productivity of capital; $w-$ wage rate; $q-$ Tobin's $q$; $r-$ capital returns.

the model's impulse response function described in Figures 19.1 to 19.6, the most important exogenous shock in the model — the productivity shock — generates almost identical responses in output and in the trade balance.

One defect of our parameterization is that, although we assumed that the contemporaneous correlation between $A_t$ and $r_t^*$ is zero, when we compute this correlation using $r_t^*$ and the model generated $A_t$ that we describe below, we obtain a value of $-0.20$. For this reason we have studied an alternative parameterization in which we introduced a contemporaneous correlation between $r_t^*$ and the innovation to the $A_t$ shock. Choosing this contemporaneous correlation to be $-0.18$ generates a correlation between $A_t$ and $r_t^*$ (after HP detrending) that is the same in the model and in the "data". This new parameterization produce moments that were almost identical to those of Table 7.

## 4.4 Impulse Responses

Figures 19.1 to 21.6 illustrate the mechanics of this economy. There are now three exogenous variables: the technological shock ($A_t$), shock to government consumption ($G_t$) and the stochastic international real interest rate ($r_t^*$).

The response to a technological shock (Figures 19.1 to 19.6) involves now permanent effects, due to the presence of a unit root in the model. The amplitude of response is much larger than in the closed economy model for all variables with the exception of consumption and wages.

The existence of an external asset, and the consequent possibility of portfolio shifts, modifies the behavior of the capital stock, whose path is almost symmetrical to the path for $B_t$.

As in the closed economy model a positive shock in $A_t$ generates an expansion in the economy, with a rise in consumption, investment, capital stock, output, wages, labor effort and in the price of capital (which is equal to Tobin's $q$).

As in section 3, the impact of a government consumption shock (Figure 20.1 to 20.6) is very small. The most important differences with respect to the closed economy is that investment and capital now rise instead of falling. An increase in government expenditures has a negative income effect that depresses both consumption and leisure. The consequent increase in hours worked enhances the productivity of capital. This shock produces a reduction in the level of $B_t$ which is larger than the increase in the domestic capital stock, leading to an overall reduction in total wealth, as in the closed economy model.

The main effects of an increase in $r_t^*$ are a decrease in domestic investment, which is accompanied by a drop in output and in labor effort.

## 4.5 The Productivity Shock

Given the model's difficulty in reproducing key moments of the data it is also not surprising that the pattern that it implies for the productivity shocks is also less plausible than that of section 3. This pattern, which is depicted in Figure 18.2, implies that total productivity $(X_0\gamma_x^t)^\alpha A_t$ falls nine times. Productivity drops more than 2% in 1974 (5.9%), 1982 (2.3%), 1983 (6.9%) and 1985 (5.3%). This has the unreasonable implication that total factor productivity fell more in 1983 than during the 1973 oil shock and the 1974 revolution! We interpret these results as casting doubts on the appropriateness of the r series that we employed. On the basis of this series we chose a stochastic process for $r_t^*$ that is i.i.d. and uncorrelated with $A_t$ and $G_t$.[28] These assumption clearly deserve further examination.

## 4.6 Long Run Multipliers

As we discussed before, in this economy temporary shocks have permanent effects. The asymptotic effect of a 1% shock to $K_t$, $B_t$, $A_t$, $G_t$ and $r_t^*$ on the model's variables are described in Table 7.

The direction of these long run effects is determined by the nature of the income effect associated with any given shock. An increase in government expenditures has a negative income effect that reduces consumption and

[28] Our measure of the world real interest rate is negatively correlated with both $Y_t$ and $G_t$. These correlations are −30% and −7%, respectively (both series were linearly detrended).

Table 7: Open economy: long run multipliers.

| | Percentage impact of a 1% variation in | | | | |
|---|---|---|---|---|---|
| | $k$ | $b$ | $A$ | $g$ | $r^*$ |
| $k$ | -0.18 | -0.22 | -0.67 | 0.01 | -0.01 |
| $b$ | 0.97 | 1.18 | 3.55 | -0.04 | 0.07 |
| $y$ | -0.18 | -0.22 | -0.67 | 0.01 | -0.01 |
| $c$ | 0.05 | 0.06 | 0.17 | -0.00 | 0.00 |
| $Ns$ | 1.62 | 1.99 | 5.97 | -0.07 | 0.12 |
| $Bs$ | -1.13 | -1.38 | -4.14 | 0.05 | -0.08 |
| $i$ | -0.18 | -0.22 | -0.67 | 0.01 | -0.01 |
| $Tb$ | -0.97 | -1.18 | -3.55 | 0.04 | -0.07 |
| $Ca$ | 0.97 | 1.18 | 3.55 | -0.04 | 0.07 |
| $N$ | -0.18 | -0.22 | -0.67 | 0.01 | -0.01 |
| $Mk$ | 0.00 | 0.00 | 0.00 | 0.00 | 0.00 |
| $w$ | 0.00 | 0.00 | 0.00 | 0.00 | 0.00 |
| $q$ | 0.00 | 0.00 | 0.00 | 0.00 | 0.00 |
| $r$ | 0.00 | 0.00 | 0.00 | 0.00 | 0.00 |

*Note:* $y$– output; $c$– private consumption; $Ns$– NIA savings; $BS$– basic savings; $i$– investment; $Tb$– trade balance; $Ca$– current account; $N$– employment; $Mk$– marginal productivity of capital; $w$– wage rate; $q$– Tobin's $q$; $r$– capital returns.

increases labor effort. This labor effort increase leads to a long run increase in the stock of capital which ensures that in the new steady state the marginal product of capital net of depreciation is equal to $r^*$. The long run effect on output of a temporary increase in public expenditures is positive but very small (0.0074%).

Increases in $K_t$, $B_t$, $A_t$, and $r_t^*$ have positive income effects and hence the sign of their long run impacts is the opposite of the sign of the long run multipliers associated with government expenditures.

# 5 Conclusions

In this paper we document the main stylized facts of the Portuguese business cycle in the period 1958–1989. These facts conform with the general pattern of fluctuations in OECD countries: investment is more volatile than output while consumption is less volatile than output; there is significant co movement among all macroeconomic variables, output, consumption, investment and employment tend to move together; finally, all variables show significant serial correlation. But a striking fact about Portuguese fluctuations is that they are more severe than those of other OECD countries.

We have compared the properties of the Portuguese data with two benchmark dynamic general equilibrium models: a closed economy model and a small open economy model. These models are extremely simple and hence should not be expected to explain all prominent features of macroeconomic data. But it is remarkable how these simple paradigms help us organize a large number of empirical regularities about business cycles and economic growth. The closed economy model that we considered produces business cycles that are remarkably similar to those experienced by the Portuguese economy in the last four decades, but it cannot obviously explain the behavior of the current account. The small open economy model did not improve on the performance of its closed economy counterpart. This model generated a variability of consumption that is too low and a counterfactual pro-cyclical behavior for the balance of trade. Some of these difficulties could be related to our measure of the international real rate of interest.

The simple models that we considered can be extended along many directions. Some of these extensions involve making the models more realistic along some dimensions. Examples include the introduction of monetary shocks (Kydland (1988), Cooley and Hansen (1988), King et al (1990) and Fuerst (1989)), imperfect credit markets (Scheinkman and Weiss (1986)), more complex tax and public expenditure structures (Wynne (1987), Braun (1988), McGrattan (1988), Baxter and King (1988) and Christiano and Eichenbaum (1990)), and modifications that allow the model to generate predictions about the level of unemployment and not solely about the total number of hours worked (Hansen (1985) and Cho and Cooley (1988), Kydland and Prescott (1989)) .

Other extensions of the basic neoclassical framework that we explored involves the consideration of "Keynesian" features such as sticky prices and wages (King (1990) and Cho and Cooley (1990)).

A third line of related research makes use of ideas developed in the "new Keynesian" macroeconomic literature to construct models that can be explored using the real business cycles methodology (Danthine and Donaldson (1989) and Rothemberg and Woodford (1989)).

It is unclear at present which of these lines of research has survival value. But that is why macroeconomics is arguably the most exciting field of research in economics today.

# Appendix: Data

- The secular data is from Nunes, Mata and Valério (1989).
- The National Accounts series (gdp, private consumption, government consumption, investment, exports and imports) measured in 1977 prices, are from Cartaxo and Rosa (1986), updated up to 1989 with Banco de Portugal (1986–89).
- The same methodology was used for the GDP and investment deflators and for Total Wages and Total Profits, Interest and Rents (at

current prices).

- Total population for 1980–89 is taken from Banco de Portugal (1980–89). For 1958–79 the series is computed with the implicit growth rates of Nunes et al (1989).

- Total Capital Stock (1977 prices) series are from Santos (1984), updated with a simplified methodology with the data from Banco de Portugal (1986–89).

- Total Employment for 1980–89 was taken from Banco de Portugal (1980–89). For the period of 1958–79, the series was computed by integrating the following series: 1975–79: INE "Inquérito Permanente ao Emprego", 1970–75: Ramos and Abecassis (1980), 1958–60: INE "Estatísticas para o Planeamento". The source for all of these series was Confraria and Monteiro (1988).

- Average interest and wage rates were computed by dividing Total Wages and Total Profits, Interest and Rents (in nominal terms) by total employment and capital, respectively. These series were then deflated by the GNP and the investment deflators, respectively.

- The measures of the money stock ($M1$, $M2$ and $MB$) are from Banco de Portugal (1982–89). For $M1$ and $M2$ there was a change in the series definition. This fact forced us to use only data for the period after 1960, and to use non–published data from the Banco de Portugal.

- For the Consumer Price Index (1980=100), the central series (1960–83) is from OECD (1984) "Consumer Price Indexes — Sources and Methods and Historical Statistics", Paris. This data was extrapolated for the periods before and after with information from INE (1960) "O Rendimento Nacional Português", Estudos 34 and INE (1972) "As Contas Nacionais Portuguesas 1958-1971", Estudos 46. After 1984, the source is Banco de Portugal (1987–89).

# Appendix: Figures

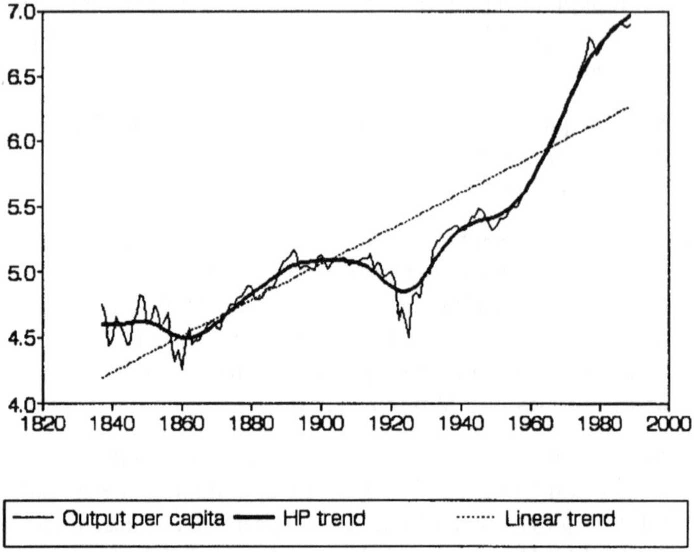


Figure 1.1: Per capita output and trends ($HP$ and linear).

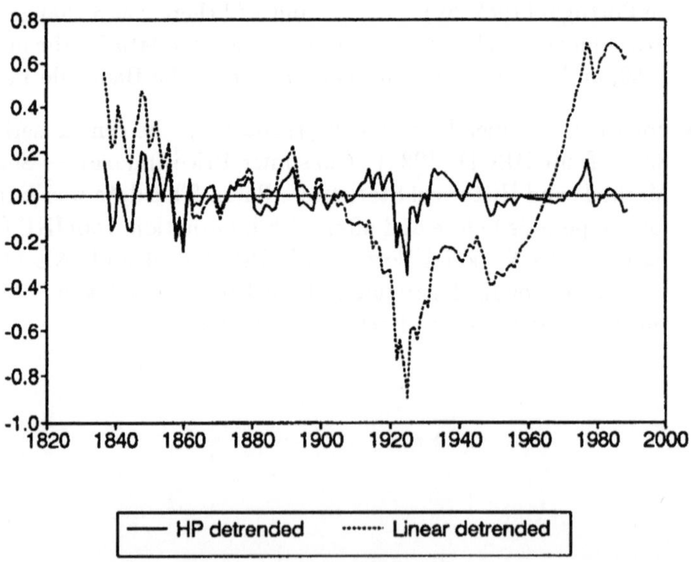


Figure 1.2: Per capita output detrended with $HP$ and linear filter.

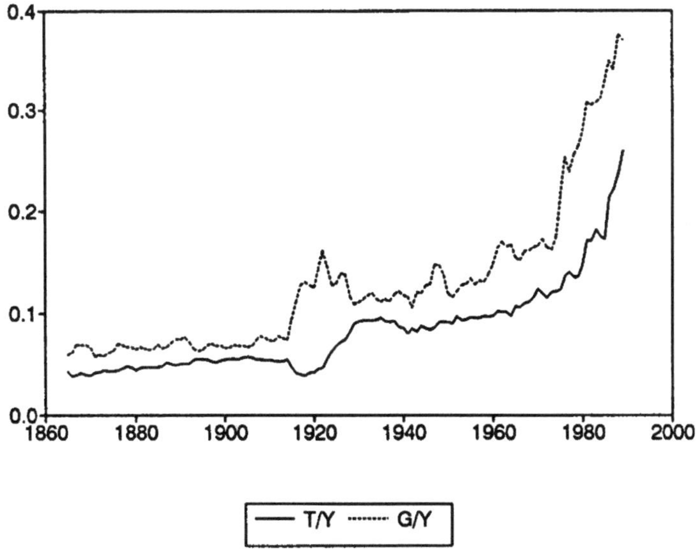


Figure 2.1: Shares in $GNP$: $T/Y$ and $G/Y$.

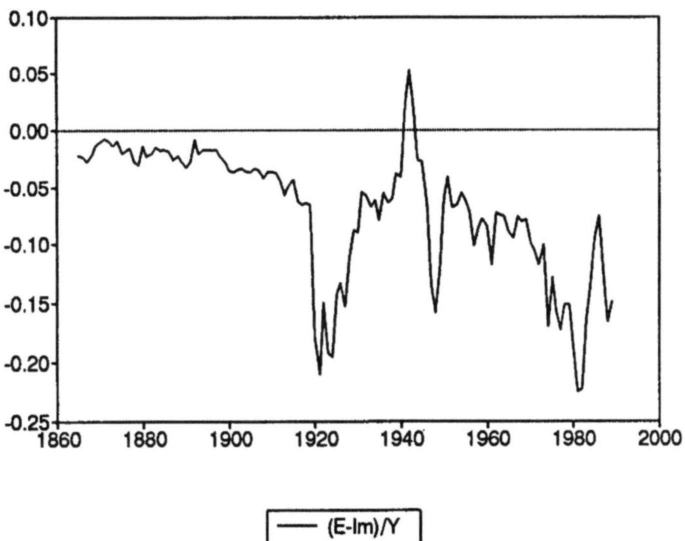


Figure 2.2: Shares in $GNP$: $(E - Im)/Y$.

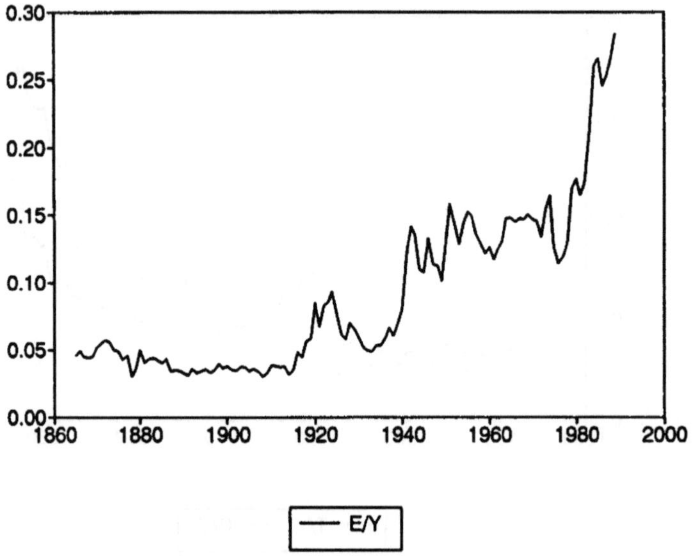


Figure 2.3: Shares in $GNP$: $E/Y$.

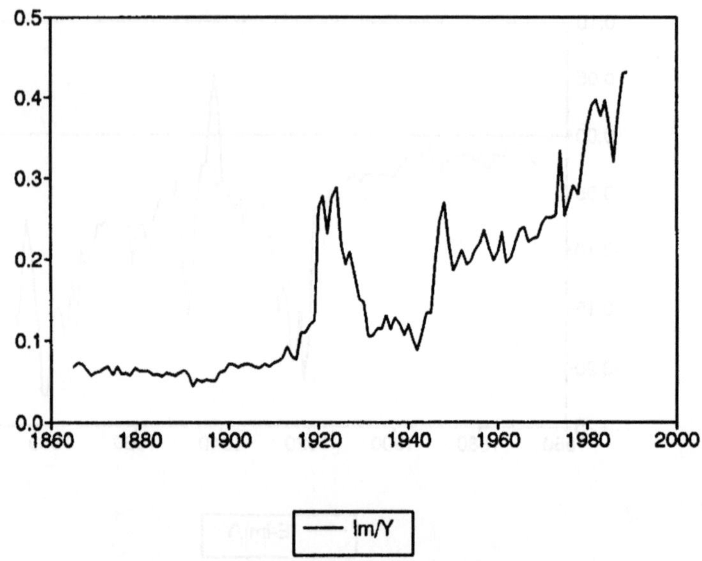


Figure 2.4: Shares in $GNP$: $Im/Y$.

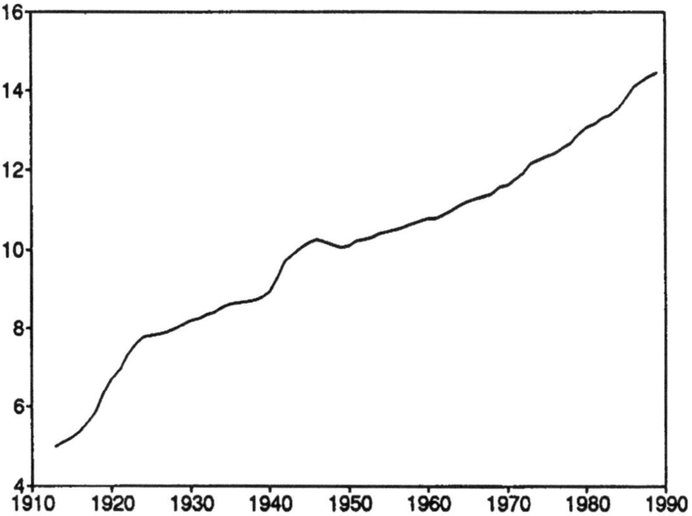


Figure 3: Secular $M1$ (logs).

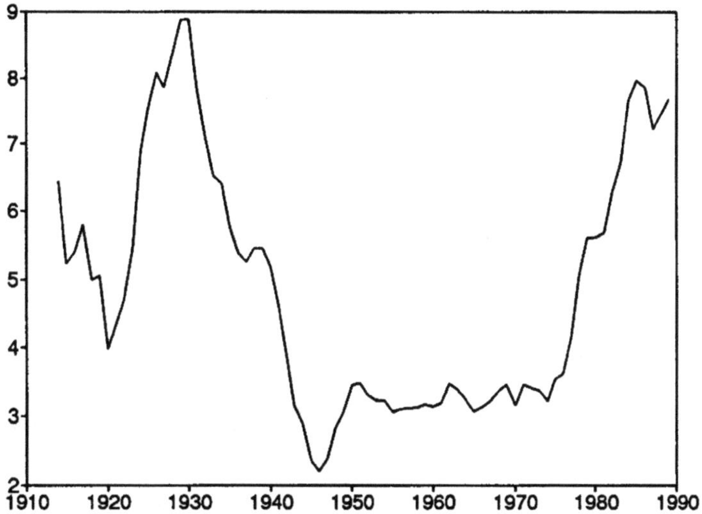


Figure 4: Secular money velocity ($PY/M1$).

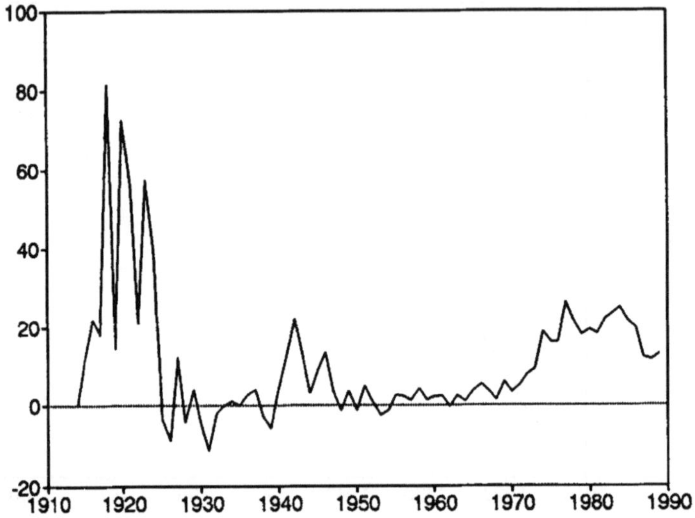


Figure 5: Secular inflation rate.

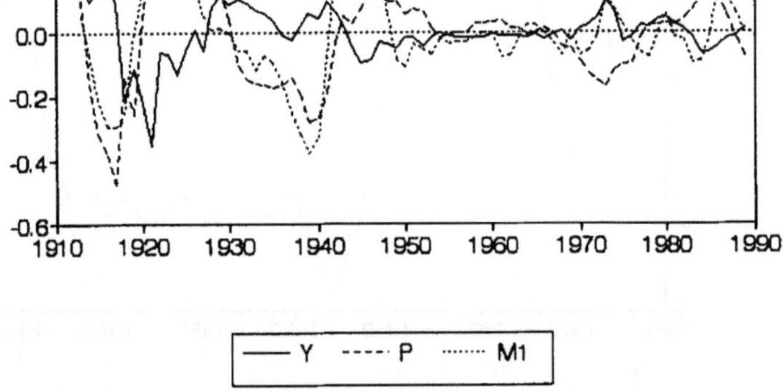


Figure 6: *GDP*, *GDP* deflator and *M*1 (*HP* detrended).

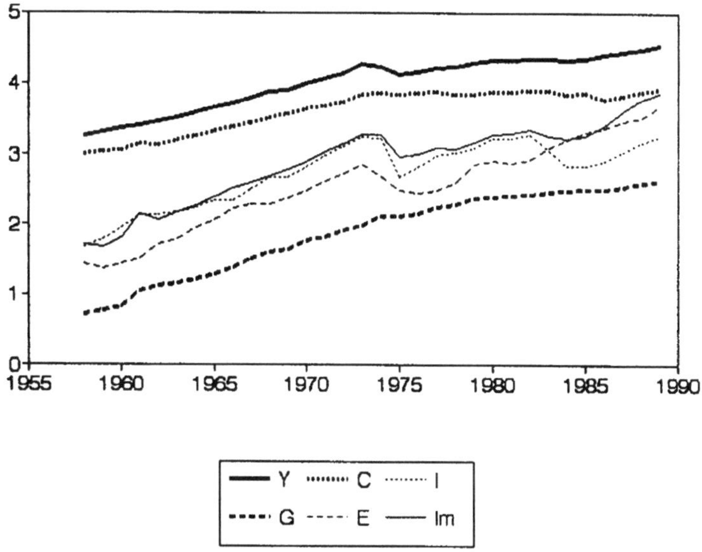


Figure 7.1: National Income Account Series (logs).

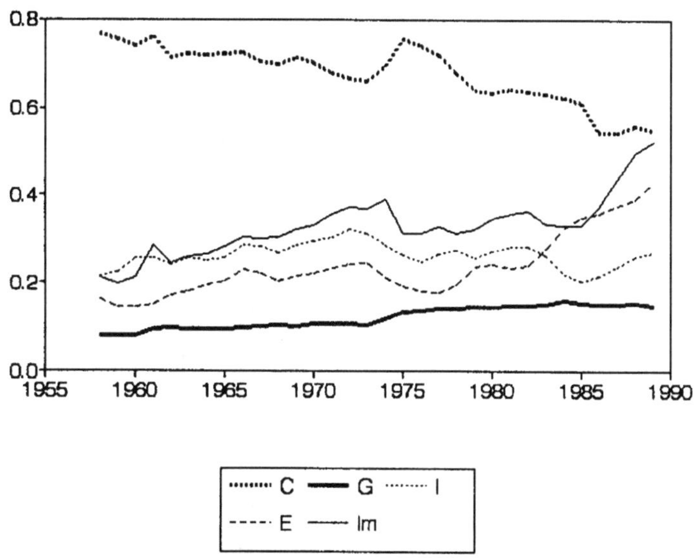


Figure 7.2: Shares of $C$, $G$, $I$, $E$, $Im$ on $Y$.

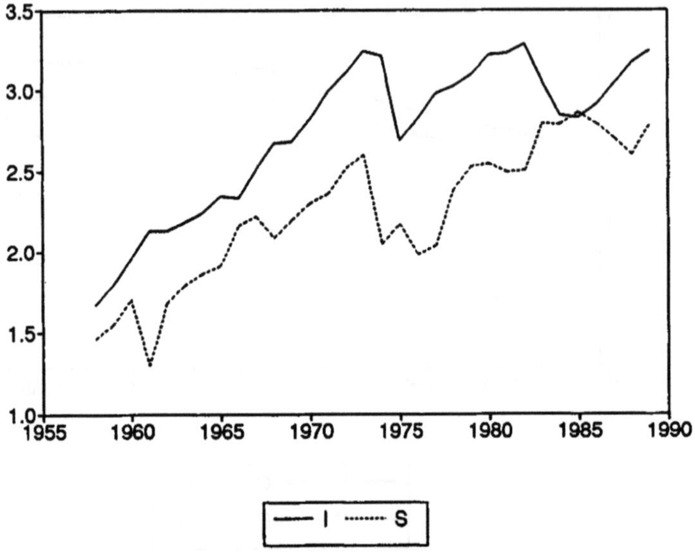


Figure 8: Savings and Investment (logs).

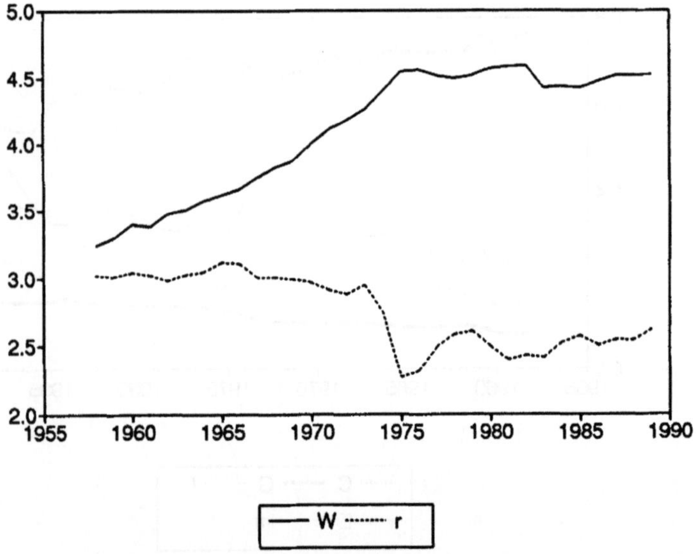


Figure 9: Wages and Interest Rates (logs).

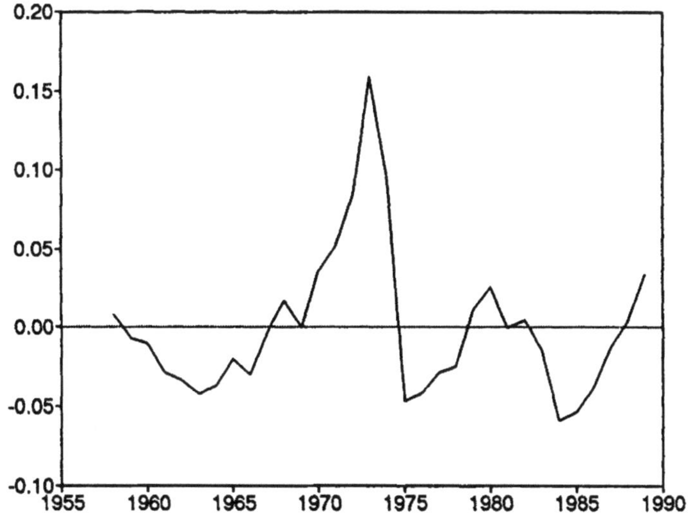


Figure 10.1: $Y$ ($HP$ detrended).

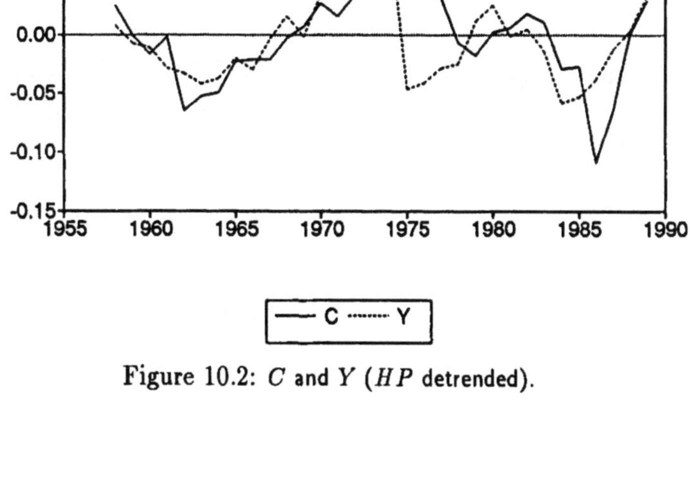


Figure 10.2: $C$ and $Y$ ($HP$ detrended).

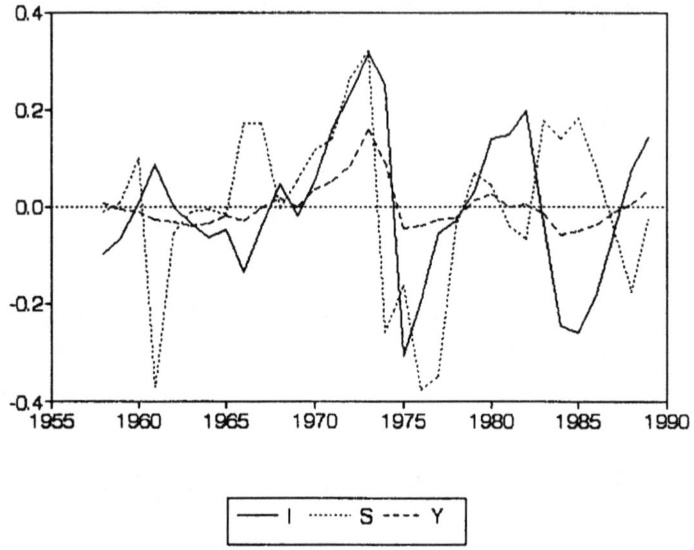


Figure 10.3: $I$, $S$ and $Y$ ($HP$ detrended).

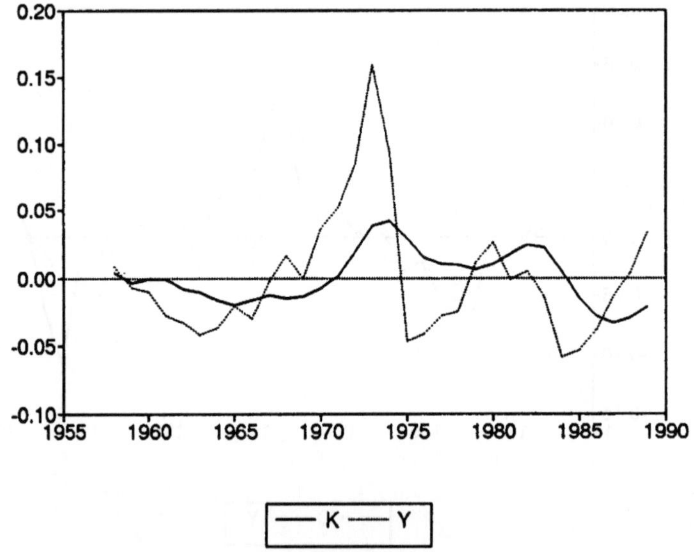


Figure 10.4: $K$ and $Y$ ($HP$ detrended).

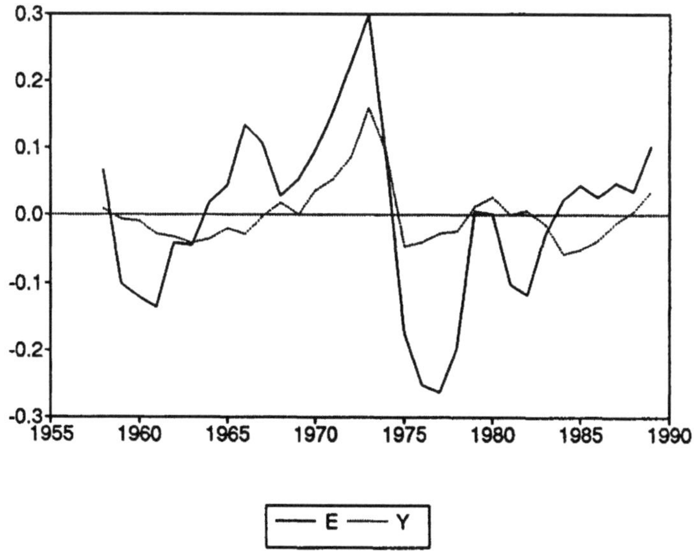


Figure 10.5: $E$ and $Y$ ($HP$ detrended).

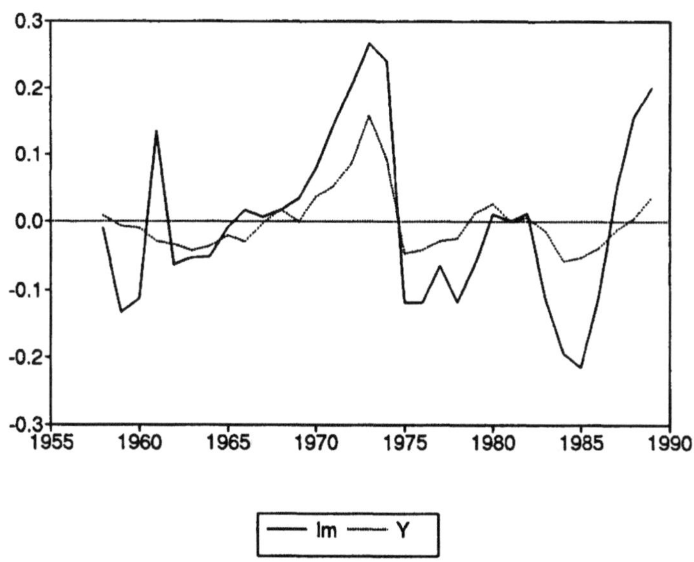


Figure 10.6: $Im$ and $Y$ ($HP$ detrended).

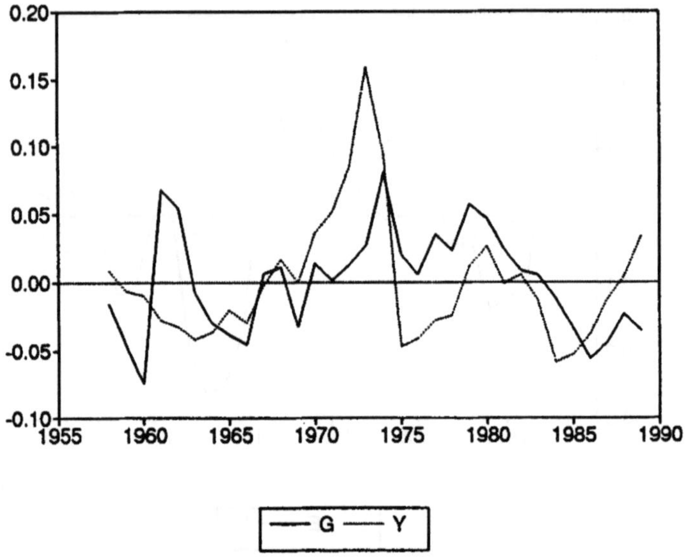


Figure 10.7: $G$ and $Y$ ($HP$ detrended).

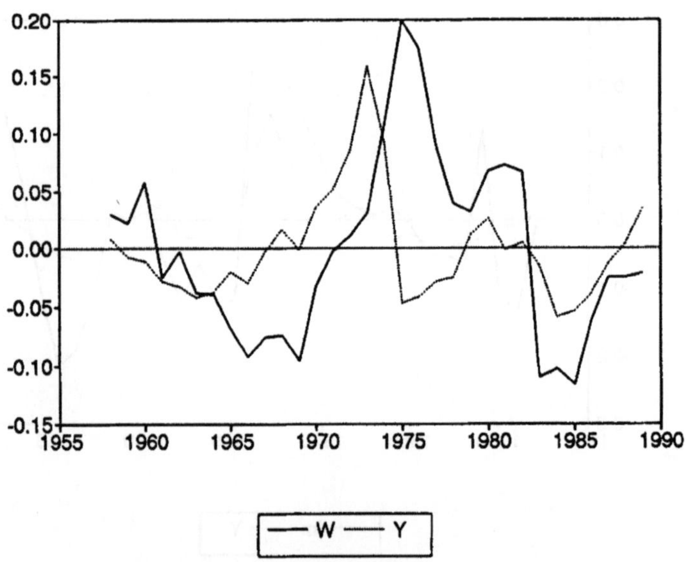


Figure 10.8: $W$ and $Y$ ($HP$ detrended).

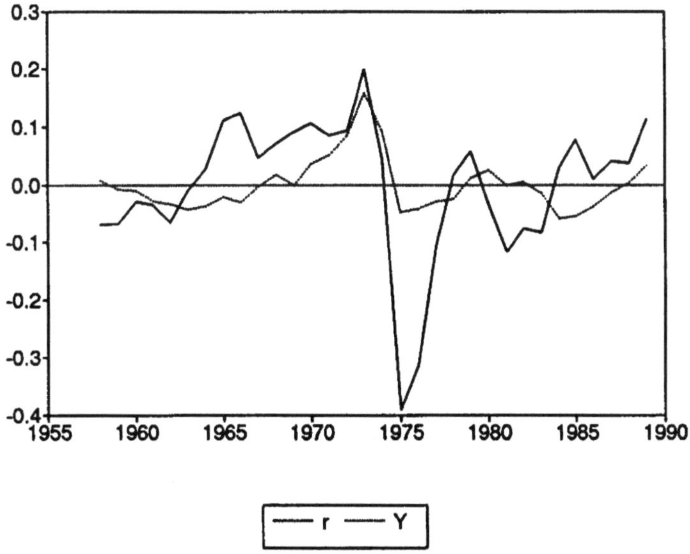


Figure 10.9: $r$ and $Y$ ($HP$ detrended).

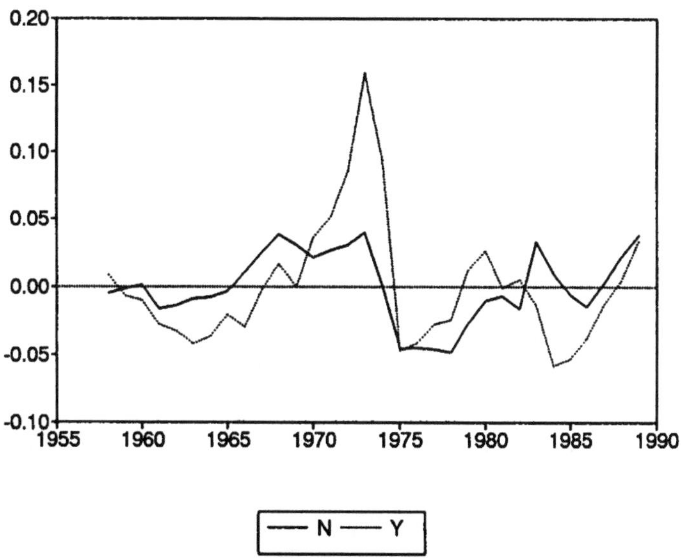


Figure 10.10: $N$ and $Y$ ($HP$ detrended).

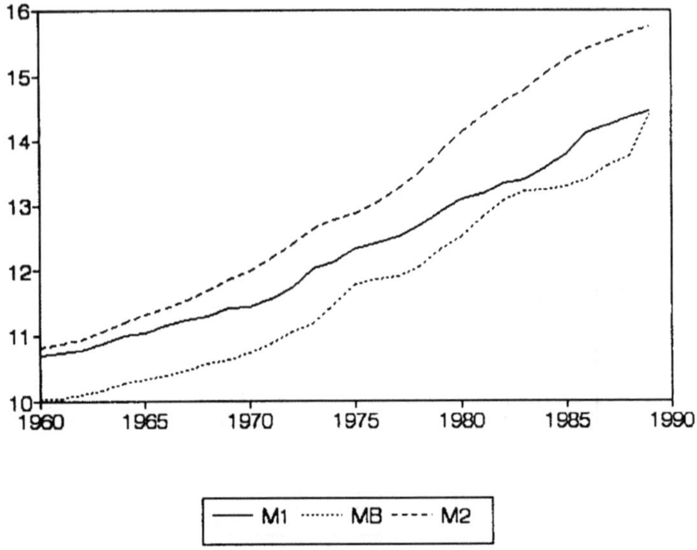


Figure 11: Monetary base, $M1$ and $M2$ (logs).

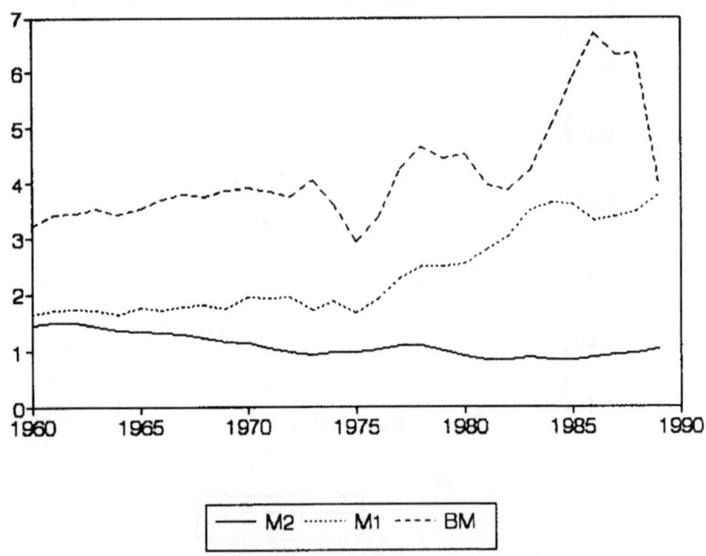


Figure 12: Velocity of circulation ($PY/M$).

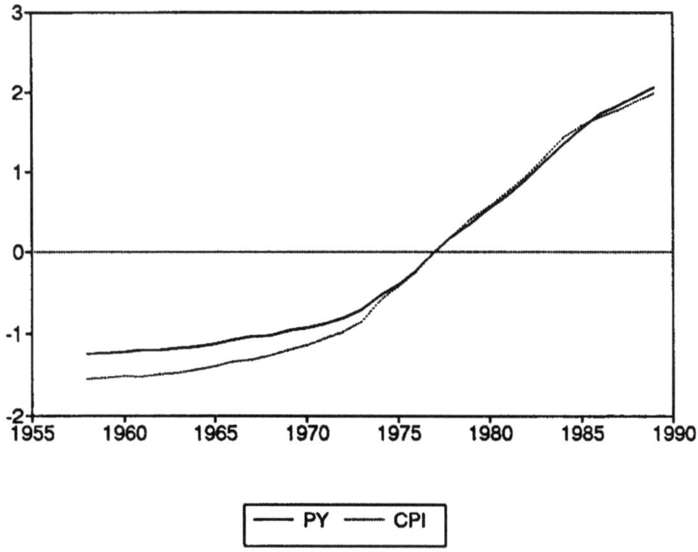


Figure 13: *GDP* deflator and *CPI* (log) (1970=0).

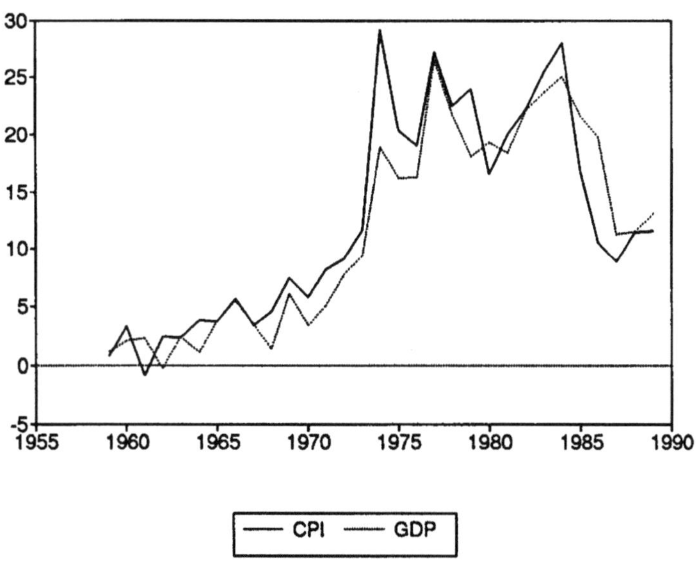


Figure 14: Inflation rates *CPI* and *GDP* deflator.

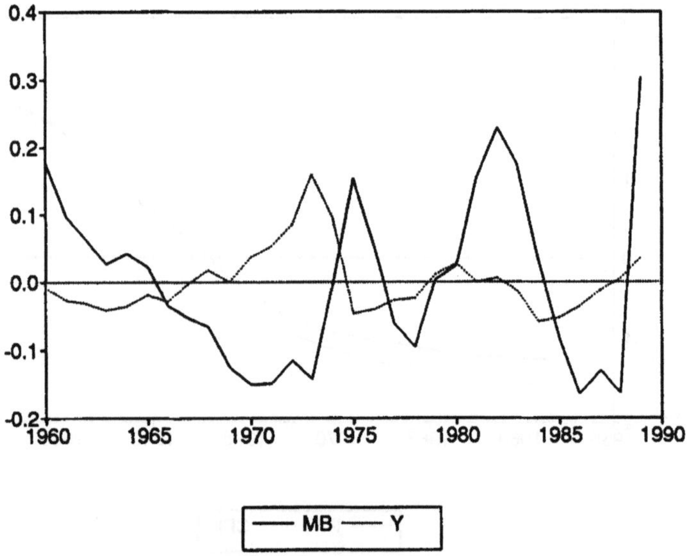


Figure 15.1: Monetary base and $Y$ ($HP$ detrended).

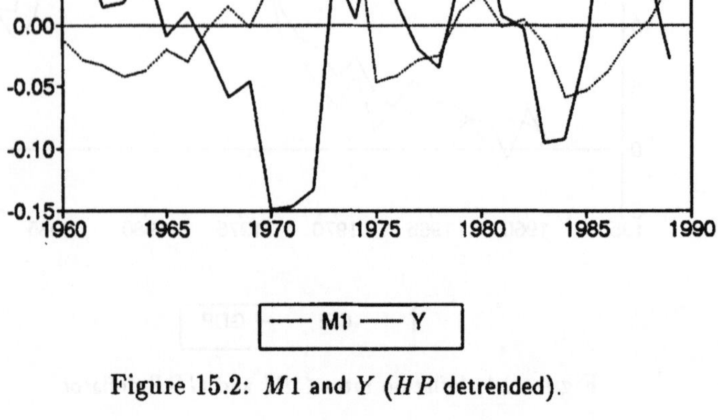


Figure 15.2: $M1$ and $Y$ ($HP$ detrended).

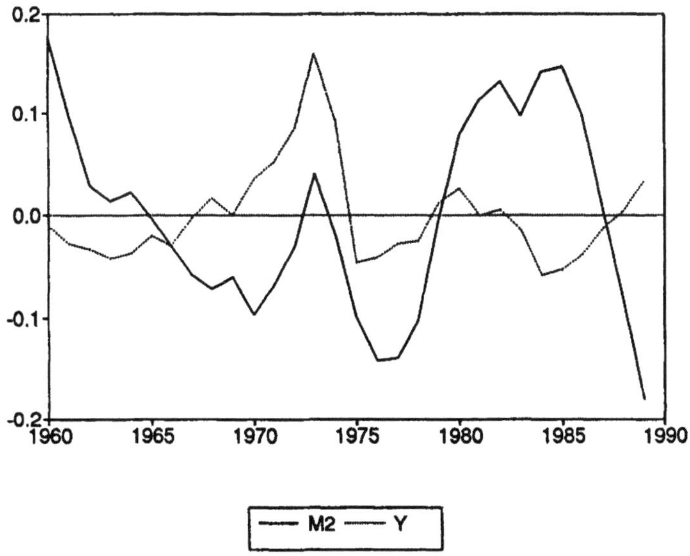


Figure 15.3: $M2$ and $Y$ ($HP$ detrended).

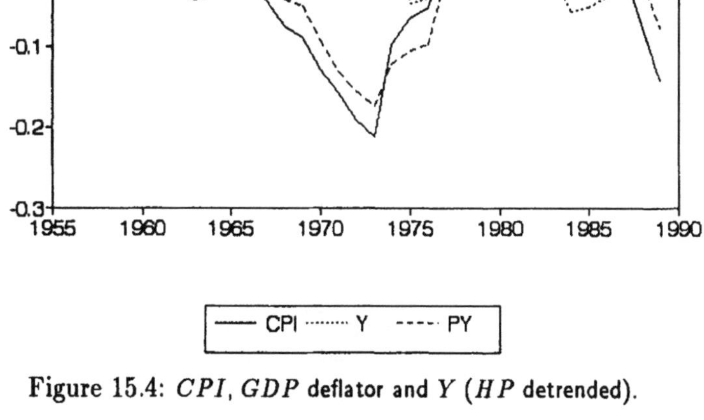


Figure 15.4: $CPI$, $GDP$ deflator and $Y$ ($HP$ detrended).

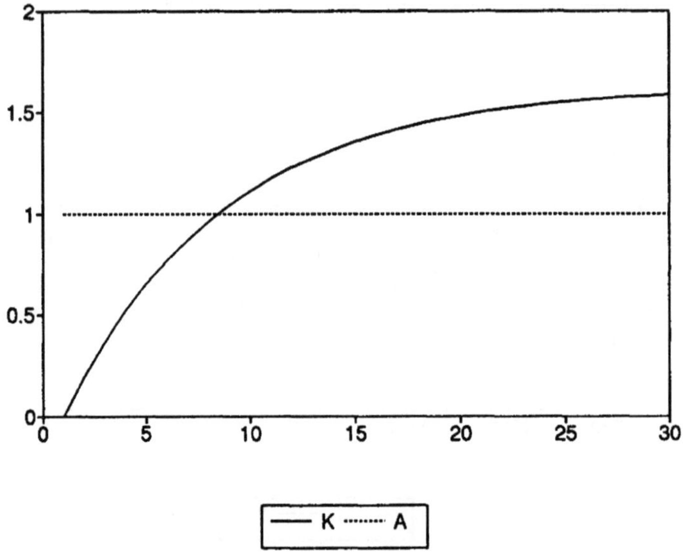


Figure 16.1: $A$ and $K$.

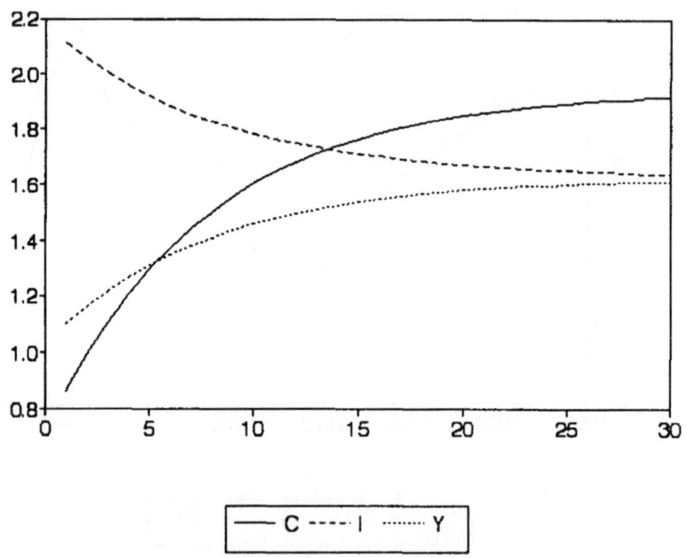


Figure 16.2: $C$, $I$, and $Y$.

Figure 16.3: Labor and Wages.

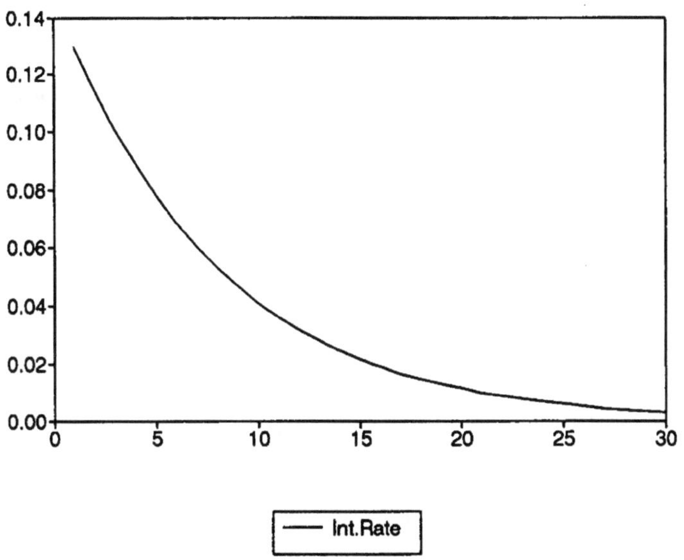


Figure 16.4: Interest Rates.

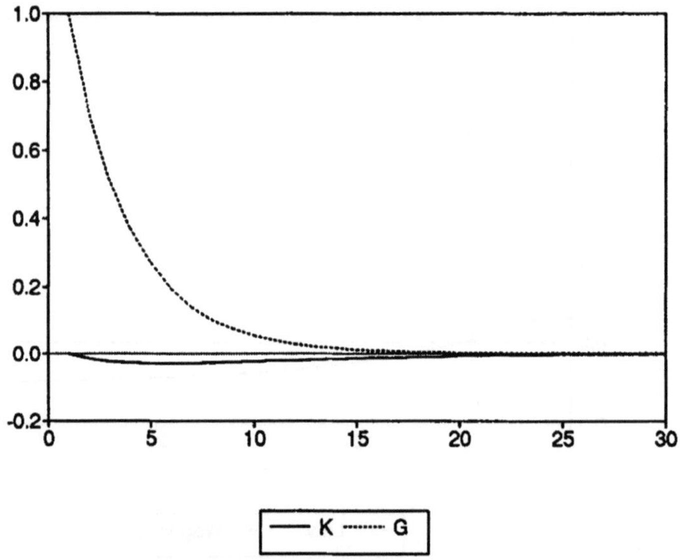


Figure 17.1: $G$ and $K$.

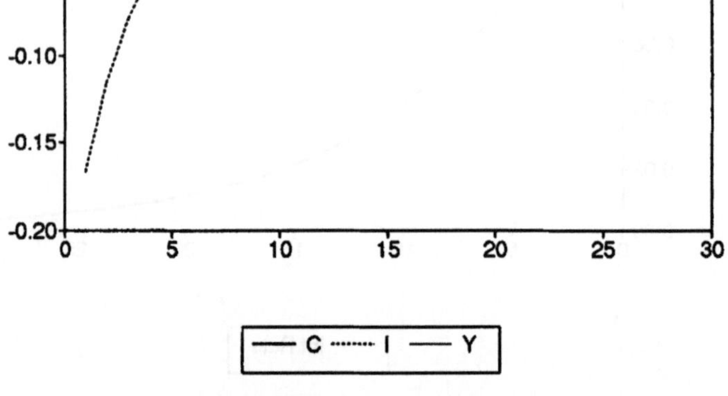


Figure 17.2: $C$, $I$, and $Y$.

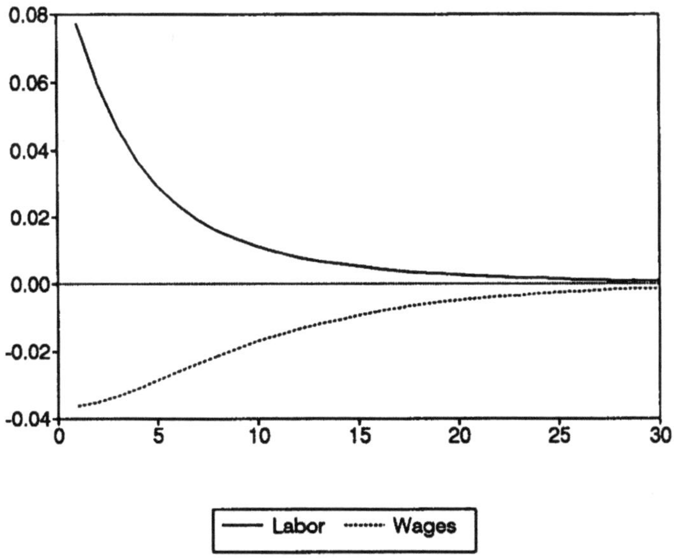


Figure 17.3: Labor and Wages.

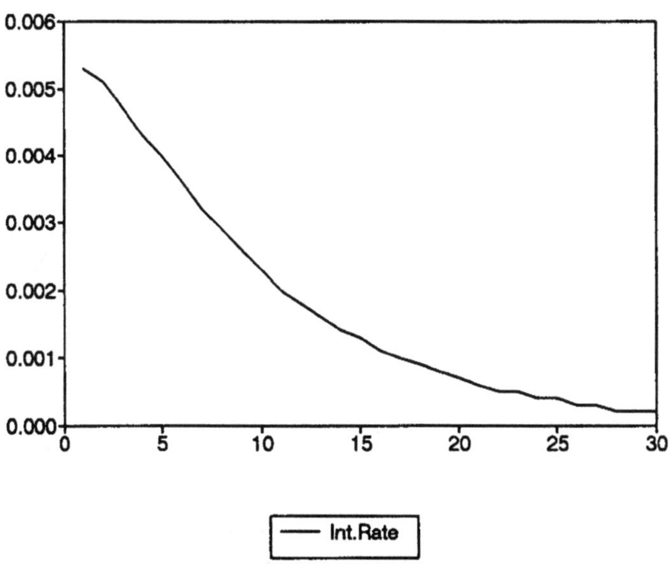


Figure 17.4: Interest Rates.

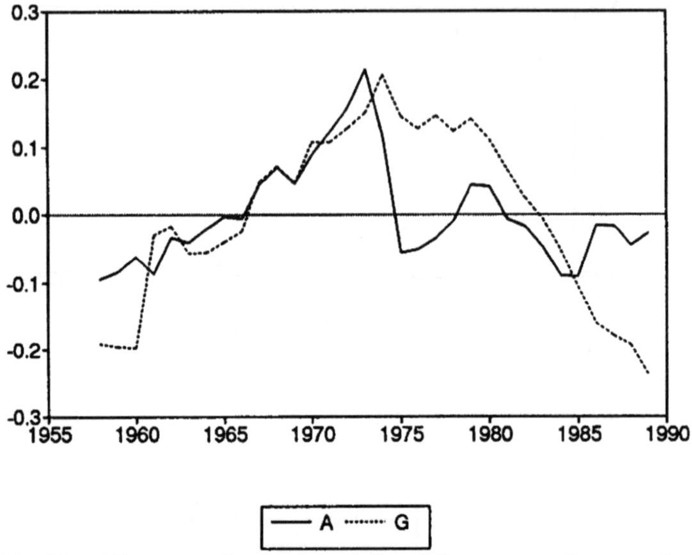


Figure 18.1: Closed Economy: Productivity ($A$) and Government Consumption ($G$) shocks.

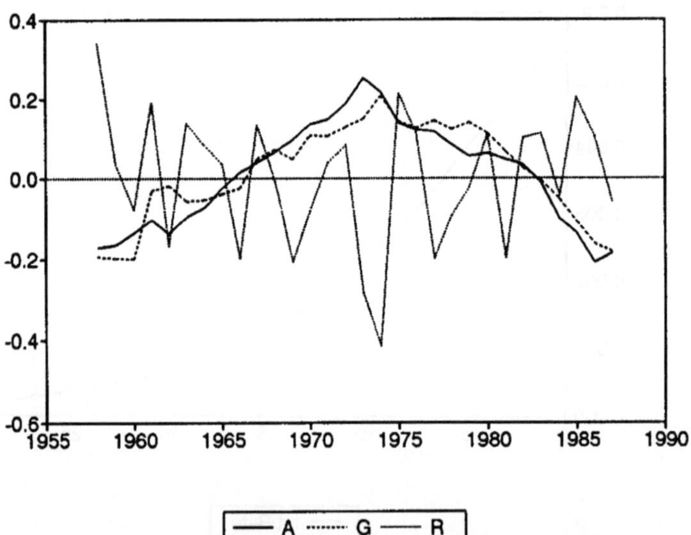


Figure 18.2: Open Economy: Productivity ($A$) and Government Consumption ($G$) and Interest Rate ($R$) shocks.

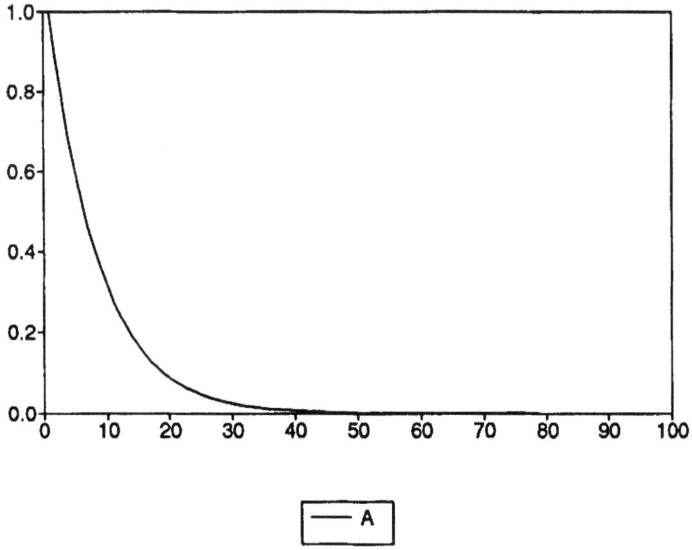


Figure 19.1: $A$, $G$ and $r^*$.

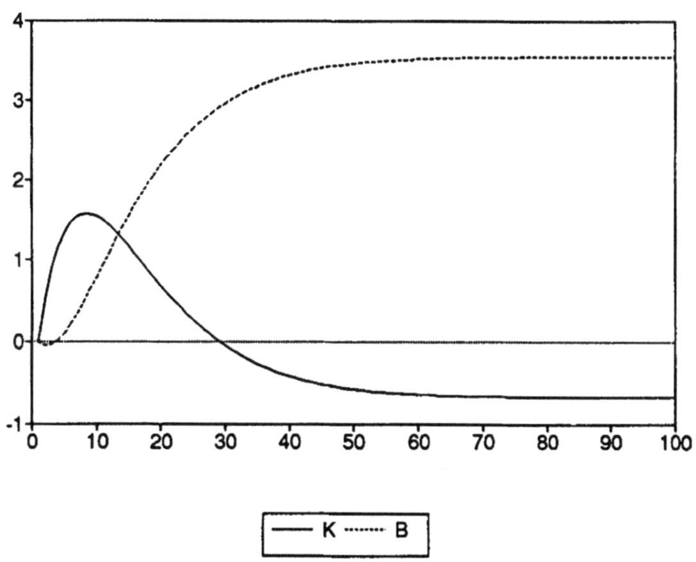


Figure 19.2: $K$, and $B$.

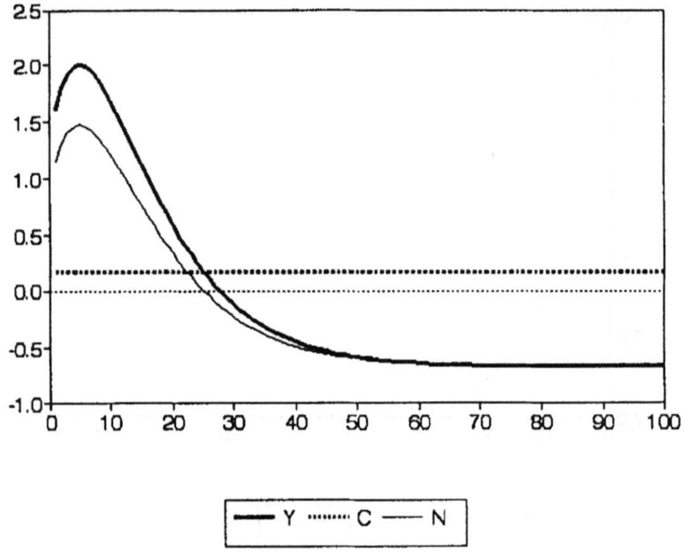


Figure 19.3: $Y$, $C$, and $N$.

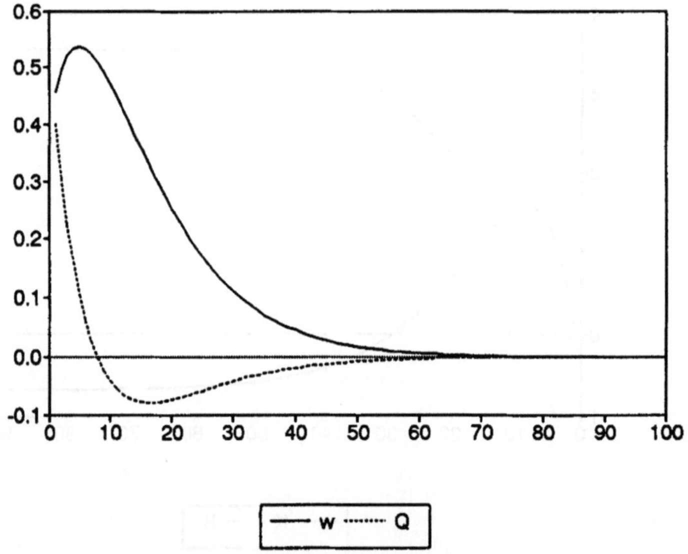


Figure 19.4: $w$ and Tobin $Q$.

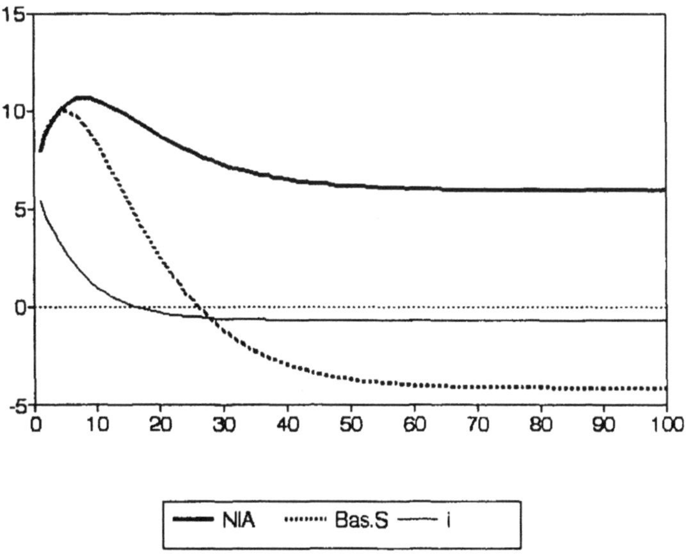


Figure 19.5: $i$, $NIA$ and Basic Savings.

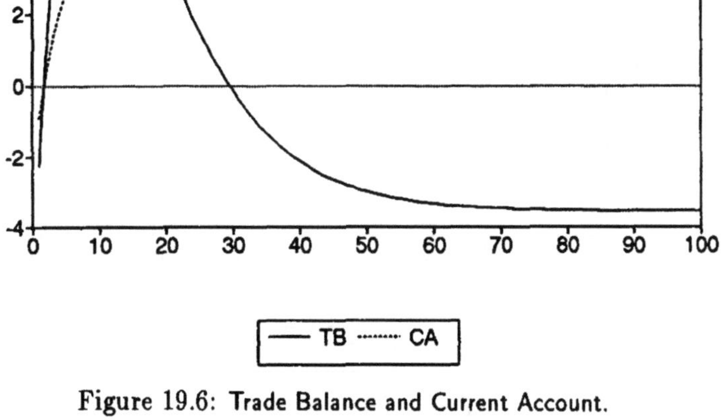


Figure 19.6: Trade Balance and Current Account.

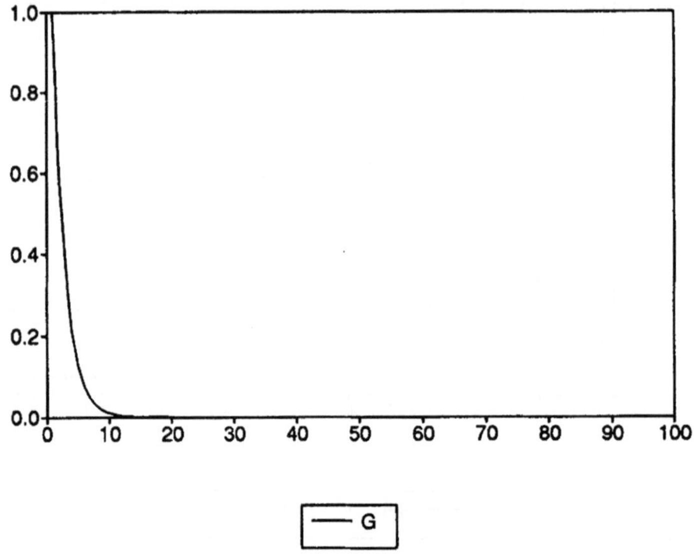


Figure 20.1: $A$, $G$ and $r^*$.

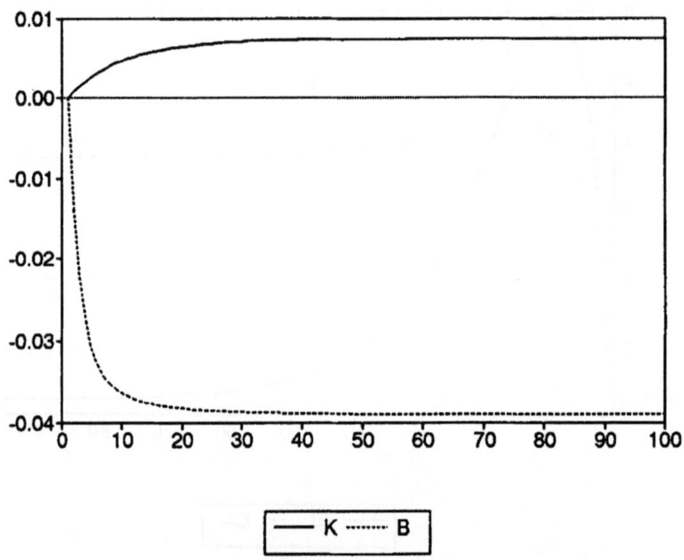


Figure 20.2: $K$, and $B$.

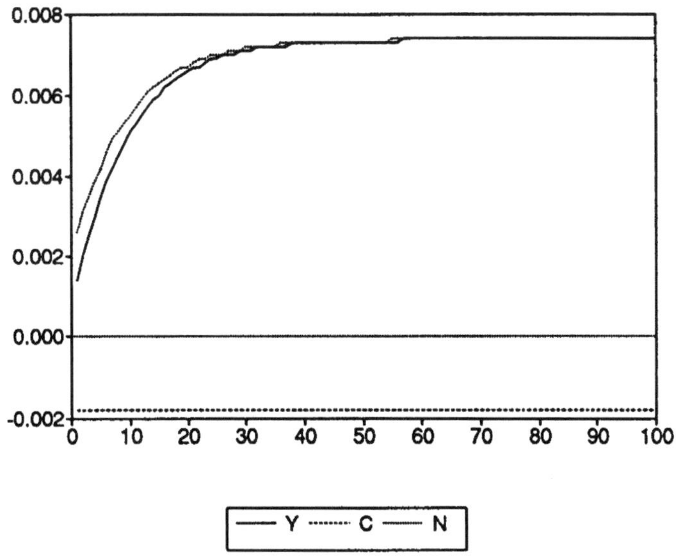


Figure 20.3: $Y$, $C$, and $N$.

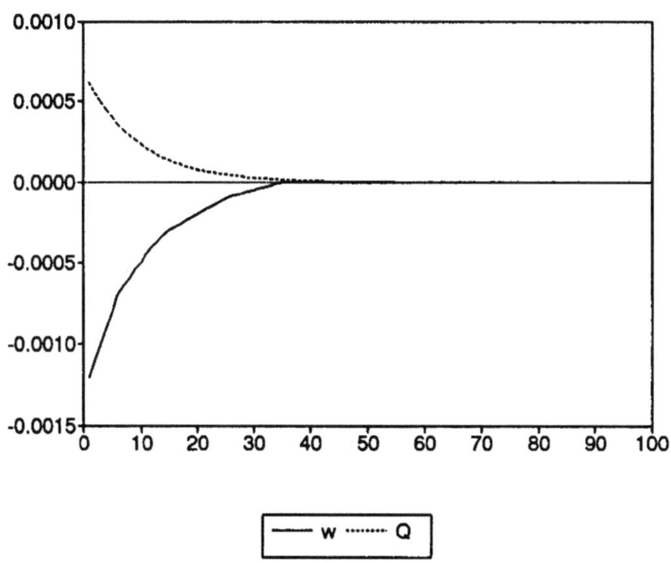


Figure 20.4: $w$ and Tobin $Q$.

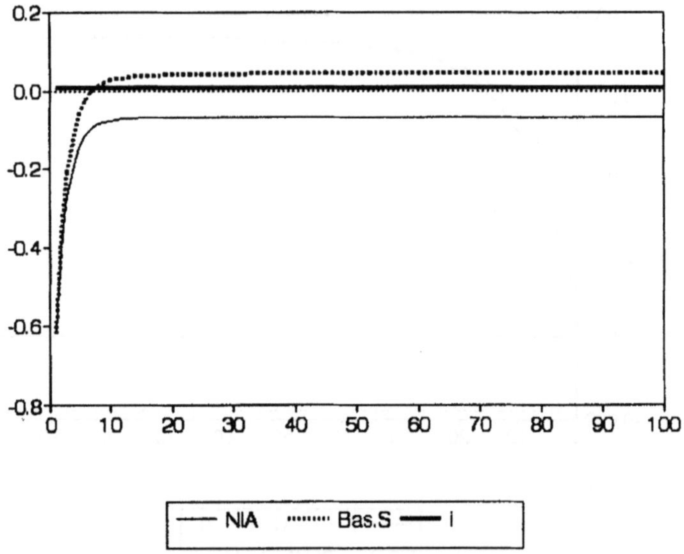


Figure 20.5: $i$, $NIA$ and Basic Savings.

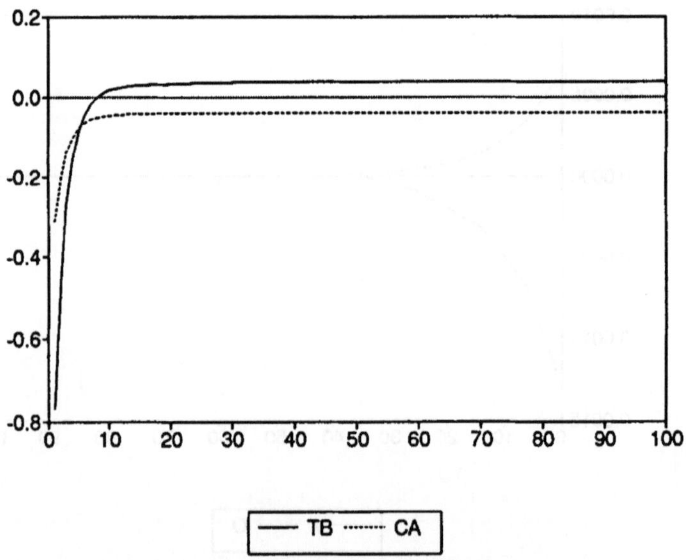


Figure 20.6: Trade Balance and Current Account.

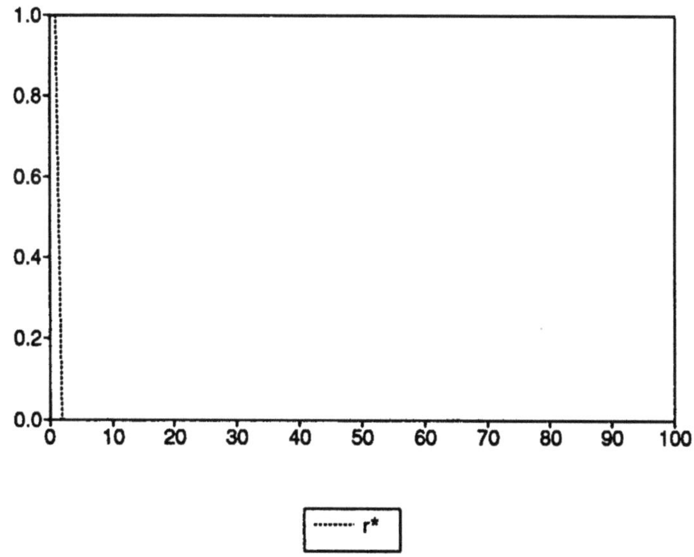


Figure 21.1: $A$, $G$ and $r^*$.

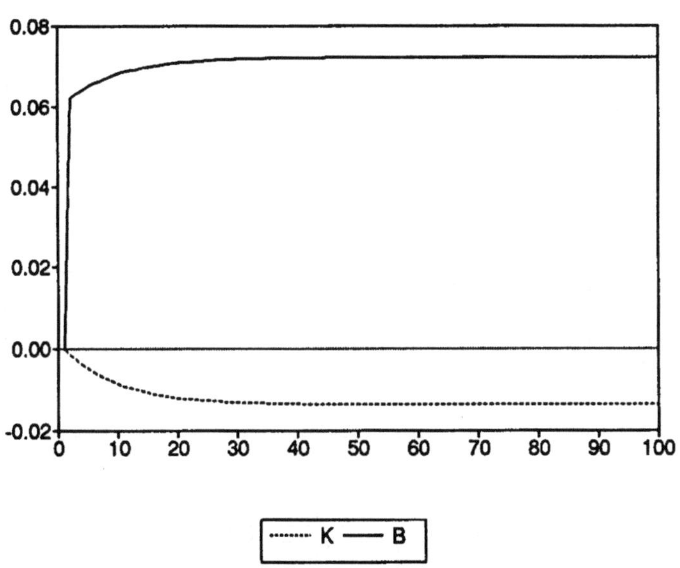


Figure 21.2: $K$, and $B$.

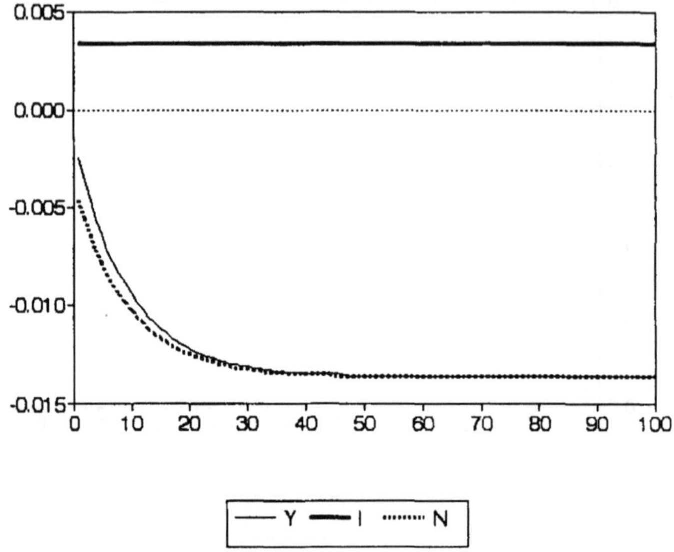


Figure 21.3: $Y$, $C$, and $N$.

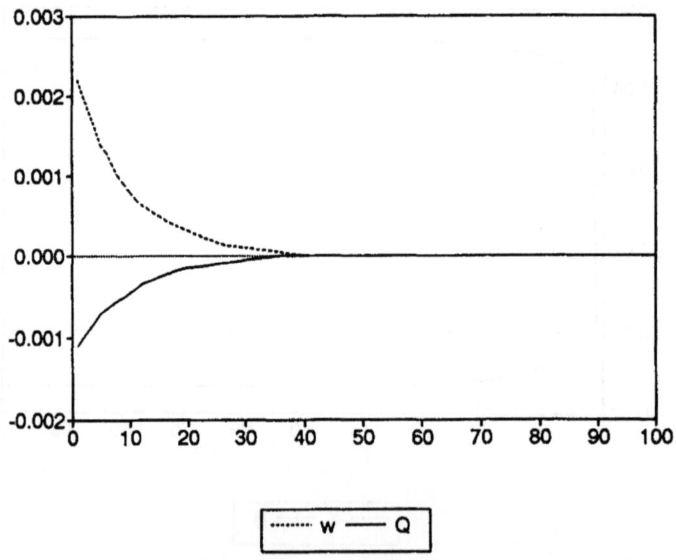


Figure 21.4: $w$ and Tobin $Q$.

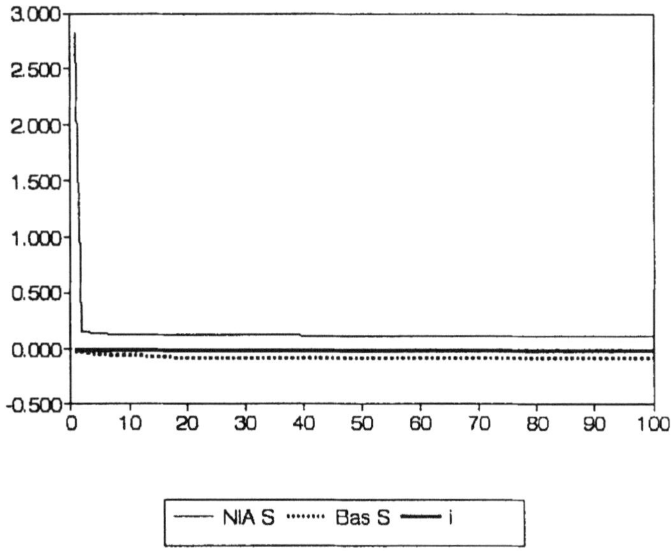


Figure 21.5: $i$, $NIA$ and Basic Savings.

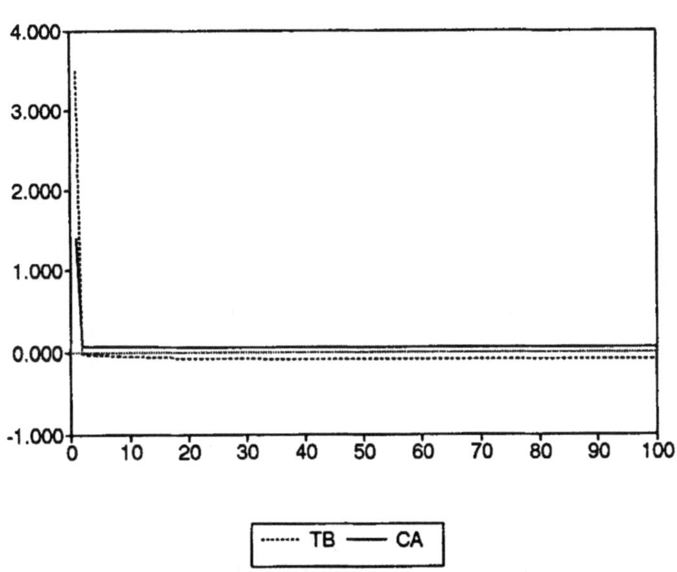


Figure 21.6: Trade Balance and Current Account.

# References


ABEL, A. AND O. BLANCHARD (1983): "An Intertemporal Equilibrium Model of Savings and Investment," *Econometrica*, **51**, 675–692.

AMBLER, S. AND A. PAQUET (1990): "Fiscal Spending Shocks, Real Business Cycles and Stabilization Policies," Université du Québec.

BACKUS, D., P. KEHOE, AND F. KYDLAND (1989): "International Borrowing and World Business Cycles," Working Paper #426R , Federal Reserve Bank of Minneapolis, Research Department.

BARBOSA, A. M. P. (1971): "Portuguese Economic Development in the Presence of Post-War Foreign Policies of the US," in *North American and Western European Economic Policies*, ed. by Kindleberger and Shonfield. London: MacMillan.

BARBOSA, A. M. P. (1972): *Speech at the 125 anniversary of the Bank of Portugal*, Banco de Portugal.

BARBOSA, A. P. (1985): "Inflação e Produto em Portugal 1953–1980," *Economia* **9**, 1.

BARRO, R. (1988,1990): *Macroeconomics*, 2nd and 3rd edition. New York: Wiley.

BARRO, R. AND G. BECKER (1989) "Fertility Choice in a Model of Economic Growth," *Econometrica*, **57**, 481–501.

BAXTER, M. (1991): "Business Cycles, Stylized Facts and the Exchange Rate Regime," forthcoming in *Journal of International Money and Finance*.

BAXTER, M. AND R. KING (1988): "Multipliers in Equilibrium Business Cycles Models," Rochester Center for Economic Research Paper #224 University of Rochester.

BAXTER, M. AND M. CRUCINI (1990): "Explaining Saving/Investment Correlations," Working Paper #224. Rochester: Rochester Center for Economic Research.

BECKER, R. (1980): "On the Long-Run Steady State in a Simple Dynamic Model of Equilibrium With Heterogeneous Households," *The Quarterly Journal of Economics*, **95**, 375–382.

BLACKBURN, K. AND M. O. RAVN (1990): "Business Cycles in the U.K.: Facts and Fictions," Working Paper, Department of Economics, University of Southampton.

BANCO DE PORTUGAL (1977–89): *Relatórios do Conselho de Administração*, Lisbon.

BRANDNER, P. AND K. NEUSSER (1990): "Business Cycles in Open Economies: Stylized Facts for Austria and Germany," Working Papers, Austrian Institute of Economic Research.

BRAUN, R. A. (1988): "The Dynamic Interaction of Distortionary Taxes and Aggregate Variables in Postwar U.S. Data," manuscript, Northwestern University.

BURNS, A. AND W. MITCHELL (1946) *Measuring Business Cycles*. New York: National Bureau of Economic Research.

CARDIA, E. (1988) "The dynamics of savings and investment in response to monetary, fiscal and productivity shocks," unpublished manuscript, University of Montreal.

CARTAXO, R. J. AND N. S. ROSA (1986): "Séries Longas para as Contas Nacionais Portuguesas 1958–1985," Documento de Trabalho #15, Banco de Portugal.

CHO, J. (1987): "Heterogeneous Agents and the Business Cycle," unpublished, University of Rochester.

CHO, J. AND T. COOLEY (1988): "Employment and Hours over the Business Cycles," unpublished, University of Rochester.

CHO, J. AND T. COOLEY (1990): "The Business Cycle with Nominal Contracts," manuscript, University of Rochester.

CHO, J. AND R. ROGERSON (1988): "Family Labor Supply and Aggregate Fluctuations," *Journal of Monetary Economics*, **21**, 233–245.

CHRISTIANO, L. (1988): "Solving a Particular Growth Model by Linear Quadratic Approximation and by Value Function Iteration," Working Paper #415, Federal Reserve Bank of Minneapolis.

CHRISTIANO, L. AND M. EICHENBAUM (1990): "Current Real Business Cycle Models and Aggregate Labor Markets," manuscript, Northwestern University.

CONFRARIA, J. AND M. MONTEIRO (1988): "Notas sobre o Problema da Precisão das Observações Estatísticas — o Caso das Estatísticas de Emprego e de Emigração em Portugal (1960–1985)," Estudos #13, Departamento de Economia, Universidade Católica Portuguesa.

COOLEY, T. AND G. HANSEN (1988): "The Inflation Tax in a Real Business Cycle Model," *American Economic Review*, **79**, 733–48.

CORREIA, I. H. J. C. NEVES, AND S. REBELO (1991): "Dynamic Small Open Economy Models," (paper in progress).

CRAFTS, N. AND T. C. MILLS (1990): "British Economy Fluctuations, 1851–1913: A Perspective Based on Growth Theory," Working Paper, University of Warwick.

DANTHINE, J. P. (1989): "Modelisation des Fluctuations Conjuncturelles: Survol de quelques Recents Developments," *Recherches Economiques de Louvain*, **55**, 213–244.

DANTHINE, J. AND J. B. DONALDSON (1988): "Efficiency Wages, and the Real Business Cycles," Cahier de Recherches Économiques 8803, DEEP, Université de Lausanne, forthcoming *European Economic Review*.

DANTHINE, J., J. B. DONALDSON, AND R. MEHRA (1989): "On Some Computational Aspects of Real Business Cycles Theory," *Journal of Economic Dynamics and Control*, **13**, 449–470.

DANTHINE, J. AND M. GIRARDIN (1989): "Business Cycles in Switzerland: A Comparative Study," *European Economic Review*, **33**, 31–50.

DOTSEY, M. AND C. S. MAO (1990): "How Well Do Linear Approximation Methods Work? Results for Suboptimal Dynamic Equilibria," Federal Reserve Bank of Richmond.

ENGLE, R. F. AND C. W. J. GRANGER (1987) "Co-Integration and Error Correction: Representation, Estimation, and Testing," *Econometrica*, **55**, 251–276.

EPSTEIN, L. G. (1983): "Stationary Cardinal Utility and Optimal Growth under Uncertainty," *Journal of Economic Theory*, **31**, 133–152.

FELDSTEIN, M. AND C. HORIOKA (1980): "Domestic Savings and International Capital Flows," *The Economic Journal*, **90**, 314–329.

FRENKEL, J. AND M. MUSSA (1985): "Asset Approach to the balance of payments and to the exchange rate determination," in *Handbook of International Economics*, ed. by R. Jones and P. Kenen. Amsterdam: North Holland.

FRISCH, R. (1933): "Propagation Problems and Impulse Problems in Dynamic Economics,"in *Economic Essays in Honor of Gustav Cassel*. London: George Allen and Unwin, Ldt. Reprinted in *Readings in Business Cycle Theory*, 155–85. Homewood, Illinois: Richard D. Irwin.

FUERST, T. (1989): "Liquidity, Loanable Funds, and Real Activity," *mimeo*, The University of Chicago.

GIOVANNINI, A. (1985): "Saving and the Real Interest Rate in LDC's," *The Journal of Development Economics*, **17**, 197–217.

GOMES, J. M. (1984): "Flutuações e Crescimento Conjunturais. Ensaio de Delimitação para a Economia Portuguesa (1950/80)," in *Evolução Recente e Perspectivas de Transformação da Economia Portuguesa*, ed. by CISEP, vol. 1, EPNC, Lisbon.

GORDON, R. (1990): "Are Procyclical Productivity Fluctuation a Figment of Measurement Error?," manuscript, Northwestern University.

HALL, R. E. (1989): "Consumption" in *Modern Business Cycle Theory*, ed. by Barro. Cambridge: Harvard University Press.

HANSEN, G. (1985): "Indivisible Labor and the Business Cycle," *Journal of Monetary Economics*, **16**, 309–327.

HANSEN, L. (1982): "Large Sample Properties of Generalized Method of Moments Estimators," *Econometrica*, **50**, 1029–1054.

HODRICK, R. AND E. PRESCOTT (1980): "Postwar U.S. Business Cycles: An Empirical Investigation," Discussion Paper #451, Carnegie-Mellon University.

IBBOTSEN, R. AND R. SINQUEFIELD (1988): *Stocks, Bonds, Bills and Inflation 1988 Yearbook*. Chicago: Ibbotsen and Associates.

JUGLAR, C. (1962): *Des Crises Commerciales et de leur Retour Périodique en France, en Angleterre et aux États-Unis*. New York: A. M. Kelley.

JUSTINO, D. (1988): *Formação do Espaço Económico Nacional Portugal 1810–1913*. Lisbon: Editorial Vega.

KING, R. (1990a): "Value and Capital in the Equilibrium Business Cycle Program," in *Value and Capital: Fifty Years Later*, ed. by L. McKenzie and S. Zamagni. London: MacMillan.

KING, R. (1990b) "Money and Business Cycles," manuscript, University of Rochester.

KING, R. AND C. PLOSSER (1989): "Real Business Cycles and the Test of the Adelmans," Working Paper #3160, National Bureau of Economic Research.

KING, R. AND S. REBELO (1989): "Low Frequency Filtering and Real Business Cycles," Working Paper #205, Rochester Center for Economic Research, University of Rochester.

KING, R. M. BAXTER, S. FISHER, AND K. G. ROUWENHORST (1990): " The Liquidity Effect in General Equilibrium," manuscript.

KING, R. C. PLOSSER, AND S. REBELO (1987): "Production Growth and Business Cycles: Technical Appendix," Working Paper, University of Rochester.

KING, R. C. PLOSSER, AND S. REBELO (1988a): "Production, Growth and Business Cycles: I— The Basic Neoclassical Model," *Journal of Monetary Economics*, 21, 195–232.

KING, R. C. PLOSSER, AND S. REBELO (1988b): "Production, Growth, and Business Cycles: II— New Directions," *Journal of Monetary Economics*, **21**, 309–341.

KOCHERLAKOTA, N. (1988): "A Note on the 'Discount' Factor in Growth Economies," manuscript, Northwestern University.

KOOPMANS, T. (1960): "Stationary Ordinal Utility and Impatience," *Econometrica*, **28**, 287–309.

KOOPMANS, T. (1965): "On the Concept of Optimal Economic Growth," in *The Econometric Approach to Development Planning*. Chicago: Rand-McNally.

KOOPMANS, T. P. DIAMOND, AND R. WILLIAMSON (1964): "Stationary Utility and Time Perspective," *Econometrica*, **32**, 82–100.

KYDLAND, F. (1984): "Labor-Force Heterogeneity and the Business Cycle," *Carnegie-Rochester Conference Series on Public Policy*, **21**, 173–208.

KYDLAND, F. "The Role of Money in a Competitive Model of Business Fluctuations," *Mimeo*, Federal Reserve Bank of Minneapolis and Carnegie-Mellon University.

KYDLAND, F. AND E. PRESCOTT (1982): "Time to Build and Aggregate Fluctuations," *Econometrica*, **50**, 1345–1370.

KYDLAND, F. AND E. PRESCOTT (1990): "Business Cycles: Real facts and a Monetary Myth," *Quarterly Review*, Federal Reserve Bank of Minneapolis, 3–18.

LONG, J. AND C. PLOSSER (1983): "Real Business Cycles", *Journal of Political Economy*, **91**, 1345–1370.

LOPES, J. S. (1981): "Factores Explicativos da Evolução do Saldo da Balança de Transacções Correntes," *Economia*, **5**.

LUCAS, R. (1977): "Understanding Business Cycles," in *Stabilization of the Domestic and International Economy*, ed. by Brunne, K. and A. Meltzer. Amsterdam: North-Holland, and Carnegie-Rochester Conference Series on Public Policy 5: 7–29.

LUCAS, R. (1980): "Methods and Problems in Business Cycles Theory," *Journal of Money Credit and Banking*, **12**, 696–715. Reprinted in *Studies in Business Cycle Theory*. Cambridge: MIT Press.

LUCAS, R. (1987): *Models of Business Cycles*. Cambridge: Harvard University Press.

LUCAS, R. (1988): "On the Mechanics of Economic Development," *Journal of Monetary Economics*, **22**, 3–42.

MACEDO, J. B. C. CORADO, AND M. PORTO (1986): *Trade Liberalization Episodes in Portugal: An Overview*, World Bank.

MADDISON, A. (1982): *Phases of Capitalist Development*. Oxford: Oxford University Press.

MANKIW, N. G. (1989) "Real Business Cycles: A New Keynesian Perspective," *Journal of Economic Perspectives*, **3**, 79–90.

MARQUES, A. AND A. ROMÃO (1983): "Croissance et Crise de l'Economie Portugaise (1960–1982)," *Estudos de Economia*, **4**, 1.

MCCALLUM, B. T. (1989): "Real Business Cycle Models," in *Modern Business Cycle Theory*, ed. by Barro. Cambridge: Harvard University Press.

MCGRATTAN, E. (1988): "The Macroeconomic Effect of a Tax Policy in an Equilibrium Model," manuscript, Stanford University.

MENDOZA, E. G. (1989): "Real Business Cycles in a Small Open Economy," forthcoming in *American Economic Review*

MOURA, F. P. (1989): *Por onde vai a Economia Portuguesa*. Lisbon: Publicações Dom Quixote.

MOURA, F. P. AND PINTO, L. M. T. (1958): *Problemas do Crescimento Económico Português*. Lisbon: Associação Industrial Portuguesa.

NELSON, C. R. AND C. PLOSSER (1982): "Trends and Random Walks in Macroeconomic Time-Series," *Journal of Monetary Economics*, **10**, 139–167.

NEVES, J. C. (1990): "O Desenvolvimento Português e o Padrão Transversal de Crescimento," forthcoming in *Análise Social*.

NEVES, J. C. AND CONFRARIA, J. (1988): "The Portuguese Economy 1948–1985: a Brief Survey," text presented at the seminar *Structural Adjustment Policies and Position of Smaller European Countries in the International Division of Labour*, Belgrade, (forthcoming).

NUNES, A. , MATA, M. E. AND N. VALÉRIO (1989): "Portuguese Economic Growth 1833–1985," *The Journal of European Economic History*, **18**, 291–330.

OBSTFELD, M. (1981): "Macroeconomic Policy, Exchange Rate Dynamics and Optimal Asset Accumulation," *Journal of Political Economy*, **89**, 1142–1161.

PEREIRA, A. M. AND GASPAR, V. (1990): "Portugal and the European Community: On the Effects of Financial Integration on Investment and Economic Growth," manuscript.

PINTADO, V. X. (1964): *Structure and Growth of the Portuguese Economy*, EFTA.

PRESCOTT, E. (1986): "Theory Ahead of Business Cycle Measurement," *Quarterly Review*, Federal Reserve Bank of Minneapolis, **10**, 9–22.

RADNER, R. (1966): "Optimal Growth in a Linear Logarithmic Economy," *International Economic Review*, 1–33.

RAMOS, AND ABECASSIS (1980): "Estudos sobre o Nível Sectorial de Emprego," Série de Estudos do Departamento de Estudos e Planeamento do Ministério do Trabalho, Lisbon.

ROCHA, E. (1981): "Especialização e Crescimento Económico em Portugal: 1960-74", *Análise Social*, **66**, vol. XVII, 2.

ROCHA, E. (1984): "Crescimento Económico em Portugal nos anos de 1960–73: alguns aspectos", *Anlíse Social*, vol. XX, 5.

ROMER, C. (1989): "The Prewar Business Cycle Reconsidered: New Estimates of Gross National Product, 1869–1908", *Journal of Political Economy*, **97**, 1–37.

ROMER, P. (1989): "Capital Accumulation in the Theory of Long-Run Growth," in *Modern Business Cycle Theory*. Cambridge: Harvard University Press.

ROTEMBERG, J., AND M. WOODFORD (1989): "Oligopolistic Pricing and the Effects of Aggregate Demand on Economic Activity," Working Paper #3206, National Bureau of Economic Research.

SACHS, J. (1981): "The current account and Macroeconomic Adjustment in the 70's," *Brooking Papers on Economic Activity*, **1**.

SALTER (1957): *External and Internal Equilibrium and the Terms of Trade.*

SANTOS, E. A. (1984a): "O Stock de Capital na Economia Portuguesa," Documento de Trabalho #6, Banco de Portugal, Lisbon.

SANTOS, E. A. (1984b): "Bens de Consumo Duradouros: Estimativas Anuais do Stock e do Consumo no Período 1958–1981," Documento de Trabalho #7, Banco de Portugal Lisbon.

SCHUMPETER, J. (1939): *Business Cycles. A Theoretical, Historical and Statistical Analysis of the Capitalistic Process.* New York: McGraw Hill.

SCHEINKMAN, J. AND L. WEISS (1986): "Borrowing Constraints and Aggregate Economic Activity," *Econometrica*, **54**, 23–45.

SIDRAUSKI, M. (1967): "Rational Choice and Patterns of Growth in a Monetary Economy," *American Economic Review*, **57**, 534–544.

SLUTSKY, E. (1937): "The Summation of Random Causes as the Source of Cyclic Processes," *Econometrica*, **5**, 105–146.

STOCKMAN, A. AND L. SVENSSON (1987): "Capital Flows, Investment, and Exchange Rates," *Journal of Monetary Economics*, **19**, 171–201.

SUMMERS, R. AND A. HESTON (1984): "Improved International Comparisons of Real Product and its Composition: 1950–1980," *Review of Income and Wealth*, **20**, 207–262.

WYNNE, M. (1987): "The Effects of Government Purchases in a Perfect Foresight Model," manuscript, University of Rochester.

# Financial Liberalization and Adhesion to EMS - Dynamics of Adjustment in Portugal

Mário Antão
Paulo Brito

## 1 Introduction

Increasing financial liberalization is one of the major influential changes in the Portuguese economy since EEC entry in 1986. The completion of the Single Market Programme which includes banking and other financial markets and full liberalization of capital movements is compulsory for Portugal from 1993 onwards, except for purely financial credits and monetary portfolio transactions, up to a transitory period not exceeding the end of 1995. This integration is likely to enhance the paradox, noticed in Gaspar and Macedo (1990), that a non-accommodating exchange rate policy and a tight monetary policy will not suffice to assure the controllability of the convergence of the domestic inflation rate to the EEC average.

Strong dynamic effects in welfare, exceeding the static ones, is the expected outcome from a process of gradual financial integration. And, as Peeters (1990) pointed out, if the efficient market hypothesis is reasonably verified during the transition, one should expect an impressive increase in gross capital cross-border transactions whereas the correspondent stock in a net basis will exhibit a small variance. Accordingly, as reported in Macedo (1990), substantial capital inflows followed EEC entry and the existing covered interest rate parity bias in favor of the dollar declined steadily. More recently, this bias, as well as its version in terms of the uncovered interest

We are particularly indebted to Victor Gaspar's comments on earlier versions of the paper. We are of course fully responsible for errors and omissions that may still remain.

rate parity, often became sizeable again but with the opposite sign. Particularly in June 1990, huge capital inflows, following expectations assuming that the entry of the Escudo in the exchange rate mechanism of EMS was imminent, forced the central bank to restore capital controls - prohibition of interbank swaps and the imposition of a non interest bearing deposit on the cost of borrowing funds abroad were the basic measures taken at the time which actually are still in force. Interestingly, Spain took before the same road and kept similar controls for a quite long time even after full entry of the Peseta in the EMS.

This evidence runs against Giavazzi and Spaventa's (1990) policy suggestion on the "new EMS" problem. They argue, on the subject of the full participation of the southern countries in the EMS, that exchange rate stability and financial integration, as well as the credibility of such commitments, would shift the loss of competitiveness towards the early stages of the dynamic process of disinflation, by raising domestic demand, and possibly inflation. However, shifting and concentrating this burden in the early stages would make the whole disinflation process shorter and less costly in terms of lost output. Therefore the implication is that the authorities should hasten the fixity of the exchange rate and accelerate financial integration, being of course out of question the reimposition of capital controls.

What would be the major consequences of such a strategy in terms of the paths of short run and long run inflation rates for a very open small capital importing economy like Portugal? Which decision would be preferable, to enter EMS now or to announce it for a given future date, in terms of the accumulated competitiveness loss and of the speed of the disinflation process? Is there a need to reinforce fiscal tightness? How deviations from purchasing power parity and from the Fisher open interest rate parity are related during the dynamic process of adjustment?

This paper attempts to provide some progress in answering to these questions.

It was firstly motivated by the policy dilemma pointed out in Krugman (1990). In short, his argument runs as follows. Capital mobility as well as exogenous shifts in the expectations of the future exchange rates will likely induce pressures for nominal exchange rate appreciation. Given the commitment to fixed exchange rates, those pressures lead to increased money supply and inflation. If the policy maker prefers to maintain the non-accommodating stance of monetary policy, the outcome will be instead nominal exchange rate appreciation. The only way out of this dilemma is to use also a tighter fiscal policy or to restore capital controls. A large degree of uncertainty about the long run equilibrium real exchange rate helps the formation of the government's preference to err on the side of undervaluation.

One of the insights brought to this discussion by Gaspar (1990) is on the determination of the long run real exchange rate. In a perfect foresight world and using a Dornbusch (1976) type model he shows that shifts in financial integration, related to decreases in risk premium and transaction costs, cause real exchange rate appreciation which, if perceived as undesirable, should be counteracted namely by stronger fiscal tightness.

As in that paper we study the case of a completely specialized small open economy with capital controls denoted by a premium over domestic assets. In addition we deal with a crawling peg regime and with a sticky price adjustment on the short run, through an expectations augmented Phillips curve. This last change makes possible to study the short and long run consequences of anticipated and non-anticipated policies.

We use a model which is rooted in the overshooting Dornbusch's model (1976). This type of models is remarkably useful for short run analyses, as Blanchard and Fischer (1989) pointed out. A synthesis about them can be found in Obstfeld and Stockman (1985). We extend that literature, **(i)**, by combining a fixed exchange rate regime (or a crawling peg regime) with a sticky price adjustment process and, **(ii)**, by studying, beyond the usual non-anticipated fixed shocks, time-varying and anticipated shocks.

In a second Part an empirical analysis of the model is performed. We deal with the adjustment process of the Portuguese economy between the half of 1985 and the end of 1989. After a preliminary study to test for the existence of co-integration of the variables, we highlight the Granger causality relationships between the most important variables of the process - the real exchange rate, the financial liberalization and the fiscal adjustment policy - and we draw some policy implications from the results.

Therefore, the plan of the paper is as follows.

Part I is composed by five sections. First, we introduce the model and study its dynamic behavior as well as its stability conditions. Then, several kinds of isolated shocks are considered: financial liberalization, changes in the exchange rate and in the fiscal policies and shifts in foreign prices. Alternative ways of performing the international financial liberalization and the EMS entry are evaluated next as combinations of some of those isolated shocks. In the sixth section we offer a brief conclusion and point out some shortcomings of our theoretical model.

Part II has also five sections. In the seventh we state the core of the relations among the variables that have to be the subject of empirical testing. The eighth section studies the integration and the possibility of co-integration among the most relevant variables, as well as the restrictions that should be imposed to a VAR (vector autoregression) representation of the data. After selecting an appropriate VAR model we proceed in the following section with its estimation. In the tenth section we analyze the predictive performance of the model as well as their derived impulse response functions. Finally, in the last section we extract several conclusions from the analysis as a whole and we suggest several directions to improve the present model and its explanatory power of the Portuguese transition to full financial integration.

# Part I

## 2 The Model

The model is introduced by Table 1 bellow. In a nutshell, it is based upon the following assumptions.

The economy is completely specialized in the production of one composite good which is an imperfect substitute to a composite good produced by the rest of the world (r.o.w.), and consumes both goods. We deal with a "semi-small" open economy case, i.e., the economy is small as far as the foreign composite good is concerned and it has some market power in the home produced good. The price of this domestic good adjusts sluggishly in the short run to imbalances between the aggregate demand and supply. In the steady state the prices permanently clear the domestic goods markets.

We also assume imperfect substitutability between domestic and foreign financial assets. This is translated in a simple way through the inclusion of a $\delta$ term in the uncovered interest parity equation. In the current context of the Portuguese economy $\delta$ can have various non exclusive interpretations: **(i)** there are capital controls with a predefined schedule for its abolition by phases; **(ii)** there is a higher risk involved in holding domestic assets as a result of lower levels of their liquidity and of the credibility of the macroeconomic policy; **(iii)** higher transaction costs.

The government budget is always balanced and the country follows a crawling peg regime. The rate of the crawl $\xi$ and, in some proportion, $\delta$ are exogenously determined by the government.

These assumptions are formally translated into Table 1.

Equation (1) denotes the uncovered nominal interest rate parity gap which equals $\delta$. Gradual financial integration is modelled here very simply by $\delta(t)$, a variable dependent of time, which, loosely defined, accounts for risk premium and abnormal transaction costs. This justifies a somewhat lengthy explanation.

Modelling risk premium is a hard task as it is shown in the very large literature on the issue. A quite common statement is that the forward

Table 1: The model.

$$i = i^* + \dot{e} + \delta \quad (1)$$

$$\dot{e} = \dot{e}^+ = \xi \quad (2)$$

$$m^d - \pi = \psi(p + y - \pi) - \lambda i \quad (3)$$

$$\pi \equiv \gamma p + (1-\gamma)(e + p^*) \quad (4)$$

$$d = \phi(e + p^* - p) - \sigma(i - \dot{\pi}) + g \quad (5)$$

$$m = m^d \quad (6)$$

$$\dot{p} = \theta(d - y) + \dot{\bar{p}} \quad (7)$$

$$y = \phi(e + p^* - \bar{p}) - \sigma(i - \dot{\bar{\pi}}) + g \quad (8)$$

$$\bar{\pi} \equiv \gamma \bar{p} + (1-\gamma)(e + p^*) \quad (9)$$

*Variables.* In levels: $i$ - nominal interest rate; $\delta$ - in a simplifying definition, the premium for holding domestic assets. In natural logs: $e$ - nominal exchange rate; $\xi$ - rate of the crawl; $m$ - nominal stock of money; $p$ - domestic good price index; $\pi$ - consumer price index; $y$ - aggregate supply of the domestic good; $d$ - aggregate demand of the domestic good; $g$ - government expenditure.

*Notation.* $\bar{x}$ - the steady state level of the variable $x$; $x^*$ - r.o.w. variables; $\dot{x}$ - time derivative; $\dot{x}^+ \equiv \lim_{t+h\to t}\left\{\frac{x(t+h)-x(t)}{h}\right\}$ - right time derivative; the time reference for all the variables was eliminated to simplify the notation.

*Parameters* (all positive). $\psi$ - real income elasticity of the real demand for money; $\lambda$ - nominal interest rate semi-elasticity of the real demand for money; $\gamma$ - absorption share of the domestic good; $\phi$ - real exchange rate elasticity of the aggregate demand, with the real exchange rate defined as the relative price of the domestic good; $\sigma$ - real interest rate elasticity of the aggregate demand; $\theta$ - speed of price adjustment to clear the domestic goods market.

premium is a biased predictor of future exchange rates due to the presence of volatile risk premia. In this vein, Krugman (1989) argues that the risk premium concept is highly elusive and does not offer, for instance, a convincing explanation for the persistent deviations from covered interest rate parity, between the DM and the USD, that arose in the 1980s, the case being that it is even legitimate to cast doubts on the validity of the usual efficient market hypothesis. Of course, we are entitled to remain even more skeptical if the case is of reinforcing the integration of the thin and emergent Escudo Euro-market with its domestic counterpart.

Besides, on this case further untractable considerations may apply. One could add to the picture several episodes suggesting the relevance of the so called "peso problem". And one could also suggest the presence of shifting expectations lagging behind long run capital movements — such as the increasing confidence on political stability and on sound macro policy management — and behind, of short run speculative capital flights of imprecise value and evading nature following, in this case, the approach developed by Lopes (1989). The point is that, taking all together, either we develop a rigorous but rather complicated model of the transition to full financial integration or we make some heroic assumptions to remain with a tractable expression.

Nevertheless, one can also find motivation to model $\delta$, as defined above, dependent of time. First, the effects on the interest rate parities from gradually removing capital controls may reasonably be captured by a time varying risk premium. The same should apply to the credibility effect that successful commitment for fixed exchange rate would likely exert. Finally, taking into consideration the remark in Branson (1990) that potential or actual entry in EMS reduces the risk of default for the entrants, the more so as they control their external debt, leads to the same suggestion.

The crawl is defined in equation (2) as the right time derivative of the nominal exchange rate. This is sufficiently general for allowing discrete devaluations.

In equation (3) the real demand for money is dependent upon the real income — nominal income deflated by the consumer price index, which is defined by equation (4) — and the nominal interest rate. The instantaneous equilibrium condition for the money market is set in equation (6). As it is well known, the supply of money is endogenous when we combine, for a small open economy, a fixed exchange rate (or a crawling peg) regime with a high level of external financial liberalization.

The aggregate demand for the home produced good is formalized by equation (5). The private demand is a function of the real exchange rate, as a result of the Marshall-Lerner condition or of the Harberger-Laursen-Metzler effect, and of the intertemporal price related to consumption in different time periods, that is, the real interest rate. The adjustment rule for the domestic good price is given by equation (7). The short term inflation rate incorporates two elements: the long run inflation rate, which will be verified with complete price flexibility, and the current disequilibrium in the domestic good market.[1] Finally, equations (8) and (9) display respectively the long run specifications of the GDP deflator and the consumer price index.

[1] According to Obstfeld and Rogoff (1984) this rule has two desirable properties: (i) it leads to a stationary equilibrium with a valid economic meaning: the fix-price model tends to the corresponding flex-price model, or, in other words, the unemployment is a short term phenomenon that must be eliminated in the long run; (ii) the stationarity feature of the model is not reduced to a stationary state and we can study time varying shocks.

# 3 Stationarity and Dynamics

After performing the suitable substitutions we get the following system of differential equations

$$\dot{p} = \frac{1}{1-\theta\sigma\gamma}\{\dot{\bar{p}} + \theta\phi(e+p^* - p) - \theta\sigma[i^* + \delta + \gamma\dot{e} - (1-\gamma)\dot{p}^*] + \theta(g-y)\} \tag{10}$$

$$\dot{\bar{p}} = \frac{1}{\sigma\theta}\{y - g - \phi(e+p^* - \bar{p}) + \sigma[i^* + \delta + \gamma\dot{e} - (1-\gamma)\dot{p}^*]\}\ , \tag{11}$$

and the equation

$$m = [\psi + (1-\psi)\gamma]p + \psi y + (1-\psi)(1-\gamma)(e+p^*) - \lambda(i^* + \dot{e} + \delta). \tag{12}$$

There are three independent endogenous variables: $p, \bar{p}$ and $m$. The first two are obtained as solutions of the system of ordinary differential equations (10)–(11). The solution for $m$ comes from the substitution upon (12) of the solution for $p$.

Table 2 shows the expressions for the general solution of the model and for the saddle path, after applying the Laplace transforms.

The saddle path was determined by taking the following into consideration. We have two real eigenvalues, one positive ($\mu_2$) and the other ($\mu_1$) with an a priori ambiguous sign. Convergence to a stationary state will only exist if $\mu_1$ is negative, that is, if the stability condition (20) holds. This is a sufficient condition for the existence and stability of the stationary equilibrium, because $p$ is a predetermined variable and $\bar{p}$ is a non-predetermined one.[2] The saddle path, which is given by equations (16)–(17), is the only one that leads to it. Any other path given by equations (13)–(14) is divergent and is a speculative bubble.

The economic content behind these mathematical properties is as follows. We have two prices: a short term and observable price which adjusts in a slow and continuous way towards a long run equilibrium price which is perfectly forecasted by agents. The divergence between these two prices is a result of the slow adjustment in the goods market.

Let us assume that we are in a situation of stationary equilibrium when an actual or anticipated future shock occurs. Then a difference between those two prices will follow which can induce two kinds of alternative consequences:

1. if the model is stable, price expectations "jump" discontinuously at once. Then, both prices will evolve along a new saddle path: instantaneously, if the shock was not anticipated, or after a certain lapse of

[2] The first paper that deals explicitly with this issue is Blanchard and Kahn (1980).

Table 2: The model's solution.

General solution

$$p(t) = [p(0) - \bar{p}(0)]e^{\mu_1 t} + \bar{p}(t) \tag{13}$$

$$\bar{p}(t) = [\bar{p}(0) + \int_0^\infty z(s)e^{-\mu_2 s}ds]e^{\mu_2 t} - \int_t^\infty z(s)e^{\mu_2(t-s)}ds \tag{14}$$

$$z \equiv -\frac{\phi}{\sigma\gamma}(e + p^*) + \frac{1}{\gamma}(i^* + \delta - \dot{p}^*) + \dot{e} + \dot{p}^* - \frac{1}{\sigma\gamma}(g - y)\,. \tag{15}$$

Saddle path

$$\tilde{p}(t) = [p(0) - \bar{p}(0)]e^{\mu_1 t} + \tilde{\bar{p}}(t) \tag{16}$$

$$\tilde{\bar{p}}(t) = e(t) + p^*(t) - \frac{1}{\gamma}\int_t^\infty [i^*(s) + \delta(s) - \dot{p}^*(s) - \frac{1}{\gamma}(g(s) - y(s))]e^{\mu_2(t-s)}ds\,. \tag{17}$$

Eigenvalues

$$\mu_1 = -\frac{\theta\phi}{1 - \theta\sigma\gamma} \tag{18}$$

$$\mu_2 = \frac{\phi}{\sigma\gamma} \tag{19}$$

Stability condition

$$1 - \theta\sigma\gamma > 0 \tag{20}$$

time, if the shock was anticipated. The short run prices will asymptotically converge to the long run prices, along that trajectory. Thus the stationary equilibrium is characterized by an equality between the observed and the expected prices, in levels or rates of growth, depending upon the behavior of the exogenous variables;

2. if the model is not stable, the prices will behave like a speculative bubble. The price anticipations would be systematically revised and the price dynamics would be divergent.

Figure 1 illustrates the phase diagram when condition (20) holds. We shall assume this from now on. The important facts are:

i) the schedule $\dot{\bar{p}} = 0$, which stands for the long run factors that are independent from the short run adjustment of prices, is vertical, and the schedule $\dot{p} = 0$ is positively slopped;

ii) the saddle path is coincident with the $\dot{\bar{p}} = 0$ schedule. This fact makes

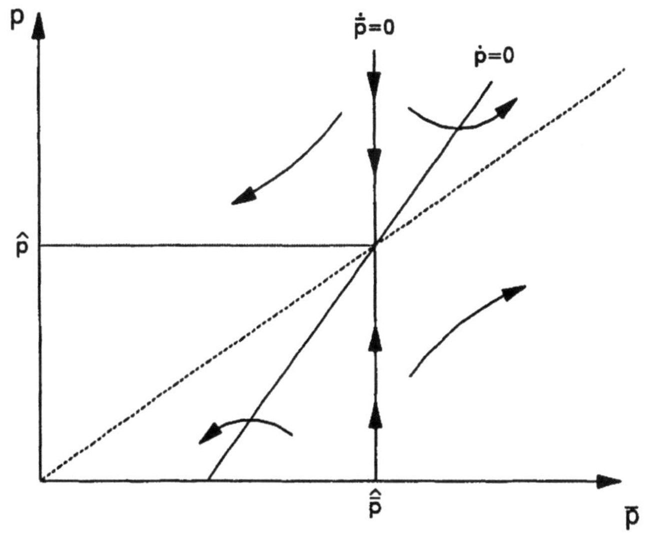


Figure 1: Phase diagram.

it possible to state the following general pattern of adjustment in this model:

— when a non-anticipated shock is exerted, the inflationary expectations "jump" to a new $\dot{\bar{p}} = 0$ curve and stay stationary afterwards. When the economy is placed in that new saddle path, the current rate of inflation adjusts along until it reaches a new stationary state;

— when the shock is anticipated, the initial equilibrium is disturbed even before the shock is produced. The "jump" of $\bar{p}$ will be smaller and will not place the model in a new saddle path but in a path determined by the condition that there will not be speculative gains when the shock finally occurs. In a more formal expression: the adjustment is determined by the condition that, when the saddle path moves at last, the anticipated prices will not jump because the economy would already be precisely placed over this new path. This kind of adjustment, though resembling, is not a speculative bubble;

**iii)** the stationary equilibrium $(\hat{p}, \hat{\bar{p}})$ will be placed over the angle bisector, in a given point (as in Figure 1), or moving along it when the crawl is different from zero or when the r.o.w. price index is not constant.

It should be noted that, in (20), $\theta$ is not only a crucial parameter to ensure that the model is stable but it is also an important factor that determines the speed of adjustment on the saddle path towards the stationary state. Given the domestic consumers' tastes and the real interest rate elasticity of the domestic aggregate demand, the stability condition calls for a slow adjustment in the goods market.[3]

# 4 Comparative Dynamics for Isolated Shocks

The current section studies the effects related to the introduction of some isolated disturbances. The dynamic multipliers are referred to deviations from an initial stationary position which is deemed to prevail before the introduction of any shock.

The shocks in isolation, here studied, are the following: the progress in international financial liberalization, formalized by a reduction of $\delta$; a nominal exchange rate overvaluation, discrete or through a reduction in the rate of the crawl; a deflationary fiscal policy; an external price shock.

## 4.1 Financial Liberalization

Three cases deserve consideration: **(i)** A set of non-announced liberalization measures; **(ii)** a pre-announced set of liberalization measures for a future date (in $t = 0$ to take place at $t = T$); **(iii)** a smooth liberalization between $t = 0$ and $t = T$.

In case **(i)** we take the following impulse function

$$\Delta\delta(t) = -\delta(0), \quad 0 \leq t \leq \infty \,, \tag{21}$$

that leads to the following expression for the multiplier related to (17)

$$\Delta\tilde{p}(t) = \frac{\sigma}{\phi}\delta(0) \,, \quad 0 \leq t \leq \infty \,. \tag{22}$$

Figures 2 and 3 illustrate, respectively, the phase diagram and the adjustment paths for the most important variables. In short, we can see that:

[3] A sufficient condition for condition (20) to hold is that $\theta$ should be small enough. The consequence of this is that the smaller $\theta$ is the smaller the adjustment over the saddle path will be, because

$$\frac{\partial \mu_1}{\partial \theta} = -\frac{\phi}{(1-\theta\sigma\gamma)^2} \,.$$

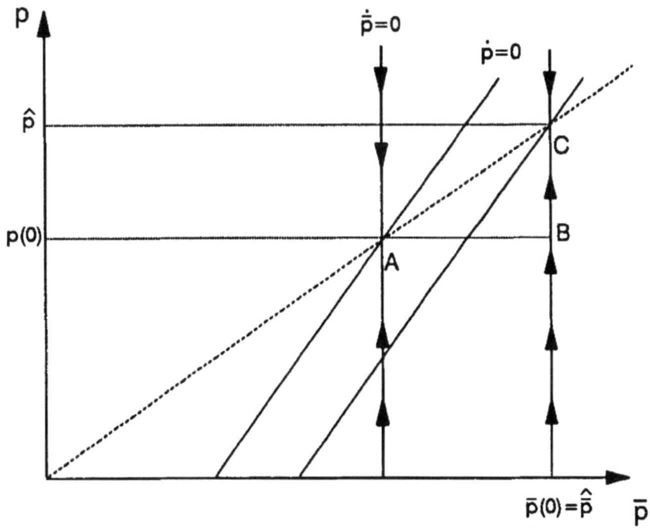


Figure 2: Non-anticipated liberalization.

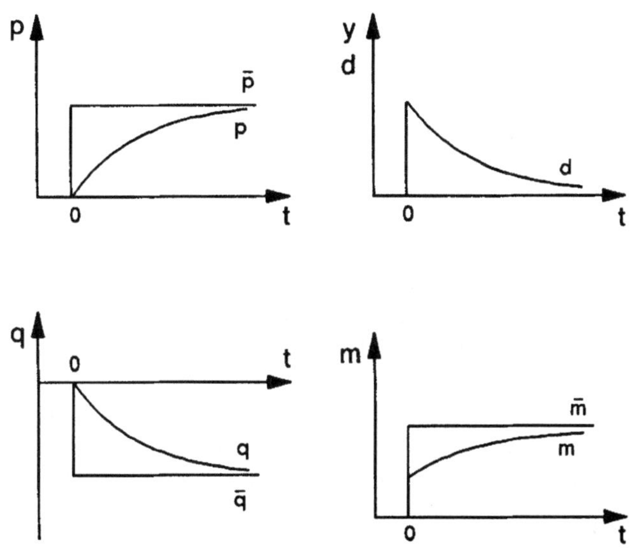


Figure 3: Non-anticipated financial liberalization.

— there is an instantaneous upward revision of the expectations over the price level to make it compatible with the new long run equilibrium level (**A** → **B**) due to the reduction of the long run real interest rate. Given the constant aggregate supply, the revision of the price expectations leads to a real long run exchange rate appreciation, $\bar{q} = e + p^* - \bar{p}$, which was already noticed by Gaspar (1990);

— after the shock had been exerted, the actual price level will gradually adjust along the new saddle path until it reaches its long run level (**B** → **C**). However, after the initial jump, the long run price level will be invariant. Therefore, the price convergence process, which is followed by a process of real exchange rate appreciation, is only a consequence of the initial excess demand.

In case (**ii**), when the financial liberalization is previously announced[4] to take place at a specific future moment $T$, we have the following impulse function,

$$\Delta\delta(t) = \begin{cases} 0, & 0 \leq t < T \\ -\delta(0), & T \leq t \leq \infty. \end{cases} \tag{23}$$

The long run price adjustment process now includes a section outside the saddle path, which is calculated from the general expression for the multiplier (14), and, another, after $T$, within the new saddle path.

$$\Delta\bar{p}(t) = \begin{cases} \frac{\sigma}{\phi}\delta(0)e^{\mu_2(t-T)}, & 0 \leq t < T \\ \frac{\sigma}{\phi}\delta(0), & T \leq t \leq \infty. \end{cases} \tag{24}$$

Figures 4 and 5 show that in this case we will have an adjustment section (**B** → **C**) which is different from the former case.

In this experiment we have the following outcome:

— the pre-announcement of the shock for a future time $t = T$ leads to a revision of the inflationary expectations at $t = 0$ and to an anticipation of a decrease in the real long run interest rates. While the liberalization is not enforced the saddle path is not moved from its initial position. Assuming that there is enough credibility that the shock will be effectively exerted at $t = T$, the size of the initial jump in expectations will be endogenously determined in such a way as to place the system at **C**, where there are no capital gains.[5]

[4]For a first study of anticipated policies within the Dornbusch (1976) model, see Wilson (1979).

[5]To have this, it is necessary that at $t = 0$ the shock is credible and the government plays fair at $t = T$.

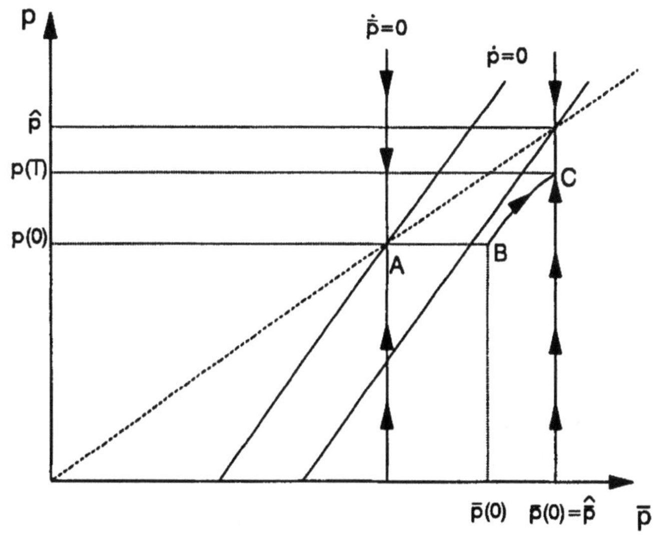


Figure 4: Announced liberalization.

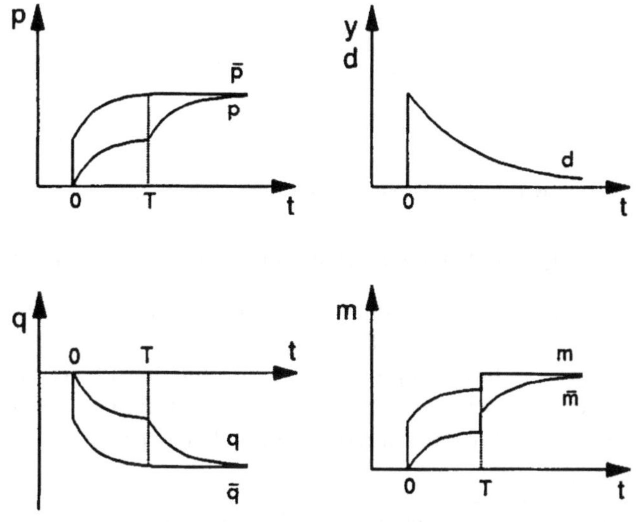


Figure 5: Announced liberalization $T$ periods before.

The larger the time lag between the announcement and the implementation, the larger the initial jump will be.[6] Besides, it is important to note that differently from the non-announced liberalization, we have a positive and decreasing inflation rate between $t = 0$ and $t = T$;

— the revision of the referred inflationary expectations starts by its own an inflationary process which is not strictly a speculative bubble. As we can see in the section (**B** $\rightarrow$ **C**), the short run inflation rate is higher than the long run one, their difference being an outcome of the inflationary expectations revision before the shock, will tend to zero. Between $t = 0$ and $t = T$, the inflation is then a pure anticipatory phenomenon and is the only effect that diminishes the real anticipated interest rate. After $t = T$ the anticipated inflation rate and the price adjustment process will be similar to that of case (**i**).

By comparison, we will have in (**ii**) a more gradual adjustment for the real exchange rate and a smaller initial disequilibrium in the goods market, and the higher the time lag between the announcement and the implementation moments, the larger the difference to the former case will be.

In case (**iii**), the liberalization process would be the elimination of $\delta$ by steps. If it was previously announced or anticipated, then we would have a higher initial jump as compared with (**A** $\rightarrow$ **B**) of Figure 4, followed by a series of sections like (**B** $\rightarrow$ **C**), of the same figure, till the completion of the adjustment. Thus, we can approximate this case by the impulse function [7]

$$\Delta\delta(t) = \begin{cases} -\delta(0)\frac{t}{T}, & 0 \leq t < T \\ -\delta(0), & T \leq t \leq \infty. \end{cases} \tag{25}$$

This case has a similar phase diagram as case (**ii**) (see Figure 4), with the important difference that, in the adjustment along section (**B** $\rightarrow$ **C**), the system will always be placed on a saddle path that is continuously moving with $\delta$.

Figure 6 displays the behavior across time of the main variables:

— the anticipated price level jumps instantaneously, then increases until $t = T$ and remains constant afterwards; the actual price level does not jump at the beginning of the exercise but it will asymptotically converge to the anticipated price level. Therefore, the actual rate of inflation will display a much more gradual behavior and will not jump as in case (**ii**);

[6] One of the desirable properties of the price adjustment rule assumed throughout this paper is that an announcement for a shock to take place at infinity will not lead to any discontinuous jump for the non-predetermined variables.

[7] A complete list of the multipliers can be found in the appendix.

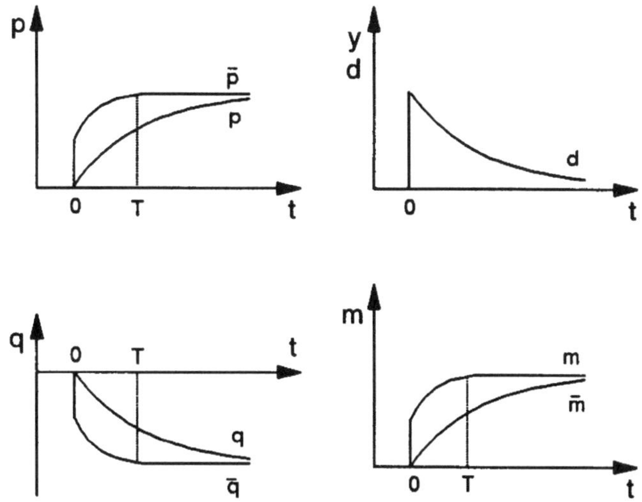


Figure 6: Gradual liberalization.

— also, the excess aggregate demand and the real exchange rate appreciation will evolve in a more gradual way between $t = 0$ and $t = T$.

## 4.2 Exchange Rate Shocks

Three cases will be of concern: **(iv)** discrete "surprise" revaluation; **(v)** non-announced elimination of the crawl; **(vi)** announcement at $t = 0$ of the elimination of the crawl to take place at $t = T$.

In the first case, the discrete nominal revaluation will have real short run effects that will not change the real long term exchange rate (see Figure 7). The impulse function and the long run price multiplier will be equalized

$$\Delta\bar{p}(t) = \Delta e(t) = -\Delta e(0)\,, \quad 0 \leq t \leq \infty\,. \tag{26}$$

There is an instantaneous downward revision of the long run price level that fully compensates the nominal revaluation (the short term real exchange rate will have a discrete appreciation). Then, we will have an excess supply in the goods market. There is, subsequently, a short run disinflation, real exchange rate depreciation and a reduction of the excess supply. In contrast to the former section, the real interest rate will remain constant.

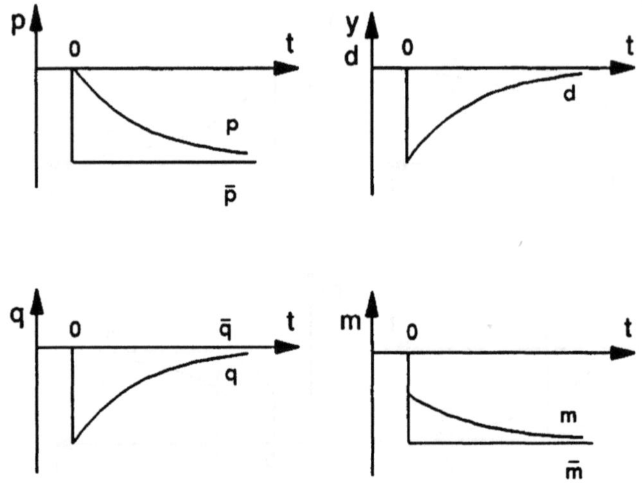


Figure 7: Non-announced discontinuous revaluation.

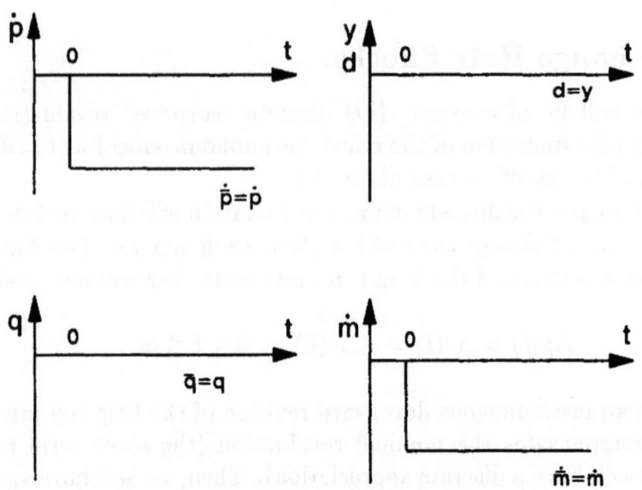


Figure 8: Non-announced elimination of the crawl.

As far as case (**v**) is concerned (see Figure 8), the real exchange rate is neutral when there is a non-announced elimination of the crawl.

$$\Delta\dot{e}(t) = -\Delta\dot{e}(0) = -\xi\ , \quad 0 \leq t \leq \infty\ . \tag{27}$$

Furthermore, the expectations concerning all the variables will be permanently fulfilled, with equal multipliers for the actual and anticipated variables (see Table 10 in the Appendix).

In contrast to the discrete revaluation case, the reduction in the rate of the crawl will simultaneously decrease the nominal interest rate and the long run inflation rate. As these two effects fully offset each other the real exchange rate adjustment to restore equilibrium in unnecessary.

In the case (**vi**) the elimination of the crawl is previously announced to take place at time $t = T$ (see the Table 11 in the Appendix for the variational dynamics of this case),

$$\Delta\dot{e}(t) = \begin{cases} 0, & 0 \leq t < T \\ -\Delta\dot{e}(0) = -\xi, & T \leq t \leq \infty. \end{cases} \tag{28}$$

We will have, synthetically, the following developments (see Figure 9):

— between $t = 0$ and $t = T$ the dynamics will have a pure anticipative nature. The announcement implies an immediate fall in the long run

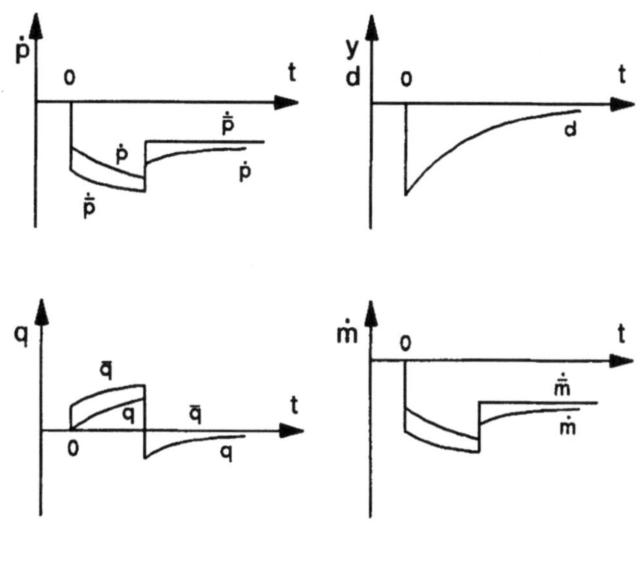


Figure 9: Pre-announced elimination of the crawl $T$ periods before.

price level in anticipation to its future behavior after the implementation of the policy. This causes an instantaneous increase in the long run real interest rate that must be countered by a real depreciation to gradually clear the goods market. As, with the proximity of $T$, the inflation rate expectations tend to stabilize the same happens to the long run real exchange rate. The downward change in the inflationary expectations will add up to the continuous reduction of the actual price level, reinforcing the disinflationary process until $t = T$;

— at $t = T$, there is a sharp real exchange rate overshooting, followed by a gradual depreciation until it reaches the same stationary equilibrium at the $t = 0$ level, as implied by the property of long run neutrality of monetary shocks, which is satisfied by the model.

## 4.3 Fiscal Policy and Foreign Price Shocks

Some other shocks may be exerted upon the economy (see Table 12 in the Appendix).

A non-anticipated contractionary fiscal policy, that can be thought as a discontinuous fall in the public expenditure share of the GDP, reduces instantaneously the long run levels of the home good price and of the real money supply. Therefore it causes, in the long run, a real exchange rate depreciation. The short run adjustment is induced by the excess supply in the goods market that occurs, which is gradually eliminated through the pressure on the price level to fall, while a continuous real exchange rate depreciation goes on, smoothing this undershooting adjustment to the new steady state.

On the other hand, a non-anticipated and permanent increase in the international price level has the opposite effects on the domestic prices, the real money stock and the imbalances in the home goods market. However, since the long run real exchange rate will not change, a depreciation arises at the beginning, which is followed by a gradual short run appreciation.

If a similar shock arises in the international inflation rate, then in the new stationary equilibrium we will have rising inflation rates, which means that the long run multipliers, when measured in levels, are dependent of time. We would have then both short run and long run inflationary processes and a real appreciation.

# 5 Financial Liberalization and Adoption of a Fixed Exchange Rate Regime

After the examination of the effects of the more relevant shocks in isolation, one should combine them to become nearer to the real problem of policy-makers. So, in this section, we make a comparative assessment of the two major alternatives that financial liberalization and EMS entry involve for the Portuguese economy.

Let us assume that:

— $t = T$ is the common horizon for both the full opening of the financial markets and the EMS entry, which means here full adhesion to the respective exchange rate mechanisms;

— the international financial liberalization process is gradual and can be simulated by a reduction of $\delta$ as in case (**iii**), section 4.1;

— there are two alternative ways to adhere to the EMS: first, immediate entry by surprise, as in case (**v**) of section 4.2 or, second, ulterior entry at $t = T_1 < T$ previously announced at $t = 0$, as in case (**vi**) of section 4.2.

Synthetically, we will consider the process of gradual financial liberalization accompanied by an immediate entry (strategy $E_1$) or by an entry at the middle of the journey (strategy $E_2$).

Their respective assessments will be made through the following criteria: consequences upon the domestic good market equilibrium, which will tend to provoke an excess supply or demand (hastening or dampening the nominal convergence towards EEC inflation rate) and consequences upon the real exchange rate (increasing further or lesser the deflationary pressures that threat the real convergence process towards EEC). We will measure these effects by the equations,[8]

$$\Delta D = \int_0^T \Delta d(s)ds \tag{29}$$

[8]Two observations are in order. Firstly, the evaluation of the two strategies makes sense only for the short run, because the long run multipliers will be equal. Then we will evaluate them between $t = 0$ and $t = T$. Secondly, as in Buiter and Miller (1982), who study a flexible nominal exchange rate model, we shall not use a discount factor. The reasons are twofold: i) since the real interest rate is endogenous in our model, if we used it as the discount rate we would further complicate the derivations, as well as the interpretation of the results, without much gain as far as the real issues faced by the policymaker are concerned; ii) on the other hand, if we decided to choose an exogenous rate we would have the same degree of arbitrariness that is involved in our choice of a zero rate of discount.

Table 3: Evaluation of strategies $E_1$ and $E_2$.

| | $\Delta D$ | | $\Delta Q$ | |
|---|---|---|---|---|
| $E_1$ | $\Omega_1$ | (+) | $-\Omega_2$ | (-) |
| $E_2$ | $\Omega_1 - \Omega_3$ | (?) | $-\Omega_2 + \Omega_4$ | (?) |

$$\Delta Q = \int_0^T \Delta \dot{q}(s) ds \, . \tag{30}$$

Next, we compare the dynamic multipliers with the two strategies $E_1$ and $E_2$.

To simplify the notation let us assume that:

$$\Omega_1 = \frac{\delta(0)\gamma\sigma^2}{\theta\phi^2 T}(1 - e^{-\mu_2 T})(1 - e^{\mu_1 T}) > 0 \tag{31}$$

$$\Omega_2 = \frac{\delta(0)\sigma}{\phi}\left[1 - \frac{\sigma\gamma}{\phi T}(1 - e^{-\mu_2 T})e^{\mu_1 T}\right] > 0 \tag{32}$$

$$\Omega_3 = \frac{1}{\theta}(\xi T_1 e^{-\mu_2 T_1})(1 - e^{\mu_1 T}) > 0 \tag{33}$$

$$\Omega_4 = \xi T_1(1 - e^{\mu_1 T - \mu_2 T_1}) > 0 \, . \tag{34}$$

Table 3 displays the multipliers under examination, from (29) and (30), which, obviously, are obtained as the sum of the correspondent ones for the shocks in isolation (see Tables 9, 10 and 11 in the Appendix).

As it is apparent, strategy $E_2$ looks unambiguously preferable in terms of the above stated criteria. In fact:

i) strategy $E_1$ is followed by a higher demand pressure across all the period, because the expansionist effect of the financial liberalization is the only at work (in this case the crawl's elimination effect is zero as we saw in case (v) of 4.2) Differently, if strategy $E_2$ is adopted, the pre-announcement of the adoption of a fixed exchange rate regime would lead to a fall in the inflationary expectations reducing the current inflation and raising the real interest rate. The aggregate demand is thus contracted and $\Omega_3$ represents the correspondent cumulative effect. However, the *rate* of instantaneous change of the aggregate demand is higher in the case $E_2$, at $t = T$.

ii) strategy $E_1$ leads to a cumulative higher real appreciation than $E_2$. In the former the only effect exerted is the inflationary effect of financial liberalization whereas the discrete elimination of the crawl is fully compensated by a reduction in prices. In the case of $E_2$, however, the effect of the financial liberalization on the real exchange rate is dampened as long as the crawl is in operation, except at $T$, as seen above in 4.2. And the higher the initial level of controls, $\delta(0)$, and the rate of crawl, $\xi(0)$, the higher the possibility of having as well a cumulated real appreciation. But, in any circumstances, $E_2$ will imply, according to the model, a smaller cumulated loss of external competitiveness as induced by the adjustments under consideration.

Finally, as it is apparent, strategy $E_1$ is a particular case of strategy $E_2$, when $T_1 = 0$ or $\xi = 0$. This means that in this model the EMS entry and the adoption of a fixed exchange rate regime without entering the EMS have the same consequences.

Therefore the model ascribes to the EMS entry neither a credibility gain nor any relief of the real adjustment costs to the entrant that can be brought by the cooperation of the other EEC members. Both effects are usually stressed as important to hasten the disinflationary process and to reduce the deflationary costs involved. We acknowledge this theoretical shortcoming which must be surpassed in a more refined version of the model, in agenda for the near future.

However it has to be remarked that the majority of the profession remains rather skeptical about the relevance of these effects in the case that Portugal decides to fully adhere to EMS in the very near future, stressing that other domestic conditions are also important to influence expectations.

# 6 Synthesis

The main preliminary conclusions to be drawn from this model are, synthetically, the following:

1. The financial liberalization will tend to have an inflationary effect, gearing pressures for the formation of excess aggregate demand, and real exchange rate appreciation.

2. An immediate EMS entry does not have, *per se*, effects on the external competitiveness and on the aggregate demand, because the crawl's reduction is completely countervailed by a change in the rate of inflation.

3. The full financial integration will be followed by lower inflationary pressures and by fewer competitiveness losses if the entry is not immediate and if it is previously announced (strategy $E_2$).

4. If it is decided to offset the precedent effects by tightening further the fiscal policy, the size of it will be also smaller if strategy $E_2$ is adopted.

The simple model that has been used does not consider some other eventually crucial dimensions. Those that seem more obvious are the introduction of supply behavioral equations and dynamical stock adjustments, namely the cumulative effect upon the balance of payments, whereas a more refined treatment of the financial integration process may also prove to be important.[9]

# Part II

## 7 The Long Run Behavior of the Real Exchange Rate

The theoretical model in Part I aims to explain essential aspects of the dynamic process of liberalization and financial integration of the Portuguese economy into the EEC Single Market.

One of its main features is that, in the presence of permanent shocks, the expectations on the long run equilibrium inflation rate adjust instantly, whereas the adjustment of the current inflation rate occurs slowly over time.

In the introduction we refer to the relation that the model has with recent literature on the policy problems that southern countries face at their entry into EMS. Clearly the consequences and the policy responses to the likely outcome of sharp and steady real exchange rate appreciation in countries with excessive inflation rates remains an open issue to debate and it is the subject of quite a number of studies. Recently Artus and Dupuy (1990) stressed the possibilities of intertemporal inconsistency between a "soft landing" of the excess of inflation and the gradual lifting of capital controls.

In those countries, and mostly in the case of Portugal, policy makers kept a tight stance of the monetary policy implying that the domestic interest rate remains in excess regarding the covered interest rate parity condition, while financial integration proceeds. The alternative, which would be an immediate and sharp increase in the tightness of the fiscal policy, has

[9]For alternative modelling of the real exchange rate see the FEREX model by Stein (1990) and an intertemporal optimizing version by Brito (1990).

been disregarded to avoid deflationary costs, estimated to be too high and uncertain.

Therefore, the probability of speculative attacks pressing for the nominal appreciation of the Escudo became high and in June 1990 the central bank had no other choice than to reintroduce capital controls.

The acceleration of financial integration is one of the implications of the Delors Report on the transition to the Economic and Monetary Union. Therefore, with the analysis of the above-mentioned trade-off between the loss of external competitiveness (or the real exchange rate appreciation, here denoted by $q$), and the *underlying* domestic real interest rate (i.e., the domestic nominal interest rate minus the sum of the rate of inflation abroad and the rate of change of the exchange rate, here denoted by $jr$), we may infer to a given extent how the policy makers have been reacting to this policy dilemma which seems crucial to explain the essentials of the behavior of the Portuguese economy in the recent past and in the next future.

In terms of our model this means to study the causal relations between $q$, $jr$ and the fiscal adjustment $(g - y)$, which are all related in Part I by equation (17). We may rewrite this equation as

$$\tilde{\bar{q}}_t = \frac{1}{\gamma}\int_t^{\infty}\left[i_s^* + \delta_s - \dot{p}_s^* - \frac{1}{\sigma}(g_s - y_s)\right] e^{(\mu_2(t-s))}ds\,. \tag{35}$$

With equation (35) we can study the long run behavior of $q$. An appropriate methodology to infer from the data some confirmation of our theoretical results is to test the existence of a relation of co-integration between the above-mentioned variables. Following namely Engle and Granger (1987) in the next sections we study the order of integration of the variables, the possibility of co-integration and Granger causality. The data is monthly, from August 1985 to December 1989, and is easily obtainable from annual reports of the central bank (Banco de Portugal) and from IMF International Financial Statistics. The variables defined below are straightforward proxies of the ones in the theoretical model.

$q$ — it is defined as $q \equiv p + e - p^*$; it is the sum of log of two composite variables, $p^*$, an weighted foreign consumer price index, and $e$, an weighted index of Escudo bilateral exchange rates, minus the log of the Portuguese consumer price index; both indexes were composed with only four major trading partners - USA, Germany, United Kingdom and France; their weights are respectively, 0.21, 0.25, 0.26 and 0.28, the same as in Macedo (1982) where this short cut is justified.

$jr$ — it is defined as $i^* - p^* + \delta = i - (p^* + e)$; therefore it corresponds to the short run domestic real interest rate if purchasing power parity would be continuously held, which in the model occurs only in the long run equilibrium; it is calculated by taking as domestic rate the Treasury Bills rate for 6 months and as the international one the Eurodollar rate for 3 months deposits; $p$ and $p^*$ are the rates of change of the corresponding variables in $q$.

$gy$ — it is the log of the ratio of public expenditure to GDP; since monthly data on GDP is not available the industrial production index was used as its proxy.

# 8 Integration

Using the definitions of integration of a series and of co-integration of two or more series (Engle and Granger, 1987), we can make a preliminary empirical assessment on the adequacy of our model, by studying the dynamic properties of the data.[10]

Our model implies the existence of a causal relation running from $q$ to $jr$ or $gy$. As an illustration, if we derive (35) with respect to time, and apply the Leibnitz's rule and the condition to preclude the existence of speculative bubbles, we obtain, eliminating $gy$ for simplicity, the differential equation

$$\dot{q}_t = \mu_2 q_t - \frac{1}{\gamma}\dot{j}r_t. \tag{36}$$

The equivalent expression in discrete time would be, taking $\dot{q} \approx q_t - q_{t-1}$,

$$q_t - \frac{1}{1-\mu_2} q_{t-1} + \frac{1}{\gamma(1-\mu_2)} \dot{j}r_t = \varepsilon_t \tag{37}$$

where $\varepsilon_t$ is assumed to be a white noise and clearly the ordering of the two pairs of variables with respect to time imply the existence of a Granger causal relation running from $q$ to $jr$. Furthermore, if $q$ is stationary only in first differences then $\mu_2$ would be close to zero. This would mean that the speed of convergence of the short run real exchange rate to its new long run equilibrium value, whenever the steady state is disturbed, would be rather low as one would expect from the usual empirical assessments on this issue. It is then convenient to check the plausibility of modeling $q$ in first differences before proceeding to the integration analysis of the series.

A crude but useful way to do it is by regressing $q_t$ in $q_{t-1}$, $jr_t$, and the sums of the correspondent lagged variables up to a given maximum number of lags. We would expect that the coefficient of $q_{t-1}$ would not be

[10] Barata (1990) studies the behavior of the Escudo-Sterling exchange rate market with the same methodology.

Table 4: **Regression:** $q_t = \alpha + \sum_{i=1}^{12} \beta_i^q q_{t-i} + \sum_{i=0}^{12} \beta_i^{jr} jr_{t-i} + \varepsilon_t$.

| Regressor | $\hat{\beta}$ | $t_{\hat{\beta}}$, $F^*$ |
|---|---|---|
| Constant | -.633 | |
| $jr_t$ | -.00109 | -5.647 |
| $q_{t-1}$ | .737 | 2.774 |
| $\sum_{i=2}^{12} q_{t-i}$ | .4004 | 1.234 |
| $\sum_{i=1}^{12} jr_{t-i}$ | -.0012 | -.0678 |
| $R^2 = 0.985$ | $Q(18) = 1.91$ (level of sign. 85.6%) | |

* The $F$-test is related to the sum of lagged $q$ and $jr$.

statistically different from one, the coefficient of $jr_t$ would be significant and have a minus sign and the remaining coefficients would not be different from zero.

In fact, as it can be seen by inspection of Table 4, the data does not seem to reject any of these assumptions whereas the Ljung-Box $Q$-statistic warrants that autocorrelation is absent.

Therefore one would expect that the integration analysis of the three variables in the model would show that: (i) $q$ is integrated of degree one and $jr$ and $gy$ are integrated of degree zero; (ii) $q$ and $jr$ or $q$ and $gy$ are not co-integrated (which immediately holds if (i) is verified).

Table 5 reports the univariate tests for unit roots, the Dickey-Fuller tests, for levels and first differences, when necessary.

The first column displays the t-statistics on $\alpha$ in the regression $\Delta x_t = \mu + \alpha x_{t-1} + \varepsilon_t$. We test the null hypothesis ($H_0 : \alpha = 0$) that $x$ follows a random walk against the alternative that it is not stationary, when $\varepsilon$ is a white noise. Critical values are tabulated in Fuller (1976, p.373). The second and third columns display, respectively, the t-statistic for $H_0 : \alpha = 0$, and the F-statistic for $H_0 : \alpha = 0, \beta = 0$ in the regression $\Delta x_t = \mu + \beta t + \alpha x_{t-1} + \varepsilon_t$. Critical values are tabulated in Fuller (1976) and Dickey and Fuller (1981).

The results in Table 5 are consistent with the univariate dynamic behavior of the variables implied by the model: $jr$ and $gy$ are integrated of order zero, $I(0)$, and $q$ is integrated of order one, $I(1)$, according to all the reported tests. These results imply that, by definition, it does not exist co-integration linking the variables either in the trivariate case of the full model or in their two bivariate simplified variants - $(q, jr)$ and $(q, gy)$. In fact, quoting Engle and Granger (1987, op.cit.)

> "...the components of a vector $x_t$ are said to be co-integrated of order $d, b$, denoted by $x_t \rightsquigarrow CI(d, b)$ if: (i) all components

of $\mathbf{x}_t$ are $I(d)$; (ii) there exists a vector $\alpha$ (diff. from 0) so that $z_t = \alpha'\mathbf{x}_t \rightsquigarrow I(d-b)$, $b > 0$; the vector $\alpha$ is called the co-integrating vector ...".

In checking whether co-integration exists or not it is important to define what sort of empirical modeling should be carried on. For co-integrated systems, a most convenient estimation procedure is to use the error correction form, (particularly if one can assume that there is no moving average term). Furthermore, if $x_t \rightsquigarrow I(1)$ are generated by an error correction model, then $\mathbf{x}_t$ is necessarily co-integrated and if a finite VAR (vector autoregression) representation is possible one should remark that: (i) vector autoregressions estimated with co-integrated data will be misspecified if the data are differenced and (ii) will have omitted important constraints if the data are used in levels.

# 9 VAR Estimation

The fact that we do not have co-integration allows us to pursue the analysis with a VAR representation not necessarily restricted as just referred. In fact the single restrictions that we would like to see in such a model would be the ones implied by the theoretical model.

We analyzed the statistical properties of several VAR variants that would be compatible with our theoretical model. Interestingly our findings suggest that: **(i)** the bivariate version of the model which tries to explain just the linkage between the real exchange rate and the *underlying* domestic real interest rate, performs better than the other bivariate case and the full trivariate model; **(ii)** lags of order higher than one do not improve significantly the forecasting capabilities of the VAR model.

Table 5: Univariate tests for unit roots.

| Variables | $t_{\hat{\alpha}}$ | $t_{\hat{\alpha}}$ | $\Phi_3$ |
|---|---|---|---|
| levels | | | |
| $q$ | 0.26 | -2.44 | 4.46 |
| $jr$ | -11.24 | -11.70 | 68.45 |
| $gy$ | -7.20 | -7.46 | 27.86 |
| First differences | | | |
| $q$ | -7.54 | -7.80 | 30.44 |
| Asymptotic critical values: 5% | -3.41 | -3.41 | 6.25 |

We have found no evidence of first order or higher order autocorrelation as tested by the Durbin-Watson or Ljung-Box $Q$-statistic in RATS.

Table 6: VAR estimates.

| Regressors | | $\hat{a}, \ldots, \hat{d}$ | $t_{\hat{a}}, \ldots, t_{\hat{d}}$ |
|---|---|---|---|
| | | Equation (38) | |
| Constant | | 1.485 | .677 |
| $\Delta jr_{t-1}$ | | -0.540 | -4.949 |
| $\Delta q_{t-1}$ | | 456.909 | 2.822 |
| | $R^2 = 0.56$ | $Q(21) = 13.9(87.3\%)$ | |
| | | Equation (39) | |
| Constant | | -0.004 | -1.621513 |
| $\Delta jr_{t-1}$ | | 0.925E-04 | 0.8454984 |
| $\Delta q_{t-1}$ | | 0.052 | 0.3196295 |
| | $R^2 = .014$ | $Q(21) = 15.458(79.9\%)$ | |

Therefore, the VAR version selected to pursue the estimation was

$$\Delta jr_t = a(L)\Delta jr_{t-1} + b(L)\Delta q_{t-1} + u_{1t} \tag{38}$$

$$\Delta q_t = c(L)\Delta jr_{t-1} + d(L)\Delta q_{t-1} + u_{2t} \tag{39}$$

and the results from the estimation are given in Table 6.

Before analyzing these results a comment on the methodology is in order. We used the RATS software and the VAR estimation procedures suggested in Doan and Litterman (1986). First, a Wold's moving average transformation of the original data was performed. Then, the impulses were normalized by equating the unitary variation of each variable to their standard deviation. To eliminate the contemporary correlations the variance-covariance matrix of the errors was diagonalized. There are however for a VAR model with $n$ variables $n!$ procedures to orthogonalize the errors that are linearly independent. Therefore the propagation effects of each impulse can be quite sensitive to the selected procedures, particularly to the order of the variables in the process of factorization. Nevertheless, adopting a Choleski decomposition in the orthonormalization, one can expect that the referred order of the variables will not influence the results. Furthermore the Choleski decomposition corresponds exactly to the Grand-Schmidt procedure, often used in non linear programming algorithms when the series are, as in this case, weakly stationary. Finally, a SUR (Zellner's seemingly unrelated regression) estimation procedure should be used, instead of OLS, commonly used in VAR estimation, to correct the estimates of the coefficients with the information eventually existing in the contemporary correlations between the residuals.

It is apparent that the results gathered in Table 6 are quite in line with the predictions from the theoretical model. Namely there is a Granger causal relation running from $\Delta q$ to $\Delta jr$ but the converse is not true. On

Table 7: Forecast statistics for $\Delta jr_t$.

| N. Obs. | RMS Error | Theil $U$ |
|---|---|---|
| 12 | 5.855 | 1.106 |
| 9 | 2.684 | 0.489 |
| 6 | 2.063 | 0.444 |
| 3 | 0.254 | 0.058 |
| 1 | 0.222 | 0.102 |

Table 8: Cumulative variation of $\Delta jr$ as a response to a surprise in $\Delta q$ (%).

| Months | Variation |
|---|---|
| 1 | 32.7 |
| 4 | 26.8 |
| 8 | 23.6 |
| 12 | 23.1 |
| 16 | 23.1 |
| 20 | 23.0 |
| 24 | 23.0 |

the other hand autocorrelation is absent in each equation and whereas $\Delta jr$ seems to be fairly explained $\Delta q$ clearly requires a more refined specification.

# 10 Forecasting Capabilities and Impulse Response Functions

One should enquire if the Granger causal relation estimated above is useful, i.e., if it allows to improve the accuracy of our predictions on future values of $\Delta jr$.

In order to do it the model was reestimated using all the data but the last year and then the accuracy of the corresponding twelve monthly predictions were evaluated in terms of statistics such us the RMSE (root mean square error) and U from Theil. As reported in the next Table 7 the results are encouraging given that the RMSE are relatively small and the forecasting capability of the model is far superior to the one of the "naive" model with static expectations.

We can now examine how the referred Granger causal relation is dynamically reproduced by calculating the correspondent impulse response function, i.e., by examining the reaction of the system to an orthonormalized shock (a "surprise") in $\Delta q$. Table 8 shows that the cumulated 24 months' response in $\Delta jr_t$ to a surprise in $\Delta q_t$ is not only significantly positive and permanent but, as one could expect, occurs mostly instantaneously.

# 11 Final Remarks

The basic explanation that the model in Part I and its empirical analysis in Part II offers, for the dynamic behavior of the Portuguese economy between the middle of 1985 and the end of 1989, can be presented in a stylized manner as follows:

- The long run real exchange rate is likely to appreciate as the process of financial integration is gradually reinforced by further liberalizations of several types of capital movements.

- This effect, which will be enhanced by the full adhesion to EMS, will not be so exacerbated if the authorities announce this decision to take place at some date in the future.

- Of the two basic possibilities to counteract this effect — to raise the fiscal adjustment tightness or to stimulate private saving, by increasing the domestic interest rate above the Fisher open parity — the latter is inconsistent with the development of financial integration, since it would provoke speculative attacks pressing for the nominal appreciation of the Escudo.

- On the other hand, if the authorities refuse also to adopt the first option, they are caught in a policy dilemma - either they support the deflationary costs associated with the real exchange rate appreciation or they have to reimpose capital controls.

- This seems to be the case of the Portuguese economy - using monthly data, the empirical analysis suggests that fiscal adjustment was not responsive to the variations of the real exchange rate between the middle of 1985 and the end of 1989.

- Putting a halt to the process of gradual financial liberalization from June onwards capital controls were reimposed, and are still in use, to prevent speculation pressing for the nominal appreciation of the Escudo; this suggests that, while the above-mentioned liberalization was going on, a causal relation between the real exchange rate and the real domestic interest rate should exist.

- The estimation of our model suggests that a significant Granger causal relation exists running from the variations of the real exchange rate to the so called *underlying* real domestic interest rate and that the effect of a surprise in the former is strong, persistent and almost instantaneous in the latter, when we cumulate the short run dynamics during a number of months.

- In this perspective, the meaning of the decision of the authorities to reimpose capital controls is to buy time until the disinflation process in course works out enough to shorten the inflation gap in EEC terms.

- The implication is that the authorities revealed a preference for maintaining capital controls possibly as long as this gap is not fully closed and, in such a case, only at that point of time the domestic nominal interest rate would be aligned with respect to the uncovered interest rate parity.

- There are at least three problems with such a strategy: firstly, over time the maintenance of capital controls will raise growing opposition from the EEC authorities; secondly, this gives a signal that reluctance to raise the tightness of the fiscal adjustment is structural - not simply dictated by the electoral cycle constraints - which in turn could undermine the credibility of the policy mix; thirdly, the speed of the disinflation process is quite slow accordingly to our model.

- Therefore, one can reasonably expect that this strategy would prove to be self defeating, becoming more and more unsustainable and inefficient as capital controls are evaded.

This problem obviously is not restricted to the Portuguese approach to full membership in the future Monetary and Economic Union. Spain kept for quite a long time this sort of capital controls and Greece is in no condition to reject its use. And in the years to come this problem will be faced by more European countries that will take the same road of financial integration with EEC-12.

It is therefore a major problem in search for a solution. Our analysis possibly brought some elements for an answer but, at the present stage, it has several important shortcomings.

In particular, as stated in Part I, it should be extended as to incorporate a supply side and cumulative disequilibria in the balance of payments and, possibly, the credibility effect associated with EEC entry.

Also the variables that were used can be refined, namely the one that tries to capture the fiscal adjustment effort, which was actually relatively important in the period at study. It meant in an important way the incorporation in the official deficit of hidden imbalances of autonomous public bodies and a sharp decrease of seigniorage and of the implicit taxation lying in Government financing below the market interest rates. It is then possible that we did not capture this effort satisfactorily, given the sort of data that we used. A similar consideration may apply to the modelling of the financial liberalization process.

Nevertheless, the results obtained so far with this simplified model look quite encouraging and one cannot rule out that the basic explanations here suggested would still stand in more refined versions.

# Appendix: Multipliers for some Chosen Cases

Table 9: Multipliers for a gradual financial liberalization process.

| | $0 \leq t \leq T$ | $T < t \leq \infty$ |
|---|---|---|
| $\Delta\delta(t)$ | $-\delta(0)\frac{t}{T}$ | $-\delta(0)$ |
| $\Delta\bar{p}(t)$ | $\frac{\sigma\delta(0)}{\phi T}[t + \frac{\sigma\gamma}{\phi}(1 - e^{\mu_2(t-T)})]$ | $\frac{\sigma\delta(0)}{\phi}$ |
| $\Delta\bar{q}(t)$ | $-\Delta\bar{p}(t)$ | $-\Delta\bar{p}(t)$ |
| $\Delta y(t)$ | $0$ | $0$ |
| $\Delta(\bar{m} - \bar{\pi})(t)$ | $\psi(1-\gamma)\Delta\bar{p}(t) + \lambda\delta(0)\frac{t}{T}$ | $\psi(1-\gamma)\Delta\bar{p}(t) + \lambda\delta(0)$ |
| $\Delta p(t)$ | $\frac{\sigma\delta(0)}{\phi T}\left\{t + \frac{\sigma\gamma}{\phi}\left[\left(1 - e^{\mu_2(t-T)}\right) - (1 - e^{-\mu_2 T})e^{\mu_1 t}\right]\right\}$ | $\frac{\sigma\delta(0)}{\phi}\left[1 - \frac{\sigma\gamma}{\phi T}(1 - e^{-\mu_2 T})e^{\mu_1 t}\right]$ |
| $\Delta q(t)$ | $-\Delta p(t)$ | $-\Delta p(t)$ |
| $\Delta d(t)$ | $\frac{\delta(0)\gamma\sigma^2}{\phi T(1-\theta\sigma\gamma)}(1 - e^{\mu_2 T})e^{\mu_1 T}$ | $\frac{\delta(0)\gamma\sigma^2}{\phi T(1-\theta\sigma\gamma)}(1 - e^{\mu_2 T})e^{\mu_1 T}$ |
| $\Delta(m - \pi)(t)$ | $[\gamma + \psi(1-\gamma)]\Delta p(t) + \lambda\delta(0)\frac{t}{T}$ | $[\gamma + \psi(1-\gamma)]\Delta p(t) + \lambda\delta(0)$ |

Table 10: Multipliers for a non-announced reduction of the crawl to zero.

| | |
|---|---|
| $\Delta\dot{e}(t)$ | $-\xi$ |
| $\bar{p}(t)$ | $-\xi t$ |
| $\Delta\bar{q}(t)$ | $0$ |
| $\Delta y(t)$ | $0$ |
| $\Delta(\bar{m} - \bar{\pi})(t)$ | $\lambda\xi$ |
| $\Delta p(t)$ | $-\xi t$ |
| $\Delta q(t)$ | $0$ |
| $\Delta d(t)$ | $0$ |
| $\Delta(m - \pi)(t)$ | $\lambda\xi$ |

Table 11: Multipliers for a reduction of the crawl to zero in $t = T_1$ announced before at $t = 0$.

| | $0 \leq t \leq T$ | $T < t \leq \infty$ |
|---|---|---|
| $\Delta\dot{e}(t)$ | $0$ | $-\xi$ |
| $\Delta\bar{p}(t)$ | $-\xi T e^{\mu_2(t-T)}$ | $-\xi t$ |
| $\Delta\bar{q}(t)$ | $-\Delta\bar{p}(t)$ | $0$ |
| $\Delta y(t)$ | $0$ | $0$ |
| $\Delta(\bar{m}-\bar{\pi})(t)$ | $\psi(1-\gamma)\Delta\bar{p}(t)$ | $\lambda\xi$ |
| $\Delta p(t)$ | $\xi T(e^{\mu_1 t-\mu_2 T} - e^{\mu_2(t-T)})$ | $\xi(Te^{\mu_1 t-\mu_2 T} - t)$ |
| $\Delta q(t)$ | $-\Delta p(t)$ | $\xi T e^{\mu_1 t-\mu_2 T}$ |
| $\Delta d(t)$ | $-\frac{\xi\phi T}{1-\theta\sigma\gamma}e^{\mu_1 t-\mu_2 T}$ | $-\frac{\xi\phi T}{1-\theta\sigma\gamma}e^{\mu_1 t-\mu_2 T}$ |
| $\Delta(m-\pi)(t)$ | $-\psi(1-\gamma)\Delta q(t)$ | $\lambda\xi - \psi(1-\gamma)\Delta q(t)$ |

Table 12: Other permanent and non-anticipated shocks.

| | $\Delta g(t)$ | $\Delta p^*(t)$ | $\Delta\dot{p}^*(t)$ |
|---|---|---|---|
| | $\Delta g(0)$ | $\Delta p^*(0)$ | $\Delta\dot{p}^*(0)$ |
| $\Delta\bar{p}(t)$ | $\frac{\Delta g(0)}{\phi}$ | $\Delta p^*(0)$ | $\Delta\dot{p}^*(0)(\frac{\sigma}{\phi}+t)$ |
| $\Delta\bar{q}(t)$ | $-\frac{\Delta g(0)}{\phi}$ | $0$ | $-\Delta\dot{p}^*(0)\frac{\sigma}{\phi}$ |
| $\Delta y(t)$ | $0$ | $0$ | $0$ |
| $\Delta(\bar{m}-\bar{\pi})(t)$ | $\psi(1-\gamma)\frac{\Delta g(0)}{\phi}$ | $\psi(1-\gamma)\Delta p^*(0)$ | $\psi(1-\gamma)\Delta\bar{p}(t)$ |
| $\Delta p(t)$ | $(1-e^{\mu_2 t})\frac{\Delta g(0)}{\phi}$ | $(1-e^{\mu_2 t})\Delta p^*(0)$ | $\Delta\dot{p}^*(0)\left[t+\frac{\sigma}{\phi}(1-e^{\mu_2 t})\right]$ |
| $\Delta q(t)$ | $-(1-e^{\mu_2 t})\frac{\Delta g(0)}{\phi}$ | $\Delta p^*(0)e^{\mu_2 t}$ | $-\Delta\dot{p}^*(0)\frac{\sigma}{\phi}(1-e^{\mu_2 t})$ |
| $\Delta d(t)$ | $\frac{\Delta g(0)}{1-\theta\sigma\gamma}e^{\mu_2 t}$ | $\phi\Delta p^*(0)e^{\mu_2 t}$ | $\Delta\dot{p}^*(0)\frac{\sigma}{1-\theta\sigma\gamma}(1-e^{\mu_2 t})$ |
| $\Delta(m-\pi)(t)$ | $\psi(1-\gamma)(1-e^{\mu_2 t})\frac{\Delta g(0)}{\phi}$ | $\psi(1-\gamma)(1-e^{\mu_2 t})\Delta p^*(0)$ | $\psi(1-\gamma)\Delta p(t)$ |

# References

ANTÃO, M. (1988): "Causal Relations Among the Sources of Money Supply: the Portuguese Case," in *Monetary Theory and Policy — Studies in Contemporary Economics*, ed. by D. Laussel, W. Marois and A. Souberyan. Berlin: Springer-Verlag.

ARTUS, P. AND C. DUPUY (1990): "Peut-il y Avoir un Nouveau SME?," Caisse des Dépôts et Consignations, Working Paper #1990/20/T, Paris.

BARATA, N. C. (1990): "Expectations of Devaluation: an Empirical Study Based on the Escudo-Sterling Forward Exchange Rate Market 1975–88," unpublished paper.

BLANCHARD, O. AND S. FISCHER (1989): *Lectures on Macroeconomics*. Cambridge: The MIT Press.

BLANCHARD, O. AND C. KHAN (1980): "The Solution of Linear Difference Models under Rational Expectations," *Econometrica*, **48**, 1305–11.

BRANSON, W. (1990): "Financial Market Integration, Macroeconomic Policy and the EMS," in *Unity with Diversity in the European Economy: the Community Southern Frontier*, ed. by C. Bliss and J. B. Macedo. Cambridge: Cambridge University Press.

BRITO, P. (1990): "Real Exchange Rate, Current Account and Capital Accumulation in an Intertemporal Optimizing Model of a Small Open Economy," Working Paper #1/90, Departamento de Economia, Instituto Superior de Economia e Gestão, Universidade Técnica de Lisbon.

BUITER, W. AND M. MILLER (1982): "Real Exchange Rate Overshooting and the Output Cost of Bringing Down Inflation," *European Economic Review*, **18**, 85–123.

DICKEY, D. A. AND W. A. FULLER (1981): "The Likelihood Ratio Statistics for Autoregressive Time Series with a Unit Root," *Econometrica*, **49**, 1057–72.

DOAN, T. A. AND R. B. LITTERMAN (1986): *User's Manual, RATS Version 2.00*. Minneapolis: VAR Econometrics.

DORNBUSCH, R. (1976): "Expectations and Exchange Rate Dynamics," *Journal of Political Economy*, **84**, 1161–76.

ENGLE R. AND C. GRANGER(1987): "Co-integration and Error Correction: Representation, Estimation and Testing," *Econometrica*, **55**, 251–76.

FULLER, W. (1976): *Introduction to Statistical Time Series*. New York: John Wiley.

GASPAR, V. (1990): "Discussion of Chapters 5 and 6," in *Unity with Diversity in the European Economy: the Community Southern Frontier*, C. Bliss and J. B. Macedo. Cambridge: Cambridge University Press.

GASPAR, V. AND J. B. MACEDO (1990): "The Case for Budgetary Restraint in Portugal: Short Run and Long Run Arguments," unpublished manuscript.

GIAVAZZI, F. AND L. SPAVENTA (1990): "The 'New' EMS," CEPR Discussion Paper, Working Paper #369.

KRUGMAN, P. (1989): *Exchange Rate Instability*, The Lionel Robbins Lectures. Cambridge: The MIT Press.

KRUGMAN, P. (1989): "Macroeconomic Adjustment and Entry into the EC: a Note," in *Unity with Diversity in the European Economy: the Community Southern Frontier*, ed. by C. Bliss and J. B. Macedo. Cambridge: Cambridge University Press.

LOPES, P. S. (1990): "A Classifying Approach and a Portfolio Perspective," Doctoral dissertation, University of South Carolina.

MACEDO, J. B. (1982): "Portfolio Diversification and Currency Inconvertibility," Doctoral dissertation, Princeton University, UNL, ed.

MACEDO, J. B. (1990): "External Liberalization with an Ambiguous Public Response: the Experience of Portugal," in *Unity with Diversity in the European Economy: the Community Southern Frontier*, ed. by C. Bliss and J. B. Macedo, Cambridge: Cambridge University Press.

OBSTFELD, M. AND K. ROGOFF (1984): "Exchange Rate Dynamics with Sluggish Prices under Alternative Price-adjustment Rules," *International Economic Review*, **25**, 159–74.

OBSTFELD, M. AND A. STOCKMAN (1985): "Exchange Rate Dynamics," in *Handbook of International Economics, II*, ed. by P. Kenen and R. Jones. Amsterdam: North-Holland.

PEETERS, T. (1990): "Intégration Financière: Pourquoi?" in *Espace Financier Européen et Coopération Monétaire*, P. Van den Bempt and Quintyn, GEPE/SEP.

STEIN, J. L. (1990): "The Real Exchange Rate," in special issue on Real and Nominal Exchange Rates, *Journal of Banking and Finance*, J. L. Stein, guest-ed., **14**, 1045–78.

WILSON, C. (1979): "Anticipated Shocks and Exchange Rate Dynamics," *Journal of Political Economy*, **87**, 639–47.

# Foreign Entry and Domestic Welfare, with an Application to Portuguese Life-Insurance

Pedro P. Barros
Luís M. B. Cabral

## 1 Introduction

Foreign investment has been one of the most important factors of growth in the Portuguese economy during the past decade. It has also been a topic of contention among a number of interested parties. The debate surrounding the virtues of foreign investment typically contrasts the benefits from technology transfer with the costs of increased dependence from foreign capital. Some say foreign investment is a condition *sine qua non* for the modernization of the Portuguese economy; others will argue that the country is being "sold to foreign powers".

In this paper, we depart from the "classical" controversy and instead examine the impact of foreign investment from the perspective of (partial equilibrium) industrial organization. Specifically, we consider foreign investment as entry into some imperfectly competitive domestic market. Our goal is to evaluate the impact of entry on market competitiveness, in particular on the level of domestic social surplus. Evidently, this is a somewhat limited analysis, since it does not consider important factors such as technology transfer, direct and indirect creation of employment, political dependence, and the like. However, we believe it to be a worthwhile exercise, especially because it looks at one aspect which is often neglected in the debate surrounding the effects of foreign investment.

We are grateful to José Mata, António S. Mello, and seminar participants at the Universidade do Minho for useful comments and suggestions. Responsibility for any errors and deficiencies is our own.

Our analysis is related to the literature on free entry and welfare. Ever since the seminal paper by von Weizsacker (1980), economists have agreed that there may be situations in which the equilibrium market structure with free entry is non-optimal from a social welfare point of view. In fact, Mankiw and Whinston (1986) have recently shown that for quite general conditions the free entry equilibrium number of firms in any given industry is greater than the socially optimum number, and thus a barrier to entry might be welfare improving. Our paper considers the case of an industry which is subject to entry by foreign firms. The impact of (foreign) entry on (domestic) we fare is different from the case considered by Mankiw and Whinston (1986), since the regulator is only concerned about consumer's surplus and *domestic* firms' profits. As we shall see, this difference may be quite substantial, and in fact the case for barriers to entry may be reversed.

In sections 2 and 3 of the paper, we present tests for the marginal and the global effects of foreign entry on domestic welfare. We show that marginal entry is welfare improving if and only if foreign firms' market share is above some threshold value. As a result, the optimum number of foreign firms is either zero or infinity. The global impact of foreign entry is positive if and only if the increase in total quantity (the consumer's surplus effect) is sufficiently greater than the decrease in the domestic firms' Herfindahl index (the profit transfer effect). Section 4 extends the results to the case of entry by acquisition (as opposed to *de novo* entry).

An important feature of the tests presented in sections 2 and 3 is that they depend only on current market share data, which is usually easy to obtain. In section 5, the tests are applied to the Portuguese life-insurance market. We find the global effect of foreign entry by 1989 to be negative. However, based on the available data, we find it plausible that the effect of marginal entry (both *de novo* entry and entry by acquisition) be positive. Therefore, although foreign entry has decreased domestic welfare, *additional* foreign entry would increase domestic welfare.

We conclude with some final remarks concerning limitations of the analysis and possible extensions.

# 2 Marginal Welfare Effect of Foreign Entry

Consider a homogeneous product $N$-firm Cournot oligopoly, with $N = D + F$, where $D$ is the number of domestic firms and $F$ the number of foreign firms competing in the domestic market. Demand is given by $P(Q)$, where $P$ is price, $q_i$ firm $i$'s output, and $Q \equiv \sum q_i$ total output.

Firm $i$'s profits are given by

$$\pi_i = P(Q)q_i - C_i(q_i), \quad i = 1, \ldots, N \tag{1}$$

where $C_i\ (q_i)$ is firm $i$'s cost function. We assume $P$ is a concave function of $q_i$. The first-order (sufficient) conditions for profit maximization are given by:

$$P(Q) + q_i \frac{\partial P}{\partial Q} - \frac{\partial C_i(q_i)}{\partial q_i} = 0, \quad i = 1, \ldots, N \tag{2}$$

and can be re-written as

$$q_i = \frac{P(Q) - c_i}{-\partial P/\partial Q}, \quad i = 1, \ldots, N \tag{3}$$

where $c_i$, stands for marginal cost.

For simplicity, though at the risk of some abuse of notation, we will use $D$ both for the *number* of domestic firms and the *set* of domestic firms. Therefore, total quantity produced by domestic firms, $Q_D$, is the sum of $q_i$ for all $i$ in $D$, $Q_D \equiv \sum_{i \in D} q_i$. A similar definition holds for $Q_F$.

Domestic welfare is defined as the sum of consumer's surplus and domestic firms' producer's surplus:

$$W = \int_0^Q P(x)dx - PQ + PQ_D - \sum_{i \in D} C_i(q_i)\,. \tag{4}$$

One can easily identify two different effects on domestic welfare following from entry by foreign firms. On the one hand, total output in the industry expands, which implies a lower price and a greater consumer's surplus. On the other hand, domestic firms' profits decrease, both because of a lower price and of a lower market share held by domestic firms. Figure 1 depicts these two effects in a simple case of linear demand and zero marginal cost. The equilibrium under autarky is given by $E_0$, whereas $E_1$ is the equilibrium with foreign entry. The effects of foreign entry on domestic welfare are given by areas $A$ (the "consumer's surplus" effect) and $B$ (the "profit transfer" effect). Conceptually, the problem we want to solve in this paper is very simple: which is greater, $A$ or $B$? Difficulties arise, however, because we have no reliable estimates of what the demand and cost functions are, not to speak of where the (hypothetical) autarky equilibrium $E_0$ would lie.

In the results that follow, we will consider changes in domestic welfare resulting from entry by foreign firms *assuming that the number of domestic firms remains fixed.* The typical sequence of events we have in mind is the following. In a first stage, the domestic country is in autarky and entry proceeds to the point where no domestic potential entrant can gain positive profits. In a second stage, entry by foreign firms is allowed. Due to absolute cost advantages, both in terms of fixed costs and of marginal costs, foreign entry does indeed occur. It is easy to see that if domestic entry was not

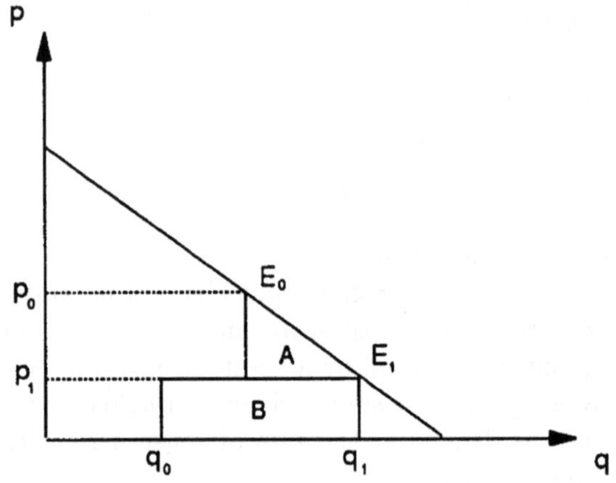


Figure 1: Effects of foreign entry on domestic welfare.

optimal at the end of stage one, than it will not be optimal during the second stage either.

Our first result is about the marginal effect on domestic welfare of entry by a foreign firm.

**Proposition 1** *At the margin, foreign entry increases domestic welfare if and only if*

$$s_F > \sum_{i \in D} \eta_i s_i \tag{5}$$

*where* $s_F \equiv \frac{Q_F}{Q'}$, $s_i \equiv \frac{q_i}{Q}$ *and (see Farrel and Shapiro (1990))*

$$\eta_i \equiv \frac{\partial P/\partial Q + q_i \partial^2 P/\partial Q^2}{\partial P/\partial Q - \partial^2 C_i/\partial q_i^2} .$$

*Proof:* The change in domestic welfare resulting from entry by a "marginal" foreign firm is given by

$$\frac{dW}{dF} = \sum_{i \in D} (P - c_i) \frac{\partial q_i}{\partial F} - Q_F \frac{\partial P}{\partial Q} \frac{\partial Q}{\partial F} . \tag{6}$$

From the first-order condition (2) we have (by the implicit function theorem)

$$\frac{\partial q_i}{\partial Q} = -\frac{\partial P/\partial Q + q_i \partial^2 P/\partial Q^2}{\partial P/\partial Q - \partial^2 C_i/\partial q_i^2} = -\eta_i \ . \tag{7}$$

Substituting (7) for $\partial q_i/\partial F$ in (6), we have

$$\begin{aligned}\frac{dW}{dF} &= \left(-\sum_{i\in D}(P-c_i)\left(\frac{\partial P/\partial Q + q_i \partial^2 P/\partial Q^2}{\partial P/\partial Q - \partial^2 C_i/\partial q_i^2}\right) - Q_F\frac{\partial P}{\partial Q}\right)\frac{\partial Q}{\partial F} \\ &= \left(\sum_{i\in D} q_i \left(\frac{\partial P/\partial Q + q_i \partial^2 P/\partial Q^2}{\partial P/\partial Q - \partial^2 C_i/\partial q_i^2}\right) - Q_F\right)\frac{\partial P}{\partial Q}\frac{\partial Q}{\partial F}\end{aligned} \tag{8}$$

where the latter equality follows from (3). Since $\partial Q/\partial F > 0$, a necessary and sufficient condition for $dW/dF > 0$ is that

$$\sum_{i\in D} q_i \left(\frac{\partial P/\partial Q + q_i \partial^2 P/\partial Q^2}{\partial P/\partial Q - \partial^2 C_i/\partial q_i^2}\right) - Q_F < 0 \tag{9}$$

which, dividing through by $Q$, gives (5). ■

Proposition 1 indicates the critical value of foreign firms' market share above which additional foreign entry is desirable. This implies that, starting from an autarky equilibrium, entry by foreign firms to a small extent necessarily decreases domestic welfare (the profit transfer effect dominates). On the other hand, if foreign entry has proceeded to a point where foreign firms hold a market share close to one, then *additional* entry by foreign firms necessarily increases domestic welfare (consumer's surplus effect dominates).

This dichotomy of effects has strong implications in terms of the optimum number of foreign firms from the point of view of domestic welfare:

**Corollary 1** *The optimum number of foreign firms is either zero or infinity.*

*Proof:* From Proposition 1, we have conclude that $dW/dF > 0$ if $s_F > k$, where $k$ is given by (9b). Since $s_F$ is itself increasing in $F$, we conclude that $W$ is a quasi-convex function of $F$, and the result follows. ■

To see how both extreme cases of Corollary 1 could possibly occur, consider the following example. Demand is linear ($P = 2 - Q$) and there is one domestic firm with zero fixed and marginal cost. Now first suppose there is an infinite number of potential foreign entrants with zero fixed and marginal costs. Clearly, infinite entry would be preferable, since total domestic surplus would increase from 3/2 to 2. Now suppose instead that foreign firms' marginal costs is 1/2, and that fixed costs are zero. Under this second set of assumptions, infinite entry by foreign firms would decrease domestic welfare from 3/2 to 3/2 – 1/4.

Unfortunately, the values of $\eta_i$ in (5) are not easy to estimate. However, based on (5) and some knowledge of the demand and cost functions, we can provide necessary and sufficient conditions corresponding to proposition 1.

**Corollary 2** *Assume that marginal cost $c_i(q_i)$ is nondecreasing and consider a marginal increase in the number of foreign firms.*

**a)** *If the demand function is convex or not too concave, then $s_F > s_D$ is a sufficient condition for an improvement in domestic welfare;*

**b)** *If the demand function is sufficiently concave, then $s_F > s_D$ is a necessary condition for an improvement in domestic welfare.*

*Proof:* From the definition of $\eta_i$, we get

$$\eta_i = \frac{\partial P/\partial Q + q_i \partial^2 P/\partial Q^2}{\partial P/\partial Q - \partial^2 C_i/\partial q_i^2} .$$

Therefore, $\eta_i < 1$ if $\partial^2 P/\partial Q^2 > -(\partial^2 C_i/\partial q_i^2)/q_i$ and $\eta_i > 1$ if $\partial^2 P/\partial Q^2$ is sufficiently negative. If $\eta_i < 1$, then $s_F > s_D$ is a sufficient condition; if $\eta_i > 1$, then it is necessary. ■

Finally, for the special case when demand and costs are linear, $s_F > s_D$ (or $s_F > .5$) is a necessary and sufficient condition for marginal foreign entry to improve domestic welfare.

# 3 Global Welfare Effect of Foreign Entry

In the previous section, we have analyzed the marginal effect of entry by foreign firms. We have seen that only when the market share of foreign firms exceeds some critical value it is desirable to have an additional foreign firm enter the domestic market. However, this "marginal" result does not tell much about the total gain from having foreign firms in the domestic market as compared to the autarky equilibrium. In this section, we focus on the global (as opposed to marginal) effect of foreign entry on domestic welfare. In order to keep the model tractable, we consider the simplest case of constant marginal costs, $c_i$, and a linear demand curve, $P = a - bQ$.

Firm $i$'s profit before entry by foreign firms is given by

$$\pi_i = \left(a - b\sum_{i\in D} q_i - c_i\right) q_i, \quad i + 1, \ldots, D\,. \tag{10}$$

In the absence of foreign entry, firm $i$'s equilibrium quantity is given by

$$q_i = \frac{1}{b}\frac{a + \sum_{j\in D} c_j - (D+1)c_i}{D+1}, \quad i = 1, \ldots, D\,. \tag{11}$$

Industry profits are $\sum_{i\in D} \pi_i = bQ^2H$ (Cowling and Waterson, 1976), where $H$ is the domestic firms' Herfindahl index before entry by foreign firms and $Q$ is total quantity produced by domestic firms before entry by foreign firms.

Once again, we define domestic welfare as the sum of consumer's surplus and total domestic profits. Before entry by foreign firms, this is given by

$$W = \frac{1}{2}bQ^2 + bQ^2H = bQ^2\left(\frac{1}{2} + H\right)\,. \tag{12}$$

The equilibrium after entry by foreign firms implies a new value for domestic welfare,

$$W = \frac{1}{2}bQ'^2 + bQ'^2H' = bQ'^2\left(\frac{1}{2} + H'\right)\,. \tag{13}$$

where $Q'$ is total quantity and $H'$ is the domestic firms' Herfindahl index after entry by foreign firms.[1]

**Proposition 2** *Domestic welfare improves with foreign entry (that is, $W' > W$) if and only if*

$$\left(\frac{Q'}{Q}\right)^2 > \frac{1+2H}{1+2H'} \tag{14}$$

*Proof:* Straightforward comparison of (12) and (13). ■

Proposition 2 reflects the trade-off, in terms of domestic welfare, referred to above. The left-hand side can be interpreted as the consumer's surplus effect. Foreign entry implies a decrease in price (an increase in quantity), and thus an increase in consumer's surplus. The right-hand side, in turn, can be interpreted as the profit transfer effect. Foreign entry implies a decrease in domestic firms' profits, which is reflected in a lower domestic firms' Herfindahl index.

[1] In general, a prime will denote equilibrium values after entry by foreign firms.

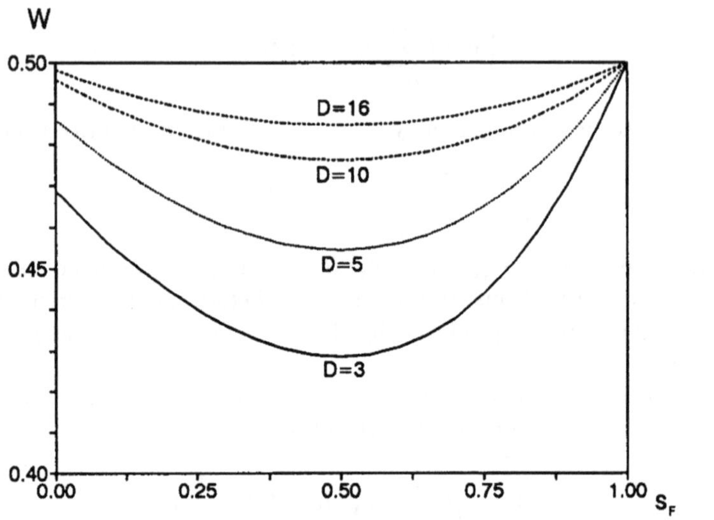


Figure 2: Domestic welfare as a function of the market share of foreign firms, for given values of the number of domestic firms.

Propositions 1 and 2 are illustrated in Figures 2 and 3. Figure 2 shows the level of domestic welfare as a function of the market share of foreign firms, for given values of the number of domestic firms. We assume demand and costs are linear, and that domestic and foreign firms' marginal costs are equal and that $(a-c)^2 = b$. It can be seen that domestic welfare is decreasing up to the point where the market share of foreign firms is 0.5, and increasing for higher values of $s_F$ (Proposition 1). The market share held by foreign firms must be quite large for additional foreign entry to be beneficial from a domestic welfare point of view. This can be seen from Figure 3, which depicts the critical value $s_F$ for $W = W'$, as a function of the number of domestic firms. We conclude that the critical market share increases rapidly as $D$ goes from one to ten, and less so for higher values of $D$.

Both Figures 2 and 3 are based on the strong assumption that domestic and foreign firms' marginal costs are equal. In general, we would expect foreign firms to be at a cost advantage relative to domestic firms. Nevertheless, if we assume that foreign firms' marginal cost is a fraction $\gamma$ of domestic firms' marginal cost, then we can show that the critical value of $s_F$ for $W = W'$, as a function of $D$, is independent of $\gamma$ (however, the critical value of $F$ depends on $\gamma$). This result is not totally surprising, considering

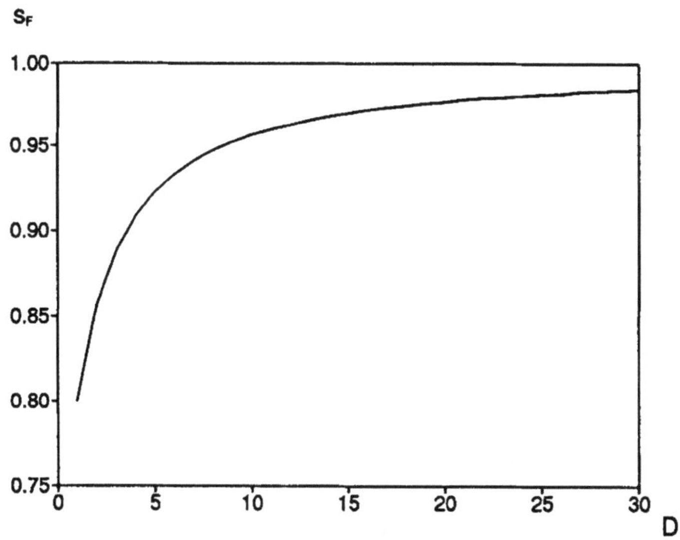


Figure 3: Critical value of foreign firms' market share such that domestic welfare is equal before and after foreign entry, for given values of the number of domestic firms.

the assumptions of linear demand and cost functions.

We should note that, from a practical point of view, equation (14) is of little use, since it depends on values $(Q, H)$ of a hypothetical autarky equilibrium. Just like in the case of the marginal welfare effect, we would like to find a test which is based only on current market data. This is the object of our last result.

**Lemma 1** *The following equations allow (14) to be written as a function of current market data:*

(i) $(\frac{Q'}{Q})^2 = (s_F \frac{D}{D+1} + s_D)^{-2}$;

(ii) $s_i = (s_F \frac{D}{D+1} + s_D)^{-1}(s_F \frac{D}{D+1} + s_i')$.

*Proof:* See Appendix. ∎

# 4 Entry by Acquisition

So far, we have only considered foreign investment in the form of *de novo* entry into the domestic market. In this section, we examine the consequences of an alternative form of entry, namely entry by acquisition. In order to appreciate the difference between the two kinds of entry, consider the case of a domestic firm which is totally acquired by foreigners. This situation can be interpreted as the process of entry by an additional foreign firm *and* simultaneous exit of an existing domestic firm. By contrast, in the case of *de novo* entry, the latter does not occur.

The first-order effects of acquisition of a domestic firm are that a fraction of domestic profits are transferred to foreigners, and, at the same time, a compensating payment is made to the previous owners of the firm. The second-order effects are that the cost function of the acquired firm is (possibly) shifted, due to changes in management, technology transfer, of some other effect. As a result, the equilibrium solution in the domestic market is (possibly) changed as well. To be more specific, suppose that a fraction $\alpha_k$ of the $k$-th domestic firm is acquired by foreigners. Putting aside the possibility of information asymmetries, an agreement between buyer and seller signals that ownership is at least as valuable to the buyer as it is to the seller. We interpret this to imply that firm $k$'s total cost is non-increasing in the value of $\alpha_k$, that is, $\partial C_i/\partial \alpha_i \leq 0$.[2] Furthermore, we make the assumption that firm $k$'s marginal cost is also non-increasing in $\alpha_k$, that is, $\partial^2 c_i/(\partial q_i \partial \alpha_i) \leq 0$.

First, let us consider the simple case when marginal costs remain unchanged upon entry by acquisition.

**Proposition 3** *If* $\partial^2 c_i/(\partial q_i \partial \alpha_i) = 0$, *then domestic welfare (weakly) improves with foreign entry by acquisition.*

*Proof:* Since marginal cost remains unchanged, the market equilibrium maintains regardless of the measure of acquisition. Therefore, the only effects to consider are the transfer of profits from the acquired firm and the corresponding price paid to domestic owners. Since information asymmetries are ruled out and agents are assumed to be rational, the price received by domestic owners must be at least as large as the foregone profits. ∎

An immediate consequence of proposition 4 is that entry by acquisition may or may not be preferable to *de novo* entry. Suppose that $\partial c_i/\partial \alpha_i = 0$ in addition to $\partial^2 c_i/(\partial q_i \partial \alpha_i) = 0$.

Then, domestic welfare remains constant with entry by acquisition regardless of the value of $s_F$. However, we have seen that domestic welfare may increase or may decrease with de novo entry, depending on the value of $s_F$. Even though there is no one-to-one relationship between the welfare

[2] An alternative possibility, which we will ignore, is that ownership has a strategic value for the buyer which it doesn't for the seller.

effects of *de novo* entry and of entry by acquisition, there is a one-way implication in terms of the marginal welfare effects.

**Proposition 4** *If domestic welfare improves with marginal* de novo *entry, then it also improves with marginal entry by acquisition.*

*Proof:* Since there is now no clear distinction between domestic and foreign firms, we will treat all firms symmetrically and let $\alpha_i (i = 1, \ldots, N)$ represent the fraction of firm $i$ which is owned by foreigners. Entry by acquisition consists of a change in the value of some $\alpha_k$, with the value of $N$ remaining fixed.

Domestic welfare is given by

$$W = \int_0^Q P(x)dx - PQ + \sum (1 - \alpha_i)(Pq_i - C_i(q_i)) \tag{15}$$

where the summation ranges over all $i$.

Consider now the impact of a marginal increase in the value of $\alpha_k$,

$$\frac{dW}{d\alpha_k} = P\frac{\partial Q}{\partial \alpha_k} - \frac{\partial p}{\partial Q}Q\frac{\partial Q}{\partial \alpha_k} - P\frac{\partial Q}{\partial \alpha_k}$$
$$+ \sum (1 - \alpha_i)\left(\frac{\partial P}{\partial Q}q_i\frac{\partial Q}{\partial \alpha_k} + P\frac{\partial q_i}{\partial \alpha_k} - \frac{\partial C_i(q_i)}{\partial q_i}\frac{\partial q_i}{\partial \alpha_k}\right) - \frac{\partial C_k(q_k)}{\partial \alpha_k}.$$

Notice that the direct derivative with respect to $\alpha_k$ cancels out with the value of the payment to domestic owners for the increase in the share of firm $k$. By analogy with the proof of proposition 1, this can be shown to be equivalent to

$$\left(\sum (1 - \alpha_i)q_i\eta_i - \sum \alpha_i q_i\right)\frac{\partial p}{\partial Q}\frac{\partial Q}{\partial \alpha k} + \frac{\partial C_k(q_k)}{\partial \alpha_k} < 0\,, \tag{16}$$

which is implied by (9), the condition for an improvement from marginal *de novo* entry. ■

Finally, we consider the global effect of foreign entry when this includes entry by acquisition. Since we do not know the relation between foreign ownership and the firm's cost function (that is, the derivative $\partial C_k(q_k)/\partial \alpha_k$), all we can hope for is to find necessary or sufficient conditions for an increase in welfare. In what follows, we consider the global impact of foreign *de novo* entry as the difference in welfare between the autarky equilibrium and the situation of *de novo* entry only. The global impact of foreign entry refers to the difference between autarky and the situation when all foreign entry (both *de novo* and by acquisition) has occurred.

**Proposition 5** *If the global effect of* de novo *entry is positive, then the global effect of foreign entry (including both types of entry) is also positive.*

*Proof:* Recall that domestic welfare is a quasi-convex function of the degree of *de novo* entry by foreign firms. (See the proof of Corollary 1). Therefore, if the global effect of foreign entry is positive, it must be that the marginal effect is positive as well. By Proposition 5, if the effect of marginal *de novo* foreign entry is positive, so is the effect of marginal entry by acquisition. But since this is valid for any measure of entry by acquisition, it follows that the global impact is positive. ■

# 5 Application to the Portuguese Life-Insurance Market

The Portuguese insurance industry has experienced profound changes in the recent past. The first major change was a consequence of the April 74 Revolution: in 1975, all domestic insurance firms were nationalized. Firms with participation of foreign capital did not fall into the State's domain; only the capital share belonging to national citizens was nationalized. Moreover, the industry was legally declared closed to private enterprise.

The second major adjustment in market structure occurred in 1980. The engine of change was, once again, the State: it declared the merger of a number of State-owned firms, thus creating six "giant" firms. In the life-insurance market, the number of public firms fell from 18 in 1979 to 7 in 1980.

The third structural change consisted of the industry's liberalization process. It began in 1984 with its opening to private enterprise. In 1986, Portugal became a member of EEC, which also implied adjustments toward freer market conditions. The process of privatization of public firms, which has recently been started, provided an additional means of entry into the market. As a result of these changes, many firms, both domestic and foreign, have entered the market. This is particularly true for the life-insurance market, which has experienced a high rate of growth in recent years.

The presence and importance of foreign capital in the Portuguese life-insurance market has been a subject of debate between domestic firms, the political power and other groups. In fact, the market share of foreign firms has significantly increased in recent years, especially after 1986, as can be seen from Figure 4.

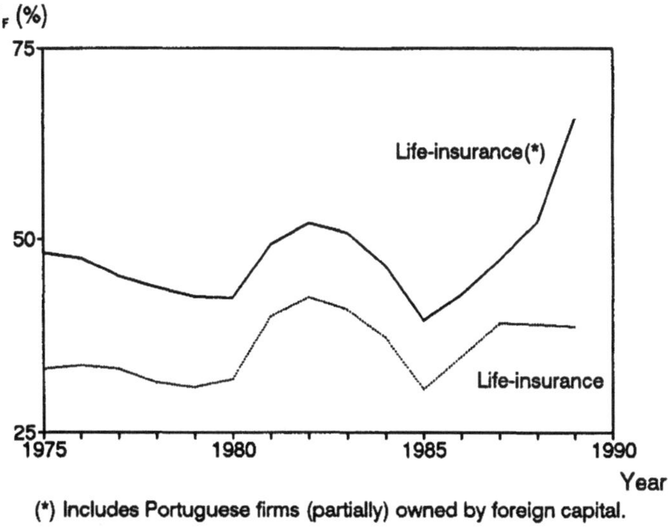


Figure 4: Foreign firms' market share (1975–89) of the Portuguese life-insurance market.

Since it is not possible to obtain the exact share of capital owned by foreigners, Figure 4 indicates a lower and an upper-bound for this value. The lower bound corresponds to the share of subsidiaries of foreign firms, whereas the upper bound also includes the share of Portuguese firms which are partially or totally owned by foreigners.[3]

The Portuguese life-insurance market seems to be a good example for application of the results developed in the previous sections. Evaluating the formulae in Propositions 1 and 2 (also using Lemma 1), we can calculate the values required for both the marginal and the total welfare tests. We will assume that demand and cost functions are linear. Since we have no exact and complete information about the shares of foreigners in Portuguese firms, we will consider the alternative concepts "subsidiaries of foreign firms" (i.e., *de novo* entry) and "subsidiaries plus Portuguese firms owned by foreign capital", which together give a lower and an upper bound

[3]A few comments are in order. First, there is a significant increase in $s_F$ during the early eighties, which can be explained by the wave of mergers between domestic firms. The sharp decline in 1985 is accounted for by the fact that a domestic firm (*Tranquilidade*) has capitalized a large fraction of future premiums in that year. Finally, the widening of the gap between the lower and the upper bound reflects an increased participation of foreigners in the capital of domestic firms.

Table 1: Values for marginal and global welfare test.

| Measure | 1989 value |
|---|---|
| $s_F$ | 38.62% |
| $s_F^*$ | 65.68% |
| $(Q'/Q)^2$ | 1.076 |
| $(1+2H)/(1+2H')$ | 1.135 |

$s_F$: Market share of foreign subsidiaries.
$s_F^*$: Market share of all firms with foreign capital.
$Q$, $Q'$: Market quantity before and after foreign entry.
$H$, $H'$: Herfindahl index of domestic firms before and after foreign entry.

of the desired value.

The results are presented in Table 1.[4] Comparison of the third and the forth values suggests that there was a global loss due to *de novo* entry by foreign firms. Not much can be said with regard to the global effect of foreign entry, since the sufficient condition of Proposition 5 is not satisfied. As to the effect of marginal entry, the relevant value is somewhere between 38.62% and 65.68%. It is thus possible that it is greater than 50%, which would imply a positive effect of marginal entry (either *de novo* or by acquisition).

To summarize, it is plausible that, as of 1989, the global welfare effect of foreign entry is negative, but the effect of marginal entry, either *de novo* entry or entry by acquisition, is positive.

# 6 Conclusion

We have developed tests for evaluating the marginal and the global effect of foreign entry on domestic welfare. For the particular case of the Portuguese life-insurance market, the results seem quite negative about the impact of foreign entry. However, one should interpret these results with caution, since they are based on somewhat arbitrary assumptions. First, at a theoretical level, we have assumed Cournot equilibrium as the relevant equilibrium concept. A model with conjectural variations, which may even be different before and after entry, would be more general and would, possibly, yield different results (cf. Spiller and Favaro (1984)). Second, the results for the Portuguese life-insurance market were based on assumptions of linear cost and demand. Third, we should note that we have considered the sum of consumer's and producer's surplus as our definition of domestic welfare. If we believe that consumer's surplus should be given a higher

[4] The numbers are for 1989, and can be found in "Estatísticas da Actividade Seguradora – Elementos Estatísticos I".

weight than profits, then our results are somewhat biased against foreign entry.

Finally, it may well be the case that the Portuguese life-insurance market is still going through a period of adjustment. It follows from our "non-convexity" result that although current welfare is lower than in the autarky equilibrium it may become greater once all foreign entry has occurred.

# Appendix

Proof of Lemma 1: Solving the first-order conditions for a Cournot equilibrium, we get

$$Q = \frac{1}{b(D+1)}\left(Da - \sum_{j\in D} c_j\right) \tag{17}$$

$$Q_D = \frac{1}{b(N+1)}\left(Da + D\sum_{j\in F} c_j - (F+1)\sum_{j\in D} c_j\right) \tag{18}$$

and

$$Q_F = \frac{1}{b(N+1)}\left(Fa + F\sum_{j\in D} c_j - (D+1)\sum_{j\in F} c_j\right) . \tag{19}$$

Using (17), (18), and (19) can be rewritten as

$$Q_D = \frac{D+1}{N+1}Q + \frac{1}{b(N+1)}\left(D\sum_{j\in F} c_j - F\sum_{j\in D} c_j\right) \tag{20}$$

$$Q_F = \frac{F}{D}\frac{D+1}{N+1}Q + \frac{D+1}{b(N+1)}\left(D\sum_{j\in F} c_j - F\sum_{j\in D} c_j\right) . \tag{21}$$

This is a system of two equations with two unknowns, $Q$ and $(D\sum_{j\in F} c_j - F\sum_{j\in D} c_j)$. Solving for $Q$, we get

$$Q = Q_F\frac{D}{D+1} + Q_D \tag{22}$$

or simply

$$\frac{Q}{Q'} = s_F\frac{D}{D+1} + s_D \tag{23}$$

which gives the first expression in the lemma.

Again from the first-order conditions for a Cournot equilibrium, we have

$$q_i = \frac{1}{b(D+1)}\left(a + \sum_{j\in D} c_j - (D+1)c_i\right) \tag{24}$$

$$q_i' = \frac{1}{b(N+1)}\left(a + \sum_{j\in N} c_j - (N+1)c_i\right) \tag{25}$$

for firm $i$'s quantity before and after entry by foreign firms, respectively. Solving these for $c_i$, we obtain

$$c_i = \frac{a + \sum_{j\in D} c_j - b(D+1)q_i}{D+1} = \frac{a + \sum_{j\in N} c_j - b(N+1)q_i'}{N+1} \,. \tag{26}$$

Upon appropriate manipulations, we get

$$Q_F = (D+1)(q_i - q_i') \,. \tag{27}$$

Solving for $q_i$ and using (23) gives the second expression in the lemma.

# References

COWLING, K. AND WATERSON, M. (1976): "Price-Cost Margins and Market Structure," *Economica*, **43**, 247–274.

FARRELL, J. AND SHAPIRO, C. (1990): "Asset Ownership and Market Structure in Oligopoly," *Rand Journal of Economics*, **21**, 275–292.

MANKIW, G. AND WHINSTON, M. (1986): "Free Entry and Social Inefficiency," *Rand Journal of Economics*, **17**, 48–58.

SPILLER, P. AND FAVARO, E. (1984): "The Effects of Entry Regulation on Oligopolistic Interaction: The Uruguayan Banking Sector," *Rand Journal of Economics*, **15**, 244–254.

VON WEIZSACKER, C. C. (1980): "A Welfare Analysis of Barriers to Entry," *Bell Journal of Economics*, **11**, 399–420.

# Concentration and Competitive Dynamics

José Mata

## 1 Introduction

The Portuguese economy is generally supposed to be extremely rigid. Red tape and lack of flexibility in the labour market, would hinder the adjustment of the economic structure to new situations, namely to the challenges created by the recent EEC membership and the future completion of the Internal Market. Bureaucracy, imposing costs and increasing the lags between detection of profit opportunities and entry into the market to exploit them, and labour law, constraining the quick response to market requirements would be, according to this dominant view the main obstacles to new firm formation, to the growth of existing firm growth and to productive investment in general.[1]

Without going into the discussion of bureaucracy or of the labour market, this paper presents statistical evidence on firm creation and growth that casts some doubt on this view of the Portuguese economy. The data, obtained from *Quadros de Pessoal* (*QP*), a major statistical source produced by the Ministry of Employment, reveal that between 1982 and 1986, firm entry and exit flows, as well as expansion and contraction of those firms that remained in the market during the period, attained very important levels. This is somewhat surprising, since Portuguese manufacturing was in 1982 relatively concentrated, and concentration levels do not exhibit an unequivocal tendency to decrease.

The data presented here, characterizing Portuguese manufacturing with respect to concentration and mobility, were computed for this effect; due

This paper was written during a semester I spent visiting Universidade Nova de Lisboa. Its hospitality and financial support provided by the Instituto Nacional de Investigação Científica are gratefully acknowledged.

[1]See Modesto and Neves (1990) for a recent text sharing this view.

to the novelty of the use of *QP* as statistical source in Industrial Organization studies, as well as to the novelty of the data themselves, source and computing process are described in some detail. This task is pursued in section 2. In section 3, an overview of the importance of mobility flows and concentration levels is displayed and, in section 4, the use of concentration measures as proxies to market structure and to the intensity of competition is discussed. From the mobility measures, a direct measure of intensity of competition is suggested, and the relationship between this direct measure and the indirect measures proxied by concentration is tentatively outlined in a simple model. The paper ends with a brief note, summarizing the most important conclusions and making some final remarks.

# 2 Data

## 2.1 Source

The statistical data employed in this paper were obtained from unpublished data from *QP*, produced by the Ministry of Employment. *QP* are the only source that inquires simultaneously firms and establishments, keeping track of the connections between them. Moreover, its identification method allows one to follow firms' paths across their lives, which makes it an excellent source for the study of firm births, deaths and growth.

For the research reported in this paper, it was possible to work directly with raw data from *QP*, and to compute several variables, which are not commonly available. For each industry, it was possible to obtain measures of the importance of firm entry and exit, as well as of continuing firms expansion and contraction. Besides, available data allowed calculation of concentration measures employing market shares computed using the set of establishments in the same industry belonging to the same firm, which is a more appropriate unit than the firm or the establishment themselves.

The data base employed to compute the measures presented in the paper included two files for each one of the years of the study (1982 and 1986). For each one of them, a file including all establishments classified in the manufacturing sector, and another containing all firms operating at least one establishment in manufacturing, were available. In both files, for each firm/plant, it was available information relative to the number of people employed, the code number (CAE six digit) of its main industry and to an firm/plant identifier.

Firms' identifiers are simply numbers sequentially supplied to firms by the first time they report to *QP*. This number remains with the firm during all its life, and will not be used again, if the firm disappears from the file.

Plants identifiers are composed by two numbers: the owner firm identifier, and the plant number itself. This identifying scheme allows us to compute concentration measures using as the computing unit the set of plants in the industry which belong to the same firm, and to obtain very precise measures of firm entry and exit. Entrants were identified by looking for those firms which were in the industry in 1986, but not in 1982. Conversely, a firm was classified as an *exitor*, if it was in the industry in 1982, but not in 1986. These definitions correspond to *industry* entry and exit, and they clearly overestimate the firm creation phenomenon (entry from the whole economy perspective), since those firms which were already operating in 1982 but changed their main activity between 1982 and 1986 are also classified as entrants. These two types of entry can however be distinguished, by recognizing a new firm if its 1986 identifier is greater than the highest identifier in 1982. By doing that, one can get an idea of the relative importance of each one of these phenomena, and this is important because they are quite different in a number of aspects.

Firstly, these two types of entrant face different barriers[2] and therefore, the relative weight of the two types of entry is not neutral to the appraisal of the degree of competition or the intensity of entry barriers. Even if, from the point of view of the whole economy, firms that change their main activity are continuing firms, in this paper, as we work at the industry level, they are considered as entrants.

Secondly, the way entry's importance is calculated is not the same for both types. In what new firm entry is concerned, we can be sure that entry corresponds to an increase in industry's employment, and that this increase is relatively important, since this activity is the most important among firm's activities. This is not necessarily true for established firm entry. In this case, the entrant firm could be already operating in the industry, and entry can even correspond to a decrease of other industries' importance rather than to a increase of firm's activities in the particular industry where entry is said to occur. Entry, a phenomenon generally associated with firm expansion, can thus correspond to a contraction movement. An obvious consequence to the interpretation of the measures presented below is that this type of entry also implies exit and therefore, the same event (exit from one industry and entry in another) is accounted twice.

## 2.2 Coverage

Only firms with paid employees are legally required to report to *QP*, which means that this source does not consider very small firms with only self

[2] See for example Gorecki (1975) and Mata (1991).

employed people or family workers. Evaluation of its degree of coverage is not normally possible but, since final data from the 1984 Census of Mining and Manufacturing have just started being released, this appraisal can now be done. Comparison between the Census and *QP* data reveal that even though *QP* investigates only 10% of the total number of firms employing less than 5 people that were considered by the Census, it reports more firms in all the other employment classes and records a greater employment figure than the Census itself. Hence, except for very small firms, it can be seen as a highly reliable source, and to avoid the introduction of biases of unknown direction and magnitude, these very small firms were excluded from the sample.

### 2.3 Sample

The original six digit CAE code given by *QP* was translated into a new code compatible with hybrid classification system usually employed by the Institute of Statistics, based on the belief that this classification is the one which conforms best to the economic definition of markets. The sample was formed from those industries which are normally included in the Institute of Statistics reports. From this set, all the "miscellaneous" industries, all those judged to be essentially of local extent, and those in which the public sector has a predominant position were excluded. To be allowed to remain in the sample an industry should also have at least three continuing firms, and thus the final sample comprehends 65 industries, including about 50% of the total number of firms operating in manufacturing in 1982, and 54% of their employment.

## 3 The Importance of Mobility and Concentration Levels

### 3.1 Mobility

In 1982, 8450 firms employing 504275 people, were in operation in the 65 industries of this paper's sample. Four years later, these figures were respectively 9447 and 521565, which represents an increase of 11.8% in the number of firms and of 3.5% in total employment. This employment increase is the net result of four simultaneous phenomena: entry, exit, and continuing firms' expansion and contraction. The first aim of this paper is to provide an overview of their importance, which is done in Table 1.

The first thing that can be seen in Table 1 is that there is an enormous

Table 1: Mobility in Portuguese manufacturing.

| | Entry | Exit | Expansion | Contraction | New firm entry |
|---|---|---|---|---|---|
| Rate (%) | 45.9 | 34.1 | 31.8 | 28.6 | 34.1 |
| Share (%) | 21.9 | 18.9 | 10.2 | 9.7 | 14.7 |

*Source:* Ministry of Employment and own calculations.

amount of industrial turbulence,[3] (responsible for about 60.7% of the initial employment), in spite of the moderate net increase in total employment. Besides, is also clear that entry and exit and not unimportant, when compared to expansion and contraction,[4] which does not fit well to the idea that incumbents' growth, rather than new firm entry, would be the true threat to market leaders.[5] To make a rigorous test of this hypothesis, one should investigate whether or not entry and incumbents' growth occurs in the same strategic groups,[6] which is clearly beyond the scope of this paper. Nevertheless, it is worth mentioning that entrants are clearly smaller than incumbents, (compare entry rates and shares), which may give some support to Shepherd's suggestion.

Given the way entry and exit figures were computed, it would be conceivable that they might result, in a great extent, from the inability of *QP* to keeping track of firms across time. If *QP* were not really able to follow firms across time, a firm that fails to report to *QP* in a certain year, would be classified as an *exitor*, and the same firm would be classified as an entrant by the time it reports to *QP* again. Although it can not be guarantied that this type of misclassification never occurred, there are a number of reasons that suggest that this was not the rule, and that the figures reported above correspond to real phenomena.

The first reason is that there is no reason to believe that such a good source, as *QP* are in 1984, may have "lost" so many firms as those implied by entry and exit figures, in only four years. The second reason is that, in what entry is concerned, this argument could only apply to *de novo* entry, and data from Table 1 reveal that established entry is responsible for a great amount of total entry. Besides, this source also records a quite high expansion movement, and, in what continuing firms are concerned, the "lost

[3] By turbulence here is meant the sum of entry, exit, expansion and contraction. See Beesley and Hamilton (1984) and Acs and Audretsch (1990) for discussions of the concept.

[4] Recall that, given the way mobility figures were computed, entry and exit are overestimated relatively to expansion and contraction. However, the figure for *de novo* entry also confirms that entry is not unimportant.

[5] See Shepherd (1984).

[6] See Caves and Porter (1977).

and found" hypothesis cannot apply. The fourth reason is that, if it was the case that most entries and exits correspond to firms that for some reason do not report to *QP* in an intermediate year, when these firms were included again in *QP* files they would be assigned to the same industry they used to belong before leaving the file; however, the low correlation between entry and exit shares (-0.05) does not support this view. Fifthly and finally, the same phenomenon of a high movement of new firm formation in the period of this study is also reported other statistical sources.[7]

## 3.2 Concentration

Table 2 shows some descriptive statistics regarding a few concentration measures in 1982 and 1986.

The "average" concentration values depicted in Table 2 reveal a relatively concentrated[8] and stable market structure. Between 1982 and 1986 the "average" concentration, regardless the measure employed, is almost constant, although it is observable a slight increase in dispersion. Standard-deviations increase, minimum values decrease, and maximum values increase, except when they depart in 1982 from the highest possible value.

[7] See Penedo (1988).

[8] Comparing concentration levels across countries is not easy; "average concentration" is sensitive to the industry classification adopted, to the industries included in the sample, and to the variable employed. The classification employed here is less disagreggated than the usual SIC 4-digit, and the industries excluded from the sample are typically highly concentrated. However, in spite of this downward bias, concentration levels are not lower than in the U. S. (Koch (1980, page 183), Baldwin (1987, page 157), McGee (1989, page 255)) the U. K. (Clarke (1985, page 22) Ferguson (1988, page 38), Curry e George (1983, page 217)), and Canada (Baldwin e Gorecki (1989)). Our figures are not corrected for international trade exposure, and thus our estimates are overestimates of the true concentration level. However, concentration values corrected for international trade presented by Corado and Leite (1990) also confirm that concentration in Portugal is probably higher than in Spain, Italy and the U. K.

Table 2: Concentration in 1982 and 1986.

| | | Average | St. dev. | Minimum | Maximum |
|---|---|---|---|---|---|
| *C*4 | 1982 | 0.471 | 0.252 | 0.051 | 0.964 |
| | 1986 | 0.468 | 0.259 | 0.041 | 0.978 |
| *C*8 | 1982 | 0.612 | 0.274 | 0.077 | 1.000 |
| | 1986 | 0.605 | 0.278 | 0.065 | 1.000 |
| *C*20 | 1982 | 0.764 | 0.250 | 0.133 | 1.000 |
| | 1986 | 0.750 | 0.258 | 0.113 | 1.000 |
| Herfindahl | 1982 | 0.107 | 0.093 | 0.002 | 0.347 |
| | 1986 | 0.107 | 0.104 | 0.002 | 0.548 |

*Source:* Ministry of Employment and own calculations.

Table 3: Correlations and ratios between concentration measures in 1986 and 1982.

| | $C4$ | $C8$ | $C20$ | Herfindahl |
|---|---|---|---|---|
| Correlation | 0.958 | 0.974 | 0.985 | 0.925 |
| Ratio | 0.989 | 0.983 | 0.986 | 1.001 |
| Standard-deviation | 0.195 | 0.132 | 0.075 | 0.347 |

*Source:* Ministry of Employment and own calculations.

To investigate if this average concentration stability corresponds to stability in all industries, or if it was the result of simultaneous and mutually compensating concentration changes across industries, correlations and ratios between the values of each concentration measure in both years were computed. These correlations, reported in Table 3, are pretty high and confirm the stability picture suggested before, which is corroborated by the ratio values close to unity. The standard-deviations are however too high to easily agree with this image of stability and besides, while standard-deviations values decrease from $C4$ to $C20$, correlations increase.

These simultaneous movements of standard-deviations and correlations, can be due to greater concentration stability when concentration is measured more broadly, which would suggest a most intense competition among leader firms, or it can be simply a consequence of the way concentration is measured. Industries which depart in 1982 from a relatively low concentration level cannot have their concentration levels much decreased and, conversely, industries departing from high concentration values cannot have their concentration levels much increased. When we use broader measures of concentration ($C8$ instead of $C4$, and $C20$ instead of $C8$) we include more such industries, and we may simply be leaving less scope for concentration changes. This hypothesis get some support by the lower standard-deviation of the ratio between 1982 and 1986 values for the Herfindahl index; unlike concentration ratios, Herfindahl index values are concentrated in the lower half of the possible spectrum, and therefore it is less sensitive to this problem.

To go a little further in exploring the possibility that the apparent stability of concentration levels is mainly due to this fallacy of numbers, some simple regressions of $C4$ values in 1986 on its values in 1982 were run. Table 4 reports results for four different regressions. The first regression was performed with the complete sample, and for the other three regressions the sample was split according to the initial concentration level, following Caves e Porter (1980). In the second regression, only low concentrated ($C4 < 0.3$) industries were included, while the third and fourth included industries with medium ($0.3 \leq C4 < 0.6$) and high ($C4 \geq 0.6$) concentration levels in 1982.

Table 4: Results of the regression of C4 values in 1986 on C4 values in 1982.

| | Intercept | $t$-stat* | Slope | $t$-stat* | $R^2$ | d.f. |
|---|---|---|---|---|---|---|
| $0 \leq C4 \leq 1$ | 0.007 | 0.484 | 0.978 | 0.742 | 0.91 | 63 |
| $0 \leq C4 < 0.3$ | -0.014 | -0.861 | 1.062 | 0.424 | 0.77 | 14 |
| $0.3 \leq C4 < 0.6$ | 0.187 | 1.950 | 0.535 | 1.897 | 0.24 | 25 |
| $0.6 \leq C4 \leq 1$ | 0.054 | 0.526 | 0.927 | 0.576 | 0.60 | 20 |

*Source:* Ministry of Employment and own calculations.
* $t$ values robust to heteroscedasticity (White (1980)) are for the null hypotheses that the the intercept is equal to 0 and the slope equal to 1.

Regression results for the whole sample show an image of high stability, which still holds for the low and high concentration samples. However, this picture does not persist for the medium concentration sample. In this sample, not only the fit is quite lower than in the other cases, as this is the only case in which the intercept is statistically different from 0 and the slope is different from 1. For these concentration levels, the stable concentration view does not hold, and since there is no reason, other than the way the concentration ratios are built, to believe that concentration changes may have been more important in this sample, one is led to the conclusion that the image of stability may be essentially a numbers' artefact.

# 4 The Relationship between Mobility and Concentration

If we tried to summarize the message conveyed by the data until now, we would say that, on the one hand, a moderate employment growth (3.5%) occults a quite considerable amount of business mobility (involving more than 60% of the initial employment) and, on the other hand, the absence of change in concentration (evaluated by the average industry concentration) masks the real picture of important changes in concentration at the industry level. In both cases, the apparent stability hides an unexpected intense competitive situation.

Even before trying to analyze in some detail each one of these phenomena, one must know how are they related to each other, and to ascertain if looking into one of them one can get a quite precise idea of how the other looks like. If this is the case, the information embodied in one of them will be redundant, after we are in possession of the information contained by the other. This is to say, that concentration would be a sufficient measure of the degree of competition in the industry, and even if there is no immediately available information on concentration levels for Portuguese manufacturing, not only it is possible to estimate them based on published data,[9] as it will always be easier to get data to compute concentration indexes than to obtain mobility measures like the ones presented here. If industry mobility is just a reflex of market concentration, concentration will be a sufficient measure of industry competition, and the payoff of collecting data on mobility will be quite low. If, on the contrary, concentration and mobility are different in a number aspects, then studies addressing both phenomena are clearly required.

Reviewing studies conducted by other authors, Scherer writes in his famous textbook (1980, page 74), that concentration is positively correlated with measures of stability of rank and market shares of dominant firms. Baldwin e Gorecki (1990a), working with a data base that includes all firm in Canadian manufacturing confirm this idea of the existence of a positive correlation between concentration and mobility, but they stress that, in their sample, the variance of mobility measures is weakly explained by concentration measures. Applying the principal components technique to a set of mobility measures and to a set of concentration measures, Baldwin e Gorecki (1990b) found that the first components being extracted from the data were quite different in the two cases, and they concluded that these type of measures, while correlated, apprehend different phenomena.

To examine the relationship between concentration and mobility, a different approach is adopted here, which tries to explore the causality links between concentration and mobility. The model sketched here views concentration as a determinant of the degree of mobility, and actual mobility determining changes in concentration levels.

The first equation, describing mobility as a function of concentration levels, is directly inspired in the classical Structure-Conduct-Performance paradigm. Concentration is usually the first condition listed in textbooks as facilitating collusion between firms, and therefore stability in their market shares. Incumbents' collusion is a necessary condition for aggressive behaviour towards new entrants (Orr, 1974), and thus concentration should also be negatively correlated with firm entry. Testing this hypothesis is actually testing the hypothesis that concentration is a good predictor to intensity of both actual and potential competition.

The second equation describes the feedback effect from mobility to market structure, and it relies on the idea that conduct, although somewhat constrained by market structure, is greatly exogenous and plays a role in determining structure itself.[10] This specification does not conform to the classical way of modelling concentration changes,[11] but seems to be an at-

[9] See Schmalensee (1977).

[10] See Donsimoni, Geroski e Jacquemin (1984).

[11] See Curry and George (1983) for a survey of this literature and also Levy (1985) and

tractive way of modelling this phenomenon, since "the *mechanism* by which concentration changes in an industry actually takes place could be one of the following: entry into the industry, exit from the industry (including exit by merger or takeover) or a change in relative sizes of firms within the industry." (Waterson, 1984, page 181-182).

Before estimating the model, the appropriate way of measuring mobility and concentration changes must be chosen. The mobility concept appropriate in this context must be close to the intensity of competition concept, and a direct measure of the intensity of competition can be obtained by adapting the volatility measure suggested by Dunne and Roberts (1991) to the availability of measures of entry, exit, expansion and contraction. The measure employed ($VOL$) was then,

$$VOL = ENT + EX + EXP + CONTR - \mid ENT - EX + EXP - CONTR \mid$$

in which $ENT$, $EX$, $EXP$ and $CONTR$ are the entry, exit, expansion and contraction shares, respectively. This measure, which is the difference between the turbulence and the net expansion shares, relies on an interpretation of the competitive process that views industry net employment increases as a part of an industry movement towards long-run equilibrium, while changes in these equilibria are due to exogenous factors (shifts in demand, changes in technology, modifications of firms' behaviour). If the industry departs from one long-run equilibrium position, and one of such alterations occurs, there will be adaptation movements taking place. These movements will persist until a new long-run position is reached, and its net volume is independent of the intensity of competition in the industry. This intensity only acts upon the magnitude of the difference between actual movements (turbulence share) and the minimum adaptation movement that would be necessary to drive industry from one long-run equilibrium to another long-run equilibrium (net expansion share).

To measure concentration changes, avoiding the aforementioned problem of spurious correlation between concentration change and the initial concentration level, the dependent variable of the second equation ($\Delta C4$) is the transformation of concentration change suggested by Wright (1978).

Obtained results confirm the hypothesis that concentration determines market volatility, which is to say, that concentration influences the degree of industry competition, and that the existence of high volatility flows has a deconcentrating effect upon market structure. However, the limited fit of the model also suggests that the industry competitive situation is far from being solely a reflex of market concentration, and that other factors intervene in their determination, which clearly points out the need of studies

---

**Geroski, Masson, and Shaanan(1987).**

Table 5: Regression results.

| Dependent Variable | Const | t-stat* | $C4$ | t-stat* | $VOL$ | t-stat* | $R^2$ |
|---|---|---|---|---|---|---|---|
| $VOL$ | 0.53 | 13.00 | -0.34 | -4.41 | | | 0.18 |
| $\Delta C4$ | 0.22 | 1.61 | | | -0.57 | -2.04 | 0.10 |

* $t$ values robust to heteroscedasticity (White, 1980).

directly concerned with the forces that determine the entry, exit, expansion and contraction phenomena themselves.

# 5 Concluding Remarks

Data presented in this paper reveal that there exists a quite high level of business mobility in Portuguese manufacturing, which does not fit well to the idea of the economy we are used at. Besides, it also shows that the apparent stability of average concentration levels does not mean that there are no important changes in concentration at the industry level. In both cases, it seems that market structure is much more dynamic that it appears to be to the casual observer.

The relationship between concentration (an indirect measure of the degree of competition) and a direct measure of this degree of competition is explored in a very simple model, which shows that market concentration inhibits market volatility, and that volatility have a feedback deconcentrating effect on market structure. However, the limited overall fit of the model indicates that, in spite of the strong existing interactions, concentration and degree of competition are not synonymous, and therefore the emergence of studies concerned with direct manifestations of the competitive process seems warranted.

Research on this issue seems to be crucial at the present moment in Portugal for a number of reasons. The high levels of the mobility flows in the period 1982–86 are probably, to a certain extent, a result from rigidities, which were present in the recent past. Past rigidities may have created a *stock* of unexploited profit opportunities by protecting very inefficient firms, and the movements we observe may, in part, be directed to exploitation of these opportunities. If this is true, the observed mobility flows may indicate that very important restructuring movements are happening now in Portugal.[12] If this is so, it is really critical to know what is exactly going

[12] If this is the case, these flows would become much less meaningful when these movements are completed. The alternative hypothesis would be that these flows are "normal", in the sense that they have been present since ever, even if we were not aware of them.

on in the industry, if one is interested on what should be done to encourage this restructuring. The study of the competitive process at the current time in Portugal will probably be much more directed to appraising and promoting firms' *competitiveness* than to detecting existence and abuses of market power. However, only having a reasonably precise idea of how do firms born, grow, compete with each other and ultimately die can one derive useful lessons to achieve this goal.

This also calls for the need of using better data than we usually do. Data employed in this paper represent a great improvement *vis a vis* the kind data which is generally available, but they still have their weaknesses. Namely, as it is not possible to identify firms' ownership, we can not use them to recognize mergers and acquisitions, and by including almost exclusively data on employment they prevent analysis of firms' relative efficiency. And these are two issues which are unquestionably relevant for assessing the competitive process. More intensive use of these data as well as production and availability of more comprehensive data bases seems to be a necessary step to successfully undertake the task of analyzing the dynamics of the competitive process.

# References

AUDRETSCH, D. AND Z. ACS (1990): "The Entrepreneurial Regime, Learning and Industry Turbulence," *Small Business Economics*, **2**, 119–128.

BALDWIN, J. AND P. GORECKI (1990a): "Concentration Statistics as Predictors of the Intensity of Competition," Research Paper #23G, Analytical Studies Branch, Statistics Canada.

BALDWIN, J. AND P. GORECKI (1990b): "The Relationship between Mobility and Concentration for the Canadian Manufacturing Sector," Research Paper #23H, Analytical Studies Branch, Statistics Canada.

BALDWIN, W. (1987): *Market Power, Competition and Antitrust Policy*. Homewood, Illinois: Richard D. Irwin.

BEESLEY, M. AND R. HAMILTON (1984): "Small Firms' Seedbed Role and the Concept of Turbulence," *Journal of Industrial Economics*, **33**, 217–232.

CAVES, R. AND M. PORTER (1977): "From Entry Barriers to Mobility Barriers: Conjectural Decisions and Contrived Deterrence to New Competition," *Quarterly Journal of Economics*, **41**, 241–261.

CAVES, R. AND M. PORTER (1980): "The Dynamics of Changing Seller Concentration," *Journal of Industrial Economics*, **29**, 1–15.

CLARKE, R. (1985): *Industrial Economics*. Oxford: Basil Blackwell.

CORADO, C. AND A. LEITE (1990): "Direct Foreign Investment and Industry Location in the Iberian Peninsula," paper presented at the fifth Conference of the European Economic Association, Lisbon.

---

Lack of data does not allow a direct test of these hypotheses, but the direct study of the nature of the competitive process may shed some light on the issue.

Curry, B. and K. George (1983): "Industrial Concentration: a Survey," *Journal of Industrial Economics*, **31**, 203–255.

Donsimoni, M.-P., P. Geroski and A. Jacquemin (1984): "Concentration Indices and Market Power: Two Views," *Journal of Industrial Economics*, **32**, 419–434.

Dunne, T. and M. Roberts (1991): "Variation in Producer Turnover across US Manufacturing Industries," in *Entry and Market Contestability: an International Comparison*, ed. by P. Geroski, and J. Schwalbach, forthcoming. Oxford: Basil Blackwell.

Ferguson, P. (1988): *Industrial Economics: Issues and Perspectives*. London: MacMillan.

Geroski, P., R. Masson and J. Shaanan (1987): "The Dynamics of Market Structure," *International Journal of Industrial Organization*, **5**, 93–100.

Gorecki, P. (1975): "The Determinants of Entry by New and Diversifying Enterprises in the UK Manufacturing Sector 1958-1963: some Tentative Results," *Applied Economics*, **7**, 139–147.

Koch, J. (1980): *Industrial Organization and Prices*, 2nd edition. London: Prentice-Hall.

Levy, D. (1985): "Specifying the Dynamics of Industry Concentration," *Journal of Industrial Economics*, **34**, 55–67.

Mata, J. (1991): "Entry and Type of Entrant: Evidence from Portugal," *Mimeo*, Universidade do Minho

McGee, J. (1988): *Industrial Organization*. Englewood Cliffs: Prentice-Hall.

Modesto, L. and J. Neves (1990): "Hysteresis and Sluggishness in Portuguese Unemployment: 1977–1988," paper presented at the fifth Conference of the European Economic Association, Lisbon.

Orr, D. (1974): "The Determinant of Entry: a Study of the Canadian Manufacturing Industries," *Review of Economics and Statistics*, **56**, 58–66.

Penedo, A. (1988): "Portugal à Beira de Ter Um Milhão de Empresas," *Revista das Empresas*, September, 19–22.

Schmalensee, R. (1977): "Using the H-index of Concentration with Published Data," *Review of Economics and Statistics*, **59**, 186–193.

Shepherd, W. (1982): "Contestability Versus Competition," *American Economic Review*, **74**, 572–587.

Waterson, M. (1984), *Economic Theory of the Industry*. Cambridge: Cambridge University Press.

White, H. (1980): "A Heteroskedastic-Consistent Covariance Matrix Estimator and a Direct Test for Heteroskedasticity," *Econometrica*, **48**, 817–838.

Wright, N. (1978): "Product Differentiation, Concentration, and Changes in Concentration," *Review of Economics and Statistics*, **60**, 628–631.

# Why Are Wages in Portugal Lower than Elsewhere in the EEC?

Fernando Branco
António S. Mello

## 1 Introduction

It is well known that nominal wages are much lower in Portugal than in other countries of the European Community. Several are the reasons that can be offered to explain the wage gap between Portugal and its European partners.

Wages can be lower because the price level in Portugal is lower. Empirical research on international price level differences has long uncovered a positive relationship between countries' price levels and real wages.[1]

Another source of differentiation is a productivity gap between Portugal and other EEC members. This can be because of many different aspects. It can be due to poor technology choice by Portugal, affecting the total factor productivity. At a distinct level, differences in factor allocations due to factor endowments or market imperfections can result in a lower capital intensity for Portugal. But it can also be a consequence of arguments developed by human capital theory: perhaps the average education of the Portuguese worker and the skills acquired through on-the-job training are too low, thereby constraining the labor force to concentrate on less productive techniques;[2] this may be seen as a specific quality problem, which can be extended to other factors of production. On the other hand, if, at the aggregate level, more people is employed in activities with low productivity, e.g., agriculture and certain services, in Portugal than in other European countries, the distinct sectoral composition of activity also accounts for differences in productivity.

We are grateful to Ana Paula Martins for comments and suggestions.

[1] See Kravis and Lipsey (1983) and Kravis (1984).

[2] The wage and labor supply implications of education and training, i.e., human capital accumulation, have been extensively analyzed in Mincer (1962) and in Mincer (1974).

Other sources for the observed differences come from the organization and functioning of the labor markets. For example, Portuguese unions may lack bargaining power; then, even if the value of the marginal product of labor was the same in Portugal and abroad, Portuguese real wages could be lower if the degree of market competition was lower in Portugal and Portuguese employers were able to extract a larger rent from workers.[3] Another plausible explanation may be that jobs in Portugal are relatively safer than in other European countries, and greater job security has a tradeoff expressed in lower salaries.[4] A third source may be asymmetrical information: adverse selection and moral hazard in the labor market may well influence the wage level. Finally, the contributions to the social security can be responsible for discrepancies of the wages across countries, depending on the elasticity of the labor supply curve.

In this paper we try to highlight some basic determinants of the differences in nominal wages, relative to the block of the other eleven countries of EEC and perform bilateral comparisons with Spain, Greece and Ireland. Being these countries' wages below the European average, it is interesting to see how the different factors fare relative to Portugal, as well as to examine how the gap has changed over time in recent years. We follow an approach similar to the one used in Saint-Paul (1989), who first studied the subject. His work is extended to a higher level of disaggregation, and the role of the various assumptions is discussed in greater detail.

In the next section we present a simple methodology for decomposing the wage gap into various components. Section 3 presents the results of a preliminary disaggregation of the nominal wage gap into three factors: real exchange rate, productivity and industrial relations. This is done without requiring specific assumptions about the production technology. Then, in section 4, we decompose the productivity and the industrial relations gaps. The productivity gap is decomposed into a capital intensity gap and a total factor productivity gap; the latter is explained by the sectoral composition of the economies. Finally, in the industrial relations gap, differences in social security payments are taken into account. Section 5 concludes the paper and discusses possible extensions and methodological refinements.

## 2 Methodology

Consider a simple model with two countries: Portugal and a foreign country. In each country the economy is described through similar aggregates and relations. Starred variables correspond to the foreign country, so that from

[3] For a survey of the literature on union-nonunion see Lewis (1984).

[4] Potential tradeoffs involving employment and wages are treated in, among others, Pencavel (1984).

the description of the structure of the Portuguese economy it must be clear the structure of the other country.

Let $F(K, L)$ be the Portuguese production function, where $K$ represents the stock of capital and $L$ the level of employment. The level of output is also represented by $Y$, so $Y \equiv F(K, L)$. Wages and prices are denoted by $W$ and $P$, respectively. The real wage can be decomposed into two terms

$$\frac{W}{P} = \frac{\partial F(K,L)}{\partial L} + \left(\frac{W}{P} - \frac{\partial F(K,L)}{\partial L}\right), \tag{1}$$

where the first term is the marginal productivity of labor and the second term is a measure symmetrically related to the employer's rent. From basic microeconomic theory we know that if labor markets were competitive the employer's rent would be zero.

Define the employer's markup, $\mu$, as

$$\mu = \frac{\frac{\partial F}{\partial L} - \frac{W}{P}}{\frac{\partial F}{\partial L}} \tag{2}$$

and expression (1) can be rewritten as

$$\frac{W}{P} = (1-\mu)\frac{\partial F(K,L)}{\partial L}. \tag{3}$$

Dividing (3) by its foreign analogue we get a first decomposition of the wage differential

$$\frac{W}{W^*} = \left(\frac{P}{P^*}\right)\left(\frac{\frac{\partial F(K,L)}{\partial L}}{\frac{\partial F^*(K^*,L^*)}{\partial L^*}}\right)\left(\frac{1-\mu}{1-\mu^*}\right) \tag{4}$$

The first factor is the real exchange rate gap, the second the productivity gap and the third the industrial relations gap.

The disaggregation in (4) requires an assumption about the functional form of the production function in both Portugal and the foreign country. As a first approximation, in order to isolate the terms that are independent of the functional form assumed for the production functions, we may get the analogue of expressions (1)–(4) using average values instead of marginal values. Accordingly, we would get the decomposition of the wage gap as

$$\frac{W}{W^*} = \left(\frac{P}{P^*}\right)\left(\frac{Y/L}{Y^*/L^*}\right)\left(\frac{1-\nu}{1-\nu^*}\right), \tag{5}$$

where $\nu$ is the employer's average mark-up, i.e.,

$$\nu = \frac{\frac{Y}{L} - \frac{W}{P}}{\frac{Y}{L}} . \tag{6}$$

This decomposition is used to estimate the wage gap, in section 3.

The next step further decomposes the components in (4). The real exchange rate gap does not have a particularly interesting decomposition, and it is already a primitive element of the wage gap. More relevant seem to be the decompositions of the productivity and the industrial relations gaps.

To decompose the productivity gap we assume that both countries have a constant returns to scale Cobb-Douglas production function, with the same labor coefficient, $\alpha$, i.e.,

$$F(K, L) = AK^{1-\alpha}L^{\alpha} \tag{7}$$

$$F^*(K^*, L^*) = A^*K^{*1-\alpha}L^{*\alpha} . \tag{8}$$

The choice of the constant returns to scale Cobb-Douglas production function to describe the Portuguese economy is consistent with recent findings in this area.[5] To allow an easier interpretation of the results we use an equivalent functional form for the production function of the foreign country. More problematic is the assumption of equal labor coefficients between countries. The main reason for that is that it allows us a straightforward isolation of the gap in total factor productivity. Moreover, from a purely theoretical perspective, it provides a simple solution to the problem of aggregating, at the European Community level, the individual countries' production functions. Similar arguments are used when we later study the effect of the sectoral composition of each economy and assume a particular technology for each sector in each country.[6]

Using (7)–(8) the productivity gap is then decomposed in several elements. First, we consider the effect of the capital intensity,[7] using the

[5] Work performed by Branco and Saint-Paul (1989) showed that, even though the point estimate of the returns to scale in the Portuguese economy was around 1.3, one could not reject the hypothesis of constant returns to scale. Moreover, estimating a CES production function the hypothesis of unit elasticity of substitution was not rejected. These results also justified similar assumptions in Saint-Paul (1989).

[6] If the labor coefficient varied across countries, we would need to estimate a production function for each country, and the aggregation would be non trivial. Moreover, the estimated coefficients would, probably, not change very much across countries.

[7] The constant returns to scale assumption implies that the marginal productivities depend only on the capital intensity coefficient, which then plays an important role in the productivity gap.

following relationship

$$\frac{\dfrac{\partial F(K/L,1)}{\partial L}}{\dfrac{\partial F^*(K^*/L^*,1)}{\partial L^*}} = \left(\frac{\dfrac{\partial F(K/L,1)}{\partial L}}{\dfrac{\partial F(K^*/L^*,1)}{\partial L}}\right)\left(\frac{\dfrac{\partial F(K^*/L^*,1)}{\partial L}}{\dfrac{\partial F^*(K^*/L^*,1)}{\partial L^*}}\right) . \tag{9}$$

The first term corresponds to the capital intensity gap, which results from differences in the capital intensity between countries, and the second term measures the total factor productivity, which corresponds to the gap that would exist even if Portugal had the same capital intensity as the foreign country. With the previous assumptions about the technologies, the disaggregation in (9) can be given by

$$\frac{\dfrac{\partial F(K/L,1)}{\partial L}}{\dfrac{\partial F^*(K^*/L^*,1)}{\partial L^*}} = \left(\frac{K/L}{K^*/L^*}\right)^{1-\alpha}\left(\frac{YK^{\alpha-1}L^{-\alpha}}{Y^*K^{*\alpha-1}L^{*-\alpha}}\right) , \tag{10}$$

where we use the fact that

$$A = YK^{\alpha-1}L^{-\alpha} .$$

The total factor productivity gap can be further decomposed,[8] by considering differences in the sectoral allocation of factors of production. We consider three sectors (agriculture, industry and services) in each economy. Again, we assume that each sector has a constant returns to scale Cobb-Douglas technology, with the same labor coefficient, i.e.,

$$F_i(K_i, L_i) = A_i K_i^{1-\alpha} L_i^{\alpha} , \quad i = A, I, S \tag{11}$$

where the subscript $i$ denotes the sector. The aggregate production function is then easily obtained,

$$F(K,L) = \left(\sum_{i=A,I,S} A_i k_i^{1-\alpha} l_i^{\alpha}\right) K^{1-\alpha} L^{\alpha} , \tag{12}$$

which represents an alternative way of writing the production function in (7). In expression (12) $k_i$ and $l_i$ are the shares of total capital and labor allocated to sector $i$. The total factor productivity gap is thus dependent on the sectoral allocation of the resources. Following an approach similar to that in the initial decomposition of the productivity gap, we can isolate the

[8] Note that the total factor productivity gap is just the ratio of the constants.

gap due to the sectoral allocation of the production factors, the sectoral composition gap, from the gap due to overall differences in productivity, the residual gap,[9] and write

$$\frac{\dfrac{\partial F(K^*/L^*,1)}{\partial L}}{\dfrac{\partial F^*(K^*/L^*,1)}{\partial L^*}} = \left(\frac{\sum_i A_i k_i^{1-\alpha} l_i^{\alpha}}{\sum_i A_i k_i^{*\,1-\alpha} l_i^{*\,\alpha}}\right)\left(\frac{\sum_i A_i k_i^{*\,1-\alpha} l_i^{*\,\alpha}}{\sum_i A_i^* k_i^{*\,1-\alpha} l_i^{*\,\alpha}}\right). \tag{13}$$

The first factor is the gap that would exist if the both countries has the same production function and capital intensity, but distinct sectoral structures; the second factor captures the gap due to differences between the production functions.

Making use of the assumptions about the technologies we get

$$\frac{\dfrac{\partial F(K^*/L^*,1)}{\partial L}}{\dfrac{\partial F^*(K^*/L^*,1)}{\partial L^*}} = \left(\frac{1}{\sum_i y_i \left(\dfrac{k_i^*}{k_i}\right)^{1-\alpha}\left(\dfrac{l_i^*}{l_i}\right)^{\alpha}}\right)\left(\frac{\dfrac{\sum_i Y_i \left(\dfrac{k_i^*}{k_i}\right)^{1-\alpha}\left(\dfrac{l_i^*}{l_i}\right)^{\alpha}}{K^{1-\alpha}L^{\alpha}}}{\dfrac{Y^*}{K^{*\,1-\alpha}L^{*\,\alpha}}}\right) \tag{14}$$

where $y_i$ denotes sector $i$'s share in output.

Next we decompose the industrial relations gap. At this stage we only isolate the effect of the contributions to the social security. Taking a very simple model of the labor market, it is clear that the effect of the contributions to the social security on the wages depends on the elasticity of the labor supply; if the labor supply is vertical, the level of wages is independent of the contributions because the workers effectively bear all the payment; on the other hand, if the labor supply is perfectly elastic, the level of wages varies one-to-one with the contributions to the social security because the employers effectively bear all the payment. Following the type of disaggregation presented in (4), the contributions to the social security only affect the industrial relations term, which can then be decomposed as

$$\frac{1-\mu}{1-\mu^*} = \left(\frac{\dfrac{W/P}{\partial F(K,L)/\partial L}(1-c)^{\gamma}}{\dfrac{W^*/P^*}{\partial F^*(K^*,L^*)/\partial L^*}(1-c^*)^{\gamma}}\right)\left(\frac{1-c^*}{1-c}\right)^{\gamma}, \tag{15}$$

where $c$ is the proportion of the wage bill representing contributions to the social security. The parameter $\gamma$ measures the effect of the contributions on

[9] The residual gap does not have a particular interpretation, mainly because it will aggregate all the errors introduced by the previous assumptions.

the real wage; if the labor supply is inelastic, the contributions do not affect the wage and $\gamma$ is equal to zero; if labor supply is perfectly elastic, variations in the contributions are totally reflected in the wage and $\gamma$ equals one; hence $\gamma$ has value in $[0, 1]$, depending on the elasticity of the labor supply curve. The first factor is the firms' rent gap and the second is the social security gap. With the assumptions about the technologies, we can compute each term in (15). The industrial relations gap is

$$\frac{1-\mu}{1-\mu^*} = \frac{\dfrac{WL}{PY}}{\dfrac{W^*L^*}{P^*Y^*}} \tag{16}$$

which uses the fact that, with a constant returns to scale Cobb-Douglas function, the marginal productivity of labor is proportional to the average productivity of labor, with proportionality constant $\alpha$, assumed to be equal across countries.

To decompose the industrial gap we then use

$$\frac{1-\mu}{1-\mu^*} = \left(\frac{\dfrac{WL}{PY}(1-c)^\gamma}{\dfrac{W^*L^*}{P^*Y^*}(1-c^*)^\gamma}\right)\left(\frac{1-c^*}{1-c}\right)^\gamma . \tag{17}$$

This disaggregation is correct if we assume that the sensitivity of the salaries to the social security contributions is virtually equal across countries.[10]

# 3 Wage Gap: Preliminary Disaggregation

In this section we provide a first disaggregation of the nominal wage gap. As a first approximation and to avoid assumptions about the production functions, we use the decomposition in expression (5), i.e., using averages,[11]

$$\frac{W}{W^*} = \left(\frac{P}{P^*}\right)\left(\frac{Y/L}{Y^*/L^*}\right)\left(\frac{1-\nu}{1-\nu^*}\right) .$$

With the data described in appendix, we computed the components of the wage gap between Portugal and the other countries, which are presented in Tables 1–4.

[10] The assumption is justified by the existence of no reason supporting different parameter $\gamma$ choices.

[11] This is also the marginal decomposition if both countries have a Cobb-Douglas production function with the same labor coefficient.

Table 1: **Wage gap between Portugal and Europe.**

| | | | | | Contribution to Wage Gap | | |
|---|---|---|---|---|---|---|---|
| Year | Wage Gap | Exch. Rate | Prod. | Indust. Relat. | Exch. Rate | Prod. | Indust. Relat. |
| 1965 | 0.245 | 0.640 | 0.464 | 0.826 | 31.8% | 54.6% | 13.6% |
| 1970 | 0.307 | 0.678 | 0.506 | 0.895 | 32.9% | 57.7% | 9.4% |
| 1972 | 0.312 | 0.641 | 0.495 | 0.981 | 38.1% | 60.3% | 1.6% |
| 1974 | 0.371 | 0.690 | 0.487 | 1.104 | 37.5% | 72.5% | -10.0% |
| 1976 | 0.411 | 0.605 | 0.520 | 1.309 | 56.6% | 73.7% | -30.3% |
| 1978 | 0.299 | 0.526 | 0.480 | 1.183 | 53.1% | 60.8% | -13.9% |
| 1980 | 0.280 | 0.498 | 0.497 | 1.132 | 54.8% | 55.0% | -9.7% |
| 1982 | 0.293 | 0.532 | 0.494 | 1.115 | 51.5% | 57.4% | -8.9% |
| 1984 | 0.247 | 0.500 | 0.450 | 1.097 | 49.6% | 57.0% | -6.6% |
| 1985 | 0.255 | 0.514 | 0.459 | 1.078 | 48.6% | 56.9% | -5.5% |
| 1986 | 0.253 | 0.499 | 0.482 | 1.054 | 50.7% | 53.1% | -3.8% |
| 1987 | 0.287 | 0.520 | 0.483 | 1.143 | 52.4% | 58.4% | -10.7% |
| 1988 | 0.297 | 0.534 | 0.480 | 1.161 | 51.8% | 60.5% | -12.3% |

Table 1 shows the nominal wage gap between Europe and Portugal and its decomposition in the real exchange rate factor,[12] the productivity factor and the industrial relations factor; the contribution due to each factor is also presented in percentage. The column Wage Gap shows that Portuguese wages have been significantly lower than the European average, roughly 70% lower. The wage gap improved briefly in the seventies, especially in the years right after the revolution of 1974. It is also apparent that the gap has deteriorated since 1978 and in 1984 it was at the level of the sixties. The deterioration was dramatic in 1978 and again in 1984. More recently there has been a slight improvement, though the situation in the late eighties is still not much different from that at the beginning of the decade. The table also shows that the wage gap has been declining since Portugal joined the EEC, at the beginning of 1986.

Across the table the contribution of each factor to the nominal wage gap is measured considering that the contribution of the other two factors was zero.[13] So, in 1986, lower prices in Portugal could account for Portuguese salaries roughly 50% of those in Europe. Similarly, for that same year, the relatively lower productivity could explain why salaries in Portugal were 48% of those in Europe. During the late sixties and early seventies the exchange rate was responsible for 35% lower wages in Portugal relative to Europe, representing around one third of the nominal wage gap; after 1974 the exchange rate increased its contribution to about 50%, mainly as a consequence of real depreciations during the periods from 1974 to 1978 and from 1982 to 1984. From the table it is apparent that the main contributor to the wage gap is the productivity. Note that this factor has kept its

[12]The gap is obtained deducing 1 to the factor.

[13]All other numbers equal to one.

Table 2: Wage gap between Portugal and Spain.

| | | | | | Contribution to Wage Gap | | |
|---|---|---|---|---|---|---|---|
| Year | Wage Gap | Exch. Rate | Prod. | Indust. Relat. | Exch. Rate | Prod. | Indust. Relat. |
| 1965 | 0.438 | 0.970 | 0.607 | 0.743 | 3.7% | 60.4% | 35.9% |
| 1970 | 0.531 | 1.013 | 0.642 | 0.817 | -2.1% | 70.1% | 32.0% |
| 1972 | 0.502 | 0.946 | 0.616 | 0.861 | 8.1% | 70.2% | 21.6% |
| 1974 | 0.529 | 0.910 | 0.581 | 0.999 | 14.8% | 85.1% | 0.1% |
| 1976 | 0.545 | 0.810 | 0.596 | 1.131 | 34.8% | 85.4% | -20.3% |
| 1978 | 0.414 | 0.728 | 0.536 | 1.062 | 36.0% | 70.8% | -6.8% |
| 1980 | 0.358 | 0.643 | 0.541 | 1.030 | 43.1% | 59.8% | -2.9% |
| 1982 | 0.373 | 0.688 | 0.528 | 1.026 | 37.9% | 64.8% | -2.6% |
| 1984 | 0.328 | 0.680 | 0.469 | 1.030 | 34.7% | 67.9% | -2.6% |
| 1985 | 0.335 | 0.690 | 0.472 | 1.029 | 33.9% | 68.7% | -2.6% |
| 1986 | 0.345 | 0.680 | 0.486 | 1.042 | 36.2% | 67.6% | -3.8% |
| 1987 | 0.398 | 0.695 | 0.503 | 1.140 | 39.6% | 74.6% | -14.2% |
| 1988 | 0.395 | 0.680 | 0.502 | 1.157 | 41.6% | 74.2% | -15.7% |

level around 50% during the sample period, suggesting the persistence of a structural disadvantage relative to Europe. Given the stability of the productivity gap, the industrial relations gap has to explain part of the fluctuations. Since the revolution, the contribution to the nominal wage gap due to industrial relations has simply disappeared: if there was no gap due to the exchange rate and productivity, labor laws and union power would have taken Portuguese wages above the European average. This contrasts with the disadvantageous but improving situation during the years that preceded the revolution. The declining trend of the industrial relations factor was reversed after 1986. This could be the result of a purely EEC effect, in which the Portuguese labor force would demand higher salaries to compensate for higher prices and lower wage differences relative to their European counterparts. To the extent that joining the EEC would improve business conditions, employers would be prepared to accommodate such demands.[14]

Tables 2–4 show the decomposition as well as the nominal wage gap relative to three European partners in a state of economic development closer to that of Portugal. The results for the different countries are remarkably different. It is quite interesting to see that the gap relative to Spain has deteriorated systematically since 1976, until both countries joined the EEC, and in 1988 it was only 10% away from the European average. This can be attributed mainly to losses in relative purchasing power as well as in relative productivity, but while the former appeared with explanatory power after the revolution, the latter has always been important. The industrial

[14] An alternative explanation is the *ex-post* renegotiation of wages imposed by the unions, in 1987, after the government failed the inflation target, as well as by the lack of credibility, reflected in a premium demanded in future salaries.

Table 3: Wage gap between Portugal and Greece.

| | | | | | Contribution to Wage Gap | | |
|---|---|---|---|---|---|---|---|
| Year | Wage Gap | Exch. Rate | Prod. | Indust. Relat. | Exch. Rate | Prod. | Indust. Relat. |
| 1970 | 0.489 | 0.701 | 0.884 | 0.789 | 49.6% | 17.2% | 33.2% |
| 1972 | 0.561 | 0.768 | 0.816 | 0.895 | 45.7% | 35.1% | 19.3% |
| 1974 | 0.673 | 0.737 | 0.832 | 1.097 | 76.9% | 46.5% | -23.3% |
| 1976 | 0.757 | 0.729 | 0.818 | 1.270 | 113.6% | 72.1% | -85.7% |
| 1978 | 0.506 | 0.664 | 0.743 | 1.025 | 60.1% | 43.6% | -3.7% |
| 1980 | 0.537 | 0.697 | 0.771 | 0.998 | 58.0% | 41.8% | 0.3% |
| 1982 | 0.485 | 0.648 | 0.819 | 0.914 | 60.0% | 27.6% | 12.5% |
| 1984 | 0.421 | 0.636 | 0.770 | 0.860 | 52.3% | 30.3% | 17.4% |
| 1985 | 0.449 | 0.698 | 0.785 | 0.819 | 44.8% | 30.3% | 24.9% |
| 1986 | 0.521 | 0.782 | 0.809 | 0.824 | 37.8% | 32.5% | 29.7% |
| 1987 | 0.667 | 0.822 | 0.861 | 0.942 | 48.2% | 37.0% | 14.8% |
| 1988 | 0.659 | 0.825 | 0.851 | 0.939 | 46.2% | 38.7% | 15.1% |

Table 4: Wage gap between Portugal and Ireland.

| | | | | | Contribution to Wage Gap | | |
|---|---|---|---|---|---|---|---|
| Year | Wage Gap | Exch. Rate | Prod. | Indust. Relat. | Exch. Rate | Prod. | Indust. Relat. |
| 1965 | 0.335 | 0.658 | 0.696 | 0.732 | 38.2% | 33.2% | 28.6% |
| 1970 | 0.417 | 0.701 | 0.757 | 0.786 | 40.6% | 31.9% | 27.5% |
| 1972 | 0.417 | 0.636 | 0.725 | 0.903 | 51.6% | 36.7% | 11.7% |
| 1974 | 0.525 | 0.771 | 0.705 | 0.966 | 40.4% | 54.3% | 5.3% |
| 1976 | 0.616 | 0.760 | 0.685 | 1.182 | 56.6% | 78.0% | -34.5% |
| 1978 | 0.435 | 0.626 | 0.641 | 1.084 | 56.2% | 53.4% | -9.6% |
| 1980 | 0.365 | 0.566 | 0.674 | 0.958 | 56.5% | 39.2% | 4.3% |
| 1982 | 0.350 | 0.539 | 0.649 | 1.001 | 58.9% | 41.3% | -0.1% |
| 1984 | 0.280 | 0.497 | 0.578 | 0.975 | 54.9% | 43.1% | 2.0% |
| 1985 | 0.282 | 0.504 | 0.580 | 0.965 | 54.1% | 43.1% | 2.8% |
| 1986 | 0.284 | 0.500 | 0.607 | 0.937 | 55.1% | 39.7% | 5.2% |
| 1987 | 0.328 | 0.529 | 0.594 | 1.047 | 57.2% | 46.9% | -4.1% |
| 1988 | 0.346 | 0.543 | 0.584 | 1.091 | 57.5% | 50.8% | -8.2% |

relations gap has, however, contributed positively to diminish the nominal wage gap between Spain and Portugal since the mid-seventies.

Relative to Greece the nominal wage gap did not change much, until Portugal joined the EEC, although it has evolved in a volatile manner throughout the period. Note that Portuguese salaries have been around one-half of those in Greece, though in recent years the difference has had a big reduction. In recent years, the contribution to the gap due to both the productivity and exchange rate has decreased. However, labor laws and union power in Greece seem to push the wage bill in Greece above the Portuguese one, which is in part compensated by small gains in the average productivity of labor in Portugal. There are two factors which differ in the comparison with Greece to that with other countries: the productivity gap is smaller and the industrial relations gap, which plays an important role, is disadvantageous to Portugal. Also the gains from joining the EEC are much more evident in the comparison with Greece.

Ireland has seen the nominal wage gap eroding rapidly until 1976, when the Portuguese wages were 38% lower. Since then the nominal wage gap started to widen and Portuguese wages finished 72% lower in 1986, very close to the European average. After that, the EEC effect has contributed to reduce the gap, mainly due to the exchange rate and the industrial relations factors, while no evidence in productivity gains is observed. As in the case of Greece, the contribution of the productivity factor has steadily lost importance to the exchange rate. Next, we attempt to further decompose the productivity gap and the industrial relations gap, following the steps outlined in section 2.

# 4 Wage Gap: Detailed Decomposition

## 4.1 Decomposing the Productivity Gap

Here we try a disaggregation of the productivity gap. In order to decompose the gap in productivity and explain its causes it is necessary to specify the production technology in both countries. It is assumed that Portugal and other European countries have constant returns to scale Cobb-Douglas production functions. As stated in section 2, it is assumed that the labor coefficient $\alpha$ is the same in Portugal and abroad; more specifically, for the basic calculations, we use a value of $\alpha$ set at 0.6.[15]

Because of the assumption of constant returns to scale, we consider two components. One reflects differences of factor endowments and uses, i.e., the effect of differences in capital and labor if the production function in Portugal and abroad was the same. This first factor is called the capital intensity factor. The other factor assumes no gap in capital intensity and reflects differences in the production function between Portugal and Europe, and is called total factor productivity. The disaggregation and computations are performed using the decomposition given in (10), i.e.,

$$\frac{\dfrac{\partial F(K/L,1)}{\partial L}}{\dfrac{\partial F^*(K^*/L^*,1)}{\partial L^*}} = \left(\frac{K/L}{K^*/L^*}\right)^{1-\alpha}\left(\frac{YK^{\alpha-1}L^{-\alpha}}{Y^*K^{*\alpha-1}L^{*-\alpha}}\right).$$

The results of this decomposition are presented in Tables 5–8.

Table 5 shows that the capital intensity in Portugal relative to the European average has deteriorated since the early seventies. If the other factors

[15] Saint-Paul (1989) reports an estimate of $\alpha$ around 0.55 for France, while Branco and Saint-Paul (1989) have estimated an $\alpha$ around 0.6 for Portugal.

Table 5: Productivity gap between Portugal and Europe.

| | | | | | | Contribution to Wage Gap | | | |
|---|---|---|---|---|---|---|---|---|---|
| Year | Prod. | Cap. Int. | Fact. Prod. | Sect. Comp. | Resid. | Cap. Int. | Fact. Prod. | Sect. Comp. | Resid. |
| 1965 | 0.464 | 0.748 | 0.620 | 0.816 | 0.760 | 20.7% | 34.0% | 14.5% | 19.5% |
| 1970 | 0.506 | 0.768 | 0.658 | 0.996 | 0.660 | 22.3% | 35.4% | 0.3% | 35.1% |
| 1972 | 0.495 | 0.765 | 0.647 | 0.967 | 0.670 | 23.0% | 37.3% | 2.9% | 34.4% |
| 1974 | 0.487 | 0.750 | 0.650 | 0.920 | 0.706 | 29.1% | 43.5% | 8.4% | 35.1% |
| 1976 | 0.520 | 0.743 | 0.699 | 0.944 | 0.741 | 33.4% | 40.3% | 6.5% | 33.8% |
| 1978 | 0.480 | 0.750 | 0.640 | 0.782 | 0.818 | 23.9% | 37.0% | 20.4% | 16.6% |
| 1980 | 0.497 | 0.745 | 0.667 | 0.800 | 0.835 | 23.1% | 31.8% | 17.7% | 14.2% |
| 1982 | 0.494 | 0.746 | 0.663 | 0.842 | 0.788 | 23.9% | 33.5% | 14.1% | 19.5% |
| 1984 | 0.450 | 0.745 | 0.604 | 0.881 | 0.686 | 21.1% | 36.0% | 9.1% | 26.9% |
| 1985 | 0.459 | 0.746 | 0.616 | 0.875 | 0.704 | 21.4% | 35.5% | 9.8% | 25.7% |
| 1986 | 0.482 | 0.745 | 0.647 | 0.885 | 0.731 | 21.5% | 31.7% | 8.9% | 22.8% |
| 1987 | 0.483 | 0.745 | 0.648 | 0.881 | 0.736 | 23.6% | 34.8% | 10.2% | 24.6% |
| 1988 | 0.480 | 0.744 | 0.645 | 0.886 | 0.728 | 24.3% | 36.2% | 10.0% | 26.2% |

had a neutral effect on the gap, namely the ratio of price levels and the industrial relations, portuguese wages should be lower (around 75%) than the European wages due to lower capital intensity in Portugal. This could be the result of many factors, such as permanent overmanning combined with low levels of net capital formation in Portugal, or even the relative underdevelopment of the Portuguese financial markets. If instead of the absolute levels we look at the percent contributions to the nominal wage gap, it is clear that the large deterioration of the capital intensity in the mid-seventies turned into an improvement in the eighties.

Although isolating the capital intensity factor helps to explain the productivity gap between Europe and Portugal, it is apparent from the tables that the contribution of the total factor productivity to the wage gap is in general more important. Because of this importance, our next exercise attempts to explain the gap in total factor productivity. This gap captures the difference in the value of the constants of the production functions between Portugal and the foreign country. It can be due to several factors, e.g., education, though at this stage we only measure the effect of the sectoral composition of the economies. Following the methodology described in section 2 we consider three sectors (agriculture, industry and services) and decompose the total factor productivity gap according to expression (14)

$$\frac{\frac{\partial F(K^*/L^*,1)}{\partial L}}{\frac{\partial F^*(K^*/L^*,1)}{\partial L^*}} = \left( \frac{1}{\sum_i y_i \left(\frac{k_i^*}{k_i}\right)^{1-\alpha} \left(\frac{l_i^*}{l_i}\right)^{\alpha}} \right) \left( \frac{\frac{\sum_i Y_i \left(\frac{k_i^*}{k_i}\right)^{1-\alpha} \left(\frac{l_i^*}{l_i}\right)^{\alpha}}{K^{1-\alpha}L^{\alpha}}}{\frac{Y^*}{K^{*1-\alpha}L^{*\alpha}}} \right)$$

Table 5 also presents the disaggregation of the total factor productivity in the case of Europe. The series has two sub-periods: from 1965 to 1976 and after this year to the end of the sample. Different sectoral composition seem to have been more important in explaining the productivity gap, and therefore the wage differential, in the last period. During the late sixties and early seventies the gap has closed dramatically relative to the European average, perhaps because this period corresponds to significant migration to other countries and urban zones by labor traditionally employed in the Portuguese agriculture. If Portugal had levels of capital intensity equivalent to the European average, there was no purchasing power parity deviations, and assuming no differences in the industrial relations gap, wages in Portugal would have been 30% to 35% lower than in Europe, for the period 1965 to 1976. From Table 1 one can see that during this period the industrial relations factor has increased monotonically in a significant manner. It is possible, therefore, that the mere reallocation of labor might have contributed to greater union power since organized labor is more evident in manufacturing and services than in agricultural related activities. To conclude that the declining trend in the industrial relations factor after 1977–78 is related to a larger sectoral composition gap is, however, incorrect. In our view the industrial relations factor has decreased due to corrective actions imposed by the market discipline. The widening of the sectoral composition gap, on the other hand, can be explained by the implementation of supply side policies in many European countries, delayed in Portugal by the successive governments. Extensive reorganization and massive layouts contributed to gains in labor productivity in the European industry relative to Portugal. And while in Europe gains were made in the industrial sector, in Portugal, since the late seventies, employment continued to decline in agriculture mainly at the expense of the services sector. This sectoral migration may not have produced significant changes in labor productivity at the aggregate level, given that agriculture and some services are in general sectors where productivity is low.

The residual factor is very important in the first half of the seventies and in the last years of the sample, explaining 25% to 30% of the nominal wage gap. This reveals the importance of further analysis that helps to understand other important factors that have been ignored here.

Looking briefly at the individual countries in Tables 6–8, Spain has made global productivity gains as well as Ireland, especially after this country joined the EEC. The situation relative to Greece has first worsen to recover slightly during the eighties. In all cases it is apparent that the capital used per unit of the labor factor is much lower in Portugal than in any other European country. The capital intensity gap has, however, an upward trend in the eighties relative to Spain and Greece, while it has declined relative

Table 6: Productivity gap between Portugal and Spain.

| | | | | | | Contribution to Wage Gap | | | |
|---|---|---|---|---|---|---|---|---|---|
| Year | Prod. | Cap. Int. | Fact. Prod. | Sect. Comp. | Resid. | Cap. Int. | Fact. Prod. | Sect. Comp. | Resid. |
| 1965 | 0.607 | 0.822 | 0.739 | 0.908 | 0.814 | 23.8% | 36.6% | 11.7% | 24.9% |
| 1970 | 0.642 | 0.839 | 0.765 | 1.089 | 0.703 | 27.8% | 42.3% | -13.5% | 55.8% |
| 1972 | 0.616 | 0.843 | 0.730 | 1.067 | 0.685 | 24.7% | 45.6% | -9.4% | 55.0% |
| 1974 | 0.581 | 0.821 | 0.709 | 1.003 | 0.706 | 31.0% | 54.0% | -0.5% | 54.5% |
| 1976 | 0.596 | 0.793 | 0.751 | 1.027 | 0.731 | 38.2% | 47.3% | -4.4% | 51.7% |
| 1978 | 0.536 | 0.776 | 0.691 | 0.863 | 0.800 | 28.8% | 42.0% | 16.7% | 25.2% |
| 1980 | 0.541 | 0.749 | 0.723 | 0.874 | 0.827 | 28.2% | 31.7% | 13.2% | 18.5% |
| 1982 | 0.528 | 0.743 | 0.711 | 0.916 | 0.776 | 30.1% | 34.7% | 8.9% | 25.8% |
| 1984 | 0.469 | 0.733 | 0.640 | 0.954 | 0.671 | 27.9% | 40.1% | 4.2% | 35.9% |
| 1985 | 0.472 | 0.731 | 0.645 | 0.950 | 0.680 | 28.7% | 40.0% | 4.7% | 35.3% |
| 1986 | 0.486 | 0.735 | 0.662 | 0.947 | 0.699 | 28.9% | 38.7% | 5.1% | 33.7% |
| 1987 | 0.503 | 0.745 | 0.676 | 0.937 | 0.722 | 32.1% | 42.6% | 7.1% | 35.42% |
| 1988 | 0.502 | 0.747 | 0.673 | 0.941 | 0.715 | 31.5% | 42.7% | 6.5% | 36.2% |

Table 7: Productivity gap between Portugal and Greece.

| | | | | | | Contribution to Wage Gap | | | |
|---|---|---|---|---|---|---|---|---|---|
| Year | Prod | Cap. Int. | Fact. Prod. | Sect. Comp. | Resid. | Cap. Int. | Fact. Prod. | Sect. Comp. | Resid. |
| 1970 | 0.884 | 1.097 | 0.806 | 1.193 | 0.675 | -13.0% | 30.2% | -24.7% | 54.9% |
| 1972 | 0.816 | 1.015 | 0.804 | 1.189 | 0.676 | -2.6% | 37.7% | -29.9% | 67.6% |
| 1974 | 0.832 | 0.946 | 0.879 | 1.118 | 0.787 | 14.1% | 32.4% | -28.1% | 60.5% |
| 1976 | 0.818 | 0.934 | 0.876 | 1.138 | 0.770 | 24.5% | 45.3% | -46.3% | 93.9% |
| 1978 | 0.743 | 0.927 | 0.802 | 0.948 | 0.846 | 11.2% | 32.4% | 7.9% | 24.5% |
| 1980 | 0.771 | 0.905 | 0.852 | 0.962 | 0.886 | 16.0% | 25.8% | 6.3% | 19.5% |
| 1982 | 0.819 | 0.916 | 0.895 | 1.004 | 0.891 | 12.2% | 15.4% | -0.6% | 15.9% |
| 1984 | 0.770 | 0.913 | 0.843 | 1.048 | 0.804 | 10.5% | 19.8% | -5.4% | 25.2% |
| 1985 | 0.785 | 0.914 | 0.859 | 1.042 | 0.824 | 11.3% | 19.0% | -5.2% | 24.2% |
| 1986 | 0.809 | 0.908 | 0.891 | 1.054 | 0.845 | 14.8% | 17.7% | -8.1% | 25.8% |
| 1987 | 0.861 | 0.907 | 0.949 | 1.025 | 0.926 | 24.0% | 12.9% | -6.1% | 19.0% |
| 1988 | 0.851 | 0.907 | 0.938 | 1.036 | 0.906 | 23.4% | 15.3% | -8.5% | 23.8% |

Table 8: Productivity gap between Portugal and Ireland.

| | | | | | | Contribution to Wage Gap | | | |
|---|---|---|---|---|---|---|---|---|---|
| Year | Prod | Cap. Int. | Fact. Prod. | Sect. Comp. | Resid. | Cap. Int. | Fact. Prod. | Sect. Comp. | Resid. |
| 1965 | 0.696 | 0.839 | 0.829 | 0.909 | 0.912 | 16.1% | 17.1% | 8.7% | 8.5% |
| 1970 | 0.757 | 0.917 | 0.825 | 1.088 | 0.758 | 9.9% | 22.0% | -9.6% | 31.6% |
| 1972 | 0.725 | 0.889 | 0.816 | 1.070 | 0.762 | 13.4% | 23.3% | -7.7% | 31.0% |
| 1974 | 0.705 | 0.858 | 0.822 | 1.017 | 0.808 | 23.7% | 30.5% | -2.6% | 33.1% |
| 1976 | 0.685 | 0.845 | 0.811 | 1.029 | 0.788 | 34.7% | 43.2% | -5.9% | 49.1% |
| 1978 | 0.641 | 0.851 | 0.753 | 0.846 | 0.890 | 19.3% | 34.1% | 20.1% | 14.0% |
| 1980 | 0.674 | 0.836 | 0.805 | 0.856 | 0.941 | 17.8% | 21.5% | 15.5% | 6.0% |
| 1982 | 0.649 | 0.823 | 0.788 | 0.897 | 0.879 | 18.6% | 22.7% | 10.4% | 12.3% |
| 1984 | 0.578 | 0.797 | 0.726 | 0.938 | 0.773 | 17.8% | 25.2% | 5.0% | 20.2% |
| 1985 | 0.580 | 0.784 | 0.740 | 0.931 | 0.795 | 19.2% | 23.8% | 5.7% | 18.2% |
| 1986 | 0.607 | 0.776 | 0.782 | 0.941 | 0.831 | 20.2% | 19.6% | 4.9% | 14.7% |
| 1987 | 0.594 | 0.761 | 0.780 | 0.934 | 0.834 | 24.6% | 22.3% | 6.0% | 16.3% |
| 1988 | 0.584 | 0.750 | 0.778 | 0.946 | 0.822 | 27.1% | 23.6% | 5.2% | 18.4% |

to Ireland. With respect to Ireland this is important because it explains a significant share of the nominal wage gap.

As expected, the contribution of the sectoral composition to the gap is lower for the three countries than for the European average. Note, also, that in the case of Greece, sectoral composition alone would justify higher wages in Portugal, situation that seemed to persist for the case of Spain in the seventies, though later reversed. More recent data would allow a more careful characterization of the sectoral composition gap, with particular attention to the effects of the funds provided under the EEC entry treaty.

The unexplained part of the productivity gap is very important in the cases of Spain and Greece. For Ireland, however, it is neither as high nor as volatile as it is for the other two countries.

## 4.2 Decomposing the Industrial Relations Gap

The industrial relations gap combines the effect of many factors, e.g., bargaining power or the trade-off between job security and salaries. At this stage, we only isolate differences in social security payments. As noted before, the effect of social contributions depends on the conditions describing the equilibrium in the labor markets and, in particular, on the elasticity of the labor supply curves in Portugal and abroad. On the one hand, if the supply of labor is perfectly elastic, differences in social security contributions are fully reflected on the nominal wage gap. If, on the other hand, the supply for labor is vertical, social security contributions have no effect on the nominal wage gap. Under the first case the industrial relations gap does not depend on the social security contributions; hence, in the analysis so far, we consider the last case, decomposing the industrial relations gap assuming the case of a flat labor supply curve. The reader should keep in mind that the analysis that follows is purely sensitive. We are not claiming that the supply curve is flat or of any other particular form, since in our work there is no evidence supporting that or any other claim. Simply, we want to measure the effects on the wage gap by means of a very crude supply side adjustment, keeping constant the contribution of the industrial relations factor. This will allow us to separate union power that is directly reflected on wages from differences in social benefits between Portugal and other European countries.[16]

[16] A more rigorous analysis of the supply effects would take into account the possibility that the labor supply curves in Portugal and abroad imply differences on the effect of social security contribution on the nominal wage.

Table 9: Industrial relations gap between Portugal and Europe.

| Year | Indust. Relat. | Firm Rent | Soc. Sec. | Cont. to Wage Gap Firm Rent | Soc. Sec. |
|---|---|---|---|---|---|
| 1965 | 0.826 | 0.859 | 0.961 | 10.8% | 2.8% |
| 1970 | 0.895 | 0.920 | 0.972 | 7.0% | 2.4% |
| 1972 | 0.981 | 1.008 | 0.973 | -0.7% | 2.3% |
| 1974 | 1.104 | 1.144 | 0.965 | -13.6% | 3.6% |
| 1976 | 1.309 | 1.358 | 0.964 | -34.4% | 4.1% |
| 1978 | 1.183 | 1.226 | 0.966 | -16.8% | 2.9% |
| 1980 | 1.132 | 1.168 | 0.969 | -12.2% | 2.5% |
| 1982 | 1.115 | 1.165 | 0.957 | -12.5% | 3.6% |
| 1984 | 1.097 | 1.162 | 0.944 | -10.7% | 4.1% |
| 1985 | 1.078 | 1.142 | 0.944 | -9.7% | 4.2% |
| 1986 | 1.054 | 1.093 | 0.965 | -6.5% | 2.6% |

Table 10: Industrial relations gap between Portugal and Spain.

| Year | Indust. Relat. | Firm Rent | Soc. Sec. | Contr. to Wage Gap Firm Rent | Soc. Sec. |
|---|---|---|---|---|---|
| 1965 | 0.743 | 0.736 | 1.010 | 37.1% | -1.2% |
| 1970 | 0.817 | 0.823 | 0.992 | 30.7% | 1.2% |
| 1972 | 0.861 | 0.873 | 0.987 | 19.7% | 2.0% |
| 1974 | 0.999 | 1.028 | 0.973 | -4.3% | 4.4% |
| 1976 | 1.131 | 1.148 | 0.985 | -22.7% | 2.4% |
| 1978 | 1.062 | 1.136 | 0.935 | -14.4% | 7.6% |
| 1980 | 1.030 | 1.114 | 0.925 | -10.5% | 7.6% |
| 1982 | 1.026 | 1.119 | 0.917 | -11.4% | 8.8% |
| 1984 | 1.030 | 1.142 | 0.902 | -11.9% | 9.3% |
| 1985 | 1.029 | 1.141 | 0.902 | -12.1% | 9.5% |
| 1986 | 1.042 | 1.131 | 0.921 | -11.6% | 7.7% |

The disaggregation uses expression (17), taking $\gamma$ equal to one,

$$\frac{1-\mu}{1-\mu^*} = \left( \frac{\frac{WL}{PY}(1-c)^\gamma}{\frac{W^*L^*}{P^*Y^*}(1-c^*)^\gamma} \right) \left( \frac{1-c^*}{1-c} \right)^\gamma .$$

and the results are presented in Tables 9–12.[17]

In Table 9 the industrial relations gap is decomposed for the average of the other eleven EEC countries. One immediately notices that after having net out social contributions, employers' rents were lower than for the case of $\gamma = 0$. This is because of higher social security contributions in Europe than in Portugal, also reflected in numbers less than 1 under the column Social Security.

Interestingly, while for Spain and Greece the social security contributions may justify lower wages in Portugal, the reverse is true for Ireland.

[17] Due to lack of data we had to stop this analysis in 1986.

Table 11: Industrial relations gap between Portugal and Greece.

| | | | | Contr. to Wage Gap | |
|---|---|---|---|---|---|
| Year | Indust. Relat. | Firm Rent | Soc. Sec. | Firm Rent | Soc. Sec. |
| 1970 | 0.789 | 0.876 | 0.901 | 18.6% | 14.6% |
| 1972 | 0.895 | 0.979 | 0.914 | 3.7% | 15.5% |
| 1974 | 1.097 | 1.193 | 0.919 | -44.5% | 21.2% |
| 1976 | 1.270 | 1.392 | 0.912 | -118.6% | 32.9% |
| 1978 | 1.025 | 1.115 | 0.920 | -16.0% | 12.3% |
| 1980 | 0.998 | 1.120 | 0.891 | -18.2% | 18.5% |
| 1982 | 0.914 | 1.065 | 0.858 | -8.7% | 21.1% |
| 1984 | 0.860 | 1.015 | 0.847 | -1.8% | 19.2% |
| 1985 | 0.819 | 0.964 | 0.850 | 4.6% | 20.3% |
| 1986 | 0.824 | 0.951 | 0.867 | 7.7% | 22.0% |

Table 12: Industrial relations gap between Portugal and Ireland.

| | | | | Contr. to Wage Gap | |
|---|---|---|---|---|---|
| Year | Indust. Relat. | Firm Rent | Soc. Sec. | Firm Rent | Soc. Sec. |
| 1965 | 0.732 | 0.683 | 1.072 | 34.9% | -6.3% |
| 1970 | 0.786 | 0.725 | 1.084 | 36.7% | -9.2% |
| 1972 | 0.903 | 0.822 | 1.098 | 22.3% | -10.7% |
| 1974 | 0.966 | 0.895 | 1.079 | 17.2% | -11.8% |
| 1976 | 1.182 | 1.099 | 1.076 | -19.5% | -15.0% |
| 1978 | 1.084 | 0.995 | 1.090 | 0.7% | -10.3% |
| 1980 | 0.958 | 0.870 | 1.101 | 13.8% | -9.5% |
| 1982 | 1.001 | 0.922 | 1.086 | 7.7% | -7.9% |
| 1984 | 0.975 | 0.899 | 1.084 | 8.3% | -6.3% |
| 1985 | 0.965 | 0.887 | 1.088 | 9.5% | -6.6% |
| 1986 | 0.937 | 0.841 | 1.115 | 13.8% | -8.8% |

Moreover, the level of the social security gap does not seem to close relative to either country. The effect relative to the case of Greece appears to be too high, which may reflect that our set of assumptions is particularly inappropriate in comparing Portugal with this country.

# 5 Conclusions

This paper is an investigation of the reasons explaining why Portuguese wages are lower relative to those in other countries of the European Community. Using a simple model the wage gap is first decomposed into an exchange rate component, a productivity component and an industrial relations component. The productivity gap is further decomposed into a capital intensity gap and a sectoral composition gap. In the case of the industrial relations gap sensitivity analysis is performed to evaluate the effect of differences in social security contributions in Portugal and Europe.

Portuguese wages are significantly lower than the European average, roughly 70% lower. After having improved in the late sixties and early seventies, followed by a dramatic improvement in the years after the 1974 revolution, wages in Portugal have been in a declining trend, with abrupt drops in 1978 and in 1984. Recent observations, however, seem to show that the gap is closing after Portugal has joined the EEC, in 1986. This effect is obvious from the exchange rate factor, displaying an approximation of price levels between Portugal and Europe. Similar reason could explain the further increase in the industrial relations factor in favor of Portugal. In any case, Portuguese salaries are still significantly lower than those in Spain, Greece and Ireland, three countries in a state of economic development below the European average. Portuguese wages are 60% to 65% lower than Spanish ones and 35% lower than in Greece.

Of the various components explaining the gap, productivity appears to be the most important, although the exchange rate has been playing a greater role since the mid-seventies. In the last twenty years there have not been gains in productivity that could help to close the gap relative to Europe, while having a continuous deterioration relative to Spain. The capital intensity explains an important part of the productivity gap. This is especially true in the case of Spain. As expected, the sectoral composition of activity is more significant in explaining the wage gap in the case of Europe than for each of the three countries considered. The industrial relations gap had a clear turning point in 1974. Since the revolution the contribution to the wage gap due to industrial relations has disappeared, except in relation to the Greece. That is, if there was no gap due to the other factors, labor laws and union power would have taken Portuguese wages above the European average.

Provided that the relevant data could be found, many other factors could be analyzed to extend and improve our investigation of the wage gap. Perhaps, a modified production function, adjusted for differences in education of the labor force, could uncover an education factor in the productivity gap. A different extension looks at the interaction between financing constraints and business investment in trying to account for differences in the functioning of the financial markets.

# Appendix: The Data

To develop the work outlined in the preceding section, we obtained the appropriate database. In order to avoid incompatibilities among the series used, we tried, whenever possible, to use data from the same sources, in particular obtaining the same aggregates, for the different countries, from the same statistics.

The main statistical sources were the EUROSTAT data from the EEC.[18] There we got series for

- Nominal Output (at current prices in ECUs) — $PY$
- Real Output (at 1980 prices and Purchasing Power Standards) — $Y$
- Wage Bill (as percentage of the of the output) — $wb$
- Wage Employment — $WE$
- Total Employment — $L$
- Sectoral Employment — $L_i$
- Sectoral Output (at current prices in ECUs) — $Y_i$
- Social Security Contributions (as percentage of output) — $ss$
- Gross Fixed Capital Formation (at current prices in ECUs) — $PI$
- Real Gross Fixed Capital Formation (at 1980 prices and Purchasing Power Standards) — $I$
- Capital Consumption (at current prices in ECUs) — $PD$

Then we computed the series we needed to implement the methodology of section 2.

The wage index was computed as

$$W = \frac{wbY}{100WE}\,;$$

the price index was computed as

$$P = \frac{PY}{Y}\,;$$

the effective share of labor in the output as

$$\frac{WL}{PY} = \frac{wbL}{100WE}\,;$$

the social security contributions relative to the wages as

$$SSC = ss\frac{PY}{WL}\,;$$

[18] Some of the data for 1987-88 was directly received from the EEC Statistics Office. We thank José António Girão for supplying us with these data.

the sectoral structure of employment as

$$l_i = \frac{L_i}{L} ;$$

the sectoral structure of output as

$$y_i = \frac{Y_i}{Y} .$$

The series for the Capital Stock were not available, so we constructed them from the available data on Investment ($I_t$) and Depreciations ($D_t$).[19] Let $K_t$ be the correspondent (unknown) series of capital, which satisfies

$$K_{t+1} = K_t + I_t - D_t .$$

We assume that capital is depreciated according to the method of perpetual inventory, with depreciation rate $\delta$, but there are shocks in the depreciation rate, $\epsilon_t$, so that

$$\frac{D_t}{K_t} = \delta + \epsilon_t .$$

The shocks are assumed to exhibit first order serial correlation

$$\epsilon_{t+1} = \rho\epsilon_t + v_{t+1} ,$$

where $v_t$ are independent and identically distributed with zero expectation.

We use a least squares approach to estimate the series of capital and the depreciation rate. Consider the problem

$$\min_{\{e_t\}} \sum_{t=2}^{T} (e_t - \rho e_{t-1})^2$$

$$\text{s.t.} \begin{cases} K_{t+1} = K_t + I_t - D_t \\ D_t = (\delta + e_t)K_t \end{cases} \qquad 1 \leq t \leq T$$

This problem can be solved by nonlinear least squares, with the usual techniques. We estimate the depreciation rate, $\hat{\delta}$, the first value of the capital stock, $\hat{K}_1$, and the correlation coefficient, $\hat{\rho}$.[20]

[19] The data on Investment and Depreciations were taken from the EUROSTAT, except for Portugal which were taken from Santos (1984).

[20] The estimation was performed for the period 1972–1988, in which we had consecutive observations. The capital stock for 1965 and 1970 was estimated as $\hat{K}_t = D_t/\hat{\delta}$. To avoid a gap between the 1970 and 1972 values of the capital stock, the estimation restricted $e_1 = 0$. For a more detailed description of the procedure see Branco (1991).

# References


BRANCO, F. (1991): "Constructing a Series of Capital from Series of Depreciations and Investment," *Mimeo.*

BRANCO, F. AND G. SAINT-PAUL (1989): "A Macroeconomic Model for the Portuguese Economy," Departamento Central de Planeamento, Lisbon.

EEC: *Eurostat National Accounts*, various issues, Luxembourg.

EEC: *Eurostat Review*, various issues, Luxembourg.

KRAVIS, I. (1984): "Comparative Studies of National Incomes and Prices," *Journal of Economic Literature*, **22**, 1–39.

KRAVIS, I. AND R. LIPSEY (1983): "Toward an Explanation of National Price Levels," Princeton Studies in International Finance, 52.

LEWIS, G. (1984), "Union Relative Wage Effects," in *The Handbook of Labor Economics*, ed. by Ashenfelter and Layard, Vol. 2, 1139–1181. Amsterdam: North Holland-Elsevier Science Publishers.

MINCER, J. (1962), "On-the-Job Training: Costs, Returns, and some Implications," *Journal of Political Economy*, **70**, S50–S79.

MINCER, J. (1974), *Schooling, Experience and Earnings.* New York: Columbia University Press.

OECD: *Historical Statistics*, various issues, Paris.

OECD: *Labour Force Statistics*, various issues, Paris.

OECD (1990): *National Accounts – Main Aggregates 1960-88*, Paris.

OECD: *Revenue Statistics*, various issues, Paris.

PENCAVEL, J. (1984): "The Tradeoff between Wages and Employment in Trade Union Objectives," *Quarterly Journal of Economics*, **99**, 215–231.

SAINT-PAUL, G. (1989), "Decomposing the Wage Gap between Portugal and other European Countries," Departamento Central de Planeamento, Lisbon.

SANTOS, E. (1984), "O Stock de Capital na Economia Portuguesa (1953-81)," Documento de Trabalho #6, Banco de Portugal.

# Some Aspects of the Portuguese Labour Market, 1977–1988: Neutrality, Hysteresis and the Wage Gap

Leonor Modesto
Manuel Leite Monteiro
João César das Neves

## 1 Introduction

The purpose of this paper is to analyze, in a simple way, the economic functioning of the portuguese labour market. Being the result of several decades of "corporatist" interference and of the changes resulting from the revolution of 74 and the entry into the EEC, the portuguese labour market deserves a rigorous and profound study. This work pretends to be just a first approximation to such an investigation.

The study of labour economics has flourished in the last years in several models and insights that have changed the way science looked at these problems. This debate, which has strong relations with the great revolution under way in macroeconomics,[1] aims at building an entirely new form, of understanding the labour market.

These new trends in research provide some very interesting results when applied to the portuguese experience. The paper highlights some of the most simple and direct ones. In section 2 a brief discussion of the trends in theoury is provided. Section 3 discusses the "neutrality" of the portuguese wage path, while section 4 applies the "insiders-outsiders" framework to

[1] See, for examples of the new trends in macroeconomics and their relations with labour economics, Blanchard and Fisher (1989), specially chapter 9, and Phelps (1990).

the portuguese reality, estimating some models of this school. In the final section the concept of wage gap is analyzed, using the results of the preceding models.

# 2 The Labour Market and the Portuguese Experience

It is frequently stated and widely believed that the problem of european unemployment is a problem of excessive real wages. Putting it in other words, european unemployment is diagnosed as being of the classical type,[2] i.e., at current real wages with the current capital stock, all the labour force, cannot be employed profitably. To support this view empirical evidence concerning the widening of the wage gap in Europe has been presented.[3]

But high real wages per se are not enough to explain the observed persistence of unemployment. This phenomenon is only observed when there is wage rigidity, i.e., if wages do not tend to respond to unemployment conditions.

One key mechanism behind the high and persistent unemployment is therefore the wage formation process. Several authors have addressed this point and several theoretical explanations have been put forward along with some empirical evidence. Among these the "hysteresis" concept by Blanchard and Summers (1987) and Lindbeck and Snower (1988) received a wide interest.

Other authors (see, e.g., Newell and Symons (1987)) have stressed the relationship between wage-setting institutions and the behaviour of unemployment. The relevant distinction to be made here is between a decentralized and a corporatist labour market. According to these authors, in a corporatist wage bargaining model, one should expect a larger effect of unemployment on the real wage and a faster adjustment of wages.

On the empirical side, one of the major findings that seems to emerge is that in Europe productivity gains tend to be rapidly fed into wage increases.[4] In Germany, for example, since the early eighties, unemployment has remained high (about 8% of the labour force). This phenomenon has been attributed, among other factors, to the compulsory collective wage policy. According to Neumann et al (1990), trade unions in Germany have been successful in shaping contract wages according to the "neutrality" doctrine, i.e., wage increases are made equal to the sum of expected inflation and productivity growth. This phenomenon, that is not present in the

[2] We mean classical in the sense of Malinvaud (1977).

[3] See for example Bruno and Sachs (1985).

[4] See for example Drèze and Bean (1990).

U.S., leads to capital-labour substitution aggravating therefore the unemployment problem. Moreover, it has also been found that in Europe, wages do not respond significantly to the level of unemployment. However this response seems to be slightly bigger in countries with corporatist labour markets.[5]

The portuguese reality and how this discussion applies to it is the specific question approached in this paper . During the eighties, the labour share declined steadily in Portugal. The real wage has followed a cyclical trajectory in the last twenty years, with strong rises and falls. Unemployment has declined lately and it is commonly believed that we are now in a situation of full employment in some sectors. But this situation is accompanied by the existence of employment with "precarious contracts", meaning that the term of the contract is very short and the conditions are not the normal ones. The recent portuguese experience contrasts therefore with the situation observed in other European countries.

This special and interesting reality has triggered a line of analysis and research to attempt an economic understanding of the mechanisms in presence. Unfortunately the important, rigorous and scientific studies that have been presented on the portuguese reality are very few and unconnected. These are directed either on the definition of the real dimension of the phenomenon, like Ramos and Abecassis (1980) and Confraria and Monteiro (1988), or on its analysis, like Santos (1980) and Barosa (1984), (1986). The present paper is simply a research program that continues this tradition of "portuguese labour economics", with some preliminary results.

The portuguese labour market has some special structural important characteristics that relate to the particular values of its indicators. Although this is not the place to analyze them thoroughly, a few comments are in line.

It can be said that the present situation of the portuguese structure is not "corporatist" in the theoretical sense used above. The social agreements between government, unions and employers confederations represent just guidelines and are not compulsory for the bargaining processes between firms and unions.[6] These are made by direct free negotiation between the parts. On the other hand, the legal framework can be said to be somewhat strict in certain aspects, specially in the firing process.[7] This is one of the explanations for the referred percentage of "precarious situations" in the labour contract, as an attempt to elude the overprotected conditions of the

[5] See on this issue Newell and Symons (1987) and also Drèze and Bean (1990).

[6] See Pinto (ed.) (1986) pages 69–75, 251–262, Castela (1984) and Cavaco Silva (ed.) (1983).

[7] See Pinto pages 89–96.

full legal contract.[8]

The following sections attempt to show how these structural characteristics have influenced the path of the indicators of the labour market in the last decade, and to highlight some of the main economic points of the functioning of the system.

# 3 Neutrality

One of the theories of contract wage determination states that wages are determined in collective negotiations between trade unions and employer's associations and are set in order to take full account of expected inflation and productivity growth. Such contracts, as Neumann, Schmidt and Schulte (1990) state, are said to be "neutral" with respect to employment and to be "fair" with respect to the distribution of income between labour and capital.

In this section we present a simple model which allows us to test whether the neutrality doctrine has been the rule in Portugal. We state that:

$$\log w_{it}^* = a_0 + a_1[\log y_{it} + \log p_t]$$

with $a_1$ equal to unity from neutrality and where $w_i^*$ is the desired level of nominal wages in industrial branch $i$, $y_i$ is the branch productivity and $p$ is the general level of prices.

The actual level of wages, $w_{it}$, is obtained through an error correction mechanism:

$$\Delta \log w_{it} = \beta_1 \Delta \log w_{it}^* + (1 - \beta_3)[\log w_{it-1}^* - \log w_{it-1}]$$

and so wages will be dependent on the current and lagged levels of productivity and prices and on the lagged wage rate:

$$\begin{aligned}\log w_{it} = A_0 + \beta_1 a_1[\log y_{it} + \log p_t] + \beta_3 \log w_{it} \\ + (1 - \beta_1 - \beta_3)a_1[\log y_{it-1} + \log p_{t-1}]\end{aligned}$$

This model was estimated for Portugal using disaggregated data for the manufacturing sector. The estimation was carried out for nine separate branches, according to the Portuguese Classification of Economic Activities of 1973. The branches considered were:

[8] On this issue note that portuguese employers organizations assessed the importance of obstacles to the termination of employment contracts as being "fundamental" while classifying the regulatory constraints of temporary work as "minor or insignificant". Source (IOE, 1985) referred in Emerson (1988).

- 31: Food, Beverages and Tobacco Industries;
- 32: Textile, Clothing, and Footwear Industries;
- 33: Wood, Cork and Furniture Industries;
- 34: Paper, Graphic Arts and Printing Industries;
- 35: Chemical Industries;
- 36: Nonmetallic Industries;
- 37: Metallurgy;
- 38: Metal Products and Transport Machinery, Equipment and Material Industries;
- 39: Other Manufacturing Industries;
- 3: Total of Manufacturing Industry.

The disaggregated data for these branches did not allow us to calculate real productivity values because data is only available at current prices, so we had to assume that the relevant price for workers is the implicit deflator of the sector's value added. It should also be noted that the wage values used in the estimations are not the negotiated ones, but the actual values, i.e., the firms wage bill divided by the number of employees.

The OLS estimation results of this model for the period 1978–1987 are presented in Table 1.

In estimating these equations, some restrictions had to be imposed (namely on the constant and on the dynamic coefficients) in order to guarantee significant estimates for the coefficients and to diminish the autocorrelation of the estimated residuals. With the incorporation of these restrictions, we estimated the "neutrality equation" with an error correction mechanism for branches 34 and 37, both with a null current impact of productivity on wages, and with a partial adjustment mechanism for all the other branches. In these, there is not an intercept for branches 32, 35, 36 and 38.

Table 2 presents the estimated values of the original coefficients for each branch.

We can see that neutrality, measured by the coefficient $a_1$, may be assumed in the long-run for some of the industrial branches. In fact, this long-term coefficient is near unity for branches 33, 37 and 38 which means that all the increases in prices and in productivity will eventually be fed into wage increases. It should be noted that this same result was obtained

Table 1: OLS estimation results.

| | | Product. | Wage$(t-1)$ | Product.$(t-1)$ | Constant |
|---|---|---|---|---|---|
| | Estimate | 0.180402 | 0.770794 | | 0.149269 |
| 31 | t-stat | 1.0925 | 3.6143 | | 5.2469 |
| | | $SSR$ = 0.00534 | $\bar{R}^2$ = 0.9980 | $DW$ = 2.187 | |
| | Estimate | 0.512188 | 0.437496 | | |
| 32 | t-stat | 12.362 | 7.4447 | | |
| | | $SSR$ = 0.00451 | $\bar{R}^2$ = 0.9995 | $DW$ = 1.463 | |
| | Estimate | 0.221775 | 0.786898 | | 0.079248 |
| 33 | t-stat | 2.6649 | 9.9680 | | 1.7873 |
| | | $SSR$ = 0.00740 | $\bar{R}^2$ = 0.9967 | $DW$ = 2.379 | |
| | Estimate | | 0.685014 | 0.258974 | 0.201759 |
| 34 | t-stat | | 3.8639 | 1.7985 | 10.040 |
| | | $SSR$ = 0.00807 | $\bar{R}^2$ = 0.9969 | $DW$ = 1.653 | |
| | Estimate | 0.459211 | 0.513618 | | |
| 35 | t-stat | 3.7776 | 2.9997 | | |
| | | $SSR$ = 0.04546 | $\bar{R}^2$ = 0.9966 | $DW$ = 1.354 | |
| | Estimate | 0.670095 | 0.258527 | | |
| 36 | t-stat | 5.9158 | 1.7037 | | |
| | | $SSR$ = 0.02016 | $\bar{R}^2$ = 0.9982 | $DW$ = 1.025 | |
| | Estimate | | 0.863074 | 0.14393 | 0.163776 |
| 37 | t-stat | | 9.6469 | 1.5167 | 5.0932 |
| | | $SSR$ = 0.01474 | $\bar{R}^2$ = 0.9943 | $DW$ = 1.981 | |
| | Estimate | 0.644054 | 0.348178 | | |
| 38 | t-stat | 9.1828 | 3.9419 | | |
| | | $SSR$ = 0.04546 | $\bar{R}^2$ = 0.9966 | $DW$ = 1.354 | |
| | Estimate | 0.108894 | 0.873782 | | 0.873782 |
| 39 | t-stat | 1.5516 | 11.441 | | 9.6268 |
| | | $SSR$ = 0.00442 | $\bar{R}^2$ = 0.9977 | $DW$ = 2.955 | |
| | Estimate | 0.286106 | 0.675328 | | 0.106902 |
| 3 | t-stat | 1.7341 | 3.6312 | | 2.5774 |
| | | $SSR$ = 0.00503 | $\bar{R}^2$ = 0.9978 | $DW$ = 1.196 | |

Table 2: Estimated values of the original coefficients.

| | $\beta_1$ | $\beta_3$ | $a_1$ |
|---|---|---|---|
| 31 | 0.229 | 0.771 | 0.787 |
| 32 | 0.563 | 0.437 | 0.911 |
| 33 | 0.213 | 0.787 | 1.041 |
| 34 | 0.000 | 0.685 | 0.822 |
| 35 | 0.486 | 0.514 | 0.944 |
| 36 | 0.741 | 0.259 | 0.904 |
| 37 | 0.000 | 0.863 | 1.051 |
| 38 | 0.652 | 0.348 | 0.988 |
| 39 | 0.126 | 0.874 | 0.863 |
| 3 | 0.325 | 0.675 | 0.881 |

Table 3: Dynamic pattern of the adjustment in wages.

| Time | 0 | 1 | 2 | 3 |
|---|---|---|---|---|
| 31 | 22.9% | 40.6% | 54.2% | 64.7% |
| 32 | 56.3% | 80.9% | 91.6% | 96.3% |
| 33 | 21.3% | 38.1% | 51.3% | 61.7% |
| 34 | 0.0% | 31.5% | 53.1% | 67.9% |
| 35 | 48.6% | 73.6% | 86.5% | 93.0% |
| 36 | 74.1% | 93.3% | 98.3% | 99.6% |
| 37 | 0.0% | 13.7% | 25.5% | 35.7% |
| 38 | 65.2% | 87.9% | 95.8% | 98.5% |
| 39 | 12.6% | 23.7% | 33.3% | 41.7% |
| 3 | 32.5% | 54.4% | 69.2% | 79.2% |

for all but one of the industrial sectors of Germany with a static model (see Neumann, Schmidt and Schulte (1990)). For the portuguese manufacturing sector as a whole, almost 90% of nominal productivity growth is transmitted into wage increases in the long run. The "neutrality" coefficients are, in some cases, smaller than one, but it should be noted that in estimation the coefficients associated with productivity were not always significantly estimated, so it can not be rejected that wage negotiations are "neutral". Despite these similarities, the dynamic process is different across the various branches. In Table 3 the reader can find the percentage of the adjustment in wages that is completed after several periods for each branch.

This table shows that the dynamic adjustment following a productivity shock varies across branches. The contemporaneous impact on wages varies from 0 to almost 3/4 of the total long-term impact. It should also be noted that for branches 32, 35, 36 and 38 more than 90% of the wage adjustment to a productivity shock is realized in not more than three years.

# 4 Hysteresis

In 1987, Blanchard and Summers, in a now classical paper, put forward the idea that the equilibrium rate of unemployment in one period depends on last period's unemployment. The existence of time dependence in the rate of unemployment was named "hysteresis" by these authors.

This theory identifies two possible sources of unemployment persistence; first, and mainly, excessive power of a few workers (insiders) in the process of wage setting (membership theories); and second, the high level of long term unemployment, associated with little pressure of long term unemployed on wage setting (duration theories).

Blanchard and Summers (1987) model is a model of wage bargaining of the "right to manage" type, i.e., workers and firms bargain over the nominal wage but the firm determines the level of employment. Employment is then always on the labour demand curve. Then they make the additional assumption that the type of workers that matters in the wage setting process are the "insiders". They assume that insiders are sufficiently strong to set the nominal wage unilaterally and that they set it so as to make expected employment equal to some desired level, that most of the time is the size of their group (measured by past employment), allowing also for some pressure from outsiders (measured by expected unemployment).

Their model contains therefore two equations.

1. The labour demand curve specified along the lines proposed by Alogoskoufis and Manning (1988) allowing for labour demand sluggishness

$$n_t = \delta n_{t-1} - (1-\delta)\lambda(w-p)_t + \epsilon_t \tag{1}$$

where $n$ is the logarithm of employment, $w$ is the logarithm of the nominal wage, $p$ is the logarithm of the price level and $\epsilon_t$ the level of other factors that influence labour demand at time $t$. $\lambda$ is the long run elasticity of labour demand relatively to the real wage and $\delta$ is the dynamic adjustment coefficient that measures the degree of labour demand sluggishness.

2. The wage setting equation

$$E[n_t] = n_{t-1} + b[\bar{Z}_t - E(n_t)]$$

that we can rewrite as

$$E[n_t] = (1-\alpha)\bar{Z}_t + \alpha n_{t-1} \tag{2}$$

where $\bar{Z}_t$ is the logarithm of the effective labour force and $\alpha = 1/(1-b)$ is the coefficient that measures the degree of unemployment hysteresis.

With $\alpha = 1$ we have the pure insider model or full hysteresis. When $\alpha = 0$ we get the case where nominal wages and set so as to employ the whole labour force.

Solving equations (1) and (2) we obtain the equilibrium values of nominal wage and employment

$$w_t = E[p_t] + \frac{1}{(1-\delta)\lambda}[(\delta-\alpha)n_{t-1} - (1-\alpha)\bar{Z}_t + E(\epsilon_t)] \tag{3}$$

$$n_t = E[n_t] + [\epsilon_t - E(\epsilon_t)] + (1-\delta)\alpha\,(p_t - E(p_t)) \tag{4}$$

or

$$(n_t - \bar{Z}_t) = \alpha\,(n_{t-1} - \bar{Z}_t) + [\epsilon_t - E(\epsilon_t)] + (1-\delta)\lambda\,(p_t - E(p_t))\ . \tag{4'}$$

According to (4) employment will deviate from its expected level only due to unexpected shocks. From (4′) we can see that deviations of employment around the effective labour force follow a first order autoregressive process where $\alpha$ measures the degree of persistence.

While very widely used, this model has been subjected to some criticisms. The main comments centered around its intrinsic static characteristics[9] and the lack of effects of expected demand shocks on employment. Modesto and Neves (1990) tried to answer this by generalizing the original work. Considering basically the same type of wage bargaining model, the generalized model introduced an additional sluggishness in the wage setting equation.[10]

It was assumed that insiders are not fully able to set the nominal wage so as to make expected employment equal to some desired level because there is a certain wage inertia. This means that equation (1) is maintained but that equation (2) is modified in the following way:

$$E[n_t] = \beta n_{t-1} + (1-\beta)\,[\delta n_{t-1} - (1-\delta)\lambda[w_{t-1} - E(p_t)] + E(\epsilon_t)] \\ + b[\bar{Z}_t - E(n_t)]$$

It is easily seen that this structure reproduces that of Blanchard and Summers if $\beta = 1$ (no wage inertia).

The two models presented can be estimated to analyze the portuguese economy. For this, some manipulation is necessary (see Modesto and Neves, 1990, pages 7-13). This includes the introduction of the unemployment rate $u_t$ and $\bar{u}_t$ the natural rate of unemployment, (assuming that $[n_t - \bar{Z}_t] = -[u_t - \bar{u}_t]$) and $(\bar{w}-\bar{p})_t$, the level of real wages that is compatible with full employment of the effective labour force, i.e.,

$$\bar{Z}_t = -\lambda(\bar{w}-\bar{p})_t + E(\epsilon_t)/(1-\delta)$$

The models to be estimated are as follows:

### Model 1

$$[u_t - \bar{u}] = \alpha[u_{t-1} - \bar{u}] - [\epsilon_t - E(\epsilon_t)] - (1-\delta)\lambda[p_t - E(p_t)]$$

$$w_t - E(p_t) = (\bar{w} - \bar{p}) - \frac{(\delta - \alpha)}{(1-\delta)\lambda}[u_{t-1} - \bar{u}]$$

---

[9] Blanchard and Summers originally considered a static labour demand schedule, i.e., $\delta = 0$.

[10] This should not be confused with labour demand sluggishness in the Alogoskoufis and Manning (1988) way.

## Model 2

$$
\begin{aligned}
[u_t - \bar{u}] = {} & [\beta + (1-\beta)\delta]\alpha[u_{t-1} - \bar{u}] \\
& -(1-\beta)(1-\delta)\alpha\lambda[(w_{t-1} - E(p_t)) - (\bar{w} - \bar{p})] \\
& -[\epsilon_t - E(\epsilon_t)] - (1-\delta)\lambda[p_t - E(p_t)] \\
w_t - E(p_t) = {} & (\bar{w} - \bar{p}) - \left[\frac{\delta - [\beta + (1-\beta)\delta]\alpha}{(1-\delta)\lambda}\right][u_{t-1} - \bar{u}] \\
& + (1-\beta)\alpha[(w_{t-1} - E(p_t)) - (\bar{w} - \bar{p})] \,.
\end{aligned}
$$

In what concerns the unexpected shock variables, instead of simply moving them into the error term of the equations, the information contained in the business surveys questionnaires was used. In Portugal, as in many other countries, manufacturing firms are asked to assess the state of their demand relatively to its normal level, i.e., firms are supposed to classify their current level of demand as being "above normal", "below normal" or "normal". Using a quantification technique[11] one can transform this qualitative information into a macroeconomic indicator that express the state of demand relatively to its normal level.[12] It is both reassuring and interesting to note that this variable, that can be interpreted as giving us a measure of unexpected nominal demand shocks,[13] follows closely the evolution of the degree of utilization of capacities in the manufacturing sector. In terms of our model we felt that this variable ($S_t$) could function as a proxy for the total effect of unexpected shocks, i.e., that

$$[\epsilon_t - E(\epsilon_t)] + (1-\delta)\alpha[p_t - E(p_t)] = \theta S_t$$

where $\theta$ is a parameter to be estimated.

The estimation results of these models, for the portuguese labour market in the period 1977–1988, can be summarized in the following equations, taken from Modesto and Neves (the simultaneous characteristics of model 2 forced the use of FIML):

## Model 1: OLS Results

$$
\begin{aligned}
[u_t - \bar{u}] &= 0.683[u_{t-1} - \bar{u}] - 0.015 S_t \\
w_t - E(p_t) &= (\bar{w} - \bar{p}) - 1.411[u_{t-1} - \bar{u}]
\end{aligned}
$$

[11] The quantification technique used in this paper is described in Modesto (1987). See also Lambert (1987) for a similar procedure.

[12] Note that we have expressed this variable in terms of deviations from its sample mean in order to have a stationary variable.

[13] This interpretation implies that we are assuming that "normal" demand in one period is expected nominal demand for that period.

**Model 2: FIML Results**

$$\begin{aligned}[u_t - \bar{u}] &= 0.7173[u_{t-1} - \bar{u}] - 0.016S_t \\ &\quad + 0.00445\,[(w_{t-1} - E(p_t)) - (\bar{w} - \bar{p})] \\ w_t - E(p_t) &= (\bar{w} - \bar{p}) - 1.227[u_{t-1} - \bar{u}] \\ &\quad + 0.177\,[(w_{t-1} - E(p)) - (\bar{w} - \bar{p})]\ .\end{aligned}$$

On the issue of whether or not there is hysteresis in portuguese unemployment we find using Blanchard and Summer's framework (Model 1) an hysteresis coefficient for Portugal of 0.68 that is roughly of the some order of those obtained by Alogoskoufis and Manning for other european countries, Japan and the USA. With the extended model the degree of unemployment hysteresis obtained is higher (0.76) but full hysteresis is still rejected by the data. Nevertheless hysteresis appears as an important source of unemployment persistence in Portugal without being the only cause.

In what concerns the comparison between the extended model and model 1, the data validates the existence of inertia in the wage setting process ($\beta \neq 1$). Therefore one should consider a model that does not rule out a priori the possibility of expected demand shocks having effects on employment. However, as we have a rather low elasticity of labour demand we obtain a very small impact of expected demand shocks on employment and also a very weak effect of real wages on employment. Therefore policies that aim at shifting the labour demand schedule or at directly reducing the real wage will have no employment gains in the short-run due to the inelasticity of labour demand.

This last problem will be worsened in the presence of labour demand sluggishness which seems to be the case of Portugal ($\delta = 0.75$). Nevertheless wage or demand policies will have effects on employment if one manages to increase the labour demand elasticity or reduce labour demand sluggishness. Therefore costs of labour adjustment and rigidities that prevent adjustments in other markets (mainly capacity adjustments) should be reduced. This point seems particularly important in the portuguese context where the labour market is severely regulated.

The model also suggests that wages are almost fully indexed with one period lag. It is also interesting to see that unexpected nominal demand shocks exert a significant impact on unemployment. The introduction of this variable, which is an original feature of our work, and the fact that its evolution matches closely the degree of utilization of capacities in the manufacturing sector can point towards the existence of spillovers between markets.

# 5 The Wage Gap

When unemployment is regarded as arising from excessive real wages the next obvious step is the calculation of wage-gaps, i.e., the amount by which wages would have to fall in order to restore full employment. The wage-gap concept we are referring to is therefore the one used by Bruno (1986), and Bruno and Sachs (1985), i.e., the percentage deviation of the actual real product wage over the marginal product of labour at full employment. Or putting it differently the percentage deviation of the actual real wage over the real wage that would be compatible with full employment of the effective labour force.

Bruno and Sachs point out that the problem of estimating wage-gaps lies in estimating the marginal product of labour at full employment. First because we only have data on average and not on marginal productivity. Secondly we have data on actual productivity and not on productivity at full employment levels. The first problem can be avoided if one is ready to believe that the underlying production function is of the Cobb-Douglas type,[14] and there are different approaches[15] to deal with the second problem. However if the production technology is not Cobb-Douglas average labour productivity is not a good proxy for marginal labour productivity and therefore wage-gaps computed using average productivity will be misleading.[16]

Taking into account these problems of estimating the marginal product of labour at full employment from the actual series of employment and value added, we note that if we turn now to the alternative but equivalent definition of wage-gap, our version of the hysteresis model provides us with a natural concept of wage-gap. Indeed $(\bar{w}-\bar{p})$ was defined as the real wage that would be compatible with full employment of the effective labour force, and we have estimates for this value. Therefore both equation (2) of model 1

[14] In the Cobb-Douglas case labour marginal productivity equals $\alpha(Y/L)$ where $\alpha$ is the labour coefficient in the production function.

[15] See also on this issue Bruno and Sachs (1985) or Bruno (1986).

[16] For example in the case of a CES with Hicks-neutral technical change

$$Y_t = A_t[\mu L_t^{-\rho} + (1-\mu)K_t^{-\rho}]^{-1/\rho} .$$

so that

$$\frac{\partial Y_t}{\partial L_t}\frac{L_t}{Y_t} = \mu\left[\mu + (1-\mu)\left(\frac{K_t}{L_t}\right)^{-\rho}\right]^{-1} .$$

This means that marginal productivity rises relatively to average productivity when $K/L$ increases and $\sigma$ (the elasticity of substitution) $< 1$ or when $K/L$ decreases and $\sigma > 1$. Therefore when calculating wage gaps using average instead of marginal productivity we are assuming that the full employment share of labour is a constant. But with capital deepening and $\sigma < 1$ the full employment labour share should in fact rise over time.

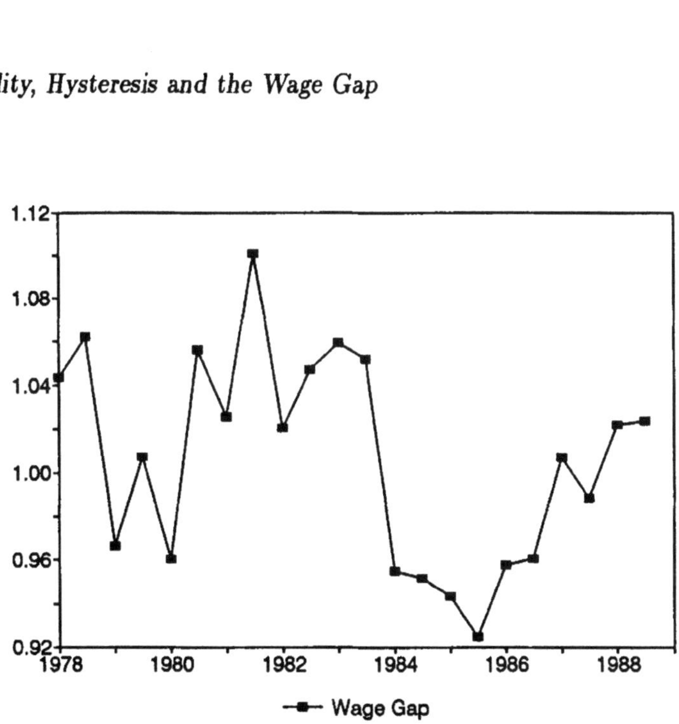


Figure 1: Wage gap series obtained from model 1.

and the long-run solution of equation (2) of model 2 (that we present below) merely state that the percentage deviation of actual expected real wage over the real wage that is compatible with full employment of the effective labour force (i.e., the wage-gap) varies negatively with deviations of unemployment from its natural rate.

$$[w_t - E(p_t)] - (\bar{w} - \bar{p}) = -1.411[u_t - \bar{u}] \quad \textbf{Model 1}$$
$$[w_t - E(p_t)] - (\bar{w} - \bar{p}) = -1.491[u_t - \bar{u}] \quad \textbf{Model 2}$$

We present our series for the wage-gap[17] in Figure 1. One can see that roughly there are four different phases: 78–80.1, 80.2–81, 82–85, 86–88 and two cycles. First the wage-gap goes down, then moves up and afterwards the pattern is repeated. Figure 2 shows the joint evolution of the wage-gap and of $-1.411[u_t - \bar{u}]$. One can see that indeed the two series vary together. The fact that the first series is more volatile than the second is due to the fact that the second series only provides us with the long-run evolution of the first one.

Another interesting representation of this phenomenon is given in Figure 3 where we have plotted equation (2) of model 1 together with the

[17] These series are obtained from model 1. For model 2 the results are almost identical and therefore we do not present them.

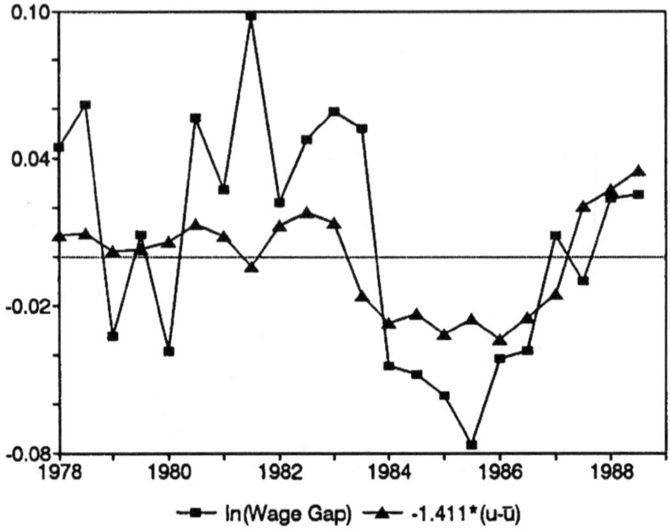


Figure 2: Actual and estimated long-run evolution of the wage gap.

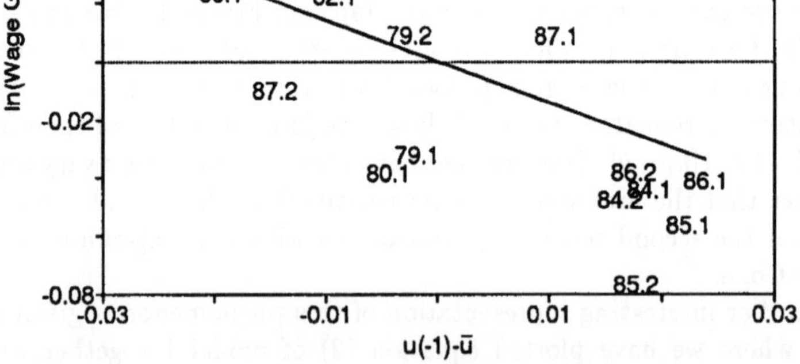


Figure 3: The wage equation: plot of equation (2) of model 1.

observed pairs (wage-gap, deviations of unemployment from the natural rate[18]) for each semester. As expected, the gross majority of points is located on the north-west and south-east zones. The west zone corresponds to the years before 1983 and 87 and 88 when the unemployment problem was not so tight. The relation depicted can be interpreted as a sort of Phillips curve, however not of the orthodox type, i.e., it does not link unemployment to the rate of change in real wages, but instead to the wage-gap. We have therefore found an empirical long-run relation for the portuguese economy that can be interpreted as a Phillips curve.[19] It turns out to be almost linear and quite flat, i.e., the downward effect of the slack labour market on wages is not very important. Our estimates imply that a one percent increase in the rate of unemployment reduces real wages by 1.4% in the long-run. This magnitude is consistent with empirical findings from other european countries and turns out to be slightly above average.[20] Nevertheless is too small to ensure that unemployment is self-correcting.[21]

At this point it is interesting to combine the wage equations of our hysteresis models with the unemployment equations and sort out the long-run adjustment implications. Below we present the long-run solution of both models.

**Model 1**

$$[u_t - \bar{u}] = -0.0473 S_t$$
$$[w_t - E(p_t)] - (\bar{w} - \bar{p}) = -1.411[u_t - \bar{u}]$$

**Model 2**

$$[u_t - \bar{u}] = -0.0553 S_t$$
$$[w_t - E(p_t)] - (\bar{w} - \bar{p}) = -1.491[u_t - \bar{u}]$$

First of all it is worth noting the striking similarities of both models which means that model 1 can be seen as the long-run solution of model 2.

---

[18] We have used the average rate of unemployment in the sample period (around 8%) as a proxy for the natural rate. It is also the value implied by our estimates. Noting that our rate of unemployment is computed as (1–Total Employment/Total Active Population) it lies, more or less, 2% points above the OECD figure and therefore seems to be a reasonable estimate for the natural rate.

[19] Or one might simply call it the wage curve.

[20] See the results presented in Drèze and Bean (1990).

[21] It is worth referring at this point that Blanchflower and Oswald (1990) report evidence, using microeconomic data for the U.S. and the U.K., that the negative trade-off between wages and unemployment flattens out at moderate to high (10% to 13%) levels of unemployment.

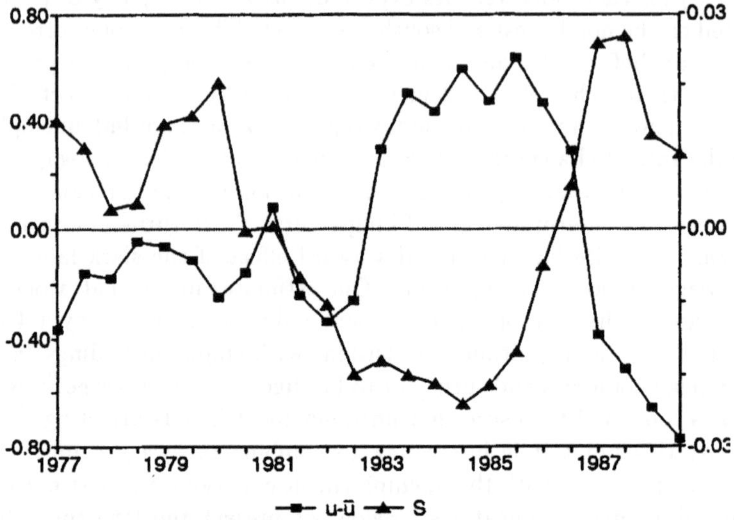


Figure 4: Evolution of unemployment and demand shocks.

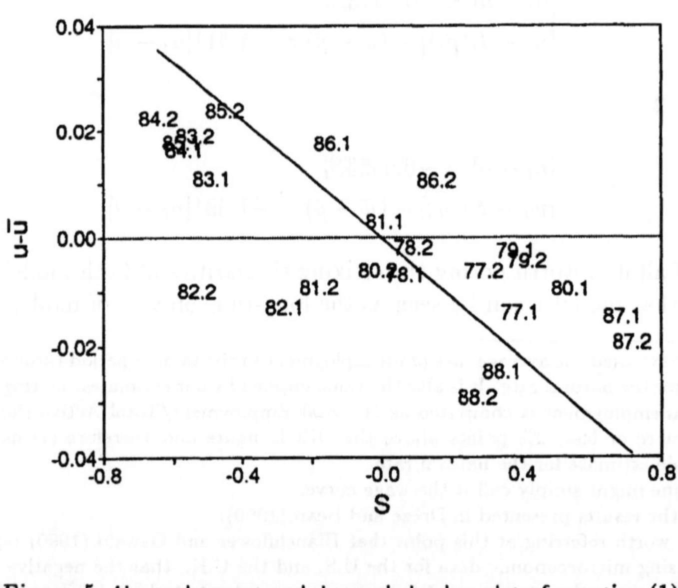


Figure 5: Unemployment and demand shocks: plot of equation (1).

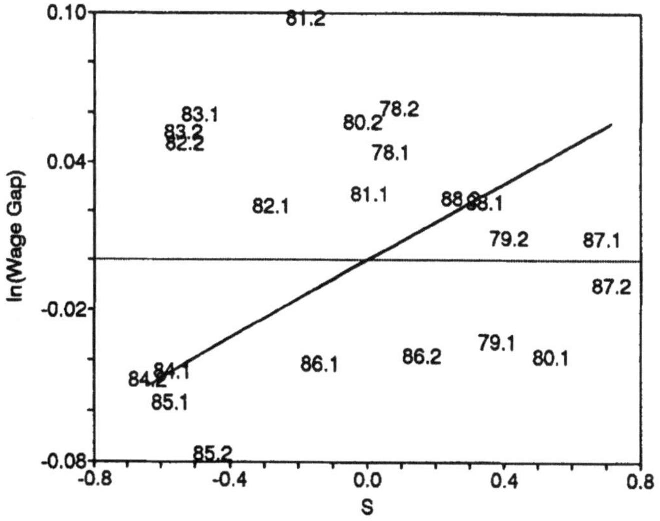


Figure 6: Wage gap and demand shocks: plot of the reduced form relation.

Now if equation (2) can be interpreted as a Phillips curve equation (1) can be seen as a sort of Okun's law. Indeed what it gives us is the relationship between the level of demand relatively to normal and deviations of unemployment from its natural rate. In this sense the estimates obtained are quite sensible. Figure 4 gives us the evolution of $(u_t - \bar{u})$ and $S_t$ along the sample period. Moreover in Figure 5 we have plotted equation (1) and the observed pairs $(u_t - \bar{u},\ S_t)$ for each semester.

Finally in Figure 6 we have plotted the final relation between the wage-gap and $S_t$, i.e.,

$$[w_t - E(p_t)] - (\bar{w} - \bar{p}) = 0.08S_t$$

together with the observed pairs of points. One can therefore tentatively conclude that ultimately the wage-gap in Portugal has been driven by demand shocks.

At this point one should try to compare our results for the evolution of the wage gap with other published wage gap series for the portuguese economy.

To our knowledge there are only two computed series for this indicator,[22] in the annual reports of the Bank of Portugal and in Barosa (1984). Both

[22]Note however that Krugman and Braga de Macedo (1979) tried to estimate the wage gap and the decline in the warranted real wage rate between 1973 and 1978.

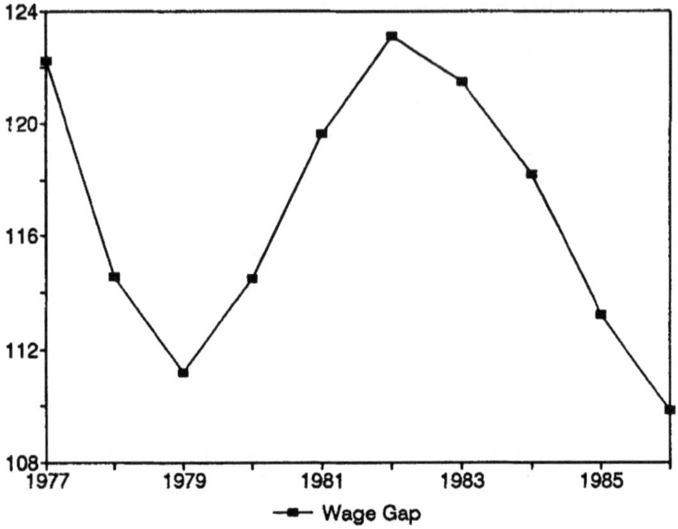


Figure 7: Bank of Portugal wage gap index.

sources use an approach that is different from ours and more similar to the one advanced by Bruno and Sachs. By this we mean that unlike us, they don't base the construction of the wage gap series on the econometric results of any model but instead they use the available employment, prices and value added series.

Moreover, the Bank of Portugal, instead of defining the wage gap as the percentage deviation of the actual real wage over the real wage compatible with full employment, define it as the percentage deviation of the actual real wage rate from what they call the "warranted real wage level". By this concept they mean the real wage compatible with the preservation of the labour share relatively to some "equilibrium" year.[23] It is straightforward to see that this definition implies that the rate of growth of the warranted real wage is nothing more than the rate of growth of average productivity.[24] Moreover it also implies that the evolution of the wage gap is the evolution of the labour share. Therefore this wage gap concept strikes us as providing little information on the situation of the labour market.[25]

[23] It happens to be the year of 1973.

[24] Actually the BP includes some correction factors to account for the discrepancies between the GDP deflator and the consumer price index, concepts at factor cost and at market prices, and domestic and national aggregates.

[25] Note however that the OECD uses a similar concept of wage gap.

Furthermore this methodology is misleading if the underlying technology is not Cobb-Douglas and if important short run shocks to productivity are present. Remember that one ideally should measure deviations of the growth rate of real wages from the growth rate of the marginal product of labour at full employment.

Barosa (1984) uses a slightly different definition of warranted real wage growth, that includes a correction for the growth rate of the labour force but the basic structure is the same and therefore the same comments apply.

Before closing this section on the wage gap one should note that if wage contracts are shaped according to the neutrality doctrine, the wage gap index computed in this way would not vary. In Figure 7 we have plotted the BP wage gap index or, which is the same, the evolution of the labour share. One can therefore conclude that for the portuguese economy as a whole, neutrality in the short run was not present. On the contrary, the labour share responded to unemployment conditions.

# 6 Conclusions

The main characteristic of the portuguese labour market, that emerges from this analysis is the relative flexibility of its structure, when compared with other european countries. The lack of rigidity in the wage determination process in the short run prevents workers from fully incorporating the productivity gains in their wage.

This means that the adjustment in the market is made rather quickly, which accounts for the low level of unemployment and small unemployment persistence registered in Portugal, when compared with other countries.

Nevertheless, these characteristics must not be exaggerated. Some persistence, "hysteresis" and labour demand sluggishness can be detected in the data, specially in the long run, when the wage level adjusts itself to the productivity shock.

We can say that these findings are in accordance with the intuition and studies of the rest of the literature on the portuguese reality. Although these results seem rather robust, they justify further research, in order to highlight the mechanisms that cause them.

# Appendix: Data

The data used in this paper has the following sources:

1) NEUTRALITY: The sectorial data used is from the Industrial Statistics

from INE.

2) HYSTERESIS: All data series used in this paper are from the Portuguese Official Statistical Institute, "INE – Instituto Nacional de Estatistica" and were published by the Bank of Portugal (BP), in its annual reports.

All the series used are semiannual and for some years we had to adjust the periodicity from three months to six months. The sample period considered was from 1977.1 to 1988.2.

The individual series are as follows. To construct the unemployment rate we used two series: "Total Active Population", and "Total Employment", in portuguese mainland (thus excluding Madeira and Azores), from the "Permanent Survey on Employment" of INE. The "Index of Average Manufacturing Nominal Wages, for 30 industry branches", was used as proxy for the level of wages. For prices we used the "Consumer Price Index, without house rents".

The data used to construct the variables $S_t$ comes from the Manufacturing Industry Survey of the INE.

# References

ALOGOSKOUFIS, G. AND A. MANNING (1988): "Wage setting and unemployment persistence in Europe, Japan and the USA," *European Economic Review*, **32**, 698–706.

BANCO DE PORTUGAL: *Annual Report*, several issues, Lisbon.

BAROSA, J. P. (1984): "A Note on the Portuguese Wage Gap: 1954-1983," Working Paper #26, Faculdade de Economia, Universidade Nova de Lisboa.

BAROSA, J. P. (1986): *Três Ensaios sobre o Mercado de Trabalho (contratos, rigidez salarial, ciclos) com aplicação à Economia Portuguesa*. Lisbon: Universidade Nova de Lisboa.

BLANCHARD, O. J. AND L. H. SUMMERS (1987): "Hysteresis in Unemployment," *European Economic Review*, **31**, 288–295.

BLANCHARD, O. J. AND S. FISHER (1989): *Lectures on Macroeconomics*. Cambridge: The MIT Press.

BLANCHFLOWER, D. G. AND A. J. OSWALD (1990): "The Wage Curve," *The Scandinavian Journal of Economics*, **92**, 215–235.

BRUNO, M. (1986): "Aggregate Supply and Demand Factors in OECD Unemployment: An Update," *Economica*, **53**, 210(S), S35–S52.

BRUNO, M. AND J. SACHS (1985): *Economics of Worldwide Stagflation*. New York: Blackwell.

CASTELA, M. (1984): "Contratação Colectiva: Negociação e Conflito," *Estudos de Economia*, **4**, 361–83.

CAVACO-SILVA, A. (ed) (1983): "Economic and Social Partnership and Incomes Policy," *Economia*, **7**.

CONFRARIA, J. AND M. L. MONTEIRO (1988): "Notas sobre o Problema da Precisao das Observacoes Estatísticas - o Caso das Estatísticas de Emprego e de Emigração em Portugal (1960-1985)," Estudos #13, Departamento de Economia, Universidade Católica Portuguesa.

DRÈZE, J. H. AND C. BEAN (1990): "Europe's Employment Problem: A Synthesis," in *Europe's Employment Problem*, ed. by Drèze, Bean, Lambert, Mehta and Sneessens, chapter 1. Cambridge: The MIT Press.

EMERSON, M. (1988): "Regulation or Deregulation of the Labour Market: Policy Regimes for the Recruitment and Dismissal of Employees in the Industrialized Countries," *European Economic Review*, **32**, 775–817.

LAMBERT, J. P. (1987): *Disequilibrium Macroeconomic Models*. Cambridge: Cambridge University Press.

LINDBECK, A. AND D. SNOWER (1988): *The Insider-Outsider Theory of Unemployment*. Cambridge: The MIT Press.

KRUGMAN, P. AND J. B. MACEDO (1979): "The Economic Consequences of the April 25th Revolution", *Economia*, **3**, 455–483.

MALINVAUD, E. (1977): *The Theory of Unemployment Reconsidered*. New York: Blackwell.

MODESTO, L. (1987): "Price, Production and Inventories Adjustments: Microfoundations and aggregate behaviour. An empirical study for the belgian manufacturing sector," Publications de la Faculté de Sciences Economiques, Sociales et Politiques de l'Université Catholique de Louvain, Nouvelle Serie #171.

MODESTO, L. AND J. C. NEVES (1990): "Hysteresis and Sluggishness in Portuguese Unemployment," paper presented at the Fifth Annual Congress of the European Economic Association, Lisbon.

NEUMANN, M. J., R. SCHMIDT AND E. SCHULTE (1990): "Determinants of contract wages in Germany," *European Economic Review*, **34**, 1233–1246.

NEWELL, A. AND J. S. SYMONS (1987): "Corporatism, Laissez-Faire and the Rise in Unemployment," *European Economic Review*, **31**, 567-614.

PHELPS, E. (1990): *Seven Schools of Macroeconomic Thought*. Oxford: Oxford University Press.

PINTO, M. (1986): *Guia Jurídico e Social para Trabalhadores*. Lisbon: Fundação Oliveira Martins.

RAMOS, A. B. AND M. ABECASSIS (1980), "Estudo sobre o Nível de Emprego Sectorial," Estudos #39, Ministério do Trabalho, DEP.

SANTOS, A. (1980), "O Salário na Indústria Transformadora — Ensaio," Estudos #41, Ministério do Trabalho, DEP.

# Trade-Off between Emigration and Remittances in the Portuguese Economy

Alfredo M. Pereira

## 1 Introduction

Portugal has traditionally been a country of emigration. In the last three decades, emigration has had as destiny the European Community (EC), in particular France and Germany. In the recent past, emigration has been hindered by legal and economic conditions both in Portugal and in the host countries. This explains why the enormous wave of emigration in the 1960s was followed by a slow-down in the late 1970s and by a virtual standstill in the 1980s. Nevertheless, the Portuguese emigrated labor force in the EC is about 13% of the total Portuguese national labor force and sends to Portugal remittances that in the 1980s averaged more than 10% of the GDP. Therefore, emigration is bound to have a strong impact in the domestic economy, both as foregone labor force and as a source of remittances.

With the integration of Portugal in the EC and the European Single Act, whereby most barriers against economic flows — including barriers against labor force movements — are to be abolished starting 1993, the issue of Portuguese emigration into the EC has again picked up momentum. In fact, while legal barriers to movements of the Portuguese labor force within the EC will soon be removed, the real wage gap between Portugal and the EC is still substantial and is not likely to disappear any time soon. In addition, the pursuit of policies tending to raise the relative real wage rate is undesirable because of their effects on the international competitiveness of Portuguese exports, and unlikely because of the concerns of the economic

I would like to thank Alan Manne and Isabel Pereira for useful comments and suggestions, Kevin Klein for skillful research assistance and Meredee O'Brien for superb editorial assistance. All the remaining errors are of my sole responsibility.

authorities with relatively high domestic inflation. All given, the upcoming liberalization of labor movements in the EC will put heavy pressure on the Portuguese economy which may lead to a further drain of the labor force into the EC.

This paper has two main objectives. The first objective is to study the effects of past emigration on the Portuguese economy under the assumption that the current barriers to further emigration are maintained. The second objective is to provide an evaluation of the potential effects on the Portuguese economy from the liberalization of the movements of the Portuguese labor force within the EC.

The answers to these two questions are of considerable relevance in terms of policy-making. Traditionally, while wailing the loss of citizens, the Portuguese governments have been always more eager to foster emigrants' remittances than to creating the conditions for the return of emigrant workers. Remittances have been perceived as an important source of financing to the domestic economy. Accordingly, several incentive schemes — higher interest rates, foreign currency-denominated bank accounts, are just two examples — have been designed to induce emigrants to remitting a fraction of their savings to Portugal. The effectiveness of these policies is an empirical matter, which is outside the scope of this paper. However, the proper policy objectives — whether to encourage remittances or to discourage emigration (or promote the return of emigrated workers) — depend on the evaluation of the net effects of past emigration. Furthermore, faced with renewed international mobility of the labor force, the Portuguese economy will have to undergo a structural adjustment process that may lead to substantial new emigration. Accordingly, the timing and impact of liberalization of labor force movements upon domestic economic growth and upon the well-being of the resident population are questions of paramount concern for the Portuguese economic authorities. This paper attempts to give answers to the questions above by emphasizing the trade-off between foregone labor force and emigrants' remittances in the Portuguese economy.

In this paper the Portuguese economy is modeled in a context of optimal growth with emigration and remittances along the lines of Macedo (1977) and Pereira (1982). In Macedo (1977), the standard neo-classical growth model — see Solow (1956) for seminal work in this area — is modified so that part of the domestic labor force is allowed to emigrate due to a wage differential between the home and the host countries. While the reduction of labor force via emigration is costly in terms of foregone domestic production, it might be more than compensated for by the increase in national income, which results from emigrants' remittances. In Pereira (1982), Macedo's model is extended to an optimal control framework and the trade-off between emigration and remittances for the home economy is presented. The optimal growth model in this paper is a discrete-time version of Pereira's (1982) model generalized to accommodate numerical implementation. This model is used to simulate the overall impact of emigration, past and future, upon the Portuguese economy under different scenarios. Such scenarios are related to the evolution of the wage gap between Portugal and the EC as conditioned by the rate of growth of the international wage rate and the domestic rate of technological progress.

This paper is organized as follows. Section 2 describes the theoretical model and characterizes the optimal trajectories for the economy. Section 3 presents the different simulation scenarios and the simulation results. Finally, section 4 provides a summary of results and some concluding remarks. In addition, the paper contains an appendix with data and parameter specification.

# 2 The Optimal Growth Model and the Optimal Trajectories

The general optimal growth model with emigration and remittances, which is an extension of the model in Pereira (1982), can be specified as follows:

$$\max_{\{C_t/L_t\}} \quad SW = \sum_{0 \leq t \leq \infty} r^t U(C_t/L_t) \tag{1}$$

where

$$U(C_t/L_t) = \ln(C_t/L_t) \tag{2}$$

subject to:

i) *National accounting identity*

$$R_t + F(K_t, L_t) = C_t + I_t \qquad t = 0, \ldots, \infty \tag{3}$$

where

$$F(K_t, L_t) = (1 + tp)^t b_0 K_t^b L_t^{1-b} \tag{4}$$

ii) *Equations of motion for the state variables*

$$K_{t+1} = I_t + (1 - d)K_t \qquad t = 0, \ldots, \infty \tag{5}$$

$$(E_{t+1} - E_t)/E_t = g + G(W_t/V_t) \qquad t = 0, \ldots, \infty \tag{6}$$

where

$$G(W_t/V_t) = h[1 - (W_t/V_t)] \tag{7}$$

iii) *Labor force equations*

$$P_t = zE_t + L_t \qquad t = 0, \ldots, \infty \tag{8}$$

$$P_t = (1 + g)^t P_0 \qquad t = 0, \ldots, \infty \tag{9}$$

iv) *Domestic wage rate determination*

$$W_t = (1 - b)(1 + tp)^t b_0 (K_t/L_t)^b \quad t = 0, \ldots, \infty \tag{10}$$

v) *Remittances equations*

$$R_t = s_e V_t E_t \qquad t = 0, \ldots, \infty \tag{11}$$

$$V_t = (1 + v)^t V_0 \qquad t = 0, \ldots, \infty \tag{12}$$

vi) *Initial conditions on the stock variables*

$$K_0 \text{ and } E_0 \tag{13}$$

vii) *Feasibility constraint on the control variable*

$$0 \leq C_t \leq R_t + F(K_t, L_t) \qquad t = 0, \ldots, \infty \tag{14}$$

The objective function (1), is a time separable social welfare indicator, $SW$. This indicator is specified as the discounted value at time 0 of the intertemporal stream of utility, as measured by a well-behaved time-invariant utility function, $U(\cdot)$. The subjective discount rate is $r$, which can be interpreted as the constant marginal rate of transformation between present and future utility. In turn, utility is defined on the space of domestic consumption, $C_t$, per unit resident labor force, $L_t$. Implicitly, emigration is treated as permanent. In the sequel, the utility function is given by (2).

The national accounting identity (3) states that total national income at any time $t$ is generated by domestic production, $F(\cdot)$, and by emigrants' remittances, $R_t$. Domestic production requires the use of installed capital stock, $K_t$, and resident labor, $L_t$. Given non-satiation, total income is to be exhausted by consumption and investment expenditures, $C_t$ and $I_t$, respectively. The domestic production function, as in (4), is a constant returns to scale Cobb-Douglas function where, $b$, is the share of capital in total production cost, $b_0$, is the output scaling parameter, and, $tp$, is the neutral rate of technical progress.

The equation of motion for capital, (5), reflects the fact that investment is the gross (net plus depreciation) increase in the capital stock. The capital stock depreciates at a rate $d$. In turn, the equation of motion for emigration, (6), captures the labor force foregone by the domestic economy in the form of emigration, $E_t$. It captures the idea that changes in the foregone labor force have an exogenous demographic component associated with the natural growth of the national labor force, $g$, and an endogenous economic component, $G(\cdot)$, related to the differential between the domestic and the international wage rates, $W_t$ and $V_t$, respectively. The emigration function, $G(\cdot)$, is required to satisfy $G(1) = 0$ (i.e., when domestic wages rise to the international level there is no economic momentum for further emigration), and $\partial G/\partial(W_t/V_t) > 0$ (i.e., the higher the wage differential, the higher the changes in emigration caused by economic factors). In particular, $G(\cdot)$ is parameterized as in (7), where, $h$, measures the responsiveness of emigration to changes in the wage differential. Notice that this specification of the emigration function allows for return migration.

Total national labor force, $P_t$, is exogenous and comprises both resident and non-resident workers as in (8), where, $z$, adjusts for different labor force participation rates between domestic and emigrated population. Total labor force, as in (9), grows at an exogenous rate, $g$, from an initial stock of $P_0$. The domestic real wage rate is consistent with cost-minimizing behavior and is determined, as in (10), as the value of the marginal productivity of labor. In addition, equation (11) establishes that remittances depend not only on the international wage rate — postulated to grow at an exogenous rate, $v$, from an initial level of $V_0$, as in (12), — but also on the exogenous savings rate of the emigrated labor force $s_e$. Equations (6) and (11) reflect endogenous emigration and remittance behavior and can be rationalized as reduced forms designed to capture optimal private decisions. Finally, (13) is the initial conditions on the stock variables $K_t$ and $E_t$, and (14) are boundary conditions on the control variable, $C_t$.

Model (1)–(14) can be re-written in a condensed form as:

$$\max_{\{C_t\}} \quad SW = \sum_{0 \leq t \leq \infty} r^t \ln\{C_t/[(1+g)^t P_0 - zE_t]\} \tag{15}$$

subject, for $t = 0, \ldots, \infty$, to

$$K_{t+1} = (1+tp)^t b_0 K_t^b [(1+g)^t P_0 - zE_t]^{1-b} + s_e V_t E_t - C_t + (1-d)K_t \tag{16}$$

$$E_{t+1} = \{1+g+h[1-[(1-b)(1+tp)^t b_0 (K_t/[(1+g)^t P_0 - zE_t])^b]/V_t]\}E_t \tag{17}$$

with initial conditions $K_0$ and $E_0$, and

$$0 \leq C_t \leq s_e V_t E_t + (1+tp)^t b_0 K_t^b [(1+g)^t P_0 - zE_t]^{1-b}\,. \tag{18}$$

The Hamiltonian function associated to this problem is given, for $t = 0, \ldots, \infty$, by:

$$H(K_t, E_t, C_t, q_{1t+1}, q_{2t+1}) = \ln[C_t/((1+g)^t P_0 - zE_t)] + rp_{1t+1}\{(1+tp)^t b_0 K_t^b [(1+g)^t P_0 - zE_t]^{1-b} + s_e V_t E_t - C_t + (1-d)K_t\} + rp_{2t+1}\{1 + g + h[1 - [(1-b)(1+tp)^t b_0 (K_t/[(1+g)^t P_0 - zE_t])^b]/V_t]\}E_t \tag{19}$$

where, $q_{it+1} = r^{t+1} p_{it+1}$ with $i = 1, 2$ are the co-state variables interpreted as the discounted shadow prices of additional capital and emigration, measured in terms of utility. Accordingly, the Hamiltonian function may be interpreted as the imputed utility value at time $t$ of income — consumption plus investment — plus the imputed utility value of additional emigration, all discounted to time zero.

The solution to the optimal growth problem, (15)–(18), is characterized by using the discrete-time version of Pontryagin's Maximum Principle (see Luenberger (1979), for example). If, $(K_t^*, E_t^*)$ and $C_t^*$ represent the optimal state and control trajectories, respectively, for the optimal control problem, (15)–(18), then there is an adjoint trajectory, $\{p_{1t}^*, p_{2t}^*\}$ such that, together $\{K_t^*, E_t^*, C_t^*, p_{1t}^*, p_{2t}^*\}$ satisfy (for $t = 0, \ldots, \infty$):

viii) *The state equations of motion as in (16) and (17).*

ix) *The initial conditions for the state variables as in (18).*

x) *The co-state equations of motion*

$$\begin{aligned} p_{1t} &= rp_{1t+1}[b(1+tp)^t b_0 (K_t/[(1+g)^t P_0 - zE_t])^{b-1} + (1-d)] \\ &\quad + rp_{2t+1}[-hb(1-b)(1+tp)^t b_0 (K_t/[(1+g)^t P_0 - zE_t])^b E_t / K_t V_t] \\ p_{2t} &= rp_{1t+1}\{-z(1-b)(1+tp)^t b_0 [K_t/[(1+g)^t P_0 - zE_t]]^b + s_e V_t\} \\ &\quad + rp_{2t+1} \partial E_{t+1}/\partial E_t + \{z/[(1+g)^t P_0 - zE_t]\} . \end{aligned} \tag{20}$$

xi) *Terminal conditions on the co-state variables*

$$\lim_{t \to \infty} r^t p_{it+1} = 0 \quad i = 1, 2 . \tag{21}$$

xii) *The Hamiltonian variational condition*

$$[(1+g)^t P_0 - zE_t]/C_t = rp_{1t+1} \tag{22}$$

These necessary conditions for optimality can be interpreted as follows. Conditions viii) and ix) solely recover the two equations of motion for capital and emigrated labor force and the respective initial conditions. Conditions x) indicate evolution of the rate of change of the Hamiltonian function derived from changes in the capital stock — equation (20) — and emigrated labor force - equation (20). Otherwise stated, conditions x) indicate the evolution of the shadow utility price of capital and emigrated labor force, respectively. In turn, conditions xi) provide terminal conditions for the shadow price variables. These conditions state that the Hamiltonian function does not change as a consequence of variations in the terminal conditions on the state variables. These transversality conditions can be interpreted as reflecting that the scrap values of capital and emigrated labor force are both zero. Finally, conditions xii) determine the optimal choice of consumption such that the utility value of income and emigrated labor force is maximized at each and every period. An interior optimal trajectory for consumption is assumed, which means that the inequalities in (18) are satisfied as strict inequalities.

The characterization of the optimal solution to problem (15)-(18) can be interpreted as a two-point boundary problem. In fact, the optimal solution can be seen as the solution to a system of four nonlinear difference equations — two for the state variables, and two for the co-state variables — in four unknowns. This system of difference equations has two initial conditions for the state variables, and two terminal conditions for the co-state variables. Given the complexity of this problem no attempt has been made to develop an analytic solution and to obtain analytic comparative dynamic results. Instead, in the subsequent sections, this optimal growth problem is solved numerically for different configurations of the crucial parameters in the economy.

# 3 Simulation Experiments and Results

The model in the previous section is implemented numerically with a time horizon of thirty-five years (see the appendix for a detailed discussion of the data set and the parameterization of the model.)

## 3.1 Design of the Simulation Experiments

The study of the effects of past emigration as well as the effects of the liberalization of labor movements requires the consideration of three sub-models nested in the general model in section 2. The first sub-model (Base Case 1 — BC1) is the standard neoclassical growth model. It ignores both emigration, in that it considers emigrated labor force as if it were resident, and remittances. The second sub-model (Base Case 2 — BC2) is obtained from the general problem by setting $(E_{t+1}-E_t)/E_t = g$ in (6) and $s_e = 0$ in (11). It differs from the first sub-model only in that it captures the effect of depopulation in the form of reduced initial total labor force. However, it does not consider emigrants' remittances. The third sub-model (Revised Case 1 — RC1) is obtained from the general problem by setting $(E_{t+1} - E_t)/E_t = g$ in (6), but allowing for $s_e \neq 0$ in (11). It differs from the second sub-model in that emigrated labor force is allowed to send remittances back to the home country. In the last two sub-models the home country is foregoing labor resources in the form of emigration. Finally, the general model (Revised Case 2 — RC2) allows for further emigration and the corresponding remittances.

The contrast between the first (BC1) and the second (BC2) sub-models identifies the effects of emigration as a pure loss of labor force. It provides a measure of the depopulation effect of past emigration. The contrast between the second (BC2) and the third (RC1) sub-models determines the net effect of emigrants' remittances given that emigration has occurred. It measures the remittances effect of past emigration. The contrast between the first (BC1) and the third (RC1) sub-models gives a representation of the global effects of emigration and an evaluation of the trade-off between emigration and remittances. Finally, the contrast between the third sub-model (RC1) and the general model (RC2) highlights the effects of liberalization of labor movements in the EC.

Several scenarios are constructed for different values of the key parameters: the domestic rate of technological progress, $tp$, and the rates of growth of the international wage rate, $v$. A higher rate of increase of the international wage rate leads to further emigration and to greater remittances. Domestic technological progress mirrors the evolution of international wages in that, all other things constant, $tp$ is the rate of growth of the domestic real wage rate. The higher the domestic technical progress the lower the differential between domestic and foreign marginal productivity of labor, and the lower the incentive for further emigration and the relative importance of remittances.

The specification of the different scenarios depends on the relevant range of values for the two key parameters. According to OECD statistics, the average annual rate of increase of real wages in the 1970s was 3.6% in France and 3% in Germany, while in the 1980s the average increase was 0.9% and 0.8% respectively. Accordingly, the following cases will be considered for international wage growth: high growth, $v = 0.03$; moderate growth, $v = 0.02$; and low growth, $v = 0.01$. The same scenarios are considered for the domestic rate of technical progress. In terms of evolution of the domestic economy, optimistic scenarios maximize the positive difference between the domestic rate of technical progress and the rate of growth of the international wages, say $tp = 0.03$ and $v = 0.01$. Pessimistic scenarios maximize the negative difference between the domestic rate of technical progress and the rate of growth of the international wages, say $tp = 0.01$ and $v = 0.03$.

Both BC1 and BC2 are simulated only for the three technical progress scenarios. Given the nature of these cases — the absence of either remittances or further emigration — the rate of change of international wages is irrelevant. In turn, both RC1 and RC2 are run for a total of nine scenarios featuring a combination of low, moderate, and high rate of growth of the international wage rate with low, moderate, and high rates of technical progress. Figures 1–7 and 9–10 depict the relationship among BC1s, BC2s, RC2s with moderate rate of technical progress and low (RC1L and RC2L), moderate (RC1M and RC2M), and high (RC1H and RC2H) rates of growth of the international wage rate.

## 3.2 The Effects of Past Emigration

This subsection focuses on the welfare and growth effects of the massive flow of emigration into the EC, which occurred in the 1960s and early 1970s. The effects of past emigration on domestic welfare and growth depend crucially on the relative importance of emigrants' remittances. Figure 1 depicts the simulated contribution of remittances to total national income (GDP plus remittances). Under all the RC1s, remittances are a declining component of national income, varying between 8% and 10% for high rate of growth of the international wages, and between 6% and 10% for low rates of growth. Naturally, remittances tend to be more important the higher the rate of growth of the international wages.

The welfare effects of past emigration under the different scenarios are summarized in Table 1. The welfare effect of emigration when remittances are ignored is consistently negative. There is a 10.4% loss of welfare in BC2 over BC1 in the pessimistic scenario ($tp = 0.01$) versus a 3.4% loss in the optimistic scenario ($tp = 0.03$). These welfare losses reflect the negative

Table 1: Welfare effects of past emigration.

| | BC1 | BC2 | RC1 | | |
|---|---|---|---|---|---|
| TP\v | | | 0.01 | 0.02 | 0.03 |
| 0.01 | 34.367 | 31.135 | 35.613 | 35.893 | 36.218 |
| 0.02 | 38.007 | 36.718 | 38.899 | 38.119 | 39.379 |
| 0.03 | 41.727 | 40.378 | 42.311 | 42.494 | 42.703 |

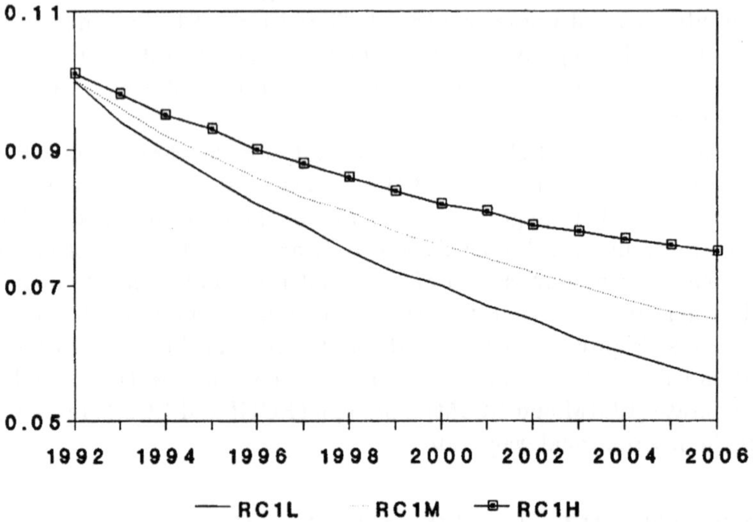


Figure 1: Effects of past emigration: remittances-national income ratio.

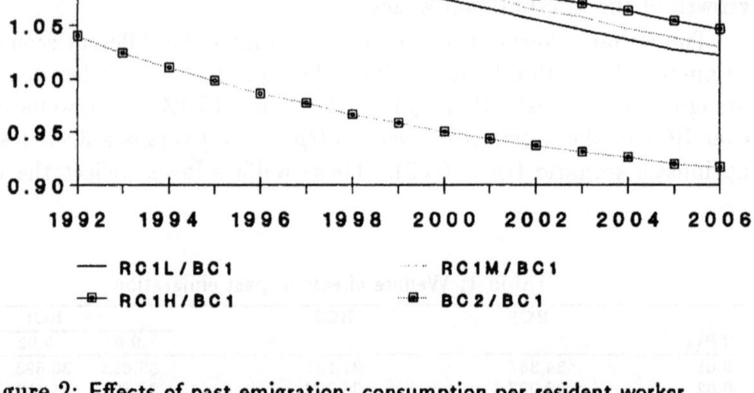


Figure 2: Effects of past emigration: consumption per resident worker.

effect of depopulation. On the other hand, the revised cases RC1s show welfare improvements over the corresponding BC2s. These welfare gains reflect the positive effect of emigrants' remittances.

Remittances act as an additional source of financing for the economy. Accordingly, remittances lead to additional current consumption and additional investment and therefore additional future consumption. The global welfare effects of past emigration, accounting for both the cost of foregone labor force and the benefits of emigrants' remittances, are always positive. It ranges from a 1.4% welfare gain in the most optimistic scenario for the evolution of the domestic economy ($tp = 0.03, v = 0.01$) to 5.4% in the most pessimistic scenario ($tp = 0.01, v = 0.03$). Such positive net effects reflect the persistently higher marginal productivity of the national labor force when in use in the host economy.

The welfare improvements due to emigration and remittances are monotonically increasing in $v$. This reflects the fact that when the international wage rate is increased one percentage point, remittances increase by $s_e E$. Also, the welfare improvements due to emigration and remittances are monotonic decreasing in $tp$. This reflects the fact that the higher the rate of technical progress the higher the marginal productivity of labor and the lower the differential between domestic and international wages. Also, the level of remittances sent back by the emigrated labor force is not affected by changes in the domestic rate of technical progress.

Under the current legal and economic barriers to further emigration, the existence of emigrated labor force that sends back remittances is welfare improving for the Portuguese resident labor force. From this standpoint the policy of the different governments in the past decade of attracting emigrants' remittances rather than attracting the emigrants back to the country seems justified.

The welfare analysis above is based on the comparison of social welfare associated with different intertemporal paths for consumption per resident worker. The simulated evolution of consumption per resident worker (BC2 and RC1s vis-a-vis BC1) is depicted in Figure 2. Foregone labor force without remittances depresses consumption per capita even though the resident labor force is also reduced. In turn, remittances clearly induce systematic improvements in the per capita consumption which are monotonic in the rate of growth of international wage. This fact is consistent with the previous welfare analysis and reflects an absolute increase in total consumption (in the different RC1s), since the resident labor force is the same in BC2 and the different RC1s.

The simulated evolution of the capital-labor ratio (in BC2 and RC1s vis-a-vis BC1) is depicted in Figure 3. The trajectory with emigration and without remittances (BC2) shows a relatively sharp decline in the capital-

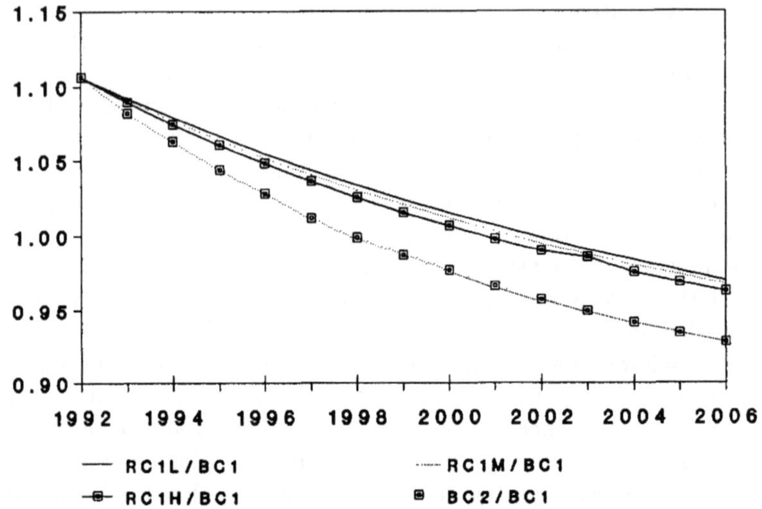


Figure 3: Effects of past emigration: capital-labor ratio.

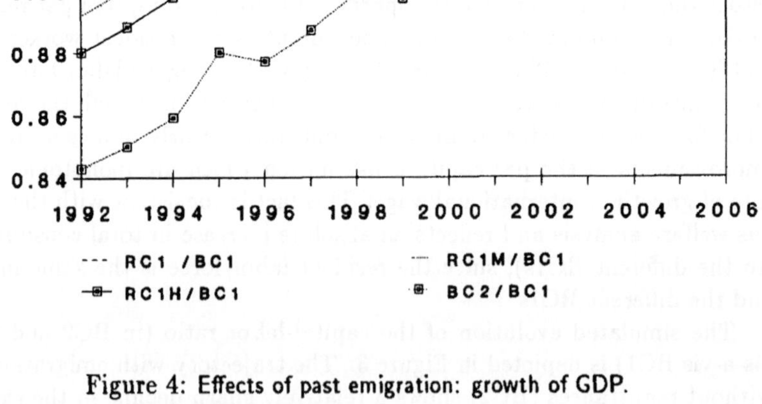


Figure 4: Effects of past emigration: growth of GDP.

labor ratio to levels below BC1. This is a measure of the effects of foregone labor force and loss in the marginal productivity of capital. The capital-labor ratios for the three RC1s do not differ significantly. However, in the RC1s the capital-labor ratio is systematically higher than in BC2. This can be accounted for by the greater availability of funds made possible by emigrants' remittances. In addition, the capital-labor ratios in RC1s show a smooth declining pattern which ultimately converges to levels below BC1. This suggests that, even in the presence of remittances, emigration leads ultimately to a more than proportional decapitalization. In fact, the higher capital-labor ratios observed in the early years tend to disappear in the long-run: the capital-labor ratios with emigration and remittances converge to about 98% of the capital-labor ratio in the absence of emigration and remittances.

The simulated rate of growth of the domestic production is depicted in Figure 4 (BC2 and RC1s vis-a-vis BC1). The net effects of foregone labor force and remittances can be identified as a decline in the annual rate of GDP growth between 9% and 12% in the short-run, and between 6% and 8% in the long-run. With the observed GDP growth rates in the last three decades (which averaged just below 5% annually) this reduction in GDP growth represents an average decline of half a percentage point per year. As expected the decline would have been much sharper in the absence of remittances.

## 3.3 The Effects of Liberalization of Labor Force Movements

In this subsection the effects of upcoming liberalization of the movements of the Portuguese labor force within the EC are analyzed. The evolution of emigrated labor force as a percent of the national labor force under the different scenarios is shown in Figure 5 (RC2 vis-a-vis RC1). Simulations under liberalization of labor force movements place the percentage of emigrants in the total labor force between 18% (in the case of low growth of international wages) and 24% (in the case of high growth of international wages) within a ten-year period, up from the current level of 13%. Given the differences in the labor force participation rates between domestic and emigrated labor force these percentages correspond to the actual emigration of between 220 and 470 thousand workers, respectively. In addition, simulations suggest that in the case of a sluggish evolution of the EC — low growth of the international wage rate and low domestic technical progress — no substantial new emigration would take place. Only 75 thousand workers would leave the country in a ten-year period. However, a substantial new wave of emigration would occur if the current trend, of low increase

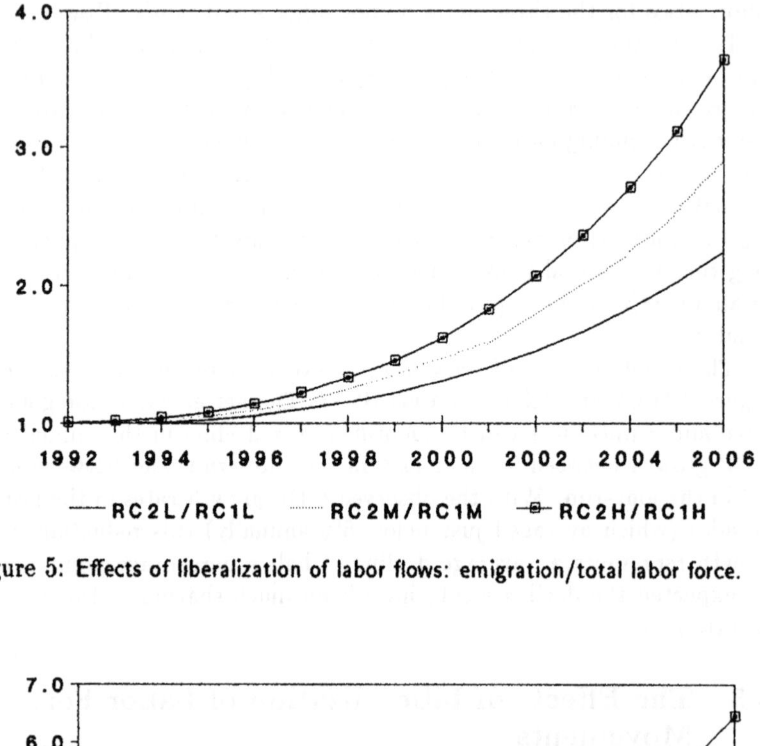


Figure 5: Effects of liberalization of labor flows: emigration/total labor force.

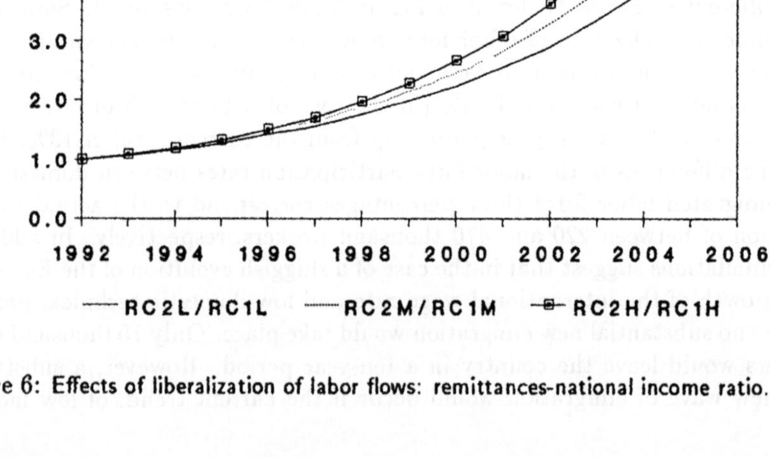


Figure 6: Effects of liberalization of labor flows: remittances-national income ratio.

of the domestic wage rate, persists. In fact, when the difference of vitality between the Portuguese and the EC economies is exacerbated — high rate of growth of the international wage rate and low domestic technical progress — about 500 thousand workers, are anticipated to emigrate within a decade.

Corresponding to the new flow of emigration, the simulations show a significant increase in the relative importance of remittances (Figure 6 depicts remittances as a fraction of total income in RC2s vis-a-vis RC1s). As a result of both the loss of domestic production and increased remittances, the economy is relying more and more on emigrants' remittances. Remittances are simulated between 18% (for low rate of growth of the international wages) and 32% (for high growth rate) after one decade, up from the current level of 10%.

The welfare analysis based on the comparisons of intertemporal social welfare derived from the path of consumption per resident population provides one measure of the potential effects of liberalization. Consumption per resident worker is represented in Figure 7 (RC2s vis-a-vis RC1s). It shows that allowing emigration and the correspondent remittances leads to a consumption spree: consumption per capita in the initial years nearly duplicates the status quo values. This is due simultaneously to the decrease in resident labor force and to a greater accessibility of funds through emigrants' remittances.

The welfare effects of liberalization of labor force movements under the different scenarios are summarized in Table 2. Lifting the legal barriers to the movements of the Portuguese labor force is, in most scenarios, welfare improving for the resident population. The only exception is the scenario reflecting the most optimistic evolution for the domestic economy — high rate of technical progress coupled with low growth of international wages, in which case welfare is reduced by about 8.5%, while the highest welfare gain is about 47% under high rate of growth of international wages and low domestic technical progress.

These welfare results follow the pattern of effects of past emigration. Again welfare gains vary directly with the rate of growth of the international wage rate. However, the welfare effects of future emigration are of a greater

Table 2: Welfare effects of future emigration.

| | RC2 | | | RC2/RC1(%) | | |
|---|---|---|---|---|---|---|
| TP\v | 0.01 | 0.02 | 0.03 | 0.01 | 0.02 | 0.03 |
| 0.01 | 44.218 | 49.255 | 53.105 | 124.1 | 137.0 | 146.6 |
| 0.02 | 41.150 | 47.098 | 51.896 | 106.8 | 120.4 | 131.8 |
| 0.03 | 38.747 | 43.844 | 49.932 | 91.6 | 103.2 | 116.5 |

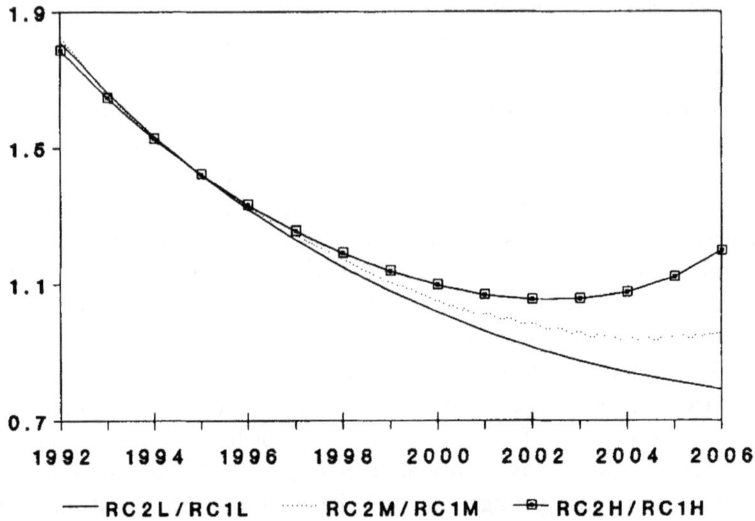


Figure 7: Effects of liberalization of labor flows: consumption per resident worker.

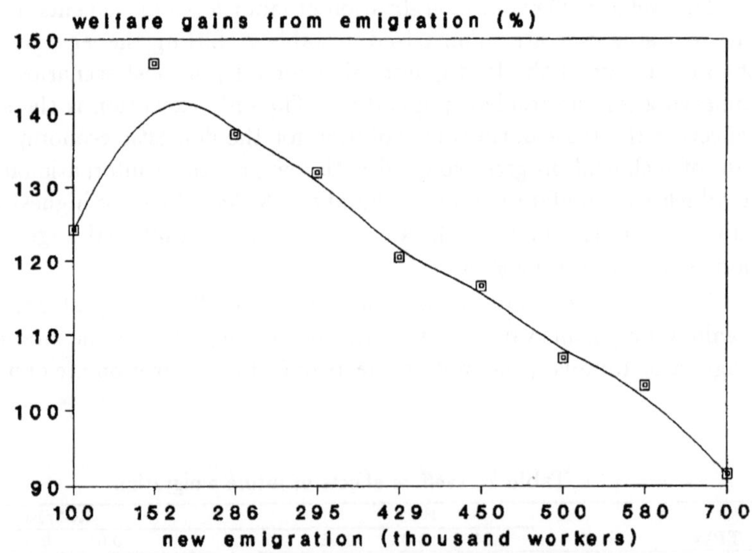


Figure 8: A Laffer curve for welfare gains.

order of magnitude than the welfare effects of past emigration. In fact, when further emigration due to the wage differential is permitted, the change in remittances due to a percentage point change in $v$ is $s_e E(1 + e_{Ev})$, where $e_{Ev}$ is the positive elasticity of emigration with respect to the international wage rate. Also, the welfare gains vary inversely with the rate of domestic technical progress. The higher is the rate of technical progress the lower is the wage differential between Portugal and the EC and the lower is future emigration and remittances.

Of great interest is the relationship between welfare gains and optimal emigration which shows a "Laffer Curve" effect (see Figure 8). For low levels of emigration increasing emigration improves welfare gains over the *status quo* (RC1). The welfare gains peak at 120 thousand new emigrants in a ten-year period and decline thereafter. For very high levels of emigration welfare gains are actually negative. This "Laffer Curve" effect suggests that for low or moderate levels of emigration, a further increase in emigration will generate high remittances relative to the domestic marginal productivity of labor. However, for high levels of emigration the marginal productivity of domestic labor becomes very high and the wage differential between home and host countries very low. The relative impact of remittances will then be minimized and eventually be dominated by the loss in domestic labor force.

This discussion now turns to other possible indicators of the effect of liberalization of labor movements. The simulated evolution of the capital-labor ratio in the RC2's vis-a-vis the corresponding RC1 are depicted in Figure 9. The simulations show clearly lower capital-labor ratios under liberalization when compared with the *status quo*. These ratios converge in the long run to about one fifth of the *status quo* values. This process of decapitalization (with investment often below replacement levels) mirrors the sharp increase in consumption per resident worker as discussed above. The idea of accelerated decapitalization is also captured in Figure 10 which depicts the rates of growth of domestic GNP under future emigration. Domestic production is systematically decreasing as a result of foregone labor force via emigration, despite increased remittances. Even in most favorable scenarios, say high technical progress and low international wage growth, the domestic production is basically stagnant.

Simulation results suggest that opening up the Portuguese economy to allow for further emigration flows into the EC is in most scenarios welfare improving for the resident population. From this standpoint the policy of integration in the EC, which provides the institutional setting for the elimination of the barriers to the movements of the Portuguese labor force, is well justified. However, it should be noted that these welfare improvements are somewhat artificial in that they are obtained at the cost of decapital-

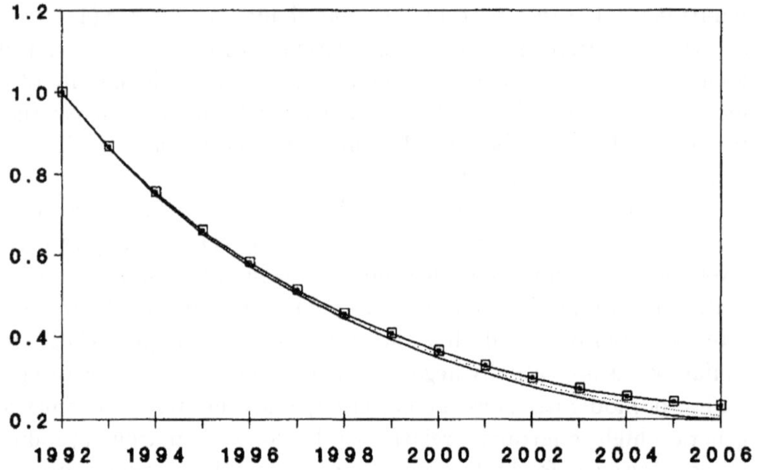


Figure 9: Effects of liberalization of labor flows: capital-labor ratio.

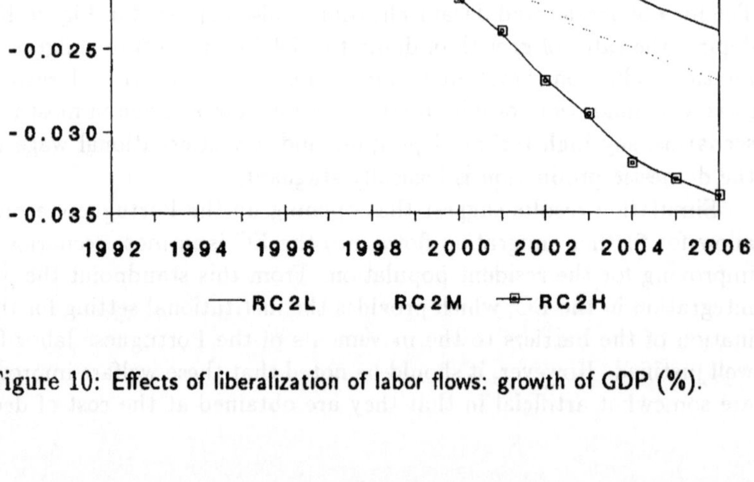


Figure 10: Effects of liberalization of labor flows: growth of GDP (%).

ization and stagnating or declining domestic production. From the policy point of view, the simulation results suggest that the Portuguese authorities should delay the liberalization of the movements of the Portuguese labor force within the EC. Liberalization should be delayed until such a time when the difference in the standards of living in Portugal versus the EC — as reflected by the domestic and foreign wage rates — will be substantially reduced. Then, only moderate emigration would be generated and the welfare gains over the current state of affairs will be maximized. Also, the delay would allow the use of the extensive community funds being channeled into the country to counteract the phenomena of decapitalization and sluggish domestic production that follow liberalization.

# 4 Summary and Concluding Remarks

This paper develops an optimal growth model in which part of the national labor force is allowed to emigrate, due to international wage rate differentials, and to send remittances to the home country. The model emphasizes the trade-off between emigration as foregone labor force and as a source of remittances. The model is numerically implemented for the Portuguese economy to study the effects on welfare and economic growth of the emigration in the 1960s and early 1970s, as well as the potential effects of liberalizing the movements of the Portuguese labor force in the EC.

The major conclusions from our simulation analysis can be summarized as follows. Past emigration has a positive welfare effects for the resident population. This suggests that the positive welfare effect of the steady flow of emigrants' remittances overrides the negative welfare effect of depopulation. In the light of these results, the traditional policies of the Portuguese governments of encouraging remittances rather than the return of the emigrants seem to be justified. However, despite the presence of remittances, past emigration leads to a decline in the capital-labor ratio and to a slowdown of domestic growth by about half a percentage point annually.

In turn, the liberalization of the movements of the Portuguese labor force in the EC is likely to provoke a substantial flow of new emigrants if the current trend of relatively low increases in the domestic real wages persists — about 300 in a decade for moderate growth of the international wages and moderate domestic technical progress. Emigrants' remittances can be anticipated to have an increasing role which boosts consumption per resident work and makes further emigration, under most scenarios, welfare-improving for the resident population. However, a further drain of the Portuguese labor force tends to depress or at best stagnate domestic production. In light of these results the Portuguese authorities should delay liberalization of the movements of Portuguese labor force in the EC until such a time when the wage rate differential between Portugal and the EC have been attenuated.

The above results and their policy implications should be considered tentative and evaluated in light of some critical assumptions and omissions in this paper. First, given the full-employment nature of the model, the optimal paths simulated represent the maximum potential of the economy and not its actual sub-utilization path. Accordingly, all the conclusions above should be interpreted as potential or full-employment properties of the economy. On the other hand, emigration can be perceived as a way of relieving unemployment pressures in the economy. Second, the determination of emigration flows and remittances follow reduced-form rules which are not directly derived from household optimizing behavior. A more rigorous approach would allow for the labor force to be optimally allocated between the domestic and foreign labor markets (for efforts in this direction with an application to the Portuguese economy see Barosa and Pereira, 1991) and for optimal savings behavior by the emigrated labor force. Third, the model does not consider international trade flows (for an optimal growth model with international borrowing applied to Portugal see Cabral, 1989). In the case of the Portuguese economy, international trade deficits are covered in good part by emigrants' remittances. In this sense emigration is instrumental in minimizing difficulties with the balance of payments. Furthermore, by not considering international trade or capital flows, the paper omits altogether the issue of the complementarity versus substitutability between international good and factor flows. This is a crucial issue when the Portuguese economy, both through the market mechanisms of financial integration and the institutional mechanisms of structural funds programs, has been experiencing substantial inflows of foreign capital (see Gaspar and Pereira, 1991, for a detailed discussion of this phenomenon).

The different issues above are difficult to tackle within the already complex framework of this model and are considered to be outside the realm of this paper. The added complexity would cloud the trade-off between emigration as foregone labor force and source of remittances and make the interpretation of the results difficult.

# Appendix: Data Set and Parameter Specification

## 1 On the Data Set

The following are the initial values for the variables in the model. The base year is 1985 and the units are billions of 1985 dollars unless otherwise indicated.

- Capital stock — $K_0 = 86,372$. There is no good data on the Portuguese capital stock. The figure above is consistent with a capital/output ratio of 3.5 and a net increase of 1% in the capital stock in 1986.

- Resident labor force — $L_0 = 4,670$ thousand workers (from Annual Report 1989, Bank of Portugal).

- Emigrated labor force — $E_0 = 660$ thousand workers (from Dados Estatísticos, Secretaria de Estado das Comunidades Portuguesas). This figure sets the emigrated labor force to about 14% of the resident labor force. In France the Portuguese community (corresponds to total population not to active labor force) is about 0.9 million people and in other EC countries about two hundred thousand. Therefore, there are approximately 1.1 million Portuguese emigrants in the EC vis-a-vis a resident population of 10 million, or 11%. The labor force figure above is obtained by applying the rate of Portuguese labor force participation in France to the whole Portuguese labor force in the EC (see below).

  It should be stressed that emigration to other areas is ignored. There are important Portuguese communities in Brazil and United States. However, these are typical cases of early emigration — 1940s and 1950s — and it is natural to assume that the ties linking these communities to Portugal are not particularly strong. It would be interesting to see how this is reflected in the flow of remittances but data is not available. In any case the main focus of this paper is the EC.

- Total national labor force — $P_0 = 5,264$ thousand workers. This figure is consistent with the model, in particular (8).

- GDP — $Y_0 = 25,227$ (from Annual Report 1989, Bank of Portugal).

- Remittances — $R_0 = 2,803$ (from Annual Report 1989, Bank of Portugal).

- Expenditure — $Y_0 + R_0 = 28,030$ (from Annual Report 1989, Bank of Portugal).
- Consumption — $C_0 = 21,984$ (from Annual Report 1989, Bank of Portugal).
- Investment — $I_0 = 6,046$ (from Annual Report 1989, Bank of Portugal).
- Domestic real wage rate — The domestic real wage rate is obtained from the model, in particular (10). Also, the initial international wage rate is derived consistently with the model, in particular (11). The initial value of the international wage rate enters in (7) in a normalized way such that no endogenous emigration occurs at $t = 1$.

## 2 Parameter Specification

The implementation of the model requires also a stylized set of structural parameters. These are the values of the parameters in the model:

- Subjective discount factor — $r = 0.97$. The long-run real rate of interest in the economy is used as a proxy for the subjective discount rate. In the base year, the nominal long run (2 to 5 years) rate of interest on loans was 25% (see Annual Report 1989, Bank of Portugal). In the same year the inflation rate was around 22% (see Annual Report 1989, Bank of Portugal).
- Share of capital in domestic expenditure — $b = 0.58$. The share of capital is obtained from Borges and Pereira (1989) as the average for the period 1970-1978 of the share of capital in the value added of the manufacturing sector.
- Output scaling factor — $b_0$. The output scaling factor is a calibration parameter. It is consistent with the economy at the base year in the sense that it is obtained form (4) given $b$, $K_0$, $L_0$ and $Y_0$.
- Labor force participation adjustment parameter — $z = 0.90$. It is accepted as a standard fact that the labor participation of the emigrated population, 50.8% in France for example, is higher than that of the resident population 46.7% (see Annual Report 1989, Bank of Portugal).
- Emigration reaction parameter — $h = 0.40$. Obtained from econometric estimation of equation (17) for the period 1959-1980. Emigration data available from Dados Estatísticos, Secretaria de Estado

das Comunidades Portuguesas, domestic wage rate and real wage in France (used as a proxy for EC wage rate) obtained from OECD Economic Outlook (several years).

- Emigrant's savings rate — $s_e = 0.20$. Applies the domestic average propensity to saving to emigrated labor force. Even though the presumption is that emigrants save at higher rate, it is questionable whether or not all savings are converted into remittances. The above figure is a subjective compromise.

- Rate of growth of the active labor force — $g = 0.008$. It is the average rate of growth of the resident labor force for the period 1978-1982. This is a good approximation under the assumption that these were years without any substantial emigration. This value is consistent with the estimated increase of the resident population for the period 1970-1980 and the forecasts in as in the World Development Report 1986, The World Bank.

- Depreciation rate — $d = 0.06$. This value is based on the depreciation rates for the manufacturing sector as reported in Borges and Pereira (1989), 0.07 for the period 1960-1978, and 0.045 for the period 1958-1974. However, one might suspect that the depreciation rates on other sectors, for example housing, are much lower, say 2%-3%.

# References


BANK OF PORTUGAL (1989): *Annual Report*, Banco de Portugal, Lisbon.

BAROSA, J. AND P. T. PEREIRA (1991): "Labor Supply in an Environment with Emigration: an Empirical Study of the Portuguese Case," in this volume.

BORGES, A. M. AND A. M. PEREIRA (1989): "Energy Demand in Portuguese Manufacturing: a Two-Stage Model," UCSD Working Paper #89-9, *Energy - The International Journal* (forthcoming).

CABRAL, L. (1989): "Optimal Timing for Repayment of Foreign Debt with an Application to Portugal," *Mimeo*, New University of Lisbon, *Economia* (forthcoming).

GASPAR, V. AND A. M. PEREIRA (1991): "On the Effects of Financial Integration and Unilateral Public Transfers on Investment and Growth," *Mimeo*, UCSD.

LUENBERGER, D. (1979): *Introduction to Dynamic Systems*. New York: John Wiley & Sons, Inc.

MACEDO, J. B. (1977): "Emigration and Remittances in Neo-Classical Steady-State," *Economia*, **1**, 95–111.

OECD (1986): *OECD Economic Outlook*, OECD, Paris.

PEREIRA, A. M. (1982): "Neoclassical Growth with Emigration and Remittances: An Extension to Optimal Control," *Economia*, **2**, 209–223.

SOLOW, R. (1956): "A Contribution to the Theory of Economic Growth," *Quarterly Journal of Economics*, **70**, 65–94.

SECRETARIA DE ESTADO DAS COMUNIDADES PORTUGUESAS (1984): *Dados Estatísticos*, Lisbon.

THE WORLD BANK (1989): *World Development Report*. Oxford: Oxford University Press.

# Labour Supply in an Environment with Emigration: an Empirical Study of the Portuguese Case

José Pedro Barosa
Pedro Telhado Pereira

## 1 Introduction

The stock of portuguese emigrants in EEC countries is at the present more than one million persons,[1] representing close to 25% of the current employment in Portugal.

Between 1965 and 1973 , more than 100 thousand people emigrated each year from Portugal to EEC countries. After 1974 emigration decreased to a virtual stop due to the emigration policies of the destination countries.

In this paper we study empirically the joint decision to emigrate and to work in the home country using portuguese data.

This analysis seems particularly relevant to the study of the consequences of the "European Single Act" whereby most barriers against the economic flows — including the barriers against the migration of workers — across EEC member states are to be abolished, starting 1993.

The phenomenon of intra Europe migration was virtually interrupted after the first oil shock in 1973/1974 but these flows can start again after the removal of the artificial barriers to free movement facing the Portuguese workers.

In this study it is shown that the emigration rate is positively related with the income in the destination countries and negatively related with the wages in the home country. The same applies to the expectations of these variables even more strongly.

[1] 1,063 thousands estimated using data from the State Department for Emigration and Portuguese Communities or 906 thousands in Eurostat estimate for 1986.

The results also demonstrate that the activity rate (rate of participation in the labour market) is significantly influenced by the income in the destination countries, strongly supporting our feeling that emigration and labour force participation , as economic decisions, belong to a single process.

This paper is organized as follows. First,conceptual issues are reviewed. Second, the data is discussed and the empirical models are presented. Third, the results are examined. The paper concludes with a brief discussion of the findings.

## 2 Conceptual Issues

There is a vast literature on the economics of the decision to supply work, either by men, women and within the family.[2] The decision to work in a environment with emigration has recently attracted more attention.[3]

Most of this studies start with an utility maximization model, where the worker decides how to allocate time and where to live within his life cycle. The main conclusions of these studies that we use here are:

1. the decisions of supplying work and or emigrating depend on real wages at home and abroad as well as its expectations; higher real wages at home imply less emigration and more participation at home, the opposite applies to foreign wages.

2. as there is no certainty about future wages some expectation hypothesis for this variable has to be used.

3. unemployment is important in the decision to migrate. If at all, people move from regions with higher unemployment to regions with lower unemployment when the wages are the same in the two regions.

4. the cost of emigration influences not only the probability to migrate but also the frequency of migration. Lower costs imply higher probability to migrate, shorter stays abroad and higher frequency of migration.

5. the information about the conditions of work in a foreign country tend to increase with the number of emigrants already there. The uncertainty cost associated with emigration therefore decreases with

[2] See Ashenfelter and Heckman (1974), Heckman (1974), Heckman (1976), Heckman and MaCurdy (1980), McCabe (1983), Moffit (1984) and Blundell and Walker (1984).

[3] Some recent studies are those of Falaris (1987), Hill (1987), Berninghaus and Seifert-Vogt (1988), Barosa and Pereira (1989), Djajič (1989), Hartog and Vriend (1990) and Pissarides and McMaster (1990).

the stock of emigrants in the destination country. The probability of migrating will increase with the stock of emigrants.

6. real wealth influences the probability of working and of migrating.

# 3 Data and Estimation Procedure

Most of data we used in this paper is from publications of the INE (National Institute of Statistics), Banco de Portugal , IMF, ILO and the State Department for Emigration. The period under study is 1958 to 1985 .[4]

Variables:

*wh* — home wages — we used the value obtained by multiplying the real wage by the probability of employment, so being an "average wage".

*ewh* — expected home wages — this variable is constructed as an weighted average of wages in the next three periods.

$$ewh(t) = a_1 wh(t+1) + a_2 wh(t+2) + a_3 wh(t+3) .$$

where:

$$a_1 + a_2 + a_3 = 1 .$$

The coefficient for $wh(t+3)$ can be considered as representing the whole future.

*wd* — wages in the destination countries — we tried to use wages in some of the main destination countries ( France, Germany and USA ). The result was not satisfactory in the sense that the coefficients where never significantly different from zero at the 10% level. We think this happened because the average wage is not a good proxy for the emigrants wage and the main destinations for the portuguese emigration has been changing with time. We used instead the real per capita income in the industrialized countries as a proxy for this variable.

*ewd* — expected wages in the destination countries — see above for *ewh*.

*a* — families' financial wealth at constant prices — as calculated by Cartaxo and Santos (1984).

[4] We used data from the period between 1958 and 1985 because data for 1986 and later is not directly comparable with the data until 1985.

*em* — emigration rate — calculated as the number of emigrants divided by total population.

*act* — activity rate — calculated as the active population divided by the total population.

*se* — stock of emigrants (previous period).

For purposes of identification of the model being estimated we decided to estimate the labour demand equation at the same time as the labour supply and emigration equations. Here is used a conditional (derived) demand function where the arguments are the cost of labour for the employer (nominal wage), the price of other inputs (oil price and interest rates) and the quantity produced.

*N* — total employment.

*o* — oil prices in escudos per barrel.

*ir* — one plus the nominal interest rate.

*y* — quantity produced.

*whn* — nominal home wages.

As there is a strong presumption of structural break in 1974, because of the above mentioned changes in emigration policies of the main european countries we estimated the equations allowing for the possibility of changes in the coefficients in 1974.

This means that we created variables that have the value one multiplied by the value of the variable until 1973 and zero afterwards. The variable $x_1$ is created from variable $x$ this way.

We started estimating the following model:

$$\begin{aligned}
\ln act = {} & \beta_1 + \beta_2 \ln wh + \beta_3 \ln ewh + \beta_4 \ln wd + \beta_5 \ln ewd \\
& + \beta_6 \ln se + \beta_7 \ln a + \beta_1' d + \beta_2' \ln wh_1 + \beta_3' \ln ewh_1 \\
& + \beta_4' \ln wd_1 + \beta_5' \ln ewd_1 + \beta_6' \ln se_1 + \beta_7' \ln a_1 + \epsilon \\
\ln em = {} & \gamma_1 + \gamma_2 \ln wh + \gamma_3 \ln ewh + \gamma_4 \ln wd + \gamma_5 \ln ewd \\
& + \gamma_6 \ln se + \gamma_7 \ln a + \gamma_1' d + \gamma_2' \ln wh_1 + \gamma_3' \ln ewh_1 \\
& + \gamma_4' \ln wd_1 + \gamma_5' \ln eqd_1 + \gamma_6' \ln se_1 + \gamma_7' \ln a_1 + v \\
\ln N = {} & \rho_1 + \rho_2 \ln whn + \rho_3 \ln y + \rho_4 \ln o + \rho_5 \ln ir \\
& + \rho_1' d + \rho_2' \ln whn_1 + \rho_3' \ln y_1 + \rho_4' lno_1 + \rho_5' \ln ir_1 + \zeta ,
\end{aligned}$$

where $d$ is a dummy variable that is zero until 1973 and 1 thereafter.

The three equations above were estimated simultaneously by three stages least squares and the significance of all the parameters was tested. All that appeared not significantly different from zero (10% level) were deleted from the equations. These were simplified to be:

$$\ln act = \beta_1 + \beta_2 \ln wh + \beta_4 \ln wd + \beta_4 \ln ewd$$
$$+\beta_6 \ln se + \beta_7 \ln a + \beta_3' \ln wh_1 + \beta_5' \ln ewd_1 + \epsilon$$
$$\ln em = \gamma_1 + \gamma_2 \ln wh + \gamma_4 \ln wd + \gamma_5 \ln ewd + \gamma_6 \ln se$$
$$+\gamma_7 \ln a + \gamma_3' \ln wh_1 + \gamma_5' \ln ewd_1 + v$$
$$\ln N = \rho_1 + \rho_2 \ln whn + \rho_3 \ln y + \rho_4 \ln o + \rho_5 \ln ir + \zeta \ .$$

The following variables were used as instruments: $\ln wd$, $\ln ewd$, $\ln ewd_1$, $\ln a$, $\ln se$, $\ln ir$, $\ln o$, $t$, $t^2$, $\ln e$, where $t$ is time and $e$ is the exchange rate.

# 4 Estimation Results

The results from the non-linear three stages estimation procedure are ($t$ values within brackets)[5] presented in Table 1.

The results of the estimation procedure show:

[5]Standard errors computed from heteroscedastic-consistent matrix.

Table 1: Non-linear three stages estimation.

| | ln *act* | | ln *em* | | ln *N* | |
|---|---|---|---|---|---|---|
| | Estimate | *t*-Stat | Estimate | *t*-Stat | Estimate | *t*-Stat |
| Const. | 0.025 | (1.00) | 0.434 | (1.71) | 0.15 | (4.14) |
| $\ln wh$ | 0.297 | (4.82) | 1.978 | (2.42) | | |
| | 0.590 | (3.00) | -14.688 | (-5.59) | | |
| $\ln ewh_1(+1)$ | 0.656 | (4.51) | 0.656 | (4.51) | | |
| $\ln ewh_1(+2)$ | -0.364 | (-1.79) | -0.364 | (-1.79) | | |
| $\ln ewh_1(+3)$ | 0.708 | (2.61) | 0.708 | (2.61) | | |
| $\ln whn$ | | | | | -0.140 | (-4.93) |
| $\ln wd$ | 1.243 | (4.81) | 8.597 | (3.12) | | |
| | -0.360 | (-1.74) | -10.567 | (-4.54) | | |
| $\ln ewd(+1)$ | 0.481 | (2.00) | 0.481 | (2.00) | | |
| $\ln ewd(+2)$ | -0.111 | (-0.35) | -0.111 | (-0.35) | | |
| $\ln ewd(+3)$ | 0.630 | (1.30) | 0.630 | (1.30) | | |
| | -0.678 | (-4.10) | 14.796 | (6.74) | | |
| $\ln ewd_1(+1)$ | 0.573 | (4.87) | 0.573 | (4.87) | | |
| $\ln ewd_1(+2)$ | -0.211 | (-1.26) | -0.211 | (-1.26) | | |
| $\ln ewd_1(+3)$ | 0.638 | (2.49) | 0.638 | (2.49) | | |
| $\ln se$ | -0.191 | (-3.19) | -0.155 | (-0.20) | | |
| $\ln a$ | -0.195 | (-9.88) | 1.052 | (4.15) | | |
| $\ln y$ | | | | | 0.154 | (4.21) |
| $\ln o$ | | | | | 0.070 | (7.48) |
| $\ln ir$ | | | | | -0.116 | (-1.34) |
| $d$ | | | | | 0.082 | (8.65) |
| $\bar{R}^2$ | 0.99 | | 0.96 | | 0.99 | |

1. Income in the destination country and emigration rate are positively related with an elasticity of 8.7.

2. Expected future income abroad and the emigration rate are positively related up to 1974 and negatively related thereafter. This shows that there was a structural break in 74, when the destination countries changed their immigration's policies and the portuguese revolution took place.

3. The emigration rate and the wages in the home country are positively related. This could be because present wages influence expected wages or because of imperfections in the capital markets.

4. Expected future wages at home and the emigration rate are negatively related until 1974. As workers expect their situation in the home country to improve they will stay in their home country instead of emigrating. The relevant elasticity was estimated to be a very high 14.7.

5. In what concerns the activity rate equation all the coefficients appear with the expected signs with the exception of the coefficient of the income in the destination country. Our preferred explanation is that people planing to emigrate will first enter the labour force and only then migrate. This could be because of the capital constraint and because it is easier to migrate after the worker has some working experience.

6. Wealth influences negatively the activity rate (leisure is a normal good) and positively the emigration rate, again the imperfections in the capital market.

7. The stock of emigrants in the previous period influences negatively the activity rate. Remittances may be increasing the reservation wages of those who stay.

8. The labour demand equation shows that labour demand is very rigid in what concerns the nominal wages and the substitutability between labour and energy ( the coefficient of the oil prices ) is positive. There is a structural break in 74 because of the institutional changes that took place as a consequence of the revolution.

9. As mentioned before the expectations should encompass all the future but, due to the sample size, we restricted the mechanism to be estimated to three coefficients only. In this case, the third coefficient was restricted and should be understood as the sum of all the coefficients

Table 2: Effects of future wages in the emigration rate.

| | Home wages | Destination wages | |
|---|---|---|---|
| | | till 74 | after 74 |
| $t+1$ | -9.635 | 3.395 | -5.083 |
| $t+2$ | 5.346 | -1.949 | 1.173 |
| $t+3$ | -10.399 | 2.783 | -6.657 |
| Total | -14.688 | 4.229 | -10.567 |

Table 3: Effects of future wages in the participation rate.

| | Home wages | Destination wages | |
|---|---|---|---|
| | | till 74 | after 74 |
| $t+1$ | 0.387 | -0.562 | -0.388 |
| $t+2$ | -0.215 | 0.183 | 0.143 |
| $t+3$ | 0.418 | -0.659 | -0.433 |
| Total | 0.590 | -1.030 | -0.678 |

referring to $time \geq t+3$. Of course, in this way, meaningful information about longer term dynamics may be lost if other coefficients for $time > t+3$ are significant.

The pattern of the effects of future wages in the emigration rate equation is given in Table 2.

The pattern of the effects of future wages in the participation rate equation is given in Table 3.

10 From the tables above we see that the future wages influence the emigration rate and the participation rate in opposite directions; for instance, an increase in wages at time $t+1$ in the home country increases the participation rate and decreases the emigration rate at time $t$.

11 The emigration rate shows much higher elasticity in relation to future wages than the participation rate.

# 5 Conclusions

From the results obtained in this paper a number of important conclusions can be drawn. In fact, if the immigration policies of the northern european EEC countries do change as a consequence of the Single Act, a substantial emigration towards these countries can be forecast.

As this happen the skill composition of labour supply will change. In the host countries we can expect a decrease in relative wages of the more unskilled work while the opposite will happen in the countries where emigration originates.

In the long run portuguese emigration will depend on perceptions of the evolution of wages both at home and abroad. If wages in Portugal are expected to increase fast this may counter the "level effect" that is the emigratory movement resulting from current wages differences. But if wages are expected to catch-up only gradually there may be important labour flows across EEC.

# 6 References


Ashenfelter, O. and J. Heckman (1974): "The Estimation of Income and Substitution Effects in a Model of Family Labour Supply," *Econometrica*, **42**, 73–85.

Barosa, J. P. and P. T. Pereira (1989): "Economic Integration and Labour Flows: The European Single Act and its Consequences," Working Paper #123, Faculdade de Economia, Universidade Nova de Lisboa.

Berninghaus, S. and H. G. Seifert-Vogt (1988): "Temporary vs. Permanent Migration: a Decision Theoretical Approach," *Journal of Population Economics*, 1, 195–211.

Blundell, R. and I. Walker (1984): "Empirical Approaches to Life Cycle Labour Supply," in *Recent Advances in Labour Economics*, ed. by G. Hutchinson and J. Treble. London: St. Martin Press.

Cartaxo, R. and E. A. Santos (1984): "Estimativas Anuais da Riqueza Financeira das Familias para o Periodo 1958–1981," Documento de Trabalho #8 , Banco de Portugal.

Djajič, S. (1989): "Migrants in a Guest-Worker System: a Utility Maximizing Approach," *Journal of Development Economics*, **31**, 327–339.

Falaris, E. M. (1987): "A Nested Logit Migration Model with Selectivity," *International Economic Review*, **28**, 429–443.

Hartog, J. and N. Vriend (1990): "Young Mediterraneans in the Dutch Labour Market: a Comparative Analysis of Allocation and Earnings," *Oxford Economic Papers*, **42**, 371–401.

Heckman , J. J. (1974): "Life Cycle Consumption and Labour Supply: an Explanation of the Relationship Between Income and Consumption Over the Life Cycle," *The American Economic Review*, **64**, 188–194.

Heckman, J. J. (1976): "A Life Cycle Model of Earnings, Learning and Consumption," *Journal of Political Economy*, **84**, S11–S43.

Heckman, J. J. and T. E. MaCurdy (1980): "A Life Cycle Model of Female Labour Supply," *Review of Economic Studies*, **47**, 47–74.

Hill, J. K. (1988): "Immigrant Decisions Concerning Duration of Stay and Migratory Frequency," *Journal of Development Economics*, **25**, 221–234.

McCabe, P. J. (1983): "Optimal Leisure-Effort Choice with Endogenously Determined Earnings," *Journal of Labour Economics*, **1**, 308–329.

MaCurdy, T. E. (1981): "An Empirical Model of Labour Supply in a Life-Cycle Setting," *Journal of Political Economy*, **89**, 1059–1086.

Moffit, R. (1984): "The Estimation of a Joint Wage-Hours Labour Supply," *Journal of Labour Economics*, **2**, 550–566.

Pissarides, C. A. and McMaster (1990): "Regional Migration, Wages and Unemployment: Empirical Evidence and Implications for Policy," *Oxford Economic Papers*, **42**, 812–831.

# Co-Integration of Macroeconomic Time Series: an Application to the Consumption Function

Vítor Gaspar
Maximiano Pinheiro

## 1 Introduction

During the eighties it was generally accepted that a correct approach to econometric modelling requires time series analysis as an important step. Nelson and Plosser (1982) and Engle and Granger (1987) have shown that, in particular in what concerns macroeconomic time series, those properties have important implications for the choice of a correct econometric approach.

It should be mentioned in this context that non-stationarity of macroeconomic time series constitutes an important departure from the assumption of classical econometric models. Nevertheless the use of first and second differences in regressions, suggested to ensure the stationarity of the underlying time series, translates on excess volatility and bad quality of the estimates and associated forecasts. These problems may however be easily overcome when it is possible to use co-integration relations between variables.[1] In this paper it will be shown that these remarks are relevant for the study of "consumption function" in Portugal.

The behavior of consumption is a matter of particular interest at present in Portugal. In fact national savings in Portugal are extremely high bring in vicinity of 30% of GDP. This figure is well above European Community averages. For this result the behavior of households savings is clearly crucial. Given the foregoing it also becomes evident that the modelling of

[1] The fundamental reference is Engle and Granger (1987). For an introduction see Hall and Henry (1988).

the "consumption function" is important to be able to gather additional information, e.g., concerning its stability (or instability) of this ratio.

Furthermore consumption is the most important component of aggregate demand which makes its relevance for macroeconomic modelling evident.

Internationalization, de-regulation and liberalization of financial markets are associated with the generalization of consumers' credit. Consumers' credit conditions have very significant consequences for consumption and savings.[2] Japelli and Pagano (1989) have argued for the relevance of credit market imperfections in the area of consumers' credit for consumption and saving.

Given the internationalization, de-regulation and liberalization of the portuguese financial system, these remarks are particularly timely (see Macedo, 1990, and Branson, 1990). All the more so given that Luz (1990) has shown that liquidity constraints are important in the portuguese case. The de-regulation of portuguese financial markets is occurring in the context of increased financial integration throughout the European Community. In fact the institutional changes associated with the Single Market Program and Economic and Monetary Union call for the removal of all barriers to trade in financial services and confer unrestricted rights of establishment for member-states financial institutions. In such a case it is possible to argue that international competition will prevent the government from retaining regulations that translate into competitive disadvantages for domestic financial intermediaries. Regulation will converge to a minimum compatible with stability of financial markets. Therefore it is likely that one of the main consequences of this process will be the gradual generalization of, inter alia, consumers' credit (see Giovaninni and Mayer, 1991).

The purpose of this paper is to present an application of the co-integration methodology. This methodology will be applied to the macroeconomic time series relevant for modelling aggregate consumption behavior. In particular a "consumption function" will be obtained. The form retained for the function is such as to make it compatible with a small macroeconometric model.

In the second section of the paper the univariate time series properties of consumption, nominal and real interest rates and income will be presented and studied. In the third section co-integration relations between these variables will be explored. It will be argued that it is useful to think about such a co-integration relation as a "long run consumption function". In section 4 Engle and Granger representation theorem will be used to obtain

[2] See, for example, *European Economy*, 42, Nov. 1989.

results on the short run dynamic behavior of consumption. The short run dynamics obtained in this fashion relate to the well known "error correction mechanisms" derived from the solution to the optimal control of dynamic systems. In this context it is relatively simple to show that given reasonable restrictions the long run relation may be recovered from the short run dynamics. Evidence will be presented suggesting that such restrictions are not rejected by the available data. Finally, we will conclude by offering some tentative conclusions and providing lines for further research.

# 2 Univariate Time Series Analysis

This section will present an analysis of time series properties of consumption, income, real and nominal interest rates and, finally, inflation rates. The choice of income and real interest rates is suggested by traditional formulations of the permanent income/life cycle hypothesis as in Blanchard and Fisher (1989). The inclusion of nominal interest rates and inflation rates in turn is suggested both by: (i) the effect of inflation on disposable income as measured according to the methodology of National Accounts; (ii) the effect on the relevance of liquidity constraints.

The relevance of this preliminary analysis stems from the fact that the classical econometric methods rely on the assumptions that the economic variables involved are generated by stationary and ergodic stochastic processes. Nevertheless the evidence presented by several authors (namely Nelson and Plosser (1982)) points out that economic time series are only stationary in first or second differences. That is macroeconomic time series are frequently integrated of first or second orders, $I(1)$ or $I(2)$.[3]

Phillips and Durlauf (1987) have shown that although in certain well specified conditions consistency of estimators is retained, the usual distributions no longer apply when regressions include integrated time series. Furthermore there is a problem with possibly "spurious regressions" when using small samples. That is, reasonable good fits may occur as consequences of non-stationarity and not as a reflex of any association between variables. Granger and Newbold (1974) have noted that "spurious regressions" correspond frequently to a Durbin-Watson statistic $d$ close to zero. This result is justified because of the non-stationarity of residuals induced by non-stationarity in the series.[4]

[3] The simpler example of a stochastic process which is integrated of the first degree is the random walk $x_t = x_{t-1} + \epsilon_t$ when $\epsilon_t$ is a white noise. In general the stochastic process $\{x_t\}_1^\infty$ is said to be integrated of order $k$ and will be noted as $x_t \sim I(k)$ if $\Delta^k x_t$ ($k$-th order difference of $x_t$) is stationary in first and second moments ($\Delta^k x_t \sim I(0)$).

[4] If $\{y_t\}$ and $\{x_t\}$ are $I(1)$ then the residual $\{\epsilon_t\}$ of the regression $y_t = x_t\beta + \epsilon_t$ will

A common solution to the problem of performing regressions involving integrated time series is simply to substitute regressions using first or second differences for the regressions in levels. The cost of this drastic solution may be high. In fact differentiation excludes information that might be reflected from the association between variables in levels. That could lead to a worsening of the quality of the fit and to instability of estimates. Perhaps more important than that, this omission may also contribute to the worsening of the forecast performance of the models.

A superior alternative is to use possible co-integration relations between the time series. In any case, the study of co-integration relations requires the univariate characterization of time series to be made before hand. That is the purpose of this section.

The following series will be considered:[5]

$LCPRIVR$: Natural logarithm (for short: ln) of real private consumption (evaluated at 1977 prices);

$LRDFR = \ln(RDF/PCPRIV)$ where $RDF$ stands for households disposable income and $PCPRIV$ for the consumption deflator (base 1977 = 1.00);

$DLPCPRIV$: First difference of the logarithm of the consumption price deflator (base 1977 = 1.00);

$LTXJDPL = \ln[1+TXJDP(1-TXIKDP)]$, where $TXJDP$ stands for the nominal interest rate on six-month time deposits and $TXIKDP$ is the corresponding withholding tax (which taxpayers have the option of regarding as final);

$LTXJDPLR = LTXJDPL - DLPCPRIV$ stands for the real interest rate.

The analysis of the above time series will be set namely on testing the existence of unit roots. For each of the above series the $\Phi_3$ Dickey and Fuller (1981) test will be presented. This test is based on the likelihood ratio. The purpose of $\Phi_3$ is, for any time series $y_t$, to test the null hypothesis:

$$\mathrm{H}_0{:}y_t = \mu + y_{t-1} + \epsilon_t \,, \quad t = 1, \ldots, T \tag{1}$$

against the alternative:

$$\mathrm{H}_1{:}y_t = \mu + \beta t + \rho y_{t-1} + \epsilon_t \,, t = 1, \ldots, T \,. \tag{2}$$

be in general $I(1)$, given that it is a linear combination of $I(1)$ processes $\epsilon_t = y_t - x_t\beta$. Granger and Newbold suggested the rule $R^2 > d$ as an indicator for spurious regressions.

[5] Sample period: (i) $LCPRIVR$ and $LRDFR$, 1958–1988; (ii) $DLPCPRIV$, 1959–1988; (iii) $LTXJDPL$ and $LTXJDPLR$, 1965–1988. Source: Banco de Portugal.

Table 1: $\Phi_3$ statistic.

| | Variable | 1st Diff. |
|---|---|---|
| *LCPRIVR* | 2.02 | 5.65 |
| *LRDFR* | 2.05 | 8.22 |
| *DLPCPRIV* | 1.42 | 19.61 |
| *LTXJDPL* | 3.03 | 4.70 |
| *LTXJDPLR* | 2.62 | 13.36 |

The inclusion of a trend in the alternative has the advantage of making the asymptotic distribution independent of the drift term $\mu$. $\Phi_3$ is the usual F-statistic associated with the OLS regression of (2) for the test $(\beta, \rho) = (0, 1)$.

Dickey and Fuller (1981) provide critical values for the test based on the asymptotic distribution. They also provide the critical values for finite samples (with 25, 50, 100, 250 and 500 observations). For finite samples the critical values were obtained through simulation methods. The critical values obtained by Dickey-Fuller for 10%, 5%, 2.5% and 1% significance levels were respectively 5.34, 6.25, 7.16 and 8.17 using the asymptotic distribution and 5.91, 7.24, 8.65 and 10.61 using the distribution corresponding to samples with 25 observations.[6] Dickey and Fuller have also shown that the asymptotic distribution is invariant when $y_t$ is generated by an auto-regressive stochastic process of order $p$ ($p > 1$) and one wants to test whether one of the roots is unitary. In such a case one would use the F-statistic corresponding to the hypothesis $(\beta, \theta_0) = (0, 0)$ in the following regression:

$$\Delta y_t = \mu + \beta t + \theta_0 y_{t-1} + \sum_{i=1}^{p} \theta_i \Delta y_{t-1} + \epsilon \ . \qquad (3)$$

Table 1 includes the values of the $\Phi_3$ statistic for the following series *LCPRIVR*, *LRDFR*, *DLPCPRIV*, *LTXJDPL* and *LTXJDPLR* and their first differences.

On Table 1 it is clear that the hypothesis of existence of unit roots is not rejected for each and everyone of the series. In fact the largest value 3.03 corresponding to *LTXJDPL* (the nominal interest rate) is still well below the critical values for the 10% significance level.

In the second column of Table 1 results are more mixed. One is able to reject clearly the existence of unit roots both for the first difference of inflation and the first difference of real interest rates. Furthermore it is still possible to search a similar conclusion for the case of real disposable income. The case of the growth rate of private consumption is less clear:

[6] One may remark that these critical values are approximately two times larger than the corresponding values for the Fisher–Snedcor distribution.

Table 2A: Correlograms.

| LAG | *LCPRIVR* | *LRDFR* | *DLPCPRIV* | *LTXJDPL* | *LTXJDPLR* |
|---|---|---|---|---|---|
| 1 | 0.904 | 0.915 | 0.858 | 0.926 | 0.600 |
| | (0.180) | (0.180) | (0.183) | (0.204) | (0.204) |
| 2 | 0.809 | 0.827 | 0.763 | 0.797 | 0.508 |
| | (0.292) | (0.294) | (0.287) | (0.336) | (0.268) |
| 3 | 0.715 | 0.739 | 0.687 | 0.659 | 0.452 |
| | (0.357) | (0.361) | (0.348) | (0.407) | (0.305) |
| 4 | 0.631 | 0.647 | 0.546 | 0.526 | 0.044 |
| | (0.400) | (0.407) | (0.391) | (0.450) | (0.332) |
| 5 | 0.537 | 0.554 | 0.478 | 0.386 | -0.001 |
| | (0.431) | (0.439) | (0.415) | (0.475) | (0.332) |
| 6 | 0.441 | 0.460 | 0.363 | 0.236 | -0.170 |
| | (0.452) | (0.461) | (0.433) | (0.488) | (0.332) |
| 7 | 0.343 | 0.362 | 0.233 | 0.083 | -0.329 |
| | (0.466) | (0.475) | (0.443) | (0.492) | (0.336) |
| 8 | 0.251 | 0.265 | 0.141 | -0.064 | -0.368 |
| | (0.474) | (0.484) | (0.447) | (0.493) | (0.349) |
| 9 | 0.162 | 0.166 | 0.031 | -0.190 | -0.394 |
| | (0.478) | (0.489) | (0.449) | (0.493) | (0.365) |
| 10 | 0.077 | 0.077 | -0.091 | -0.295 | -0.387 |
| | (0.480) | (0.491) | (0.449) | (0.496) | (0.382) |
| 11 | -0.004 | -0.011 | -0.203 | -0.371 | -0.403 |
| | (0.480) | (0.491) | (0.450) | (0.504) | (0.398) |
| 12 | -0.084 | -0.093 | -0.302 | -0.481 | -0.267 |
| | (0.480) | (0.491) | (0.453) | (0.515) | (0.415) |
| 13 | -0.159 | -0.167 | -0.381 | -0.442 | -0.185 |
| | (0.481) | (0.492) | (0.459) | (0.529) | (0.422) |
| 14 | -0.230 | -0.235 | -0.421 | -0.432 | -0.117 |
| | (0.483) | (0.494) | (0.470) | (0.544) | (0.425) |
| 15 | -0.292 | -0.290 | -0.444 | -0.408 | 0.061 |
| | (0.486) | (0.497) | (0.482) | (0.588) | (0.426) |

the null hypothesis is rejected only at the 10% significance level and for the case in which the asymptotic distribution is used.

Finally we were unable to reject (even at the 10% significance level) the existence of a unit root for the first difference of the nominal interest rate.

The previous results should be regarded with particular caution. Firstly because one is working in the context of a small sample; secondly because the power of unit roots tests is limited. It is therefore justified to try to obtain additional information from the estimated auto-correlation coefficients. These are reported in Table 2A for the original series and in Table 2B for the corresponding first differences.

In fact additional information is readily available from the estimated auto-correlation coefficients. These are reported in Table 2A for the original series and in Table 2B for the corresponding first differences.

Comparing Table 1 with Tables 2A and 2B one may propose the following conclusions:

(i) The results on the first column of Table 1 are confirmed by Table 2A. The only exception concerns real interest rates. For this series the

Table 2B: Correlograms.

| LAG | $\Delta LCPRIVR$ | $\Delta LRDFR$ | $\Delta DLPCPRIV$ | $\Delta LTXJDPL$ | $\Delta LTXJDPLR$ |
|---|---|---|---|---|---|
| 1 | 0.458 | 0.411 | -0.188 | 0.536 | -0.425 |
| | (0.183) | (0.183) | (0.186) | (0.209) | (0.209) |
| 2 | 0.219 | 0.197 | -0.109 | 0.026 | -0.038 |
| | (0.218) | (0.211) | (0.192) | (0.262) | (0.243) |
| 3 | 0.083 | 0.222 | 0.309 | -0.214 | 0.451 |
| | (0.225) | (0.217) | (0.194) | (0.262) | (0.244) |
| 4 | 0.113 | 0.082 | -0.311 | -0.054 | -0.420 |
| | (0.226) | (0.225) | (0.210) | (0.269) | (0.277) |
| 5 | 0.133 | 0.122 | 0.164 | 0.111 | 0.158 |
| | (0.228) | (0.226) | (0.226) | (0.270) | (0.304) |
| 6 | 0.128 | 0.210 | 0.122 | 0.082 | -0.015 |
| | (0.230) | (0.228) | (0.237) | (0.272) | (0.307) |
| 7 | 0.124 | 0.040 | -0.159 | -0.114 | -0.150 |
| | (0.233) | (0.234) | (0.232) | (0.273) | (0.307) |
| 8 | -0.019 | 0.111 | -0.004 | -0.286 | -0.005 |
| | (0.235) | (0.234) | (0.236) | (0.275) | (0.311) |
| 9 | -0.099 | 0.211 | 0.104 | -0.227 | 0.014 |
| | (0.235) | (0.236) | (0.236) | (0.287) | (0.311) |
| 10 | -0.270 | -0.095 | -0.057 | -0.214 | -0.010 |
| | (0.236) | (0.242) | (0.237) | (0.295) | (0.311) |
| 11 | -0.334 | -0.303 | -0.079 | -0.175 | -0.072 |
| | (0.246) | (0.244) | (0.238) | (0.302) | (0.311) |
| 12 | -0.106 | -0.224 | -0.050 | -0.090 | 0.003 |
| | (0.261) | (0.256) | (0.239) | (0.306) | (0.311) |
| 13 | -0.088 | -0.187 | -0.183 | 0.012 | -0.005 |
| | (0.262) | (0.262) | (0.239) | (0.307) | (0.311) |
| 14 | -0.187 | -0.186 | -0.017 | 0.020 | -0.033 |
| | (0.263) | (0.267) | (0.244) | (0.307) | (0.311) |
| 15 | -0.128 | -0.078 | 0.006 | -0.006 | 0.059 |
| | (0.268) | (0.271) | (0.244) | (0.307) | (0.311) |

auto-correlation coefficients points clear to stationarity. This result is more on line with *a priori* beliefs on the behavior of real interest rates.

(ii) Table 2B gives further information that is useful to settle some unclear results presented on Table 1. In fact both the growth rate of real consumption and the first difference of nominal interest rates appear to be stationary.

Table 3A: Co-integrating regressions without imposing unit elasticity.

| | (3.1) | (3.2) | (3.3) | (3.4) | (3.5) | (3.6) |
|---|---|---|---|---|---|---|
| Constant | 1.1827 | 1.1827 | 1.0386 | 2.2056 | 2.3185 | 2.2825 |
| *LRDFR* | 0.8936 | 0.8936 | 0.9054 | 0.8127 | 0.8036 | 0.8059 |
| *LTXJDLR* | -0.5923 | | | | | -0.2721 |
| *DLPCPRIV* | -0.4464 | 0.1459 | | -0.0477 | | |
| *LTXJDL* | | -0.5923 | -0.5118 | | | |
| $R^2$ | 0.987 | 0.987 | 0.986 | 0.979 | 0.979 | 0.982 |
| $\bar{R}^2$ | 0.985 | 0.985 | 0.985 | 0.977 | 0.978 | 0.981 |
| *SE* | 0.030 | 0.030 | 0.030 | 0.036 | 0.036 | 0.034 |
| *CRDW* | 0.897 | 0.897 | 0.993 | 0.735 | 0.699 | 0.667 |
| *ADF* | -3.47 | -3.47 | -3.70 | -2.69 | -2.68 | 2.61 |

# 3 Co-Integration Relations / Co-Integration Tests

In this section evidence will be presented on the existence of a co-integration relation between real private consumption, real disposable income and nominal interest rate.

A vector $x_t$ $(k \times 1)$ of variables is said to be co-integrated if a vector $\alpha \in \mathbf{R}^k$, $\alpha = (\alpha_1, \ldots, \alpha_i, \ldots, \alpha_k)$ with $\alpha_i \neq 0 \quad (i = 1, \ldots, k)$, exists such that $\alpha' x_t = z_t$ with $z_t$ stationary (that is $I(0)$). With no loss of generality one may normalize in the first component of $x_t$ and write $z_t = \mu + v_t$ with $E(v_t) = 0$ to obtain:

$$x_{1t} = \beta_1 + \beta_2 x_{2t} + \ldots + \beta_k x_{kt} + \epsilon \tag{4}$$

where $\epsilon_t = v_t/\alpha_1$, $\beta_1 = \mu/\alpha_1$ and $\beta_j = -\alpha_j/\alpha_1 \quad (j = 2, \ldots, k)$. From a statistical view point the normalization chosen is entirely arbitrary. Nevertheless, given that the purpose of this paper is to study a "consumption function", a "natural" normalization in *LCPRIVR* is suggested.

It is shown in Stock (1987) that OLS estimates are "super-consistent" when applied to a co-integration relation. That is:

$$\hat{\beta}_{OLS} - \beta = O_p(T^{-1}) \,.$$

It should be noted that, because of this "super-consistency" result, the traditional simultaneity bias does not exist for co-integration relations. Nevertheless given that the series are non-stationary, the conventional distributions for the estimators no longer apply.

Tables 3A and 3B present OLS estimates for different possible formulations.

CRDW stands for "Co-integrating Regression Durbin-Watson Test" and ADF for the statistic corresponding to the "Augmented Dickey-Fuller Test".

Table 3B: Co-integrating regressions imposing unit elasticity.

| | (3.7) | (3.8) |
|---|---|---|
| Constant | -0.1695 | -0.1678 |
| *DLPCPRIV* | 0.0456 | |
| *LTXJDL* | -0.8802 | -0.8421 |
| $R^2$ | 0.773 | 0.772 |
| $\bar{R}^2$ | 0.752 | 0.762 |
| *SE* | 0.034 | 0.033 |
| *CRDW* | 0.890 | 0.927 |
| *ADF* | -4.15 | -4.21 |

The purpose of these tests is to consider whether the residual of the relation is stationary. Furthermore given that the involved variables are $I(1)$, the stationarity of the associated residual is equivalent to the existence of a co-integration relation. In other words, one will not reject the existence of a co-integration relation between $I(1)$ variables if one rejects the hypothesis that the corresponding residuals display a unit root. What complicates the test is the fact that residuals are not susceptible of direct observation.

The CRDW test was proposed by Sargan and Bhargava (1983). Its intuition is clear. If the residuals were $I(1)$ the statistic $d$ (Durbin-Watson) will be close to zero. The drawback of this test is that the distribution of the CRDW statistic is most sensitive to the parameters of the co-integrating relation. For significance levels of 1% and 5% the critical values are of the order of respectively 0.5 and 0.4.

The ADF statistic corresponds exactly to the Dickey-Fuller statistic for observable time series. The difference is that it is applied to the residuals of the co-integration equation. Significantly the ADF statistic corresponds to the t-ratio (OLS) of the coefficient of $\hat{\epsilon}_{t-1}$ in the regression:

$$\Delta\hat{\epsilon}_t = (\rho - 1)\hat{\epsilon}_{t-1} + \alpha\Delta\hat{\epsilon}_{t-1} + \eta_t \ .$$

Since the variables in this regression are estimated residuals, it was shown that Dickey-Fuller's critical values would lead to an over-rejection of the unit root hypothesis. Engle and Granger (1987) provided the corrected critical values for the case of a regression involving two variables. For the case where three variables are involved, Hall and Henry (1988, chap.2) present the respective critical values as being -2.83, -3.13 e -3.89, for, respectively, 10%, 5% e 1% significance levels. The critical values of the ADF test are relatively insensitive to the number of variables and the true co-integrating vector. These facts may be regarded as important advantages for the test.

For all the regressions (presented on Tables 3A and 3B) the CRDW and ADF statistics point to the existence of a co-integration relation. The exceptions being provided by regressions (3.4), (3.5) and (3.6) under the ADF test even at a 10% significance level.

The regressions in which real interest rates are involved have to be interpreted with special care given the mixed evidence presented in section 2 concerning its stationarity. This point is all the more important given that the stationarity of real interest rates seems more compatible with theoretical *a priori* concerning the behavior of this variable. Furthermore the regressions including real interest rates seem to be dominated, from a statistical viewpoint, by regressions involving nominal interest rates.

In fact the best of the regressions presented on Table 3A is (4.3) including consumption, disposable income and nominal interest rates. The criteria used as foundation for this judgment were the CRDW and ADF tests. Furthermore this conclusion was also backed by the more traditional indicators also presented ($\bar{R}^2$ and $SE$, where $SE$ standing for standard deviation of the error of the regression).

For the regressions presented on Table 3B a homogeneity condition was imposed. Specifically a unit income elasticity of consumption was imposed. The statistical indicators of co-integration improved when this restriction was imposed, lending some support for its validity.[7] The previous result pointing to the superiority of regressions involving nominal rather than real interest rates is preserved under this restriction suggesting some robustness for the result.

From the perspective of co-integration analysis the best regressions would be (3.3) without imposing the unitary income elasticity of consumption and (3.7) imposing such a constraint.

# 4 Short-Run Dynamics and Engle-Granger Representation Theorem

Engle and Granger's representation theorem implies the existence of a dynamic relation between the first differences of co-integrated variables and the co-integrating regression's lagged error term.[8]

[7] It should be clear that given that the right-hand side variable is not the same, it is meaningless to use indicators such as $R^2$ and $\bar{R}^2$ to compare regressions presented on Table 3A with regressions on Table 3B.

[8] Engle and Granger (1987) representation theorem states that it is possible to write (with $\Delta x_{jt} = (1 - L)x_{jt}$ and having normalized in the first element of the co-integrated vector $x_t$ $(k \times 1)$):

$$\Delta x_{1t} = b_1(L)\Delta x_{1\,t-1} + \sum_{j=2}^{k} b_j(L)\Delta x_{jt} - b_0\epsilon_{t-1} + u_t$$

All these variables are stationary. The inclusion of the lagged error term may be interpreted as corresponding to an error correction mechanism. This interpretation allows one to relate the co-integration literature to results from optimal control of dynamic systems.

Engle and Granger suggest a two stage estimation procedure based on this result.

First the co-integration relation is estimated following the procedure outlined in the previous section. Given the estimated co-integration relation one proceeds to the second stage. This involves a regression including the first differences of co-integrated variables and the co-integrating regression estimated lagged error term.

When all the regressors involved in the second stage are pre-determined, it was shown by Engle and Granger that OLS estimators are consistent. Furthermore there is an asymptotic equivalence between the OLS estimators distribution and the estimators distribution that would be obtained if the true lagged error term was used. Engle and Granger's argument may be slightly modified to show consistency in the case of simultaneity. In fact that is the case when using instrumental variables (IV). Furthermore the traditional asymptotic distribution for IV estimators is still valid.

The results are presented in Table 4. As already pointed out, the IV method was used. The instruments retained were those ensuring the best possible fit.[9]

In Table 4, $\Pi^2$ is the statistic proposed by Godfrey (1976) to test the first order autocorrelation of residuals when the IV method is used.[10] This statistic $\Pi^2$ is $\chi_1^2$ asymptotically distributed under the null hypothesis of absence of autocorrelation.

CHOW(-3) is the Chow's statistic for testing structural break in the last three years of the sample period. Under the null hypothesis of no structural

---

where $b_j(L)$, $j = 1, \ldots, k$, are finite polynomials in the lag operator $L$, $u_t$ is a stationary residual, $b_0$ is a positive scalar and $\epsilon_{t-1}$ is the lagged error from the co-integrated regression. In their 1987 paper, Engle and Granger impose $b_j(0) = 0$ for $j = 2, \ldots, k$. However, the extension for the case $b_j(0) \neq 0$ is trivial and it has been used in the literature.

[9] The set of instruments is presented on Table 4. Results from section 2 and 3 show that, with the exception of $\Delta LCPUBR$, the remaining instrument are stationary. For the case of $\Delta LCPUBR$ (first difference of the logarithm of real public consumption, at 1977 prices) a value $\Phi_3 = 14.62$ enables one to reject the existence of a unit root.

[10] Take $y_t = x_t'\beta + u_t$ as the regression equation, let $T$ be the number of observations and let $\hat{u}_t$ be the IV estimated residuals. One has $\Pi^2 = T\hat{\hat{u}}'P_W\hat{\hat{u}}/\hat{u}'\hat{u}$ where $P_W = W(W'W)^{-1}W'$, $W$ is the instruments matrix and $\hat{\hat{u}}$ is the estimation of $\hat{u}$ given by the regression:

$$\hat{u}_t = \alpha_0 \hat{u}_{t-1} + \alpha' x_t + \xi_t$$

using IV method with the same instruments $W$. This test can be used only when the number of instruments is strictly superior to the number of regressors in $x_t$.

Table 4: Short Run Dynamics.

| | (4.1) | | (4.2) | | (4.3) | |
|---|---|---|---|---|---|---|
| $\gamma_0$ | 0.56469 | (5.5156) | 0.50086 | (4.4116) | 0.55504 | (5.7456) |
| $\gamma_1$ | 0.38531 | (4.1605) | 0.43519 | (4.4141) | 0.44596 | (4.6165) |
| $\gamma_2$ | -0.56342 | (-3.0008) | -0.55476 | (-2.9698) | -0.60194 | (-3.3946) |
| $\gamma_3$ | -0.31338 | (-2.7551) | -0.30103 | (-2.8623) | -0.27602 | (-2.7522) |
| $SE$ | 0.01330 | | 0.01336 | | 0.01318 | |
| $\Pi^2$ | 2.14 | | 1.11 | | 1.31 | |
| $CHOW(-3)$ | 4.74 | | 3.36 | | 2.37 | |

$\Delta LCPRIVR = \gamma_0 \Delta LCPRIVR_{-1} + \gamma_1 \Delta LRDFR + \gamma_2 \Delta LTXJDPL + \gamma_3 ERROR_{-1}$

$ERROR$: estimated OLS residual from the co-integrating regression ((4.1): residuals from (3.3); (4.2) and (4.3): residuals from (3.8))

Sample Period: 1967–1988

Estimation Method: Instrumental Variables. Instruments: $\Delta LCPRIVR_{-1}$, $\Delta LRDFR_{-1}$, $\Delta LRDFR_{-2}$, $\Delta LTXJDPLR_{-1}$, $ERROR_{-1}$,

$\Delta LCPUBR$ ($LCPUBR$: logarithm of real public consumption at 1977 prices.)

Standard deviations in parenthesis

$SE$: Standard deviation of the estimated residual

$\Pi^2$: Godfrey's statistic for testing first order autocorrelation of the residuals

$CHOW(-3)$: Chow's statistic for the last three observations

change, CHOW(-3) is asymptotically distributed as $\chi^2_3$.[11]

The lagged error terms in (4.1) and (4.2) are, respectively, the lagged estimated residuals of the co-integrating regressions (3.3) and (3.8). Recall that this last equation imposes a unit income elasticity of consumption. Given that the fit in regressions (4.1) and (4.2) is similar, the unit income elasticity appears to conform with the evidence provided by the sample.

Engle and Granger's two-step estimation procedure does not guarantee that the dynamic equation, obtained by imposing steady state conditions on short run equations, allows to reproduce the long run equation. Conditions for having this "dynamic homogeneity" are usually rather complicated

[11] Denote by $X^*$ and $W^*$ the augmented matrices obtained by joining to $X$ (the regressors matrix) and to $W$ (the instruments matrix) three dummies, one for each year (1986, 1987 and 1988). Let $SS = \tilde{u}'P_{W^*}\tilde{u}$, $RSS = \tilde{u}_c'P_{W^*}\tilde{u}_c$ and $SE^* = (\tilde{u}'\tilde{u}/T)^{1/2}$, where $P_{W^*} = W^*(W^{*\prime}W^*)^{-1}W^{*\prime}$, $\tilde{u} = y - X^*\hat{\gamma}_{IV}$, $\tilde{u}_c = y - X\hat{\beta}_{IV}$, $\hat{\gamma}_{IV} = (X^{*\prime}P_{W^*}X^*)^{-1}X^{*\prime}P_{W^*}y$ and $\hat{\beta}_{IV} = (X'P_{W^*}X)^{-1}X'P_{W^*}y$. One has

$$CHOW(-3) = \frac{RSS - SS}{(SE^*)^2} .$$

and strongly non-linear.[12] However, in the case of (4.2), this problem is simplified. When assuming a unit income elasticity, allows one to postulate identical means for the logarithms of real consumption and disposable income. Let $\mu$ be this common mean. Further assuming a zero mean for the first difference of the nominal interest rate $\Delta LTXJDPL$, the complete dynamic equation:

$$\begin{aligned}\Delta LCPRIVR_t &= \gamma_0 \Delta LCPRIVR_{t-1} + \gamma_1 \Delta LRDFR_t + \gamma_2 \Delta LTXJDPL_t \\ &+\gamma_3(LCPRIVR_{t-1} - LRDFR_{t-1} - \alpha_0 - \alpha_2 LTXJDPL_{t-1})\end{aligned}$$

generates the following long run solution:

$$\mu = \gamma_0\mu + \gamma_1\mu + \gamma_2 \times 0 + \gamma_3(LCPRIVR - LRDFR - \alpha_0 - \alpha_2 LTXJDPL)\,.$$

The co-integrating equation (3.7) will be reproduced whenever $\gamma_0+\gamma_1 = 1$. Imposing this linear constraint on (4.2), one obtains (4.3) on Table 4. A first look seems to indicate an improvement comparing to (4.2). A formal test of the homogeneity constraint may be performed using the statistic:

$$F = \frac{SS_{(4.3)} - SS_{(4.2)}}{SE^2_{(4.2)}} \xrightarrow{d} \chi^2_1$$

where $SS = \hat{u}' P_W \hat{u}$, $\hat{u}$ is the vector of estimated residuals, $P_W$ is the projection matrix $W(W'W)^{-1}W'$ and $W$ is the instruments matrix. The value of 0.86 was obtained for this statistic. Meaning that the dynamic homogeneity hypothesis is not rejected given the available data.

# 5 Concluding Remarks

The paper shows that by using co-integration relations between macroeconomic time series one is able to obtain empirically relevant results for traditional "macroeconomic functions" such as the "consumption function".

The methodology retained seems particularly promising for use in the context of building a small macroeconomic model of the portuguese economy for short/medium term simulation. The use of such model to perform economic policy simulations however has to be considered with due care given the relevance of Lucas's (1976) critique.

The results obtained when modelling the "consumption function" presented in the paper seem clearly satisfactory. In fact the results obtained in estimating the co-integration relation point clearly to the existence and relevance of such relations between the chosen variables. This was the case

[12] See, for example, Hall and Henry (1988, chap. 2).

both with the unrestricted form and when a unit income elasticity was imposed. As a matter of fact the statistical indicators of co-integration improved when the restriction was imposed lending some support for its validity.

Furthermore the results in section 3 pointed to the superiority of regressions involving nominal rather than real interest rates. This is an interesting result which may be in line with the relevance of liquidity constraints for the behavior of consumption in Portugal found in previous studies (Silva (1988) and Luz (1990)). It should be recognized however that the liquidity constraints necessary to reproduce the type of results obtained in our paper would have to be formulated in quite a different way. [13] These results are entirely in line with those previously obtained, albeit using quite different a methodology, by Rosa (1988) on the relevance of the nominal interest rates or real interest rates *plus* inflation as determinants of savings in Portugal.

Engle and Granger's representation theorem was explored to obtain information relevant to the modelling of short run dynamics. The results obtained are of course crucial for adequate forecasting ability. In general Engle and Grangers's two-step estimation procedure does not guarantee that the dynamic equation, obtained by imposing steady state conditions on short run equations, allows one to reproduce the long run equation. Conditions for having this "dynamic homogeneity" are usually rather complicated and strongly non-linear. In the case of this paper, using the unit income elasticity constraint, it is relatively easy however to test for dynamic homogeneity. The result of the test provides evidence against rejection of dynamic homogeneity.

All results obtained on consumption sensitivity to its various determinants conform with theory. One should however conclude the paper with a word of caution concerning the interpretation of the results given the small dimension for the sample used.

# References

BLANCHARD, O. J. AND S. FISHER (1989): *Lectures on Macroeconomics*. Cambridge: The MIT Press.

BRANSON, W. (1990): "Financial Market Integration, Macroeconomic Policy and the EMS," in *Unity with Diversity in the European Economy*, ed. by C. Bliss and J. Macedo. Cambridge: Cambridge University Press.

[13] One such a possibility could arise from the use of debt servicing to current income ratios as an indicator of credit-worthiness. It may be useful to quote from Cooper and Sachs (1985) in a different context: "Indicators such as the debt to GDP ratio or the debt servicing ratio are often used to signal when external debt is reaching dangerous levels. So far as such indicators are widely used they of course become important in establishing credit-worthiness".

COOPER, R. AND J. SACHS (1985): "Borrowing Abroad: the Debtor's perspective," in *International Debt and Developing Countries*, ed. by G. Smith and J. Cudington. Washington: The World Bank.

DEATON, A. AND J. MUELLBAUER (1980): *Economics and Consumer Behavior*. Cambridge: Cambridge University Press.

DICKEY, D. A. AND W. A. FULLER (1981): "Likelihood Ratio Statistics for Autoregressive Time Series With a Unit Root," *Econometrica*, **49**, 1075–1072.

ENGLE, R. F. AND C. W. GRANGER (1987): "Co-integration and Error Correction: Representation, Estimation, and Testing," *Econometrica*, **55**, 251–276.

FRIEDMAN, M. (1957): *A Theory of the Consumption Function*. Princeton: Princeton University Press.

FULLER, W. A. (1976): *Introduction to Statistical Time Series*. New York: John Wiley and Sons.

GIOVANINNI, A. AND C. MAYER (1991): *European Financial Integration*. Cambridge: Cambridge University Press.

GODFREY, L. (1976): "Testing for Serial Correlation in Dynamic Simultaneous' Equations Models," *Econometrica*, **44**, 1077–1084.

GRANGER, C. W. AND P. NEWBOLD (1974): "Spurious Regressions in Econometrics," *Journal of Econometrics*, **2**, 111–120.

HALL, R. (1989): "Consumption," in *Modern Business Cycle Theory*, ed. by R. Barro. Cambridge: Harvard University Press.

HALL, S. G. AND S. G. HENRY (1988): *Macroeconomic Modelling*, chapter 2. Amsterdam: North-Holland.

JAPELLI, T. AND M. PAGANO (1989): "Consumption and Capital Market Imperfections: an International Comparison," *American Economic Review*, **79**, 1088–1105.

KING, M. (1985): "The Economics of Savings: a Survey of Recent Contributions" in *Frontiers of Economics*, ed. by K. Arrow and S. Honkapohja. New York: Blackwell.

LUCAS, R. E. (1976): "Econometric Policy Evaluation: a Critique," in *The Phillips Curve and the Labour Markets*, ed. by K. Brunner and A. Meltzer, Vol. 1, Carnegie-Rochester Conferences on Public Policy, *Journal of Monetary Economics*, Suppl., 19–46.

LUZ, S. (1990): "Consumo e Restrições de Liquidez: uma Aplicação a Portugal," *manuscript*, DEE, Banco de Portugal.

MACEDO, J. (1990): "External Liberalization with Ambiguous Public Response: the Experience of Portugal" in *Unity with Diversity in the European Economy*, ed. by C. Bliss and J. Macedo. Cambridge: Cambridge University Press

NELSON, C. R. AND C. I. PLOSSER (1982): "Trends and Random Walks in Macroeconomic Time Series — Some Evidence and Implications," *Journal Monetary Economics*, **10**, 139–162.

PHILLIPS, P. C. B. AND S. N. DURLAUF (1986): "Multiple Time Series Regression with Integrated Processes," *Review of Economic Studies*, **53**, 473–495.

ROSA, N. (1988): "A Função Consumo e a Taxa de Poupança em Portugal," *manuscript*, DEE, Banco de Portugal.

SARGAN, J. D. AND A. BHARGAVA (1983): "Testing Residuals From Least Squares Regression for Being Generated by the Gaussian Random Walk," *Econometrica*, **51**, 153–74.

SILVA, A. S. (1988): "Função Consumo: Alguns Desenvolvimentos Recentes e Análise do Caso Português," Master's Dissertation, Instituto Superior de Economia, Lisbon.

STOCK, J. H. (1987): "Asymptotic Properties of Least Squares Estimators of Co-integrating Vectors," *Econometrica*, **55**, 1035–1056.

# Allocation of Common Costs in Portuguese Telephone Service

Diogo Lucena
António P. N. Leite
Vítor Gaspar

## 1 Introduction

There are three operators of telephone services in Portugal: Telecom Portugal, TLP and CPRM. Their networks have always been interconnected, and for many calls each operator uses infrastructure which is property of other(s) operator(s). This *status quo* has prompted the need to develop a methodology to allocate common costs among these three companies. Typically this was done by employing non-optimal *ad hoc* procedures, leading inevitably to sub-optimal outcomes. The purpose of this paper is to apply the methodology first developed by Billera and Heath (1982), Mirman and Tauman (1982), and Mirman, Saumet and Tauman (1983) to this particular problem. Following this seminal work, we present an axiomatic approach to allocate the full cost of production of these multiproduct firms to all the services (outputs) they supply. The use of this axiomatic approach results in an allocation mechanism which associates a vector of cost sharing prices to each admissable cost function and output vector. These prices, known in the literature as Aumann-Shapley (AS) prices (Aumann and Shapley, 1974), can be computed simply by collecting information regarding both cost structure and output vectors. Since their computation does not require the knowledge of demand functions, AS prices avoid the cross subsidization of commodities which would be the case if the price mechanism were also to depend upon demand behavior. Nevertheless, there will exist a vector of outputs and corresponding AS prices for which markets clear (Mirman and Tauman, 1982).

The remainder of the paper is organized as follows. In section 2 we present a general methodology to allocate costs through prices for multi-product firms. We go on to apply this general methodology to the case in which we consider two operators: TLP and Telecom Portugal (sections 3 through 5). Section 6 provides an extension of the original application by means of also considering the third operator (CPRM). The conclusions are presented in section 7.

# 2 The Allocation of Common Costs through AS Prices

Any cost allocation scheme must fulfill certain properties, ensuring its uniqueness. In particular, consider the problem in which one has to allocate costs relative to a firm producing n products. Let $\Phi^n$ be the family of cost functions of $n$ products and let $\Phi = \sum_{n=1}^{\infty} \Phi^n$.

Denote by $\Omega^n$ the set $\Phi^n \times \Psi^n_+$, where $\Psi^n$ is the product space. Let $\Omega = \sum_{n=1}^{\infty} \Omega^n$. An element of $\Omega$ is a pair $(\Phi, b)$ where $b$ is the products vector. We are interested in finding a pricing mechanism for $\phi$, i.e., a function $\Pi$ which assigns to each pair $(\Phi, b)$ in $\phi^n$, a vector of prices $(\Pi_1(\Phi, b), \dots, \Pi_n(\Phi, b))$, satisfying the following properties.

1. *Exact cost sharing.* The prices determined by $\Pi$ for the pair $(\Phi, b)$ cover the cost of production $\Phi(b)$.

2. *Rescaling.* Let $\lambda \times b = (\lambda_1 b_1, \dots, \lambda_n b_n)$ for $\lambda, b \in \Psi^n$. Assume that $(\Gamma, b)$, $(\Phi, \lambda \times b) \in \phi^n$, and $\Gamma(x) = \Phi(\lambda \times x)$. Then $\Pi(\Gamma, b) = \lambda \times \Pi(\Phi, \lambda \times b)$, i.e., if the scales of measurement of the commodities are changed, then the prices determined by $\Pi$ are changed accordingly.

3. *Consistency.* Let $\Phi(x_1, \dots, x_n) = \Gamma\left(\sum_{j=i}^{n} x_j\right)$ for each $x \in \Psi^n_+$. If $(\Phi, b)$ and $\Gamma(\sum_{j=i}^{n} b_j)$ are in $\phi^n$ and $\phi^1$, respectively, then for each $i$, $1 \leq i \leq n$, $\Pi_i(\Phi, b) = \Pi\left(\Gamma\left(\sum_{j=i}^{n} b_j\right)\right)$.

4. *Positivity.* Let $(\Phi, b)$ and $(\Gamma, b)$ be two elements in $\phi$ such that $\Phi(0) \geq \Gamma(0)$. If $\Phi - \Gamma$ is nondecreasing on $\gamma_b = \{x \in \Psi^m_+ : x_j \leq b_j, j = i, \dots, n\}$, then $\Pi(\Phi, b) \geq \Pi(\Gamma, b)$.

   This property solely asserts that if $\Phi$ increases at least as rapidly as $\Gamma$ on $\gamma_b$, then the prices determined for $(\Phi, b)$ are at least as high as those determined for $(\Gamma, b)$.

5. *Additivity.* If $(\Phi, b)$, $(\Gamma, b)$, and $(\Phi, \Gamma, b)$ are elements of $\phi$, then $\Pi(\Phi\Gamma, b) = \Pi(\Phi, b) + \Pi(\Gamma, b)$.

Now consider $\phi_0$, the subset of $\Omega$ which contains all pairs of the form $(\Phi, b)$, where $\Phi$ is continuously differentiable and $\Phi(0) = 0$. Proposition 1 states de existence and uniqueness of a price mechanism which obeys to properties 1 through 5 for continuously differentiable cost functions in the absence of a fixed component.

**Proposition 1** *There exists one and only one price mechanism* $\Pi^*(.)$ *for* $\phi_0$ *which obeys to properties 1–5. This is the AS price mechanism given by:*

$$\Pi_i^*(\Phi, b) = \int_0^1 \frac{\partial \Phi}{\partial x_i}(tb)\, dt \,, \tag{1}$$

*for each* $(\Phi, b) \in \phi_0$.

*Proof:* Mirman and Tauman (1982). ■

The above presented axiomatic approach to the determination of cost-sharing prices is applied only to the family $\phi_0$ of continuous cost functions $\Phi$ satisfying $\Phi(0) = 0$. Given the nature of the specific question we have in hand we have to extend the axiomatic approach in order to determine cost-sharing prices for cost functions which include a fixed cost component. Such extension is provided by Mirman, Saumet and Tauman (1983). Having fixed costs in the model implies that there is no cost-sharing price mechanism compatible with properties 1–5. It turns out that only a minor change in the additivity property is necessary to generate conditions in which there exists a unique cost-sharing price mechanism.

The idea is to limit the way in which the fixed cost is allocated between additive components of the variable cost. It happens that it is sufficient to require only that there exists a way to split the fixed cost between the various variable cost components. This constitutes properties 5$a$ and 6.

5$a$. Let $\Phi$ be a function in $\Phi_+^n$ and let $R$ be a nonnegative number. then, for each $\Gamma$ in $\Phi_+^n$ such that $\Gamma \leq \Phi$, there is a nonnegative number $R_\Gamma$ such that if $\Phi = \sum_{i=1}^m \Gamma_i$ and $G_i \in \Phi_+^n$, then $R = \sum_{i=1}^m R_{\Gamma_i}$ and $\Pi(\Phi + R, b) = \sum_{i=1}^m \Pi(R_i + R_{\Gamma_i}, b)$.

The following property asserts that the part $R_{\Gamma_i}$ of the fixed cost $R$ which is associated with the component $\Gamma_i(b)$ in the total variable cost $\Phi(b)$ is at least as large as $\Gamma_j(b)$.

6. Let $\Phi, \Gamma_1, \ldots, \Gamma_m$, and $R$ be as stated in property 5a. Then $\Gamma_i(b) \geq \Gamma_j(b)$ implies $R_{\Gamma_i} \geq R_{\Gamma_j}$.

**Proposition 2** *There exists a unique price mechanism* $P(.,.)$ *on* $\phi_1$ *obeying properties 1,2,3,4,5a and 6. It is given by*

$$P(\Phi + R, b) = \Pi^*(\Phi, b) + \frac{R}{\Phi(b)}\Pi^*(\Phi, b) = \left[1 + \frac{R}{\Phi(b)}\right]\Pi^*(\Phi, b) \quad (2)$$

*where* $\Pi^*$ *is the AS price vector associated with the variable part* $\Phi$ *for the quantity vector* $b$.

*Proof:* Mirman, Saumet and Tauman (1983). ■

It is this generalized methodology that we are going to apply to our specific problem of allocating common costs among Portuguese telephone operators.

# 3 The Two-Operator Model

There are three telecommunication operators (TO) in Portugal. Telecom Portugal (part of CTT) has the monopoly over all traffic in Continental Portugal except for two regions centered in Lisbon and Oporto, which belong to TLP. Telecom has also the international traffic to Europe and the local traffic in Azores and Madeira. CPRM is a third TO operating the intercontinental traffic, including the liaison between the continent and Azores and Madeira.

A call originating in Lisbon and Oporto and ending somewhere else in Portugal or directed to Europe will use equipment both from TLP and Telecom Portugal. By legal definition all income from such traffic belongs to Telecom Portugal. The question then arises of how to compensate TLP for the use of their equipment. The first model we develop tries to answer this question through the use of AS pricing. When the study was begun both TLP and Telecom Portugal were under the same board of directors. It was agreed then that sharing of income would be proportional to the costs allocated by each company to the relevant service. The problem became then one of cost allocation. First we allocate the total costs of Telecom Portugal to "local" traffic and to long-distance and international traffic. Local traffic is defined as the traffic within each local area network. Long-distance and international traffic will use the long-distance network, belonging to Telecom; part of it is directed or originates in Lisbon and Oporto; part will belong entirely to Telecom. Then we do the same to TLP traffic by using a geographic unit which is similar in size (number of lines) to the local area networks of Telecom Portugal ("network area"). As the problems are similar we will describe only the procedure applied to Telecom Portugal.

The cost function is defined as dependent of the following arguments: local traffic ($T_i^L$) and long-distance and international traffic ($T_i^I$), for each LAN, indexed by $i$.

$$C_i = C_i(T_i^L, T_i^I), \quad i = 1, \ldots, N . \tag{3}$$

These costs must include the investment costs.

Similarly there are some costs which are specific to the long-distance and international traffic: the long-distance network, which is owned and operated by Telecom:

$$C^* = C^*(T_1^I, \ldots, T_N^I, T_{N+1}^I, T_{N+2}^I, T_{N+3}^I) \tag{4}$$

where $T_{N+3}^I$ refers to international traffic, which is here assimilated to an extra LAN, and $T_{N+1}$ and $T_{N+2}$ are the Lisbon and Oporto "LAN's", where traffics can originate or end. By using AS pricing, the cost we must allocate to $T_j^I$ is given by:

$$AS_j^I = \int_0^1 \frac{\partial C_j(tT_j^I, tT_j^I)}{\partial T_j^I} dt + \int_0^1 \frac{\partial C^*(tT_1^I, \ldots, tT_N^I, tT_{N+1}^I)}{\partial T_j^I} dt . \tag{5}$$

A similar method is used to allocate the costs of TLP. In this case we use the "network areas" defined by TLP as our unit and the first part is similar to Telecom Portugal. Then we must add

$$\sum_{j=1}^{2} \int_0^1 \frac{\partial C^*(tT_1^I, \ldots, tT_{N+3}^I)}{\partial T_{N+j}^I} dt \tag{6}$$

to include the allocation of the long-distance network to Lisbon and Oporto, but bearing in mind that this is a TLP cost that is actually paid by Telecom Portugal.

# 4 Data and Estimation

Telecom Portugal was able to give the relevant data by LAN. We could obtain costs — current and investment costs — by local area and the relevant traffics, measured in erlangs. The investment costs were disaggregated by type of equipment and could be annualized by using an estimate of their useful life.

We could then try to fit a cost function giving the total cost of LAN as a function of the levels of local and "non-local" traffics. We had the data for 23 LANs, and after testing

$$C_i = \beta_o + \beta_1 T_i^L + \beta_2 T_i^I + \epsilon_i \tag{7}$$

and

$$C_i = \beta_0 \, T_i^{L\beta_1} \, T_i^{L\beta_2} \, \epsilon_i \tag{8}$$

with $\epsilon_i$ distributed according to normal and log-normal distributions respectively, we finally adopted the form

$$C_i = \beta_0 \, (T_i^L + T_i^I)^{\beta_3} \, \epsilon_i \ . \tag{9}$$

The results are presented in Table 1

We could not reject, at the 1% level the hypothesis that $\beta_1 = \beta_2$. This confirms the long-lasting practice of adding local and non-long erlangs, which is generally adopted in applied work in telecommunications.

For similar reasons, in the TLP case the form finally adopted was

$$C_i = \beta_0 \, (\textstyle\sum_j T_j^i)^{\beta} \, \epsilon_i \ . \tag{10}$$

The results are summarized in Table 2.

To obtain the long-distance cost-function,

$$C^* = C^*(T_1^I, \ldots, T_N^I, \ldots, T_{N+3}^I) \ ,$$

we could not use an econometric approach, for we could not observe the cost associated with different traffic levels. The engineering of Telecom Portugal

Table 1: Estimation of the Cost Function (9).

| | Estimate | t-ratio |
|---|---|---|
| $\beta_0$ | 4967.142 | 32.589* |
| $\beta_3$ | 0.77427 | 17.864* |
| $R^2 = 0.878$; $\bar{R}^2 = 0.876$; $F = 319.134$* | | |

* significance at 1% level.

Table 2: Estimation of the Cost Function (10).

| | Estimate | t-ratio |
|---|---|---|
| $\beta_0$ | 7.2801 | 4.6672* |
| $\beta$ | 0.7739 | 25.786* |
| $R^2 = 0.890$; $\overline{R}^2 = 0.889$; $F = 664.94$* | | |

* significance at 1% level.

suggested the use of a function of the type (1989 prices) $C^* = 10^7 \times 225\,c$ where $c$ is the number of circuits.

This function does not contain the relevant information. We want to distinguish the impact on $C^*$ of the traffic relative to each LAN and the international traffic. Telecom Portugal was able to give some additional elements:

- a factor allowing to convert cost per circuit to cost per erlang;
- the information that the "fixed cost" of $10^7$ could be allocated to the different LANs in a way proportional to the distance among them. We could obtain a matrix of distance among LANs. The international traffic and the traffic between the continent and Azores/Madeira (CAM) was treated as being in Lisbon;
- detailed information on the cost of equipment dedicated to international traffic;
- volume of the relevant traffics in erlangs.

We believe that the linear form presented by Telecom Portugal is the main informational limitation to the reliability of the results. We would expect some economies of scale, and thus a concave function to be the relevant description.

The final form we could estimate was therefore of the type:

$$C^* = \sum(\alpha_i + \phi_i)T_i^I + \gamma T_{CAM} + \varphi T_{int} \,. \tag{11}$$

The coefficients have the meaning presented:

1. $$\alpha_i = \lambda \frac{\sum_{j,k} D_{kj} + \sum_{j,k} D_{jk}}{\sum_{j,k} T_{kj} + \sum_{j,k} T_{jk}}$$

   where $D_{kj}$ is the distance between LANs $k$ and $T_{kj}$ is the long-distance traffic originating in $k$ and ending in $j$ and

   $$\lambda = \frac{10^7}{\sum_{j,k}(D_{kj}/2)} \,;$$

2. $\phi_i$: incremental cost, per erlang, common to all long distance traffic;
3. $\gamma$: incremental cost, per erlang, specific to CAM traffic;
4. $\varphi$: incremental cost, per erlang, specific to international traffic.

## 5 Results

Using 1989 data regarding both traffic and costs, we applied the described methodology to allocate common costs from long-distance and international traffic between TLP and Telecom. In 1989 total costs for long-distance and international traffic were $53672543.6 \times 10^3$ escudos. $45444391.6 \times 10^3$ escudos (84.67%) were allocated to Telecom while only $8228152.3 \times 10^3$ (15.33%) were allocated to TLP.

## 6 The Three Operator Model

In a final stage the above presented methodology was extended to include CPRM. Regarding both TLP and Telecom we employed the same procedure as in the two-operator case. CPRM was seen as one network area but to both intercontinental traffic and CAM traffic we distinguished between traffic originating or ending in Lisbon and Oporto (Area 1) and traffic originating or ending in the Telecom jurisdictional area (Area 2). This was done by multiplying the costs relative to intercontinental (CAM) traffic by a factor indicating the relative weight of Area 1 and Area 2 traffic in total intercontinental (CAM) traffic.

Using this methodology, for 1989 traffic we obtained the results presented in Table 3.

## 7 Conclusions

There is an inherent arbitrariness in the problem of allocating common costs. Economists argue that the problem is irrelevant, but it keeps appearing again and again in the daily life of multiproduct business firms. The axiomatic approach taken here has the advantaged of making clear what the rules of the game are. The five axioms are quite appealing and were accepted as reasonable by all parts involved. The fact that they lead to a unique allocation mechanism makes the approach very useful. Notice

Table 3: Three operator costs.

| Type of traffic | Allocated cost* |
|---|---|
| Intercontinental traffic starting/ending in Area 1 | 836014.6 |
| Intercontinental traffic starting/ending in Area 1 | 1157590.4 |
| CAM traffic: Area 1 | 1019840.8 |
| CAM traffic: Area 2 | 898836.2 |

* Unit: $10^3$ escudos

that the problem is a problem on fairness and not on pricing. We are not arguing here that consumers should be billed according to AS prices.

# References

BILLERA, L. AND D. HEATH (1982): "Allocation of Shared Costs: a Set of Axioms Yielding a Unique Procedure," *Mathematics of Operations Research*, **7**, 32–39.

MIRMAN, L. AND Y. TAUMAN (1982): "Demand Compatible Equitable Cost Sharing Prices," *Mathematics of Operations Research*, **7**, 40–56.

MIRMAN, L., D. SAMET AND Y. TAUMAN (1983): "An Axiomatic Approach to the Allocation of Fixed Costs Through Prices", *Bell Journal of Economics*, **14**, 139–151.

# Comparative Advantage and Structural Change in the Portuguese Pattern of Trade in Manufactures

Anthony S. Courakis
Fátima Moura Roque

## 1 Introduction

How to explain observed trade patterns is a subject that has absorbed a great deal of the human capital of the economics profession for many years. In the last three decades, a large part of this effort has been in the form of econometric investigations of the relationship between the composition of trade and various supply determinants, suggested by theory as important in accounting for trade patterns. Some of these investigations take the form of *cross-country* studies.[1] Others,[2] focus on the trade patterns of *individual countries*, relating these to the particular country's factor endowments and production characteristics. Most of the latter, not surprisingly, deal with the experience of highly developed economies. But whether for highly developed or less developed economies, it is generally assumed, and with varying success the empirical evidence confirms, that factor inputs and other supply determinants are important in the explanation of trade patterns. At the same time, the empirical evidence available has often produced surprises, regarding the relationship between particular determinants and trade per-

We are grateful to Guisepe Mazarino and Cláudia Rodrigues for computing assistance.

[1] Inter alia, Balassa (1979a), Leamer (1984), Maskus (1985), Balassa and Bawens (1988), Bowen et al (1987), and Noland (1987).

[2] As cited in section 2 below.

formance, leading in turn to further conceptual and empirical research.[3] Moreover, with the passage of time, and the corresponding accumulation of data, empirical studies have become more ambitious, aiming to explain not only the composition of a country's trade in some particular year, but also the evolution of trade patterns over time.[4]

What follows in this paper is an inquiry into the pattern and evolution of trade of the small, highly open, semi-developed Portuguese economy, in the years 1972 to 1985. The stylized facts about Portugal in this period, include

(a) a highly diversified composition of exports and imports

(b) a wide range of trading partners

(c) low income per capita compared to its major trading partners

(d) relative abundance of unskilled labour and relative shortage of skilled labour and physical capital

(e) shifting patterns of government intervention in external transactions

(f) marked changes in the country's circumstances, in the form of socio-political developments, external shocks and changes in domestic micro and macro economic policies.

Section 2 describes the main features and intellectual antecedents of the class of models relied upon in this inquiry to account for the pattern of Portugal's trade across industries and over time. The statistical performance of these models in explaining experience during the period under review, is examined in Section 3, where also the pattern of comparative advantage described by the estimated parameters is discussed in some detail, in the context of the broader body of available evidence about Portugal's relative factor endowments and production characteristics. In Section 4 we explore the possibility of structural change in the relationship between supply determinants and pattern of trade, and attempt to relate the picture that emerges to the broader economic experience of the country during the period under review. The main findings of the study are summarized in the concluding section.

---

[3] The Leontief Paradox for the U.S. springs easily to mind in this context, creating a bandwagon on which many authors have since embarked. But seemingly paradoxical results have been found for other countries; as, for instance, Japan in the second half of the 1970's appears to exhibit comparative advantage in unskilled labour intensive commodities, Vestal (1989, p. 570, Table 2), while the same has been claimed for the UK in the pre-first world war and inter-war years by Crafts and Thomas (1986) queried by Courakis (1987).

[4] Viz. Wolter (1977), Rodrik (1982), Maskus (1983), Bowen (1983), Baruh (1986), Han and Park (1989), and Vestal (1989).

## 2 A Model of Net Exports and its Pedigree

The following linear relationship encompasses the various determinants of net exports $(X - M)$ considered:[5]

$$(X - M)_i = a_0 + a_1 K_i + a_2 L_i + a_3 LS_i + a_4 H_i + a_5 TC_i + a_6 ES_i \quad (1)$$

where $a_j$ $(j = 1, \ldots, 6)$ and $a_0$ are parameters, $i$ denotes the $i$-th industry, $K$ is the stock of physical capital, $L$ is the number of units of raw labour and $LS$ the number of units of skilled labour, $H$ is the stock of human capital, $TC$ is an index of "technological influences", and $ES$ is a proxy aiming to capture the effects of economies of scale.

Physical capital, labour and its quality composition or human capital are determinants of trade stressed by the neo-factor proportions theory — where, as in the traditional two factor Heckscher-Ohlin-Samuelson model, a country would tend to export the products of those industries that use relatively intensively the country's relatively abundant factor.[6] In other respects, however, equation (1) strictly parts company from the factor proportions mould. For, in contrast to the factor proportions model's assumptions of costless universal availability of technology of production and constant returns to scale for all industries, it ventures to allow for: (i) the fact that since technology is not for each and every commodity freely and instantaneously available to all countries, a country's pattern of trade may reflect differences across industries and for each industry across countries in the capacity to create new products or devise new lower cost techniques of production, or in ability to assimilate such developments in its production patterns;[7] and also for (ii) the possibility that trade patterns reflect departures from constant returns to scale (perfect competition).[8] With regard to (i), it is generally assumed that innovational advantage will tend to concentrate in countries with higher per capita income and higher relative wages.[9] For (ii) it is envisaged that "large" countries will tend to display

[5]Although other dependent variables have been used in the literature, see Ballance et al. (1987) for a survey, there is fair consensus in favour of $(X - M)$.

[6]See Vanek (1968), Leamer (1980) and Deardorf (1984).

[7]Posner (1961), Vernon (1966), Hirsch (1967), Keesing (1967), Finger (1975), Krugman (1979a, 1985), Jensen and Thursby (1986), Succar (1987), and Courakis and Moura Roque (1988).

[8]Krugman (1979b, 1980) and Markusen and Melvin (1981).

[9]In what may be termed its Hicksian variant — after Hicks (1932) who first noted the relationship between factor endowments and innovation and concluded that innovators were sensitive to the relative supply of factors of production in their local economy — "innovative activity will be concentrated in industries which intensively use a nation's relatively expensive factors of production" (Davidson, 1979, p. 765), thus rendering the very opposite prediction regarding the factor content of exports to that implied by the H-O-S model.

comparative advantage in industries with significant economies of scale.[10]

Similar specifications can be found in a number of studies of the US (Baldwin, 1971; Branson and Junz, 1971; Branson, 1971; Finger, 1975; Branson and Monoyios, 1977; Stern and Maskus, 1981; Maskus, 1983), Germany (Stern, 1976; Wolter, 1977), Japan (Urata, 1983; Vestal, 1989), the UK (Crafts and Thomas, 1986; Courakis, 1987), Sweden (Gavelin, 1983), the Netherlands (Hulsman-Vejsova and Koekek, 1983), Italy (Momigliano and Siniscalco, 1984; Onida, 1987), and Israel (Baruh, 1986). Both in terms of precise form and in terms of interpretation, however, in the context of equation (1) certain distinctions between our work and other studies should be emphasized.

## 2.1 Elaborations on the Neo-Factor Proportions Theory Components of Net-Exports Functions[11]

With regard to the neo-factor proportions theory components of equation (1) it will be noticed that (unlike, for instance, Branson, Stern, Wolter, Maskus, Crafts and Thomas, Baruh and others) in addition to raw labour and human capital, skilled labour *also* appears in our specification.

To appreciate the reason for this, consider an economy with three perfectly homogeneous categories of labour, notably, unskilled, low-skill and high-skill. The linear form of the neo-factor proportions paradigm can then be expressed by *either*

$$(X - M)_i = \alpha_0 + \alpha_1 K_i + \alpha_2 LU_i + \sum_n \alpha_{3n} LS_{ni} \tag{2}$$

where $n = 1,2$ denote, respectively, the low-skill and high-skill labour groups, *or*, exactly equivalently,

$$(X - M)_i = \beta_0 + \beta_1 K_i + \beta_2 L_i + \sum_n \beta_{3n}(h_n LS_{ni}) \tag{3}$$

where $L_i = (LU_i + \sum_n LS_{ni})$, while $h_n = (w_n - w_u)r^{-1}$ describes the human capital per unit of labour of each of the two homogeneous across industries skilled labour groups — $w_n$ being the wages pertaining to each of these two groups, $w_u$ being the wage of unskilled labour, and $r$ the appropriate discount factor.

Empirically, these equations are identical and the estimates of $\alpha_2$ and each $\alpha_{2n}$ derived from (2) will certainly replicate those derived from (3) in

[10] Hufbauer (1970), Baldwin (1971), Katrak (1973), Krugman (1979b, 1980), Markusen and Melvin (1981), and Deardorf (1984).

[11] This subsection draws heavily on Courakis (1986).

the form $\alpha_2 = \beta_2$ and $\alpha_{3n} = \beta_2 + \beta_{3n} h_n$. On the other hand, if instead of equation (2) or equation (3), we estimate, in keeping with the authors cited above, a relationship of the form

$$(X - M)_i = \beta_0 + \beta_1 K_i + \beta_2 L_i + \beta_3 H_i \quad , \quad H_i = \sum_n h_n LS_{ni} \tag{4}$$

we run the risk of mispecification bias, since compared to (3) equation (4) implies $\beta_{3n} = \beta_3$ for all $n = 1, 2$, and hence the constraint that the composition of net exports is independent of the *composition* of human capital.

In terms of empirical strategy, the above implies that, in the absence of any prior reasoning that may be said to *universally* commend such a constraint,[12] we have no choice but to begin (in any empirical enquiry) from a specification that involves as detailed a decomposition of the labour force as data will permit, with the view to (laboriously) proceeding thereafter, to testing the validity of more specific hypotheses pertaining to aggregation of different qualities of labour.

Sometimes, however, as in the case of the present study, the available data regarding the composition of the labour force and/or human capital, is limited to merely the total labour input, $L_i$, the total input of skilled labour of various levels of skill, $LS_i$, and the total amount of human capital, $H_i$. In this eventuality an equation that encompasses both $LS_i$, and $H_i$ can be used to infer the qualitative relationship of net exports to the unobservable categories of skilled labour or human capital.

Specifically, suppose that with the true relationship being described by (2) or (3) above, we estimate

$$(X - M)_i = a_o + a_1 K_i + a_2 L_i + a_3 LS_i + a_4 H_i \tag{5}$$

Compared to (3) equation (5) implies

$$a_3 = (\beta_{31} - \beta_{32}) h_1 h_2 (h_2 - h_1)^{-1} \tag{6}$$

$$a_4 = (\beta_{32} h_2 - \beta_{31} h_1)(h_2 - h_1)^{-1}$$

where $h_1$ denotes the amount of human capital per unit of low-skill labour and $h_2$ denotes the amount of human capital per unit of high-skill labour, with $h_1 < h_2$ unambiguously.

Accordingly, if $a_3 = 0$ then, since this implies $\beta_{31} = \beta_{32}$, the effect of human capital on net exports is independent of the composition of human capital. On the other hand, if $a_4 = 0$, and hence $\beta_{32} h_2 = \beta_{31} h_1$, then the composition of human capital bears on net exports in such a way as for

[12] See Courakis (1986) for further discussion on this point.

variations across industries in the average amount of human capital per unit of skilled labour employed to have no effect on net exports at all. Except in these extremes, however, the composition of human capital/skilled labour is important. Moreover, by looking at the pattern of signs of $a_2$ and $a_3$ we can infer the implicit signs of $\beta_{31}$ and $\beta_{32}$.

Specifically, since $h_2 h_1^{-1} > 1$, we find that

(i) if both $a_3$ and $a_4$ are negative then $\beta_{31}$ and $\beta_{32}$ are both negative and $|\beta_{31}| > |\beta_{32}|$;

(ii) if both $\alpha_3$ and $\alpha_4$ are positive then $\beta_{31}$ is certainly positive while $\alpha_{32}$ may be either positive or negative, since $\alpha_3, \alpha_4 > 0$ requires only $0 < \beta_{31} < \beta_{32}$;

(iii) if $\alpha_3$ is positive and $\alpha_4$ is negative then either $\beta_{31}$ and $\beta_{32}$ are both positive and $\beta_{31} > \beta_{32}$, or $\beta_{32} < 0$ and $|\beta_{32}| > |\beta_{31}|$; finally

(iv) if $\alpha_3$ is negative and $\alpha_4$ is positive then either $\beta_{31}$ and $\beta_{32}$ are both positive, or they are both negative, or $\beta_{31}$ is negative and $\beta_{32}$ is positive — in other words in this case the only possibility precluded by the signs of the estimated coefficients is that of $\beta_{31} > 0$ and $\beta_{32} < 0$.

It will be noticed that without first confirming that $a_3 = 0$ when $a_4 = 0$ nothing much can be said about the factor content of trade by looking at $a_4$ alone; for $a_4 < 0$ is consistent both with $\beta_{31}$, $\beta_{32} < 0$ and with $\beta_{31}$, $\beta_{32} > 0$, depending on whether $a_3$ is positive or negative; and $a_4 > 0$ is consistent with every conceivable combination of signs of $\beta_{31}$ and $\beta_{32}$. Similarly, without first confirming that $a_4 = 0$ when $a_3 = 0$ nothing can be said by just looking at the sign of $a_3$. And since this kind of reasoning also applies when $n > 2$, it follows that, except for a circumstance where the available data relates to perfectly homogeneous across industries groups of skilled labour, it is certainly inefficient, and may even lead to erroneous inferences, to disregard the additional information that equation (5) and hence also (1) afford when compared to the more standard specifications.

## 2.2 Technological Innovation and Technological Adaptation

Extensions of the neo-factor proportions model, designed to allow for departures from the universal costless availability of technology assumption, are common to many empirical studies of trade patterns.

With theory offering no firm guide as to how technology should be measured or how it should combine with other variables to explain the sectoral composition of trade, technology variables are generally appended to linear relationships that otherwise purport to capture the insights of the factor proportions model.[13]

In so doing, across industries technological influences have been proxied by measures of research and development expenditures, technology payments, skilled labour intensity, value or number of patents, innovation lists, counts of scientific papers, and first trade date, and for performance among countries (as we have noted above) it is generally supposed that technological advantages will tend to lie with countries characterized by higher per capita income and higher relative wages.

From the latter viewpoint for a country such as Portugal the literature encourages us to expect that regressions pertaining to the composition of trade will record non-positive coefficients for each and all of the technology indices described.[14] Such a position, however, fails to distinguish between two facets of the technology process, that may respectively be described as the ***propensity to innovate*** and ***the propensity to adapt.***

Dominated by the image of US, Japan, Germany, Britain and other such "technology-leaders", the traditional literature has emphasized the former of these, while adopting a view of technology transfer that confines all initiative to the "technology-leader" countries.[15] Although, therefore, existing technology theories do capture important elements of the technology transfer problem, they neglect the importance of *"technology-follower" ability to adapt*, in the sense of propensity to respond to innovation by translating new developments into products and/or processes more compatible with the follower's comparative advantage. This ability, we maintain,[16] will depend on the same set of technology input variables that with regard to technology-leaders we generally invoke to explain technological advantage.

In the context of a semi-developed country our proposition implies that the pattern of trade will reflect differences across industries in the ability to adapt to technological improvements as a direct function of the quality composition of the labour force of different industries and of research and development expenditures, since both these will determine the degree of facility of adaptation.[17] Thus, for a semi-developed/technology-follower

[13] See, for instance, Baldwin (1971), Branson and Junz (1971), Branson (1971), Finger (1975), Stern (1976), Wolter (1977), Stern and Maskus (1981), and Maskus (1983).

[14] Hufbauer (1970), Baldwin (1979), Deardorf (1984), Onida (1987).

[15] This is particularly true of Vernon.

[16] Courakis and Moura Roque (1988).

[17] Ibid. Our hypothesis, we may note, is consistent with the analysis of Magee (1977), who in focussing on the appropriability problem of new technology invokes an inverse relationship between appropriability and skilled labour intensity, and with the work of Teitel (1982, 1984), who stresses technological adaptation as an important feature of experience of semi-industrialized countries (1984) and reasons that "The transfer of

country, *domestic* technology indices should exhibit positive coefficients in equations pertaining to net exports.

# 3 Supply Determinants and the Pattern of Portugal's Comparative Advantage

The data sample employed comprises *twenty industries* for each of the *fourteen years* 1972–1985. Physical capital, labour and human capital relate to each industry's direct inputs;[18] labour is split into two groups, namely unskilled (operários) and skilled, with "raw" labour being the sum of the two, i.e., total industry employment; and human capital, as already described, is measured by the discounted present value of the difference in earnings accruing to labour in each industry from the earnings that will accrue to an equal size unskilled labour force. Technology is proxied for each industry by the across years average ratio of skilled labour to total labour, expressed in percentage terms, while economies of scale are proxied by a concentration index relating to the ratio of the number of firms in the industry with more than one hundred employees to the total number of firms in the industry.

In the interests of statistical efficiency estimates are based on pooled (cross-section and time series) samples.[19] Accordingly, in order to avoid systematic biases arising from measurement of some of the variables (notably exports, imports, physical capital and human capital) in value terms and some in volume terms (notably unskilled and skilled labour), the current values of the former group of variables are converted to constant prices by dividing across years by the GDP deflator. Such adjustment of the raw data in no way provides for the feature of heteroscedasticity that differences in sizes across industries generally imply. Hence, with regard to the standard errors of the estimated coefficients we adopted the procedure described in White (1980) in computing heteroscedasticity consistent standard errors, in terms of which the $t$ values reported in the tables that follow are calculated.

Equations were estimated for net exports as well as gross exports and gross imports. Tables 1–3 present the detailed parameter estimates and

technology requires agents capable of learning the relevant technical information and modifying it for adaptation to local conditions" (1982, p. 333).

[18] Queries can be raised about the appropriateness of using direct inputs (rather than direct plus indirect inputs); see Baldwin (1971) and Deardorf (1982). Except for Baldwin (1971), Momigliano and Siniscalco (1984) and Baruh (1986), however, authors generally rely on "direct" inputs; and in the absence of reliable input-output coefficients corresponding to our data sample this practice is also (willy nilly) followed here.

[19] See Maddala (1977) and Hsiao (1986).

Table 1: Net-exports $(X - M)$ functions: estimates for alternative sample periods.*†

Estimated equation: $T_{it} = a_0 + \sum_j a_j J_{jit}$, where $T = (X - M)$ and $J_j = (K, L, H, LS, TC, ES)$

| $t$ | 1972-3 | 1974-5 | 1976-7 | 1978-9 | 1980-1 | 1982-3 | 1984-5 | 1972-85 |
|---|---|---|---|---|---|---|---|---|
| Const. | -3.30 | -3.76 | -2.73 | -1.54 | -1.72 | -2.12 | -0.61 | -2.95 |
| | (3.59) | (4.10) | (2.28) | (0.97) | (1.20) | (2.20) | (0.48) | (4.81) |
| $K$ | -3.95 | -5.12 | -2.27 | -1.09 | -0.07 | 1.59 | 0.34 | 0.69 |
| | (2.34) | (3.06) | (1.65) | (1.05) | (0.59) | (1.08) | (0.35) | (1.30) |
| $L$ | 0.20 | 0.22 | 0.20 | 0.16 | 0.15 | 0.15 | 0.19 | 0.17 |
| | (7.06) | (7.81) | (6.30) | (4.84) | (5.63) | (7.57) | (11.46) | (10.09) |
| $LS$ | -0.80 | -1.04 | -1.26 | -0.76 | -0.78 | -0.61 | -0.83 | -1.03 |
| | (3.60) | (4.38) | (4.96) | (1.97) | (2.41) | (2.24) | (3.46) | (6.51) |
| $H$ | -0.13 | -0.03 | -0.07 | -0.22 | -0.26 | -0.41 | -0.04 | -0.13 |
| | (1.30) | (0.72) | (1.28) | (2.09) | (1.91) | (2.56) | (1.69) | (3.61) |
| $TC$ | 0.20 | 0.24 | 0.23 | 0.08 | 0.12 | 0.15 | 0.03 | 0.18 |
| | (2.87) | (3.28) | (2.58) | (0.56) | (1.15) | (2.10) | (0.39) | (4.46) |
| $ES$ | -0.32 | -0.21 | -0.44 | -0.05 | -0.15 | -0.44 | -0.22 | -0.35 |
| | (1.52) | (1.39) | (1.74) | (0.35) | (0.93) | (2.22) | (1.14) | (3.57) |
| $R^2$ | 0.57 | 0.57 | 0.58 | 0.63 | 0.62 | 0.76 | 0.85 | 0.57 |
| $SE$ | 2.627 | 2.382 | 2.538 | 2.858 | 3.142 | 2.613 | 2.385 | 2.923 |
| $F(6,33)$ | | 7.294 | 7.203 | 7.697 | 9.563 | 8.879 | 17.693 | 30.602 |
| $F(6,273)$ | | | | | | | | 60.219 |
| $F(7,26)$ | | 0.245 | 0.669 | 0.134 | 0.151 | 0.006 | 0.149 | 0.306 |
| $F(42,231)$ | | | | | | | | 2.351 |
| $F(91,182)$ | | | | | | | | 1.010 |

* Figures in parentheses denote ratios of the estimated coefficients to their respective White (1980) heteroscedasticity corrected standard errors.

† $F(7,26)$ denote the $F$ values of the Chow tests for intertemporal parameter constancy for the corresponding two-year sample; $F(42,231)$ and $F(91,182)$ denote the $F$ values of the Chow tests for intertemporal parameter constancy corresponding to the seven two-year and to the fourteen yearly samples. The 5% critical values are: $F(7,26) = 2.39$; $F(42,231) = 1.39$; $F(91,182) = 1.26$.

related statistics for the sample as a whole and for each of the seven two-yearly sub-periods.[20]

Focusing on *net exports*, it will be noticed that with very few exceptions the estimated coefficients, shown in Table 1, are highly significant. Moreover, there is a striking consistency of pattern of parameters across sample periods. Indeed, aside from one odd (and statistically insignificant) coefficient for human capital in 1974–75, (explicable, perhaps, by the circumstances of the time),[21] the only sign reversals appearing in this table relate to the coefficient of physical capital.

[20] Notice that with regard to the two-yearly samples the $F$ tests for intertemporal parameter constancy, $F(7,26)$, shown in these three tables, reveal that (subject to the caveat that the residual sums of squares have not been purged for heteroskedasticity) the hypothesis of sample homogeneity cannot be rejected for any of the pairs of years considered.

[21] See section 4, below.

On the face of it, therefore, we can conclude that for the period 1972 to 1985 the Portuguese pattern of trade reflects:

(i) Comparative *advantage* in products of industries that are intensive in unskilled labour and/or display relatively high values of the "technological adaptation" proxy; coupled with

(ii) Comparative *disadvantage* in products of industries that are intensive in skilled labour/human capital and/or display economies of scale (in the sense of high concentration ratios)

In terms of skilled labour/human capital, furthermore, the specific parameter estimates shown in Table 1 can be interpreted to imply (in line with the reasoning of section 2 above) that thinking of two classes of human capital/skilled labour inputs we can add that

(iii) The comparative *disadvantage* in skilled labour/human capital intensive products is more pronounced in products that are intensive in *"lower"* quality skilled labour than in products that are intensive in *"higher"* quality skilled labour.

On the other hand

(iv) With regard to physical capital, the results reveal that whereas in the 1970's the Portuguese pattern of trade is characterized by comparative disadvantage in physical capital intensive commodities, in the 1980's this comparative *disadvantage* yields to physical capital *neutrality*.

For the most part this pattern of comparative advantage/disadvantage accords well with (and augments) the available background evidence on Portugal that reveals,[22] [23] (a) relative scarcity of skilled labour/human capital, and for the 1970's, at least, also in physical capital; (b) a multilateral trading-partner pattern geared mainly towards countries characterized by higher physical capital and human capital/skilled labour ratios; (c) distinctly low skilled labour content of exports; (d) lack of conditions conducive to exploiting economies of scale. Moreover, the change in the coefficient of physical capital is itself consistent with policies that since the

[22] See Balassa (1979a) p. 263, Table 1; Bowen (1983) pp. 403 and 404, Tables 1 and 2; Noland (1987), p. 685, Table 1; Hufbauer (1970), pp. 153–7, Tables 2–4; Keesing (1971), pp. 448 and 449, Tables 3 and 4; and Courakis and Moura Roque (1990).

[23] As established by Leamer and Bowen (1981) in a world of more than two factors there is no guarantee that the signs of the regression coefficients will correspond to factor abundance. It follows that one is not entitled to infer factor abundance by looking at the signs of the regression coefficients. Yet, aside from the positive coefficients for physical capital traced in Table 1 for the last two sub-periods of our sample, the signs of the coefficients of all factor inputs correspond exactly to what from direct evidence on relative factor abundance we know to be true of Portugal.

Table 2: Gross exports ($X$) functions: estimates for alternative sample periods.*†

Estimated equation: $T_{it} = a_0 + \sum_j a_j J_{jit}$, where $T = X$ and $J_j = (K, L, H, LS, TC, ES)$

| $t$ | 1972-3 | 1974-5 | 1976-7 | 1978-9 | 1980-1 | 1982-3 | 1984-5 | 1972-85 |
|---|---|---|---|---|---|---|---|---|
| Const. | -0.44 | -1.15 | -0.20 | -0.32 | -0.06 | -1.10 | -0.55 | -1.10 |
| | (0.89) | (2.26) | (0.36) | (0.34) | (0.08) | (0.98) | (0.35) | (2.34) |
| $K$ | 0.82 | 0.35 | 0.09 | 0.87 | 2.28 | 2.25 | 2.32 | 2.52 |
| | (0.87) | (0.36) | (0.13) | (1.72) | (3.78) | (7.44) | (2.57) | (6.89) |
| $L$ | 0.08 | 0.09 | 0.07 | 0.08 | 0.08 | 0.10 | 0.15 | 0.09 |
| | (5.81) | (5.63) | (5.28) | (3.85) | (5.88) | (3.83) | (5.20) | (6.22) |
| $LS$ | -0.13 | -0.37 | -0.14 | -0.08 | -0.36 | -0.23 | -0.48 | -0.40 |
| | (1.16) | (3.82) | (1.43) | (0.38) | (1.82) | (0.69) | (1.43) | (3.68) |
| $H$ | -0.09 | 0.02 | -0.02 | -0.15 | -0.11 | -0.11 | -0.07 | -0.06 |
| | (1.53) | (0.51) | (0.57) | (2.43) | (2.22) | (1.10) | (1.36) | (2.69) |
| $TC$ | 0.03 | 0.09 | 0.03 | 1.91 | 0.05 | 0.05 | 0.04 | 0.08 |
| | (0.86) | (2.46) | (0.86) | (0.30) | (0.81) | (0.60) | (0.35) | (2.91) |
| $ES$ | 0.42 | -0.03 | 0.13 | 0.03 | 0.02 | 0.14 | 0.18 | -0.04 |
| | (0.43) | (0.51) | (0.02) | (0.40) | (0.12) | (0.73) | (0.88) | (0.98) |
| $R^2$ | 0.88 | 0.85 | 0.83 | 0.88 | 0.87 | 0.85 | 0.87 | 0.77 |
| $SE$ | 0.998 | 1.009 | 0.992 | 1.141 | 1.338 | 1.853 | 2.333 | 1.799 |
| $F(6,33)$ | 41.050 | 30.518 | 25.981 | 41.958 | 35.534 | 31.765 | 35.435 | |
| $F(6,273)$ | | | | | | | | 152.011 |
| $F(7,26)$ | 0.213 | 0.552 | 0.142 | 0.774 | 0.072 | 0.270 | 0.353 | |
| $F(42,231)$ | | | | | | | | 3.782 |
| $F(91,182)$ | | | | | | | | 1.920 |

* Figures in parentheses denote ratios of the estimated coefficients to their respective White (1980) heteroscedasticity corrected standard errors.

† $F(7,26)$ denote the $F$ values of the Chow tests for intertemporal parameter constancy for the corresponding two-year sample; $F(42,231)$ and $F(91,182)$ denote the $F$ values of the Chow tests for intertemporal parameter constancy corresponding to the seven two-year and to the fourteen yearly samples. The 5% critical values are: $F(7,26) = 2.39$; $F(42,231) = 1.39$; $F(91,182) = 1.26$.

late 1960s have favoured capital intensive industrial development,[24] and which by the late 1970s result in rather substantial increase in the stock of physical capital.[25] At the same time, while from a conventional standpoint both the evidence on skilled labour and human capital scarcity and the ranking that one would be inclined to assign to Portugal in the product cycle/technological sophistication order,[26] query the positive coefficient of the proxy for technological influences, such a positive coefficient is precisely what our technological *adaptation* hypothesis predicts.

These inferences about the pattern of comparative advantage/disadvantage are, of course, tautologically replicated by the union of estimates

[24] Courakis (1984).

[25] Over the period under review both the capital/labour ratio and the capital/output ratio rose steeply.

[26] See Hufbauer (1970) pp. 153–7, Tables 2–4; and Soete (1980), pp. 10–20, Tables 1, 4 and 5.

Table 3: Gross imports ($M$) functions: estimates for alternative sample periods.*†

Estimated equation: $T_{it} = a_0 + \sum_j a_j J_{jit}$, where $T = M$ and $J_j = (K, L, H, LS, TC, ES)$

| $t$ | 1972-3 | 1974-5 | 1976-7 | 1978-9 | 1980-1 | 1982-3 | 1984-5 | 1972-85 |
|---|---|---|---|---|---|---|---|---|
| Const. | 2.86 | 2.61 | 2.53 | 1.51 | 1.66 | 1.03 | 0.60 | 1.85 |
| | (3.16) | (2.65) | (2.24) | (0.81) | (1.04) | (0.88) | (0.39) | (3.78) |
| $K$ | 4.76 | 5.47 | 2.86 | 1.96 | 2.35 | 0.66 | 1.98 | 1.83 |
| | (3.25) | (2.99) | (1.63) | (1.63) | (1.75) | (1.91) | (0.45) | (3.78) |
| $L$ | -0.12 | -0.13 | -0.13 | -0.08 | -0.07 | -0.05 | -0.05 | -0.08 |
| | (4.52) | (4.70) | (3.76) | (2.00) | (1.99) | (2.07) | (1.97) | (6.60) |
| $LS$ | 0.67 | 0.68 | 1.12 | 0.68 | 0.42 | 0.38 | 0.35 | 0.63 |
| | (2.86) | (3.36) | (3.80) | (1.50) | (1.10) | (1.25) | (1.21) | (4.48) |
| $H$ | 0.04 | -0.01 | 0.05 | 0.08 | 0.15 | 0.30 | -0.03 | 0.07 |
| | (0.34) | (0.20) | (0.71) | (0.60) | (1.10) | (0.67) | (0.75) | (1.83) |
| $TC$ | -0.17 | -0.15 | -0.02 | -0.06 | -0.07 | -0.10 | 0.40 | -0.10 |
| | (2.35) | (1.91) | (2.10) | (0.36) | (0.57) | (1.19) | (0.04) | (2.62) |
| $ES$ | 0.36 | 0.19 | 1.44 | 0.08 | 0.14 | 0.58 | 0.40 | 0.30 |
| | (1.44) | (1.13) | (1.59) | (0.47) | (0.62) | (3.14) | (1.91) | (3.09) |
| $R^2$ | 0.31 | 0.35 | 0.44 | 0.32 | 0.34 | 0.44 | 0.44 | 0.32 |
| $SE$ | 2.777 | 2.534 | 2.548 | 3.084 | 3.329 | 3.048 | 2.713 | 2.767 |
| $F(6,33)$ | 2.471 | 2.963 | 4.266 | 2.577 | 2.891 | 4.312 | 4.346 | |
| $F(6,273)$ | | | | | | | | 21.692 |
| $F(7,26)$ | 0.261 | 0.684 | 0.113 | 0.030 | 0.024 | 0.051 | 0.182 | |
| $F(42,231)$ | | | | | | | | 0.522 |
| $F(91,182)$ | | | | | | | | 0.281 |

* Figures in parentheses denote ratios of the estimated coefficients to their respective White (1980) heteroscedasticity corrected standard errors.

† $F(7,26)$ denote the $F$ values of the Chow tests for intertemporal parameter constancy for the corresponding two-year sample; $F(42,231)$ and $F(91,182)$ denote the $F$ values of the Chow tests for intertemporal parameter constancy corresponding to the seven two-year and to the fourteen yearly samples. The 5% critical values are: $F(7,26) = 2.39$; $F(42,231) = 1.39$; $F(91,182) = 1.26$.

derived from equations pertaining separately to *gross exports* and *gross imports*, that feature the same set of determinants. However, looking separately at gross exports and gross imports additional information about the pattern of trade can be had.

In Tables 2 and 3, we again find mostly significant coefficients with only two reversals in sign, both pertaining to human capital in 1974–5. Overall, the results here suggest that the pattern of comparative advantage/disadvantage described above, reflects a composition of trade where *gross exports* are physical capital cum unskilled labour cum adaptive technology intensive and human capital scarce, while *gross imports* are physical capital cum human capital cum economies of scale intensive but unskilled labour and adaptive technology scarce.

# 4 Internal and External Shocks, Policy and Structural Change

With regard to temporal pattern our attention so far has focussed only on the signs of the coefficients of the various determinants obtained for the different sub-periods considered. In terms of these signs we can conclude that, during the period under review, the only *qualitative* change in the relationship between trade determinants and net exports is that pertaining to the coefficients of physical capital as between the 1970's and 1980's. This is so notwithstanding:[27]

(a) marked changes in the labour force resulting from repatriation in 1974–75 of large numbers of colonial residents (retornados) and, subsequently, also large reduction in the size of the armed forces;

(b) sharp movements in real wages, which increased by more than 25% between 1973 and 1975 and declined systematically thereafter;

(c) contraction in the share of exports to the old escudo area from more than 16% of total exports in 1972 to some 5% of total exports in 1979, and to 4% in 1985, while conversely the share of the EEC Nine rose from 48% in 1972 to 57% in 1979 and 58% in 1985;

(d) large changes in income distribution and in the share of government in national income, with the latter rising from less than 20% of GDP in 1972 to more than 35% by 1976 and to 45% by 1984;

(e) marked government direct intervention in the structure of wages and prices and in the capital markets; and

(f) considerable apparent changes in degree and pattern of nominal and effective protection and in non-tariff barriers to trade.

On the other hand, the absence of other *qualitative* changes clearly does not imply absence of significant *quantitative* change in the relationship between the rest of the trade determinants considered and trade performance during the period under review.

With regard to the latter, Tables 4–6 and 7–8 present estimates from equations that allow for over time *shift parameters* for each of the independent variables featured in equation (1). Specifically, in Table 4-6 we

[27] See OECD Economic Outlook Portugal, and the Bank of Portugal Annual Reports, for the period under review; Courakis and Moura Roque (1990); Courakis, Moura Roque and Tridimas (1990); and Macedo, Corado and Porto (1988).

Table 4: On temporal change: consecutive post-revolution periods relative to the pre-revolution period.*

Estimated equation: $T_{it} = \sum_j a_j J_{jit} + \sum_j b_{j\gamma} D_\gamma J_{jit} + b_0 D_\gamma + a_0$, where $T = (X - M)$, $J_j = (K, L, H, LS, TC, ES)$, $t$ denotes four yearly observations combining 1972–3 and consecutive post revolution two yearly periods, and $D_\gamma$ is a dummy variable taking the value 0 for 1972–3 and 1 for each consecutive $\gamma$ (74–5, 76–7, ..., 84–5) period.†

| $t$ | 1972-3 | 1974-5 | 1976-7 | 1978-9 | 1980-1 | 1982-3 | 1984-5 |
|---|---|---|---|---|---|---|---|
| Const. | -3.30 | -0.47 | -0.57 | 1.76 | 1.58 | 1.17 | 2.69 |
| | (3.59) | (0.36) | (0.38) | (0.96) | (0.92) | (0.88) | (1.71) |
| $K$ | -3.95 | -1.18 | 1.17 | 2.85 | 3.87 | 5.53 | 4.28 |
| | (2.34) | (0.50) | (0.59) | (1.44) | (1.85) | (2.48) | (2.20) |
| $L$ | 0.20 | 0.02 | 0.00 | -0.04 | -0.05 | -0.04 | -0.00 |
| | (7.06) | (0.61) | (0.12) | (0.85) | (1.21) | (1.28) | (0.04) |
| $LS$ | -0.80 | -0.24 | -0.46 | 0.05 | 0.02 | 0.20 | -0.04 |
| | (3.60) | (0.74) | (1.35) | (0.10) | (0.06) | (0.56) | (0.09) |
| $H$ | -0.13 | 0.16 | 0.06 | -0.09 | -0.13 | -0.28 | 0.09 |
| | (1.30) | (1.49) | (0.51) | (0.65) | (0.77) | (1.49) | (0.89) |
| $TC$ | 0.20 | 0.04 | 0.03 | 0.12 | -0.08 | 0.05 | -0.17 |
| | (2.87) | (0.39) | (0.29) | (0.79) | (0.61) | (0.48) | (1.57) |
| $ES$ | -0.32 | 0.11 | -0.12 | 0.27 | 0.17 | 0.12 | 1.00 |
| | (1.52) | (0.42) | (0.36) | (1.06) | (0.63) | (0.41) | (0.35) |
| $R^2$ | 0.57 | 0.58 | 0.61 | 0.60 | 0.70 | 0.78 | |
| $SE$ | | 2.507 | 2.583 | 2.745 | 2.896 | 2.620 | 2.509 |
| $F(13,66)$ | | 6.697 | 6.914 | 7.880 | 7.626 | 11.810 | 17.760 |
| $F(7,66)^‡$ | | 0.283 | 0.337 | 0.494 | 0.595 | 2.640 | 5.925 |

* Figures in parentheses denote ratios of the estimated coefficients to their respective White (1980) heteroscedasticity corrected standard errors.

† Estimating the equation for consecutive combinations of four yearly samples all involving 1972-3 implies that $a_j$ is in all cases the same, while the shift parameters $b_{j\gamma}$ may change.

‡ $F(7,66)$ denote the $F$ values of the Chow tests for intertemporal parameter constancy between 1972-3 and each consecutive two-yearly period; the 5% critical value is $F(7,66) = 3.29$.

examine the extent to which the coefficients of each particular independent variable for each of the six more recent two-yearly sub-periods, differs significantly from the corresponding coefficient of the first two-yearly sub-period.[28] On the other hand, Table 7–8 present a sample of estimates from regressions that allow for the possibility that the coefficient of each independent variable in a two-yearly sub-period deviates significantly from the corresponding coefficient pertaining to the period as a whole.

Compared to pre-revolution Portugal, our results in Table 4 reveal three significant shift parameters at the 5% level, pertaining to physical capital in the last three sub-periods of our sample. These coefficients confirm the tendency towards reduced comparative disadvantage in physical capital

[28] Tables 4, 5 and 6 also report the $F$ values for regression homogeneity between the first two-yearly sub-period and each of the six subsequent two-yearly sub-periods.

Table 5: On temporal change: consecutive post-revolution periods relative to the pre-revolution period.*

Estimated equation: $T_{it} = \sum_j a_j J_{jit} + \sum_j b_{j\gamma} D_\gamma J_{jit} + b_0 D_\gamma + a_0$, where $T = (X - M)$, $J_j = (K, L, H, LS, TC, ES)$, $t$ denotes four yearly observations combining 1972-3 and consecutive post revolution two yearly periods, and $D_\gamma$ is a dummy variable taking the value 0 for 1972-3 and 1 for each consecutive $\gamma$ (74-5, 76-7, ..., 84-5) period.†

| $t$ | 1972-3 | 1974-5 | 1976-7 | 1978-9 | 1980-1 | 1982-3 | 1984-5 |
|---|---|---|---|---|---|---|---|
| Const. | -0.44 | -0.72 | -0.24 | 0.40 | 0.37 | -0.66 | 0.11 |
| | (0.89) | (1.02) | (0.32) | (0.38) | (0.39) | (0.54) | (0.07) |
| $K$ | 0.82 | -0.47 | -0.73 | 0.05 | 1.46 | 1.43 | 1.50 |
| | (0.87) | (0.35) | (0.62) | (0.04) | (1.31) | (1.09) | (1.15) |
| $L$ | 0.08 | 0.01 | -0.01 | 0.00 | 0.00 | 0.02 | 0.07 |
| | (5.18) | (0.62) | (0.50) | (0.03) | (0.24) | (0.67) | (2.15) |
| $LS$ | -0.13 | -0.23 | -0.01 | 0.05 | -0.22 | -0.09 | -0.35 |
| | (1.16) | (1.58) | (0.08) | (0.21) | (0.99) | (0.27) | (0.98) |
| $H$ | -0.09 | 0.11 | 0.07 | -0.06 | -0.02 | -0.02 | 0.02 |
| | (1.53) | (1.55) | (1.02) | (0.71) | (0.28) | (0.20) | (0.29) |
| $TC$ | 0.03 | 0.06 | -0.00 | -0.01 | 0.02 | -0.02 | 0.00 |
| | (0.86) | (1.13) | (0.00) | (0.16) | (0.25) | (0.20) | (0.04) |
| $ES$ | 0.04 | -0.07 | -0.04 | -0.01 | -0.57 | 0.09 | 0.14 |
| | (0.43) | (0.62) | (0.32) | (0.10) | (0.36) | (0.44) | (0.61) |
| $R^2$ | 0.87 | 0.86 | 0.88 | 0.87 | 0.87 | 0.88 | |
| $SE$ | | 1.003 | 0.995 | 1.072 | 1.180 | 1.488 | 1.794 |
| $F(13, 66)$ | | 33.001 | 31.004 | 38.554 | 35.372 | 32.669 | 36.583 |
| $F(7, 66)$‡ | | 0.380 | 1.548 | 0.210 | 0.851 | 2.150 | 6.552 |

* Figures in parentheses denote ratios of the estimated coefficients to their respective White (1980) heteroscedasticity corrected standard errors.

† Estimating the equation for consecutive combinations of four yearly samples all involving 1972-3 implies that $a_j$ is in all cases the same, while the shift parameters $b_{j\gamma}$ may change.

‡ $F(7, 66)$ denote the $F$ values of the Chow tests for intertemporal parameter constancy between 1972-3 and each consecutive two-yearly period; the 5% critical value is $F(7, 66) = 3.29$.

intensive products, evidenced since the late 1970's and leading to a pattern of physical capital neutrality. As can be seen from Tables 5 and 6, again at the 5% significance level, a significant shift parameter for physical capital appears only on the imports side. But a broad tendency for improvement in trade performance in physical capital intensive commodities, both in terms of gross imports as well as in terms of gross exports is certainly there, though stronger and, as one might have expected, emerging earlier for gross imports, than for gross exports.

Some more shift parameters are significant, at the 10% level, notably in Table 4 skilled labour in 1976-77 and human capital in 1974-75 and 1982-83. Evidently, though, these do not appear to form part of any systematic tendency, being instead of the "now you see it now you don't" kind, and thus, probably, reflecting the influence of particular episodes specific to the sub-periods in question.

Table 6: On temporal change: consecutive post-revolution periods relative to the pre-revolution period.*

Estimated equation: $T_{it} = \sum_j a_j J_{jit} + \sum_j b_{j\gamma} D_\gamma J_{jit} + b_0 D_\gamma + a_0$, where $T = X$, $J_j = (K, L, H, LS, TC, ES)$, $t$ denotes four yearly observations combining 1972–3 and consecutive post revolution two yearly periods, and $D_\gamma$ is a dummy variable taking the value 0 for 1972–3 and 1 for each consecutive $\gamma$ (74–5, 76–7, ..., 84–5) period.†

| $t$ | 1972-3 | 1974-5 | 1976-7 | 1978-9 | 1980-1 | 1982-3 | 1984-5 |
|---|---|---|---|---|---|---|---|
| Const. | 2.86 | -0.25 | -0.33 | -1.36 | -1.20 | -1.83 | -2.80 |
| | (3.16) | (0.19) | (0.23) | (0.65) | (0.66) | (1.24) | (1.57) |
| $K$ | 4.76 | 0.71 | -1.90 | -2.18 | -2.41 | -4.11 | -2.78 |
| | (3.25) | (0.30) | (0.83) | (1.52) | (1.26) | (1.99) | (1.61) |
| $L$ | -0.12 | -0.01 | -0.01 | 0.04 | 0.05 | 0.06 | 0.07 |
| | (4.52) | (0.27) | (0.34) | (0.78) | (1.22) | (1.73) | (1.99) |
| $LS$ | 0.67 | 0.01 | 0.44 | 0.01 | -0.25 | -0.29 | -0.31 |
| | (2.86) | (0.02) | (1.18) | (0.01) | (0.56) | (0.75) | (0.85) |
| $H$ | 0.04 | -0.05 | 0.01 | 0.04 | 0.11 | 0.26 | -0.07 |
| | (0.34) | (0.39) | (0.77) | (0.02) | (0.60) | (1.20) | (0.55) |
| $TC$ | -0.17 | 0.02 | -0.03 | 0.11 | 0.09 | 0.07 | 0.17 |
| | (2.35) | (1.16) | (0.28) | (0.62) | (0.64) | (0.59) | (1.32) |
| $ES$ | 0.36 | -0.18 | 0.08 | -0.28 | -0.23 | 0.21 | 0.04 |
| | (1.44) | (0.59) | (0.21) | (0.93) | (0.67) | (0.68) | (0.12) |
| $R^2$ | 0.33 | 0.37 | 0.32 | 0.33 | 0.39 | 0.38 | |
| $SE$ | | 2.695 | 2.666 | 2.935 | 3.066 | 2.917 | 2.746 |
| $F(13,66)$ | | 2.496 | 3.039 | 2.339 | 2.536 | 3.222 | 3.136 |
| $F(7,66)$‡ | | 0.169 | 0.242 | 0.367 | 0.197 | 0.679 | 0.914 |

* Figures in parentheses denote ratios of the estimated coefficients to their respective White (1980) heteroscedasticity corrected standard errors.

† Estimating the equation for consecutive combinations of four yearly samples all involving 1972-3 implies that $a_j$ is in all cases the same, while the shift parameters $b_{j\gamma}$ may change.

‡ $F(7,66)$ denote the $F$ values of the Chow tests for intertemporal parameter constancy between 1972-3 and each consecutive two-yearly period; the 5% critical value is $F(7,66) = 3.29$.

For human capital, the improvement in 1974–75, in particular, may be said to reflect changes in the composition of expenditures associated with the changes in the distribution of income and in population patterns, resulting from the revolution and colonial independence, and eventually largely dissipated. Such an interpretation is consistent both with the significant, at the 10% level, positive shift parameter for 1974–75 in the gross export equation, and with the negative but insignificant shift parameter for these years in the gross import equations. The negative and again significant at the 10% level shift parameter for skilled labour for these years, can also to be said to point in the same direction, since changes in income distribution favouring the lower income groups may have resulted in increased expenditures on products embodying lower quality skilled labour and decreased expenditures on products embodying higher quality skilled labour.[29] The same perhaps applies to the consumption patterns of the "retornados". With regard to lower quality skilled labour products, this tendency appears to continue into 1976–77, as evidenced by the negative net exports shift parameter for *LS* in that year; though the results for exports of lower quality skilled labour intensive commodities also suggest a switch from reduced exports of such commodities in 1974–75 to increased exports of such commodities in 1976–77.

The 1982–83 negative and significant, at the 10% level, shift parameter for human capital, on the other hand, appears to be part of a sequence of deteriorating performance in human capital intensive products, relative to the base years pre-revolution sub-period. Reflecting as it does (see Tables 5 and 6) mainly a higher human capital content of imports, this pattern is consistent with a process of trade liberalization, recorded during this period, vis a vis the countries of the European Community — relative at least to the original nine of which Portugal exhibits markedly lower levels of human capital per unit of labour. Over the same period, moreover, that is to say in the late 1970's and the 1980's, there is some deterioration in net export performance of unskilled labour intensive commodities — though in this case, as can be seen from Table 4, even for 1982–83, the shift coefficient carries a $t$ statistic that is marginally below the 10% significance level. The deterioration in unskilled labour performance, however, is pronounced and significant at the 5% level, when we look at the values of the shift parameters for gross imports recorded in Table 6.

Finally with regard to Tables 4, 5 and 6, at the 10% significance level, a significant negative shift parameter for 1984–85, relative to the pre-revolution period, is found for adaptive technology, and this reflects, as can be seen from Table 6, *entirely* a deterioration in gross import performance.

Broadly speaking, the same patterns are confirmed by the sample of comparisons presented in Tables 7 and 8.

Compared to the entire post-revolution period (i.e., 1974–1985) the pre-revolution period is characterized by a significantly higher comparative disadvantage in physical capital intensive products. This reflects not only significantly worse gross export performance but also significantly worse gross import performance in such products. Moreover, the results reveal that — in line with the loss of the colonies and the changes in trading partnerships noted above — export performance in lower quality skilled labour

---

[29] By equation (6 above we have $(da_3/d\beta_{31}) > 0$ and $(da_4/d\beta_{31}) < 0$. Thus a decrease in comparative advantage in lower quality skilled labour intensive products, such as may result from increased domestic absorption of such products, will (other things being equal) cause $a_3$ to fall (i.e., in our case, become more negative) and $a_4$ to rise (i.e., in our case become less negative, zero or positive). See also Courakis (1986).

Table 7: On temporal change: 1972–73 relative to the whole sample.*

Estimated Equation: $T_{it} = \sum_j c_j J_{jit} + \sum_j b_{j\gamma} D_\gamma J_{jit} + d_{0\gamma} D_\gamma + c_0$, where $t$ = 1972 – 1985, and $D_\gamma$ is a dummy variable taking the value 1 for the period $\gamma$ 1972-73 and 0 for the rest of the $t$ years.

| | $(X-M)$ | | $X$ | | $M$ | |
|---|---|---|---|---|---|---|
| | $c$ | $d$ | $c$ | $d$ | $c$ | $d$ |
| Const. | -2.77 | -0.53 | -1.18 | 0.74 | 1.59 | 1.27 |
| | (4.01) | (0.46) | (2.20) | (1.03) | (2.82) | (1.19) |
| $K$ | 0.84 | -4.79 | 2.60 | -0.78 | 1.76 | 3.00 |
| | (1.53) | (2.70) | (6.78) | (1.76) | (3.46) | (1.94) |
| $L$ | 0.17 | 0.03 | 0.10 | -0.02 | -0.07 | -0.04 |
| | (9.36) | (0.79) | (5.84) | (0.78) | (5.88) | (1.51) |
| $LS$ | -1.06 | 0.26 | -0.44 | 0.31 | 0.62 | 0.05 |
| | (6.14) | (0.92) | (3.63) | (1.85) | (4.05) | (0.18) |
| $H$ | -0.13 | 0.00 | -0.06 | -0.02 | 0.07 | -0.03 |
| | (3.50) | (0.01) | (2.56) | (0.40) | (1.80) | (0.21) |
| $TC$ | 0.18 | 0.02 | 0.09 | -0.06 | -0.09 | -0.08 |
| | (3.89) | (0.23) | (2.80) | (1.23) | (2.01) | (0.92) |
| $ES$ | -0.35 | 0.03 | -0.06 | 0.10 | 0.30 | 0.07 |
| | (3.36) | (0.13) | (1.22) | (0.90) | (2.82) | (0.25) |
| $R^2$ | 0.58 | | 0.77 | | 0.33 | |
| $SE$ | 2.917 | | 1.804 | | 2.787 | |
| $F(13, 266)$ | 28.565 | | 70.174 | | 10.121 | |

* Figures in parentheses denote ratios of the estimated coefficients to their respective White (1980) heteroscedasticity corrected standard errors.

intensive commodities is significantly better in the pre-revolution period than in the post-revolution period.

Comparing the last sub-period of our sample to the rest of the sample, we find four coefficients that are significant, at the 5% level, notably for unskilled labour and human capital, and one that is significant at the 10% level, notably for adaptive technology.

With regard to unskilled labour, net export performance in 1984–85 is significantly better, than in previous years;[30] and, in line with the results in Table 5, this relative improvement in the unambiguous comparative advantage of Portugal in unskilled labour, reflects a significant improvement in export performance in unskilled labour intensive commodities. Yet, for those that believe that Portugal exhibits a comparative advantage in skilled labour intensive products,[31] there is also some consolation to be found in Table 8. For with regard to human capital, the shift parameter for 1984–85 in the net exports equation is positive and unambiguously significant. As we know from Table 1–3 this still does not imply that Portugal exhibits,

[30] Again in line with changes in trading partnerships towards more skilled labour abundant countries.

[31] As has been claimed, for instance, by Balassa (1979b, 1984) and also in World Bank (1977).

Table 8: On temporal change: 1984–85 relative to the whole sample.*

Estimated Equation: $T_{it} = \sum_j c_j J_{jit} + \sum_j b_{j\gamma} D_\gamma J_{jit} + d_{0\gamma} D_\gamma + c_0$, where $t$ = 1972 – 1985, and $D_\gamma$ is a dummy variable taking the value 1 for the period $\gamma$ 1984-85 and 0 for the rest of the $t$ years.

| | $(X - M)$ | | $X$ | | $M$ | |
|---|---|---|---|---|---|---|
| | $c$ | $d$ | $c$ | $d$ | $c$ | $d$ |
| Const. | -2.62 | 2.01 | -0.77 | 0.22 | 1.85 | -1.79 |
| | (4.72) | (1.45) | (2.06) | (0.14) | (3.83) | (1.11) |
| $K$ | -0.11 | 0.44 | 1.88 | 0.44 | 1.99 | -0.00 |
| | (0.17) | (0.38) | (4.35) | (0.44) | (3.66) | (0.00) |
| $L$ | 0.16 | 0.38 | 0.08 | 0.07 | -0.08 | -0.03 |
| | (9.97) | (1.63) | (6.81) | (2.15) | (5.86) | (1.04) |
| $LS$ | -0.89 | 0.57 | -0.30 | -0.18 | 0.59 | -0.24 |
| | (5.74) | (0.20) | (3.32) | (0.51) | (4.05) | (0.73) |
| $H$ | -0.16 | 0.12 | -0.05 | -0.02 | 0.11 | -0.14 |
| | (3.29) | (2.27) | (1.82) | (0.28) | (2.27) | (2.26) |
| $TC$ | 0.16 | -0.13 | 0.06 | -0.02 | -0.10 | 0.11 |
| | (4.00) | (1.43) | (2.54) | (0.22) | (2.55) | (0.91) |
| $ES$ | -0.26 | 0.04 | -0.02 | 0.20 | 0.25 | 0.15 |
| | (2.92) | (0.20) | (0.44) | (0.94) | (2.59) | (0.67) |
| $R^2$ | 0.64 | | 0.84 | | 0.35 | |
| $SE$ | 2.715 | | 1.539 | | 2.755 | |
| $F(13, 266)$ | 36.150 | | 104.094 | | 10.826 | |

* Figures in parentheses denote ratios of the estimated coefficients to their respective White (1980) heteroscedasticity corrected standard errors.

for any part of our period, a comparative advantage in human capital intensive, or in high quality skilled labour intensive, commodities. Rather, what the significant positive shift parameter for human capital shown in the net exports equation in Table 8 reflects, is that in the years 1984–85 Portugal was able to achieve, relative to the rest of the years in our sample period, a significant gross import improvement in human capital intensive commodities. In the same period, though, one must count the deterioration in adaptive technology advantage, recorded by the shift parameter for this variable in the net exports equation also shown in this table.

# 5 Summary and Conclusions

Our aim in this study has been to identify the contribution of various factors, suggested by theory as important determinants of international trade, in explaining the Portuguese pattern of trade in manufactures in the years 1972-1985, and further to examine whether in this period of profound change in the country's economic circumstances significant changes over time can be traced in the relationship between these determinants and the composition of trade.

Throughout the years 1972 to 1985 the Portuguese pattern of trade exhibits comparative advantage in products of industries that are intensive in unskilled labour, and comparative disadvantage in products of industries that are intensive in skilled labour/human capital. Within the latter category, moreover, our results suggest that the comparative disadvantage in skilled labour/human capital products, is more pronounced in products that are intensive in lower quality skilled labour than in products that are intensive in higher quality skilled labour. In addition, throughout these years the Portuguese pattern of trade reflects positive trade performance in industries that are better able to adapt, and negative trade performance in industries that show high concentration ratios.

A more varied picture is found with regard to comparative advantage/ disadvantage in physical capital, where our results reveal a pattern of comparative disadvantage in physical capital intensive commodities in the 1970's, yielding to physical capital neutrality in the 1980's.

In our judgement this is the most pronounced change regarding trade performance, during the period under review. Though our results highlight a number of other changes, some of these, as we explained, relate to particular episodes, while others, that are perhaps more permanent, do not imply a qualitative change in the pattern of comparative advantage. Yet, this being said, we must also hasten to emphasize that our results indicate that in accounting for the temporal pattern of Portugal's trade over the period under review, domestic policies, changes in expenditure patterns, changes in trading partnerships and trade distortions, all seem to have something to add.

# References

BALASSA, B. (1979a): "The Changing Pattern of Comparative Advantage in Manufactured Goods," *Review of Economics and Statistics*, **51**, 259–266.

BALASSA, B. (1979b): "Portugal in the Face of the Common Market," in *2a Conferência Internacional sobre Economia Portuguesa.* Lisbon: Fundação Calouste Gulbenkian and the German Marshall Fund of the US.

BALASSA, B. (1984): "Medium Term Economic Policies for Portugal," *Economia*, **8**, 543–567.

BALASSA, B. (1986): "Comparative Advantage in Manufactured Goods: A Reappraisal," *Review of Economics and Statistics*, **68**, 315–319.

BALASSA, B. AND L. BAUWENS (1988): *Changing Trade Patterns in Manufactured Goods.* Amsterdam: North Holland.

BALDWIN, R. E. (1971): "Determinants of the Commodity Structure of US Trade," *American Economic Review*, **61**, 126–146.

BALDWIN, R. E. (1979): "Determinants of Trade and Foreign Investment: Further Evidence," *Review of Economics and Statistics*, **61**, 40–48.

BALLANCE, R. H., H. FORSTNER AND T. MURRAY (1987): "Consistency Tests of Alternative Measures of Comparative Advantage," *Review of Economics and Statistics*, **69**, 157–161.

BARUH, J. (1986): "Factor Proportions and Israel's Manufacturing Trade," *Journal of Development Economics*, **24**, 131–139.

BOWEN, H. P. (1983): "Changes in the International Distribution of Resources and their Impact on U.S. Comparative Advantage," *Review of Economics and Statistics*, **65**, 402–414.

BOWEN, H. P., E. E. LEAMER, AND L. SVEINKAUSKAS (1987): "Multicountry, Multifactor Tests of the Factor Abundance Theory," *American Economic Review*, **77**, 791–809.

BRANSON, W. H. (1971): "US Comparative Advantage: Some Further Results," *Brookings Papers on Economic Activity*, **2**, 754–759.

BRANSON, W. H. AND H. B. JUNZ (1971): "Trends in US Trade and Comparative Advantage," *Brookings Papers on Economic Activity*, **2**, 285–346.

BRANSON, W. H. AND N. MONOYIOS (1977): "Factor Inputs in US Trade," *Journal of International Economics*, **7**, 111–131.

COURAKIS, A. S. (1984): "Reflections on Government Intervention in the Portuguese Financial System," mimeo, Oxford University.

COURAKIS, A. S. (1986): "Labour Skills and Human Capital in the Explanation of Trade Patterns," Unidade de Investigação em Comércio Internacional (UICI) ISE, Working Paper #2. Forthcoming, *Oxford Economic Papers*.

COURAKIS, A. S. (1987): "U.K. Manufacturing Trade 1910-1935: Where Did Comparative Advantage Lie?," mimeo, Oxford University, Institute of Economics and Statistics.

COURAKIS, A. S. AND F. MOURA ROQUE (1988): "On the Informational Content of Technology Variables in Explaining Trade Patterns," *Greek Economic Review*, **10**, 287–298.

COURAKIS, A. S. AND F. MOURA ROQUE (1990): "Changing Trade Partnerships and the Factor Content of Portugal's Trade in Manufactures," work in progress.

COURAKIS, A. S., F. MOURA ROQUE AND G. TRIDIMAS (1990): "Public Expenditure Growth in Greece and Portugal: Wagner's Law and Beyond," University of Oxford, Applied Economics Discussion Paper, #90.

CRAFTS, N. AND M. THOMAS (1986): "Comparative Advantage in UK Manufacturing Trade: 1910-1935," *Economic Journal*, **96**, 629–645.

DAVDISON, W. H. (1979): "Factor Endowment, Innovation and International Trade Theory," *Kyklos*, **32**, 764–774.

DEARDORF, A. V. (1982): "The General Validity of the Heckscher-Ohlin Theorem," *American Economic Review*, **72**, 683–694.

DEARDORF, A. V. (1984): "Testing Trade Theories and Predicting Trade Flows," in *Handbook of International Economics*, ed. by R. W. Jones and P. B. Kenen, vol. 1, 467–517. Amsterdam: North Holland.

DONGES, J. B. AND K. W. SCHATZ (1985): "The Iberian Countries Facing EC Membership: Starting Conditions for Their Industry," *Weltwirtschaftlisches Archiv*, **121**, 756–778.

FINGER, J. M. (1975): "A New View of the Product Cycle Theory," *Weltwirtschaftlisches Archiv*, **111**, 79–99.

HAN, A. K. AND D. PARK (1989): "Testing for Structural Change in Panel Data: Application to a Study of U.S. Foreign Trade in Manufactured Goods," *Review of Economics and Statistics*, **71**, 135–142.

HICKS, J. R. (1932): *The Theory of Wages*. Oxford: Clarendon Press.

HIRSCH, S. (1967): *Location and International Competitiveness*. Oxford: Clarendon Press.

HIRSCH, S. (1978): "The Leontief Paradox in a Multi-Country Setting," *Weltwirtschaftlisches Archiv*, **113**, 407– .

HSIAO, C. (1986): *Analysis of Panel Data*. Cambridge: Cambridge University Press.

HUFBAUER, G. C. (1970): "The Impact of National Characteristics and Technology on the Commodity Composition of Trade in Manufactured Goods," in *The Technology Factor in World Trade*, ed. by R. Vernon, 145–232. New York: Columbia University Press.

HULSMAN-VEJSOVA, M. AND K. A. KOEKKOEK (1980): "Factor Proportions, Technology and Dutch Industry's International Trade Patters," *Weltwirtschaftlisches Archiv*, **116**, 162–177.

JENSEN, R. AND M. THURSBY (1986): "A Strategic Approach to the Product Life Cycle," *Journal of International Economics*, **21**, 269–284.

KATRAK, H. (1973): "Human Skills, R&D and Scale Economies in the Exports of the United Kingdom and the United States," *Oxford Economic Papers*, **25**, 337–360.

KEESING, D. (1967): "The Impact of Research and Development on US Trade," *Journal of Political Economy*, **75**, 38–48.

KRUGMAN, P. (1979a): "A Model of Innovation, Technology Transfer and World Distribution of Income," *Journal of Political Economy*, **87**, 253–267.

KRUGMAN, P. (1979b): "Increasing Returns, Monopolistic Competition, and International Trade," *Journal of International Economics*, **9**, 469–479.

KRUGMAN, P. (1980): "Scale Economies, Product Differentiation, and the Pattern of Trade," *American Economic Review*, **70**, 950–959.

KRUGMAN, P. (1985): "A Technology Gap Model of International Trade," in *Structural Adjustment in Developed Open Economies* ed. by K. Jungenfelt and D. Hague, 24–35. London: MacMillan.

LEAMER, E. E. (1980): "The Leontief Paradox Reconsidered," *Journal of Political Economy*, **88**, 495–503.

LEAMER, E. E. (1984): *Sources of International Comparative Advantage: Theory and Evidence*. Cambridge: MIT Press.

LEARMER, E. E. AND H. P. BOWEN (1981): "Cross-section Tests of the Heckschel-Ohlin Theorem: Comment," *American Economic Review*, **71**, 1037–1048.

LINDER, S. B. (1961): *An Essay on Trade and Transformation*. New York: John Wiley and Sons.

MACEDO, J. B., C. CORADO AND M. PORTO (1988): "The Timing and Sequencing of Trade Liberalisation Policies: Portugal 1948-1986," Universidade Nova de Lisboa, Working Paper #114.

MADDALA, G. S. (1977): *Econometrics*. Tokyo: McGraw-Hill.

MAGGE, S. P. (1977a): "Application of the Dynamic Limit Pricing Model to the Price of Technology and International Technology Transfer," *Carnegie Rochester Conference Series on Public Policy*, 203–224.

MAGEE, S. P. (1977b): "Information and the Multinational Corporation: An Appropriability Theory of Direct Foreign Investment," in *The New International Economic Order*, ed. by J. Bhagwati, 317–343. Cambridge: MIT Press.

MARKUSEN, F. R. AND J. R. MELVIN (1981): "Trade, Factor Prices, and the Gains from Trade with Increasing Returns to Scale," *Canadian Journal of Economics*, **14**, 450–469.

MASKUS, K. E. (1983): "Evidence on Shifts in the Determinants of the Structure of U.S. Manufacturing Foreign Trade: 1958-1976," *Review of Economics and Statistics*, **65**, 415–422.

MASKUS, K. E. (1985): "A Test of the Heckscher-Ohlin-Vanek Theorem: The Leontief Commonplace," *Journal of International Economics*, **19**, 201–212.

MOMIGLIANO, F. AND D. SINISCALCO (1984): "Technology and International Specialization" *Banca Nazionale del Lavoro Quarterly Review*, **37**, 257–284.

NOLAND, M. (1987): "Newly Industrialising Countries' Comparative Advantage in Manufactured Goods," *Weltwirtschaftliches Archiv*, **122**, 679–696.

ONIDA, F. (1987): "Italian Patterns of Trade: Some Econometric Cross-Sector and Cross-County Evidence," presented to the UICI conference on *Trade Patterns and Policies in Southern Europe*, Instituto Superior de Economia, Lisbon.

POSNER, M. V. (1961): "International Trade and Technical Change," *Oxford Economic Papers*, **13**, 323–341.

RODRIK, D. (1982): "Comparative Advantage and Structural Change: A Quantitative Analysis," UNCTAD Discussion Papers.

SOETE, L. (1980): "The Impact of Technological Innovation on International Trade Patterns: The Evidence Reconsidered," mimeo, University of Sussex.

STAIGER, R. W. (1988): "A Specification Test of the Heckscher-Ohlin Theory," *Journal of International Economics*, **25**, 129–141.

STERN, R. M. (1976): "Some Evidence on the Factor Content of West Germany's Foreign Trade," *Journal of Political Economy*, **84**, 131–141.

STERN, R. M. AND K. E. MASKUS (1981): "Determinants of Structure of US Foreign Trade: 1958–1976," *Journal of International Economics*, **11**, 207–224.

SUCCAR, P. (1987): "International Technology Transfer: A Model of Endogenous Technological Assimilation," *Journal of Development Economics*, **26**, 375–395.

TEITEL, S. (1982): "The Skills and Information Requirements of Industrial Technologies: On the Use of Engineers as a Proxy," in *Trade Stability, Technology and Equity in Latin America*, ed. by M. Syrquin, and S. Teitel, 333–348. New York: Academic Press.

TEITEL, S. (1984): "Technology Creation in Semi-Industrial Economies," *Journal of Development Economics*, **16**, 39–61.

URATA, S. (1983): "Factor Inputs and Japanese Manufacturing Trade Structure," *Review of Economics and Statistics*, **65**, 678–684.

VANEK, J. (1968): "The Factor Proportions Theory: The n-Factor Case," *Kyklos*, **4**, 749–756.

VERNON, R. (1966): "International Investment and International Trade in the Product Cycle," *Quarterly Journal of Economics*, **80**, 190–207.

VESTAL, J. E. (1989): "Evidence on Determinants and Factor Content Characteristics of Japanese Technology Trade 1977–1981," *Review of Economics and Statistics*, **71**, 565–571.

WHITE, H. (1980): "A Heteroscedasticity-Consistent Covariance Matrix Estimator and a Direct Test for Heteroscedasticity," *Econometrica*, **48**, 817–838.

WOLTER, F. (1977): "Factor Proportions, Technology and West German Industry's International Trade Patterns," *Weltwirtschaftliches Archiv*, **113**, 250–267.

WORLD BANK (1977): *Manufacturing Export Industries in Portugal*, IBRD Report #1695a-Po, Washington.

# List of Participants

**João Ferreira do Amaral** *Instituto Superior de Economia e Gestão and National Institute of Statistics.*

**Mário Antão** *Instituto Superior de Economia e Gestão and Portuguese Ministry of Finance.*

**António S. Pinto Barbosa** *Universidade Nova de Lisboa.*

**José Pedro Barosa** *Universidade Nova de Lisboa.*

**Pedro P. Barros** *Universidade Nova de Lisboa.*

**Fernando Branco** *Massachusetts Institute of Technology.*

**Paulo Brito** *Instituto Superior de Economia e Gestão.*

**Luís M. B. Cabral** *Universidade Nova de Lisboa.*

**Isabel Horta Correia** *Universidade Católica Portuguesa and Banco de Portugal.*

**Anthony Courakis** *Oxford University.*

**Vítor Gaspar** *Universidade Nova de Lisboa.*

**António P. N. Leite** *Universidade Nova de Lisboa.*

**Diogo Lucena** *Universidade Nova de Lisboa.*

**José Ferreira Machado** *Universidade Nova de Lisboa.*

**Ana Paula Martins** *Universidade Católica Portuguesa.*

**José Mata** *Universidade do Minho.*

**António S. Mello** *Massachusetts Institute of Technology.*

**Leonor Modesto** *Universidade Católica Portuguesa.*

**Manuel Leite Monteiro** *Universidade Católica Portuguesa.*

**João César das Neves** *Universidade Católica Portuguesa and Banco de Portugal.*

**Vasco D'Orey** *Universidade Nova de Lisboa and Espírito Santo Investment Bank.*

**Alfredo M. Pereira** *University of California, San Diego.*

**Pedro Telhado Pereira** *Universidade Nova de Lisboa.*

**Maximiano Pinheiro** *Universidade Nova de Lisboa and National Institute of Statistics.*

**João Pontes** *Instituto Superior de Economia e Gestão.*

**Sérgio Rebelo** *Universidade Católica Portuguesa, Northwestern University and Banco de Portugal.*

**Fátima Moura Roque** *Universidade Nova de Lisboa.*

**Vasco Santos** *Universidade Nova de Lisboa.*

**Victor Santos** *Instituto Superior de Economia e Gestão.*

**George Tridimas** *University of Reading.*

MIX
Papier aus verantwortungsvollen Quellen
Paper from responsible sources
FSC® C105338

If you have any concerns about our products,
you can contact us on
**ProductSafety@springernature.com**

In case Publisher is established outside the EU,
the EU authorized representative is:
**Springer Nature Customer Service Center GmbH**
**Europaplatz 3, 69115 Heidelberg, Germany**

Printed by Libri Plureos GmbH
in Hamburg, Germany